D1552559

SOLZHENITSYN

ALSO BY JOSEPH PEARCE

LITERARY CONVERTS
TOLKIEN: MAN AND MYTH
TOLKIEN: A CELEBRATION

SOLZHENITSYN
A SOUL IN EXILE

JOSEPH PEARCE

Baker Books

A Division of Baker Book House Co
Grand Rapids, Michigan 49516

Published in 2001 by Baker Books
a division of Baker Book House Company
P.O. Box 6287, Grand Rapids, MI 49516-6287

Originally published in English by HarperCollins Publishers Ltd. under the title *Solzhenitsyn: A Soul in Exile.* The author asserts the moral right to be identified as the author of this work.

Printed in the United States of America

Library of Congress Cataloging-in-Publication Data

Pearce, Joseph.
    Solzhenitsyn : a soul in exile / Joseph Pearce.
      p.   cm.
    Includes index.
    ISBN 0-8010-1204-X (cloth)
    1. Solzhenitsyn, Aleksandr Isaevich, 1918– 2. Authors, Russian—20th century—Biography. I. Title.
PG3488.O4 Z833   2001
891.73′44—dc21   00-045512

For current information about all releases from Baker Book House, visit our web site:
http://www.bakerbooks.com

FOR AIDAN AND DORENE MACKEY
IN GRATITUDE AND FRIENDSHIP

CONTENTS

Acknowledgements IX

Preface XI

1. Child of the Revolution 1

2. Blissful Ignorance 13

3. Man and Wife 34

4. Man of War 44

5. Arrested Development 61

6. Hell into Purgatory 71

7. Profit from Loss 86

8. Life and Death 104

9. Beautiful Exile 118

10. Ivan the Terrible 136

11. Too Hot to Handle 154

12. Old Enemies and New Friends 168

13. 'I Feel Sorry for Russia' 184

14. Out in the Cold 196

15. Cold-Shouldered 214

16. Champion of Orthodoxy 230

17. Russia Reborn 246

18. Rebuilding on Green Foundations 260

19. A Prophet at Home 278

20. Solzhenitsyn at Eighty: Pessimistic Optimist 297

Appendix: New Prose Poems 315

Index 329

ACKNOWLEDGEMENTS

First and foremost I must acknowledge a debt of gratitude to the subject of this book. Without the full and generous co-operation of Alexander Solzhenitsyn my efforts would have floundered in an ocean of secondary sources. That is not to say that I have not made use of an extensive array of such sources. I have, of course, and the principal published sources have been acknowledged in the Notes, but without Solzhenitsyn's personal involvement I would not have had the benefit of the insight into his life and work which, I hope and trust, is conveyed in this volume. I am acutely conscious of the privileged nature of my access, not least because of the Russian writer's well-known distrust of Western biographers and journalists, and this only serves to accentuate my feelings of gratitude. I am mindful, for instance, that a previous biographer met with no success whatsoever in securing Solzhenitsyn's aid, to the extent that even his letters were not answered. (It was a tribute to that particular biographer's powers as a writer that the book he produced was still of exceptional quality.) I don't know why Solzhenitsyn broke his boycott of Western writers in my case, and this is not the place to conjecture, but I am nonetheless delighted to be the beneficiary of his assistance.

During my visit to Russia, I was the recipient of Natalya Solzhenitsyn's warm hospitality as well as being the eager and hungry recipient of her traditional Russian cuisine. Subsequently she has helped me considerably with details of her own life and that of her husband. I am grateful also to Yermolai Solzhenitsyn, not only for his patient and gruelling work as simultaneous translator during the interview with his father, but also for the impromptu guided tour of Moscow which followed. Yermolai continued to help me in the following months, replying to my questions at length and sharing his childhood memories of life in Vermont and in England, and his impressions of his father's return to Russia and subsequent reception by the Russian people.

Ignat Solzhenitsyn, Yermolai's brother, was tireless in his assistance throughout the months that the book was in preparation. In spite of his own busy schedule in the United States, where he is a highly accomplished and much sought-after concert pianist, he never failed to respond to my pleas for help, replying by phone, fax, e-mail and even, on occasion, by the old-fashioned postal service. Without his help in arranging my visit to Moscow, in acting as go-between and translator for his father and mother, and in offering his own memories and opinions, this biography would scarcely have been possible. I am, indeed, deeply indebted.

I am grateful to Alexander Solzhenitsyn for permission to quote from his works and to his Paris agent, Claude Durand, for permission to publish the first English translation of the prose poems which Solzhenitsyn has written since his return to Russia. I am both delighted and honoured to be able to include these beautiful poems as an appendix to this work and am indebted to Michael A. Nicholson for his work on the translation, in which he was assisted by Alexis Klimoff. I am indebted to Michael Nicholson for the other help he has given me during the writing and researching of the book, both at University College, Oxford, and during numerous telephone conversations. He was also kind enough to translate twenty-four lines of Solzhenitsyn's verse from the Russian edition of *The Gulag Archipelago Volume Two*.

Finally I must express my thanks to Sarah Hollingsworth for her invaluable critical appraisal of the original manuscript, to Alfred Simmonds for his continuing encouragement, to Katrina White for help with translation, and to James Catford, Elspeth Taylor, Kathy Dyke and the rest of the people at HarperCollins who have laboured to bring my efforts to fruition.

PREFACE

If any twentieth-century literary figure has been the victim of media typecasting it is Alexander Solzhenitsyn. Whenever his name is mentioned it is almost invariably accompanied by the same stereotypical characterization. He is, we are reliably informed, a prophet of doom, an arch-pessimist, a stern Jeremiah-like figure who is out of touch, out of date and, worst of all in our novelty-crazed sub-culture, out of fashion. He is also, we are told, irrelevant to the modern world in general and modern Russia in particular.

Perhaps this attitude to the Russian Nobel Prize winner was epitomized by George Trefgarne in an article entitled 'Solzhenitsyn Loses the Russian Plot' in the business section of the *Daily Telegraph* on 6 June 1998. 'Alexander Solzhenitsyn proved again that he is never happier than when he is thoroughly miserable,' Trefgarne wrote. 'His impassioned critique of the new Russia displays the sense of doom, disaster and history you would expect from a survivor of the Soviet Union and a Nobel prizewinner. Solzhenitsyn believes Russia has overthrown the evils of communism only to replace them with the evils of capitalism.'

Mr Trefgarne's article ended with the statement that 'Alexander Solzhenitsyn is a better writer than he is an economist'. Yet why, one is tempted to ask, should this disqualify the writer from commenting on his country's problems? Did Dickens have nothing of importance to say about the squalor of Victorian England? Did George Orwell have nothing to say about the dangers of totalitarianism? Compared with the literary light which these writers were able to throw on controversial issues, the weakness of much of the analysis in the business sections of newspapers is only too apparent. Indeed Mr Trefgarne's own article was a case in point. He stated that 'Solzhenitsyn and the doom-mongers could have exaggerated their case' because the new and dynamic Russian prime minister, Sergei Kiriyenko, was revitalizing the ailing Russian economy with a 'decisive package of measures'. With an ingenious use of statistical data, Trefgarne painted a rose-tinted picture of Russia's future which reminded one of Solzhenitsyn's complaint that his country's troubles were forever being 'covered up ... by mendacious statistics'.

Only two months after Trefgarne's article had predicted that Russia would soon live happily ever after, Sergei Kiriyenko was sacked, his 'decisive package of measures' was abandoned, and the whole Russian economy collapsed cataclysmically sending shockwaves around the world. George Trefgarne had become only the latest in a long line of critics who had discovered to their own cost that it was perilous to dismiss Solzhenitsyn so lightly.

Yet even if Solzhenitsyn is right, the critics insist, he is still irrelevant because nobody is listening to him. 'It is little consolation that his prophecies of catastrophe are fulfilled,' wrote Daniel Johnson in the *Daily Telegraph* on 12 December 1998. 'He is unheard.' These words, written the day after Solzhenitsyn's eightieth birthday, were not completely true. To commemorate his birthday two documentaries were shown on Russian television, one of which was broadcast in hourly instalments on three consecutive nights. A third documentary was blocked at the last moment after Solzhenitsyn complained that it included unauthorized footage of his private life. In the same week, the celebrated cellist and composer Mstislav Rostropovich conducted a concert in Solzhenitsyn's honour at the Moscow Conservatory, and a dramatized version of Solzhenitsyn's novel *The First Circle* was being staged at one of Russia's leading theatres. Finally, when, as part of the birthday celebrations, President Yeltsin sought to award Solzhenitsyn the Order of St Andrew for his cultural achievements, the writer controversially refused to accept the honour in protest at Yeltsin's role in Russia's collapse. 'In today's conditions,' he said, 'when people are starving and striking just to get their wages, I cannot accept this reward.' He added that perhaps, in many years' time when Russia had overcome its seemingly insurmountable difficulties, one of his sons would be able to collect it for him posthumously. Clearly Solzhenitsyn, even as an octogenarian, was still capable of causing a great deal of controversy. Furthermore, the intense interest which his eightieth birthday aroused both in his homeland and in the media around the world contradicts the claims that he is either forgotten or irrelevant. On the contrary, seldom has a writer attracted so much publicity, both good and bad, throughout his life. Vilified or vindicated, loved or hated, Solzhenitsyn remains a provocative figure. Now, as he approaches the twilight of his life, it would seem timely to look back over the past eighty years. With the added insight provided by a recent in-depth interview with the writer himself, it is hoped that this book will help unravel Solzhenitsyn in a way which gets beyond the facts to the underlying truths which have underpinned his life, his work and his beliefs.

Exactly who *is* Alexander Solzhenitsyn? The following pages will not only address this beguiling question but will hopefully provide the beginnings of the answer.

CHAPTER ONE

CHILD OF THE REVOLUTION

The eighty years that have elapsed since the murder of Tsar Nicholas, the Empress Alexandra, three of their children and four servants have been the bloodiest in Russia's troubled history. It has been the destiny of Alexander Solzhenitsyn to live through all of them. Lenin ordered the execution of the imperial family in July 1918; just five months later Solzhenitsyn was born, and even while he nestled innocently in his mother's womb, the world which he was about to enter was itself pregnant with change. In the nine months up to his birth on 11 December 1918 Russia was transformed beyond recognition. In March the Bolshevik government, still consolidating its power after the October Revolution in the previous year, had fled from St Petersburg beyond reach of the German artillery which had advanced to within range of the city. Proclaiming Moscow as the new capital of the fledgling Soviet state, Lenin moved into the Kremlin, while the *Cheka*, the Soviet secret police, took over the Rossiya Insurance Company building on Lubyanka Square. In August, a month after the tsar and his family were murdered, the Bolsheviks destroyed their socialist rivals in a wave of repression known as the Red Terror, during which thousands of hostages were imprisoned and shot.

Meanwhile a bloody civil war was raging across Russia. The newly formed Red Army, set up by the Bolsheviks, and the various anti-Soviet forces, known collectively as the Whites, were evenly matched in terms of numbers. Crucially, however, the Bolsheviks had control of the railways emanating from Moscow, which enabled them to switch resources from one battlefront to another. The Red Army also drew upon the experience of ex-Tsarist officers forced to serve under the vigilant eye of regimental commissars. Similar force was used throughout the country as Trotsky travelled round Russia shooting commanders who failed to hold their ground at all costs. By contrast, the Whites lacked the ideological fervour which was the basis of Bolshevik unity, encompassing within their ranks a wide range of political ideologies, from monarchists to anti-Soviet socialists. They had neither a unified command nor centralized lines of communication. Such factors were to contribute significantly to the eventual Soviet victory, although the war was still at its fiercest at the time of Solzhenitsyn's birth.

Success in the economic sphere was not so simple for the post-revolutionary government. Soviet policies were causing chaos. Since money was almost worthless, the rural peasantry had no incentive to sell their scarce produce in the cities. The Bolshevik response was to send Red Guards into the countryside to seize food and to set up 'committees of the poor' which in turn incited class war against the wealthier peasants, or *kulaks*. In the cities a form of labour discipline was introduced under the guise of 'War Communism' which differed little in its harshness from the pre-trade union days under the tsar. This was a reflection of Lenin's demands, voiced in the first months after the October Revolution, for 'the most decisive, draconic measures to tighten up discipline'.[1] In December 1917 he suggested several means by which discipline could be imposed: 'confiscation of all property ... confinement in prison, dispatch to the front and forced labour for all who disobey the existing law'.[2]

On 23 July 1918 the Bolshevik government passed legislation which stipulated that 'those deprived of freedom who are capable of labour must be recruited for physical work on a compulsory basis'. Writing half a century later, Solzhenitsyn affirmed that 'the camps originated and the Archipelago was born from this particular instruction of July 23, 1918'.[3] On 5 September 1918 the Decree on the Red Terror, in addition to a call for mass executions, authorized the Soviet Republic to defend itself 'against its class enemies by isolating them in concentration camps'.[4]

'At that time,' Solzhenitsyn wrote in *The Gulag Archipelago*, 'the authorities used to love to set up their concentration camps in former monasteries: they were enclosed by strong walls, had good solid buildings, and they were empty. (After all, monks are not human beings and could be tossed out at will.) Thus in Moscow there were concentration camps in Andronnikov, Novospassky, and Ivanovsky monasteries.'⁵ Neither were monks the only victims. Nuns also warranted eviction. The *Krasnaya Gazeta* of 6 September 1918 reported that the first camp in St Petersburg 'will be set up in Nizhni Novgorod in an empty nunnery', adding that 'initially it was planned to send five thousand persons to the concentration camp'.

Thus it was that Alexander Solzhenitsyn and the Gulag Archipelago were born within weeks of each other, children of the same revolution.

The turbulent and tyrannical world which Solzhenitsyn entered in the winter of 1918 was made even less hospitable by the absence of his father, killed in a hunting accident six months before his son's birth. Consequently, Solzhenitsyn could remember his father 'only from snapshots, and the accounts of my mother and people who knew him'.⁶ From these accounts Solzhenitsyn had gleaned that his father, Isaaki Solzhenitsyn, had gone from the university to the front as a volunteer and had served in the Grenadier Artillery Brigade. He recounts with pride the story of his father's bravery in pulling ammunition boxes away from a fire which had been started by enemy shells. For this act of heroism he was mentioned in dispatches. When almost the entire front had collapsed in the face of the German advance, the battery in which his father served remained in the front lines right up until the Treaty of Brest-Litovsk in March 1918. He and Taissia Shcherbak, Solzhenitsyn's mother, were married at the front by the brigade chaplain. He ended the war with three officers' decorations, including the George and Anna crosses, but died soon after his return home in spring 1918. If he had lived, Isaaki Solzhenitsyn would have been twenty-seven years old at the time of his son's birth at Kislovodsk, a fashionable Caucasian resort. His wife was twenty-three.

Such was the volatile nature of the times into which the young Solzhenitsyn was born that his father's war medals were considered dangerously incriminating and he remembered helping his mother bury them.

His mother, Solzhenitsyn recalled many years later, raised him 'in incredibly hard circumstances'. Although widowed at such a young age and so tragically, she never remarried, which Solzhenitsyn believed was 'mainly for fear that a stepfather might be too harsh with me'. Soon after he was born, his mother took him to live in Rostov where they would remain for nineteen years, until the start of the Second World War. For the first fifteen of these they were unable to obtain a room from the state and were forced to live in rented accommodation, normally overpriced dilapidated shacks. When they finally did secure a room, it was part of a cold and draughty converted stable, heated by coal, itself a scarce commodity in Russia during the twenties and thirties. There was no running water. 'I learned what running water in an apartment means only recently,' Solzhenitsyn told correspondents from the *New York Times* and the *Washington Post* in March 1972.[7]

Taissia Solzhenitsyn knew French and English well, and also learned stenography and typing, but she faced consistent discrimination in employment because of her social origin. She was purged on these grounds from her job at Melstrio (the Flour Mill Construction Administration), her dismissal including restrictions on her future right to employment. Forced to take poorly paid jobs, she had little option but to seek extra work in the evenings, and to do her housework late at night when she got home. Looking back on this period, Solzhenitsyn recalled that his mother was always short of sleep.

Taissia Solzhenitsyn's father had come from the Crimea as a young boy to herd sheep and work as a farmhand. Says Solzhenitsyn,

> He started with nothing, then became a tenant farmer, and it is true that by the time he was old he was quite rich. He was a man of rare energy and industry. In his fifty years of work he gave the country more grain and wool than many of today's state farms, and he worked no less hard than their directors. As for his workers, he treated them in such a way that after the Revolution they voluntarily supported the old man for twelve years until he died. Let a state farm director try begging from his workers after his dismissal.[8]

Before her marriage, Taissia was the least religious member of the Shcherbak family.[9] Her parents had raised her in an atmosphere of piety and devotion and her aunt Ashkelaya was a nun, but this did not prevent the young Taissia from abandoning her childhood faith, largely through the secularizing influence of the progressive boarding school she attended in Rostov. Returning home during school holidays, she was patronizingly embarrassed by the religious devotion displayed by her family and treated the rites of the Orthodox Church with the amused contempt of one who perceived in them only the superstitious practices of an abandoned cult. The disdain for religious faith was reinforced during her time as a student in Moscow where she followed the prevailing trends of atheism and anticlericalism with all the enthusiasm of her contemporaries. By 1918, however, events had drawn her back to the church. The tragic death of her husband so soon after their marriage, the presence of a child in her womb, and the fear and uncertainty engendered by the Red Terror and the Civil War, all contributed to a rekindling of faith.

The émigré writer Nikolai Zernov, who was living in the neighbouring resort of Essentuki at the time, twelve miles from Kislovodsk, described the widespread return to the church of people in the area: 'The atmosphere created in the Caucasian resorts encouraged our religious enthusiasm ... It seemed to us that Russia was on the eve of a spiritual renaissance, that the church, purified by her suffering, would reveal to a penitent people the radiant lineaments of our Saviour, and teach Russians how to found their lives on brotherly love.'[10]

The new wave of religious zeal which had swept through the region, taking Taissia with it, was the product of a potent mixture of hope and fear. By the summer of 1919, with the White armies of Denikin and Wrangel liberating the south from the Bolsheviks, hope was in the ascendancy. It was short-lived. In March 1920 the White resistance finally collapsed. Bolshevik rule now returned to the Caucasus to stay, bringing with it a wave of revenge killing throughout the following months. In the winter of 1920 Taissia and the rest of her family had virtually starved, like everyone else in the area, selling furniture and possessions at derisory prices in order to buy food. The famine, so hard to endure in the Caucasus, was even worse in other parts of Russia, most notably in the Volga area where starving peasants turned to cannibalism, eating their own children. Russia had never known such a famine, even in the Time of Troubles in the early seventeenth century.[11] In the new desperate circumstances hope was seemingly vanquished and fear triumphant.

The infant Solzhenitsyn, scarcely two years old, was too young to appreciate the desperate nature of the situation. Instead, one of his earliest memories would always fill him with a sense of warmth and security. Almost sixty years later he was to recall the reassuring icon that hung in one corner of his room, suspended in the angle between wall and ceiling and tilting downwards so that its holy face seemed to be gazing directly at him. At night the candle in front of it would flicker and shudder while he lay in bed staring sleepily upwards. In the magic moment between waking and sleeping, the radiant visage seemed to detach itself and float out over his bed, like a true guardian angel. In the mornings, under the direction of his grandmother Evdokia, he would kneel before the icon and say his prayers.

Throughout this period, Taissia's family lived in fear of losing far more than their property, most of which had been sold or confiscated already. Although they now possessed very little, the fact that they had once been relatively wealthy made them 'class enemies' which, in the new reign of terror, was punishable by death.

By 1921, however, it was not only the rich who went in fear of their lives. Soviet Russia was economically devastated, and the Bolsheviks found themselves confronted with worker unrest. In February 1921, sailors at the Kronstadt naval base – who had been among the Bolsheviks' staunchest supporters since 1905 – staged a protest against worsening economic conditions. The Kronstadt sailors' revolt precipitated a general strike in St Petersburg. The Bolsheviks rejected calls for negotiations and, oblivious to the previous loyal support of the Kronstadt sailors, accused the protestors of treason and brutally crushed the revolt.

Meanwhile, Lenin was presiding over the Tenth Party Congress, at which he abolished democratic debate within the Party and banned all factions. In real terms, power had now passed from the purely theoretical 'dictatorship of the proletariat' to the utterly practical dictatorship of the Secretariat, the governing body of the newly emerging Party bureaucracy. The first General Secretary of the Secretariat, appointed towards the end of 1922, was a Georgian Bolshevik by the name of Josef Stalin. At the same Congress, Lenin unveiled his New Economic Policy which was destined to become increasingly unpopular, particularly with the urban working class who dubbed the NEP the 'New Exploitation of the Proletariat'.

It was also in 1922 that the Bolsheviks began to turn their resentful glare on the Orthodox Church.

In August 1921 the church had created diocesan and all-Russian committees for aid to the starving in the Volga region. The committees were banned and the funds collected were confiscated and turned over to the state treasury. Patriarch Tikhon had also appealed to both the Pope and the Archbishop of Canterbury for assistance, but was rebuked by the Bolshevik authorities on the grounds that only the Soviet government had the right to enter into negotiation with foreigners. Discussing this in the first volume of *The Gulag Archipelago*, Solzhenitsyn pointed his accusing finger at the cynical way that the Soviets sought to turn the suffering in the Volga region to their own advantage:

> But political genius lies in extracting success even from the people's ruin. A brilliant idea was born: after all, three billiard balls can be pocketed with one shot. *So now let the priests feed the Volga region!* They are Christians. They are generous!
>
> 1. If they refuse, we will blame the whole famine on them and destroy the church.
> 2. If they agree, we will clean out the churches.
> 3. In either case, we will replenish our stocks of foreign exchange and precious metals.[12]

In December 1921, Pomgol – the State Commission for Famine Relief – proposed that the churches should help the starving by donating church valuables. The Patriarch agreed and on 19 February 1922 he issued a pastoral letter permitting parish councils to make gifts of objects that had no liturgical and ritual significance. A week later, on 26 February, the All-Russian Central Executive Committee decreed that *all* valuables were to be forcefully requisitioned from the churches – for the starving. Two days later the Patriarch issued a new pastoral letter stating that such a measure was sacrilege and that he could not approve the forced requisition of objects needed for the sacred liturgy.

Immediately a campaign of persecution began in the press, directed against the Patriarch and the church authorities who, it was claimed, 'were strangling the Volga region with the bony hand of famine'. The concerns of the church were expressed by Bishop

Antonin Granovsky who explained to Mikhail Kalinin, Chairman of the All-Russian Central Executive Committee, that 'believers fear that the church valuables may be used for other purposes, more limited and alien to their hearts'.[13] Such concerns fell on deaf ears and on 26 April 1922 a trial of seventeen members of the church, ranging from archpriests to laymen, began in Moscow. The defendants were accused of disseminating the Patriarch's proclamation, with the Patriarch himself being summoned to give evidence. The principal defendant, archpriest A. N. Zaozersky, had actually surrendered all the valuables in his own church voluntarily, but he was charged nevertheless because he defended in principle the Patriarch's assertion that forced requisition was sacrilege. His principles were to cost him his life. Along with four of the other defendants, he was condemned to be shot. 'All of which went to prove that what was important was not to feed the starving but to make use of a convenient opportunity to break the back of the church,' wrote Solzhenitsyn in *The Gulag Archipelago*.[14]

In the course of his own evidence at the trial the Patriarch had stated that he only considered the laws of the state obligatory 'to the extent that they do not contradict the rules of piety'. This led to a debate about church law. The Patriarch explained that if the church itself surrendered its valuables, it was not sacrilege. But if they were taken against the church's will, it was. He stressed that his appeal had not prohibited giving the valuables at all, but had only declared that seizing them against the will of the church was to be condemned. In a vain attempt to instil a little logic into the proceedings the Patriarch spoke of the philological significance of the word *svyatotatstvo*, meaning 'sacrilege'. The word, he explained, derived from *svyato*, meaning 'holy', and *tat*, meaning 'thief'.

'So that means,' exclaimed the Accuser, 'that we, the representatives of the Soviet government, are thieves of holy things? So you call the representatives of the Soviet government, the All-Russian Central Executive Committee, thieves?' To this the Patriarch replied that he was merely citing church law.

A week later the Patriarch was removed from office and arrested.

Two weeks after that, the Metropolitan Veniamin was arrested in St Petersburg. He was charged, along with several dozen others, with resisting the requisition of church valuables. As the trial, which lasted from 9 June to 5 July 1922, reached a climax, Accuser Smirnov demanded 'sixteen heads'. Not to be outdone, Accuser Krasikov cried out: 'The whole Orthodox Church is a subversive organization. Properly speaking, the entire church ought to be put in prison.'[15] In the event the tribunal condemned ten of the defendants to death but later pardoned six of them. The other four, including Metropolitan Veniamin, were executed on the night of 12 August.

The Soviet persecution of the Orthodox Church had now begun in earnest. Over the following weeks and months there were a further twenty-two church trials in the provinces. 'Here and there in the provincial centres,' Solzhenitsyn wrote, 'and even further down in the administrative districts, metropolitans and bishops were arrested, and, as always, in the wake of the big fish, followed shoals of smaller fry: archpriests, monks, and deacons. These arrests were not even reported in the press ... Men of religion were an inevitable part of every annual "catch", and their silver locks gleamed in every cell and in every prisoner transport en route to the Solovetsky Islands.'[16]

Other victims of the newly declared war on religion included the 'Eastern Catholics' – followers of Vladimir Solovyev – and ordinary Roman Catholics such as Polish priests, as well as believers in a multitude of different religious sects ranging from theosophists to spiritualists. Later, as the manic effort to eradicate Christianity gathered pace throughout the twenties and thirties, the Soviet regime began the mass arrest of ordinary Orthodox believers. Again, Solzhenitsyn described this intensification of state-organized persecution in *The Gulag Archipelago*: 'Monks and nuns, whose black habits had been a distinctive feature of Old Russian life, were intensively rounded up on every hand, placed under arrest, and sent into exile. They arrested and sentenced active laymen. The circles kept getting bigger, as they raked in ordinary believers as well, old people, and particularly women, who were the most stubborn believers of all and who, for many long years to come, would be called "nuns" in transit prisons and in camps.'[17]

The grim irony of the situation was that religious *faith*, technically speaking, was still not a crime. The crime was in mentioning it. In the twenties, for instance, the religious education of children was classified as a political offence under Article 58-10 of the Code – in other words, counter-revolutionary propaganda. All persons convicted received ten-year sentences, the longest term then given. The absurdity beggars belief: a person was allowed by law to be convinced that he possessed spiritual truth but was required, on pain of imprisonment, to conceal the fact from everyone else, even his own children.

The bitter humour of this state of affairs was not lost on the poet Tanya Khodkevich:

> You can pray *freely*
> But just so God alone can hear.

She too received a ten-year sentence for expressing her sense of humour in this way.

George Orwell, of course, was to develop the concept of 'double-think' one step further: in *Nineteen Eighty-Four* the thought itself became a crime. Yet, although Orwellian thought-crime had not, at this stage, entered the Soviet criminal code, the fact would have come as cold comfort to those languishing in prison camps throughout the Soviet Union.

Although the young Solzhenitsyn remained oblivious to the suffering inflicted on an older generation of Russians, it is significant that his earliest memory relates to an incident connected to the state persecution of the church. It occurred in 1922 or 1923, at the very height of the wave of attacks on the church which followed the show trials of leading churchmen in Moscow and St Petersburg. Solzhenitsyn was three or four years old and he was attending church in Kislovodsk with his mother. 'There were lots of people, candles, vestments ... then something happened: the service was brusquely interrupted. I wanted a better view, so my mother held me up at arm's length and I looked over the heads of the crowd. I saw, filing arrogantly down the central aisle of the nave, the sugar-loaf "Budenny" hats of Soviet soldiers. It was the period when the government was confiscating church property all over Russia.'[18] The soldiers 'sliced through the dumbstruck crowd of worshippers', invaded the sanctuary beyond the altar screen and stopped the service.

For the toddler, held aloft by his mother to get a better view, it was all too much to take in and way beyond his childish powers of comprehension. Yet even to the adults in the congregation the rude interruption by armed soldiers must have seemed incomprehensible, a bad dream. To those beleaguered believers it must have seemed that the world about them had gone mad.

Nevertheless life retained some sort of normality and throughout the twenties Solzhenitsyn was able to enjoy a childhood relatively unimpeded by events in the world at large. Even by the end of the decade, when he had developed an interest in politics, he remained blissfully unaware of the hidden horrors unfolding around him:

> even as a callow adolescent I ... was staggered by the fraudulence of the famous trials – but nothing led me to draw the line connecting those minute Moscow trials (which seemed so tremendous at the time) with the huge crushing wheel rolling through the land (the number of its victims somehow escaped notice). I had spent my childhood in queues – for bread, for milk, for meal (meat was a thing unknown at that time) – but I could not make the connection between the lack of bread and the ruin of the countryside, or understand *why* it had happened. We were provided with another formula: 'temporary difficulties'. Every night, in the large town where we lived, hour after hour after hour people were being hauled off to jail – but I did not walk the streets at night. And in the daytime the families of those arrested hung out no black flags, nor did my classmates say a word about their fathers being taken away.
>
> According to the newspapers there wasn't a cloud in the sky. And young men are so eager to believe that all is well.[19]

NOTES

1. V. I. Lenin, *Sobrannye Sochineniya* (Collected Works), 5th edn., vol. 36, p. 217, as quoted in Alexander Solzhenitsyn, *The Gulag Archipelago Volume Two*, London: Collins & Harvill Press, 1975, pp. 9–10.
2. Ibid., vol. 35, p. 176, as quoted in Solzhenitsyn, *The Gulag Archipelago Volume Two*, p. 10.

3. Solzhenitsyn, *The Gulag Archipelago Volume Two*, p. 14.
4. *Sobraniye Uzakonenii za 1918 (Collection of Legislative Acts for 1918)*, No. 65, p. 710, as quoted in *The Gulag Archipelago Volume Two*, p. 17.
5. Solzhenitsyn, *The Gulag Archipelago Volume Two*, p. 19.
6. Alexander Solzhenitsyn, *The Oak and the Calf*, London: Collins & Harvill Press, 1980, p. 510.
7. Ibid., p. 510.
8. Ibid., p. 511.
9. Michael Scammell, *Solzhenitsyn: A Biography*, London: Hutchinson, 1985, p. 39.
10. Nikolai Zernov, *Na perelome (At the Breaking-point)*, Paris, 1970, p. 322.
11. Alexander Solzhenitsyn, *The Gulag Archipelago Volume One*, London: Book Club Associates, 1974, p. 342.
12. Ibid., p. 343.
13. Ibid., p. 345.
14. Ibid., p. 347.
15. Ibid., p. 351.
16. Ibid., pp. 36–7.
17. Ibid., p. 37.
18. Scammell, *Solzhenitsyn: A Biography*, p. 42.
19. Alexander Solzhenitsyn, *The Gulag Archipelago Volume Three*, London: Collins & Harvill Press, 1978, p. 21.

CHAPTER TWO

BLISSFUL IGNORANCE

In spite of the hardships he suffered as a child, Solzhenitsyn was lucky compared with many children his own age. For millions of children in Russia during the 1920s life had become a living nightmare. In an unpublished memoir, Prof. Dr W. W. Krysko recalls the horrific scene he encountered as a ten-year-old in the spring of 1920. As the snows melted in the field outside his father's factory in Rostov, mounds of corpses and skeletons appeared. Thousands of bodies had been dumped there for eventual burial. Among the human remains were the carcasses of horses, whose rib cages became the dens of hundreds of wild dogs, wolves, jackals and hyenas. And worst of all, among the corpses and the dogs, lived bands of equally wild children, orphaned and abandoned.[1]

These were the *bezprizornye*, the uncared-for, the unwanted by-product of revolution and civil war who could be seen all over Russia. In 1923 Lenin's wife, Krupskaya, estimated their number at around eight million. Almost a decade later, Malcolm Muggeridge, working in the Soviet Union as the *Guardian*'s Moscow correspondent, witnessed these children 'going about in packs, barely articulate or recognizably human, with pinched animal faces, tangled hair and empty eyes. I saw them in Moscow and Leningrad, clustered under bridges, lurking in railway stations, suddenly emerging like a pack of wild monkeys, then scattering and disappearing.'[2] Some as young as three years old, the *bezprizornye* survived by thieving and scrounging and many, both boys and girls, were prostitutes. Realizing that these hordes of street children were a social embarrassment, especially when observed by astute and horrified Western news correspondents, the state rounded up as many as could be caught and placed them in so-called 'children's republics' from which they later emerged as the brutalized, amoral wretches responsible for keeping order in the camps of the Gulag Archipelago. As Solzhenitsyn's friend Dmitri Panin wrote:

> A huge country, basically Christian, had been made over into a nursery for rearing a new breed of men under conditions of widescale terror and atheism. A new society, governed by primitives, began taking shape. Without asking the consent of the peasants or anyone else, the party heads, to achieve their own ends, unleashed their thugs over our vast land and fettered it in slavery. The young Communist state proceeded to mutilate and crush whatever opposed it, secular or sacred, to bury human lives under atrocities.[3]

All of this was completely beyond the experience of the young Solzhenitsyn. When he arrived at Rostov, a wide-eyed six-year-old, early in 1925, life in the city seemed, on the surface at least, to have improved immeasurably from the nightmare reality that the ten-year-old Krysko had faced five years earlier in the same place. There were no horrific scenes of unburied corpses; even the street children, it seems, had been 'tidied away'. Instead Solzhenitsyn remained blissfully ignorant of the events unfolding around him until, almost twenty years later, they swallowed him up with the millions of others who had gone before him. In the meantime the child would become a precocious schoolboy at the top of his class.

Solzhenitsyn started school in 1926 at the former Pokrovsky College, a highly respected establishment in the centre of the city which was renamed after the Soviet minister Zinoviev following the civil war. Colloquially, however, the local people called it the 'Malevich Gymnasium' after its popular and talented headmaster, Vladimir Malevich. It was generally considered the best school in Rostov.

Malevich had been headmaster of the school since before the Revolution and, as such, was considered politically unreliable. Although he was still in charge when Solzhenitsyn arrived he was forced out in 1930, by which time most of the other pre-revolutionary teachers had also been removed. Malevich was eventually arrested in 1937 or 1938 and sent to the labour camps. It is thought that Solzhenitsyn may have sought him out and interviewed him when he was collecting material for *The Gulag Archipelago*.

The future purge of Solzhenitsyn's teachers was no more than a malevolent threat on the horizon when he started school. His first teacher, Elena Belgorodtseva, was a devout woman who was known to have icons hanging in her home. She would have had no objection to the cross around her new pupil's neck which he had worn since infancy. Nevertheless, state education was becoming increasingly atheist in nature and the Christianity of the young boy's home life began to contrast ever more starkly with the fundamental tenets of what he was being taught at school.

At home the influence of his mother's religious faith was reinforced during the school holidays by visits to his Uncle Roman and Aunt Irina. Most particularly, the devotion of his aunt exerted a lasting influence. 'Solzhenitsyn,' writes his biographer, Michael Scammell, 'appears to have come deeply under the spell of his intrepid and romantic aunt.'[4] In many ways she was a true mystic, deriving sense and sustenance from the mysteries of the Gospels and the richness of the Orthodox liturgy. The lavishness of Orthodox ritual fired her imagination, nourished by the belief that manifestations of beauty were themselves manifestations of truth, that beauty and truth were inseparable. In this devotion she had much in common with her pious mother-in-law, Evdokia, Solzhenitsyn's grandmother with whom he also stayed during holidays. Both women had icons hanging in virtually every room, and both were strict in their observance of daily prayer and the many fasts and acts of worship which Orthodox practice demanded.

Irina was an avid communicant at the local church and Solzhenitsyn, when staying with her, usually accompanied her to the services. Her enduring influence on Solzhenitsyn was emphasized by Michael Scammell:

> She taught him the true beauty and meaning of the rituals of the Russian Orthodox church, emphasizing its ancient traditions and continuity. She showed him its importance to Russian history, demonstrating how the history of the church was inextricably intertwined with the history of the nation; and she instilled into the boy a patriotic love of the past and a firm faith in the greatness and sacred destiny of the Russian people. Irina thus supplied him with a sense

of tradition, of family, and of roots that was otherwise severely attenuated.[5]

Irina was also an avid aficionado of the arts and she instilled in her nephew an early and lasting love for literature. She had an extensive library and encouraged Solzhenitsyn to use it to satisfy his increasingly voracious appetite for reading. It seems that he needed little encouragement. During stays with his aunt he introduced himself to Pushkin, Gogol, Tolstoy, Dostoyevsky, Turgenev, and most of the Russian classics. He first read *War and Peace* as a ten-year-old and then reread it several times in the course of ensuing summers. It was during this formative period that he first envisaged the figure of Tolstoy as the archetypal Russian writer, a secular icon to be revered and an example to be imitated. Irina also presented him with a copy of Vladimir Dahl's celebrated collection of Russian proverbs, on which he would draw heavily in his own work in later years.

Aunt Irina's library was not restricted to Russian literature. Shakespeare, Schiller, and particularly Dickens, also made an impression. Another favourite was Jack London, who was enormously popular in Russia both before and after the Revolution. Solzhenitsyn's admiration for London found expression many years later when, during his first visit to the United States, he sought out his childhood hero's home in California and made a brief pilgrimage.

Other than religion, the subject which highlighted the stark contrast between Solzhenitsyn's youthful home life and that of the world at large was politics. 'Everyone, of course, was anti-Bolshevik in the circle in which I grew up,' he recalled many years later. Both his mother and his aunt frequently dwelt on the horrors of the civil war and the suffering it had caused the family. No effort was made to hide from him any of the outrages of the immediate past and he was often present when members of the family made bitter and candid criticisms of the Soviet regime. As a boy he learned all about family friends who had been arrested or killed; he knew of his Uncle Roman's temporary detention under sentence of death and of the confiscation of his grandfather's estate. Yet at school the Bolsheviks were glorified and he remembered how he and his friends would 'listen with such wide eyes to the exploits of the Reds, wave flags, beat drums, blow trumpets'.[6]

This struggle with the conflicting claims of home and state was to have a profound impact on his adolescent years, demanding a degree of Orwellian double-think which resulted in a sort of psychological schism, almost a split personality:

> The fact that they used to say everything at home and never shielded me from anything decided my destiny. Generally speaking ... if you want to know the pivotal point of my life, you have to understand that I received such a charge of social tension in childhood that it pushed everything else to one side and diminished it ... inside me I bore this social tension – on the one hand they used to tell me everything at home, and on the other they used to work on our minds at school. Those were militant times, not like today ... And so this collision between two worlds ... somehow defined the path I was to follow for the rest of my life ... [7]

The problem was resolved, at least temporarily, by the victory of the state over the family. Solzhenitsyn bowed under the combined force of peer group pressure and Soviet propaganda, turning his back on the 'reactionary' teaching of his family and embracing Marxist dogma. It was a triumph for the architects of the Soviet education system which, as part of its indoctrination strategy, had virtually abolished the teaching of history except in a highly selective and slanted way, and had replaced it with propaganda and ideological training. Faced with such unscrupulous ingenuity the youth of Russia quickly succumbed to the mythology surrounding the Revolution. The heroes of the Bolshevik Revolution, like a band of modern day Robin Hoods, had overthrown the cruel oppressors of the Russian people. Their spirit was marching onwards into a just and glorious future, handing over the ill-gotten gains of the rich to the world's poor. It was all so simple, so good, so unstoppable: the triumph of communist fairness over capitalist greed. So it was that Solzhenitsyn and his schoolfriends learned to 'wave flags, beat drums, blow trumpets', taking their place in the ranks of those destined to 'complete the Revolution'.

Solzhenitsyn took the first decisive step away from the beliefs of his family and towards the teaching of the state in 1930 when, at the age of eleven, he joined the Young Pioneers. This was the junior wing of the Communist Party's youth movement, the Komsomol, founded in 1918. Although no older than Solzhenitsyn himself, the Young Pioneers were virtually omnipresent in the life of Russia's children by the beginning of the thirties. In fact, it was easier to become a member than not. Everyone joined, to be with friends, to go camping, to learn to tie knots, to sing rousing revolutionary songs, to parade in the Pioneers' red tie and red badge with its five logs representing the five continents ablaze in the flames of world revolution. From the Young Pioneers it was a natural, and expected, progression to the Komsomol, and then to the final achievement of full Party membership when one was old enough. In this way, almost imperceptibly, the Communist Party was tightening its grip on the nation's life; and in this way it was tightening its grip ever more on the young life of Alexander Solzhenitsyn.

Initially Solzhenitsyn had been a reluctant recruit. At the age of ten the cross he had worn since infancy had been ripped from his neck by jeering Pioneers and the resentment this must have caused, coupled with the remnants of ambivalence towards Bolshevism inherited from his family, led him to refrain from joining even after most of his friends had done so. For over a year he was ridiculed and pressurized at school meetings, and repeatedly urged by his friends to join. Eventually the need to conform was greater than any remaining reservations and Solzhenitsyn succumbed to convention.

In the winter of 1930, a matter of months after Solzhenitsyn had joined the junior wing of the Communist Party, the visit of his grandfather was to serve as a reminder that the boy's conformity at school could not resolve the continuing conflict between his family and the state. Upon arrival Grandfather Zakhar sat down dejectedly in the corner and, leafing through the pages of the Bible he was carrying, began bewailing the ill fortune that had fallen on the family since the accursed Revolution. Not only had the old man endured the confiscation of his estate, but he faced recurrent harassment and repeated questioning by the Soviet authorities. Like many of his generation he still clung to the belief, the forlorn hope, that the Communists would soon be overthrown and that life would return to normal. When this happened he was concerned that his estate should be properly cared for so that he could hand it on to the young Solzhenitsyn, his only grandchild. In a naïvely inspired effort to comfort his grandfather, Solzhenitsyn had assured him that there was no need to worry: 'Don't worry about it, grandad. I don't want your estate anyway. I would have refused it on principle.'[8] One can only imagine the cold comfort, the pain, that the old man must have felt as the eleven-year-old displayed his communist sympathies and his belief in the evils of property.

The cramped conditions in which Solzhenitsyn and his mother lived meant that any visitors to their tiny shack were forced to sleep on the floor. Early next morning, the seventy-two-year-old woke from an uncomfortable and restless night and crept out to go to church while mother and child still slept. Soon after his departure they were rudely awakened by the sound of boots kicking against their door. Two Soviet secret policemen burst into the room and demanded to see Zakhar, who was wanted for questioning in connection with the illegal hoarding of gold. These agents had followed the old man from his home in Georgievsk where he had already been detained twice and questioned on the same subject. Surprised to find that he was not there, they turned on Solzhenitsyn's mother, abusing her as a 'class enemy' and demanding that she hand over any money, gold, or other valuables. Taissia informed them that she had none, whereupon she was threatened with imprisonment. The agents ordered her to sign a statement swearing that she had no gold in the house, warning her that she would be arrested immediately if their search proved that she had lied. Terrified, she asked whether the statement included wedding rings. The agents nodded and sheepishly she handed over both her own wedding ring and that of her dead husband.

At that moment Zakhar returned from church to be greeted by a torrent of abuse from the agents who demanded that he hand over his gold. Ignoring them, he fell to his knees before the icon in the corner and began to pray. The agents hauled him to his feet and conducted a thorough body search, but found nothing. Cursing, they stormed out, threatening to catch him on a future occasion.

Zakhar returned home and, two months later, in February 1931, his wife Evdokia died. Unable to attend the funeral in Georgievsk,

Taissia arranged a memorial Mass for her mother in Rostov Cathedral. This involved great courage and carried with it considerable personal risk. Churchgoers were now spied on and if reported to the authorities could lose their jobs. For this reason Taissia had ceased attending church on a regular basis, but she felt duty-bound to go to the Mass and duly attended with her son. Although his mother was fortunate enough to escape retribution, Solzhenitsyn was reported to the headmaster by a fellow pupil and was severely reprimanded for conduct unbecoming of a Young Pioneer.

Grief-stricken after the death of his wife, Zakhar had wandered back to the district where his confiscated estate was, in the vicinity of Armavir, pursued incessantly by the secret police who remained convinced that he had a secret hoard of gold. Driven half mad by grief and by the persistent harassment, he is said to have hung a wooden cross round his neck and gone to the secret police headquarters in Armavir. 'You have stolen all my money and possessions,' he is purported to have said, 'so now you can take me into your jail and keep me.' Whether he was indeed imprisoned or whether he collapsed and died elsewhere would remain a mystery. It was some time before news of his death, a year after that of his wife, filtered through to Taissia, who dutifully arranged another memorial Mass at Rostov Cathedral.

In March 1932, at around the time that his heartbroken and impoverished grandfather was dying in mysterious circumstances, the thirteen-year-old Solzhenitsyn witnessed his first arrest. With the slushy remains of the winter's snow still on the ground he had gone round to the home of the Fedorovskys, who were close family friends. As he arrived he stopped, startled, in his tracks at the sight of Vladimir Fedorovsky, the nearest person in his life to a father, being escorted by two strangers to a waiting car. He watched as Federovsky got into the car and was driven away. Entering the flat, Solzhenitsyn was greeted by a scene of utter devastation. Drawers and cupboards had been emptied on to the floor, rugs and carpets torn up and tossed aside, and books and ornaments were scattered everywhere. This was the aftermath of a search of the flat by the secret police which had lasted twenty-four hours.

It transpired that Fedorovsky's 'crime' was to have appeared in the same photograph as Professor L. K. Ramzin, an engineer imprisoned two years earlier for allegedly plotting against the government. The photograph, taken during an engineers' conference both men had attended, was the only 'evidence' discovered during the day-long search and was insufficient to put Fedorovsky on trial as an accomplice in Ramzin's plot. He was released after a year's detention and interrogation, but was completely broken in health and spirits and never returned to his former employment. He lived for another ten years, more or less aimlessly, and died in 1943.

If this had been Solzhenitsyn's first experience of an actual arrest, he received regular daily reminders of the presence of the Soviet prison system. Every day on his way home from school he passed the enormous building in the centre of Rostov which had been taken over by the Soviet authorities to be used as a prison. Each day he passed the back entrance to the prison where a permanent line of desolate women waited to make inquiries or to hand in food parcels. There were also the columns of prisoners marched through the streets under armed guard, accompanied by the chilling shouts of the escort commander: 'One step out of line and I'll give the order to shoot or sabre you down!' The young Solzhenitsyn would occasionally see these columns and be reminded of the existence of an incomprehensible twilight world. Yet he was too young to understand the implications. On another occasion he heard how a man had clambered out on to the sill of a top floor window of the prison and hurled himself to his death on the pavement below. His mangled body was hastily removed and the blood washed away with hosepipes, but news of the suicide spread through the town.

Later, Solzhenitsyn learned that the dungeons of the prison at Rostov were situated under the pavement, lit by opaque lights set into the asphalt. Almost daily, as a child and then as an adolescent, he had been walking unwittingly over the heads of the prisoners incarcerated beneath his feet.

At school he was an exceptional pupil, excelling in both the arts and the sciences, encouraged by his mother who, like her gifted son, had been top of the class as a child. The precocious schoolboy became close friends with two other gifted pupils in his class. His friendship with Nikolai Vitkevich and Kirill Simonyan was to last through the rest of their school years and through their years at Rostov University. Soon they were so inseparable that they referred to themselves jokingly as 'The Three Musketeers'. Their other close friend, admitted as an honorary fourth member of the intimate circle, was Lydia Ezherets, known to her friends as Lida. The four were drawn together principally by their love of literature. They wrote essays on Shakespeare, Byron and Pushkin, each trying to outdo the other in friendly competitiveness; and they wrote 'very bad, very imitative poetry'.[9] Encouraged by their literature teacher Anastasia Grunau, they collaborated on the writing of a novel which was dubbed 'the novel of the three madmen', and started producing a satirical magazine in which they wrote poems and epigrams on each other and on the teachers. Later, they developed an infatuation with the theatre, organizing a drama club and rehearsing plays by Ostrovsky, Chekhov and Rostand.

Aside from literature, Solzhenitsyn's other great love during these years was cycling, having obtained a bicycle in 1936 in somewhat unorthodox circumstances. During his last year at school he had been nominated by the headmaster for a civic prize for outstanding pupils. Normally the award of the prize was a mere formality once the nominations were made but Solzhenitsyn's nomination was blocked on account of his social background. The headmaster was incensed and demanded that the injustice be rectified. Reluctantly the officials consented to award Solzhenitsyn a bicycle as an extraordinary consolation prize.

Solzhenitsyn was more than happy with his 'consolation'. Bicycles were a rare luxury in those days and neither he nor his mother would ever have been able to afford one. His other friends also owned bicycles and thereafter cycling became a favourite hobby. The next three summers were devoted to touring holidays and the first, in 1937 when Solzhenitsyn was eighteen years old, took the friends, five boys and two girls, to Tbilisi via the most scenic and spectacular passes of the Caucasus Mountains.

Inspired by his new-found love of cycling, Solzhenitsyn indulged his other love for literature in what he called his *Cycling Notes*. These were composed in the autumn, shortly after his return from the tour of the Caucasus in July and August, and were contained in three school exercise books labelled 'My Travels, Volume IV, Books 1, 2, and 3'. The *Notes*, written in naïve schoolboy prose, were nonetheless full of high spirits and infectious humour, notably in a description of a series of punctures and other mishaps in the pouring rain when the group was en route to Stalin's birthplace at Gori. In an unintentionally amusing display of post-pubescent indignation, Solzhenitsyn waxed lyrical on the arrogant sex discrimination of Georgian men while simultaneously displaying jealousy of their easy southern charm. The Georgian men, he complained puritanically, exhibited an insufferably patronizing attitude towards Russian women, regarding them as easy conquests and therefore of easy virtue.

More disturbingly, the *Notes* displayed a political naïveté which illustrated the extent to which Solzhenitsyn's generation had soaked up Soviet propaganda. Their very thoughts, it seemed, were saturated with Stalinist slogans and jargon. 'Two things cause tuberculosis – poverty and the impotence of medicine,' he stated glibly, referring to a TB sanatorium that the cyclists had come across on their travels. 'The Revolution has liquidated poverty. Medicine, why are you lacking behind? Tear these unfortunates from death's grasping paws!'

These and similarly trite declarations throughout the *Notes* confirmed that Solzhenitsyn and his friends were now utterly convinced of the correctness of Stalinism. Their pilgrimage to the place of Stalin's birth, achieved in spite of the combined endeavours of the elements and sundry protesting bicycle tyres to prevent their arrival, was an act of homage befitting true and trusted – and trusting – children of the Revolution. Solzhenitsyn's own devotion to the father of the nation was confirmed by the motto he selected to adorn the cover of one of the exercise books in which he had written his *Cycling Notes*: 'We shall have excellent and numerous cadres in industry, agriculture, transport, and the army – our country will be invincible (Stalin).' It was almost as though only the immortal words of Stalin himself deserved place of honour on the cover of any of Solzhenitsyn's literary works. The Soviet education system had triumphed indeed.

There was, however, one notable redeeming passage in the *Notes*, inspired by a visit to the grave of Alexander Griboyedov, described by Solzhenitsyn as 'that radiant genius, that pride of the Russian nation'. *Woe from Wit*, Griboyedov's masterpiece, a verse comedy in the manner of Molière written in 1822–3, was one of Solzhenitsyn's favourite plays and he often declaimed passages from it when, as a student, he took part in readings. While in Tbilisi he had taken the opportunity to visit Griboyedov's resting place and the poignancy of the occasion inspired thoughts more worthy of the selfless and incisively introspective writer who was to emerge triumphant from the Gulag Archipelago almost twenty years later:

> I love graveyards! ... Sitting in a graveyard you involuntarily cast your mind back over all your past life, your past actions, and your plans for the future. And here you do not lie to yourself as you do so often in life, because you feel as if all those people sleeping the sleep of peace around you were somehow still present, and you were conversing with them. Sitting in a graveyard you momentarily rise above your daily ambitions, cares and emotions – you rise for an instant even above yourself. And then, when you leave the graveyard, you become yourself again and subside into the morass of daily trivia, and only the rarest of individuals is able to leap from that morass onto the firm ground of immortality.[10]

In 1937 there were early signs that Solzhenitsyn was destined to become one of these 'rarest of individuals'. It was at this time that he conceived the idea for an epic work which, more than sixty years later, he was to consider 'the most important book of my life'.[11] Eventually, under the collective title of *The Red Wheel*, this would run to several volumes, the fruit of a lifetime's labour:

> I conceived it when I was eighteen years old and in sum, including thinking it through, collecting materials, writing, I worked on *The Red Wheel* for a total of fifty-four years. I finished *The Red Wheel* when I was seventy-two years old. The subject is the history of our Revolution. Initially, I had assumed that its centre would be the October events of 1917, the Bolshevik Revolution, but in the course of immersing myself deeper in the material in studying these events I realized that the main event was in fact the February revolution of 1917.[12]

24

At its conception, the eighteen-year-old Solzhenitsyn did not have the benefit of the wisdom which his seventy-nine-year-old counterpart had accrued. Nevertheless when, on 18 November 1936, he first resolved to write 'a big novel about the Revolution', he envisaged it on the grandest of scales, modelled in scope on Tolstoy's *War and Peace*. It would be not merely a novel but a true epic in multiple volumes and parts. It would be his masterpiece. What a tribute it is to Solzhenitsyn's vision, his determination and, indeed, his genius that this wildest and most arrogantly ambitious of teenage dreams was brought to fruition through half a century of careful and considered reflection coupled with superhuman endeavour.

Provisionally labelled *R-17*, its principal focus being the Revolution of 1917, the young Solzhenitsyn's epic had originally been planned to reflect the orthodox communist point of view. 'From childhood on, I had somehow known that my objective was the history of the Russian Revolution and that nothing else concerned me. To understand the Revolution I had long since required nothing beyond Marxism. I cut myself off from everything else that came up and turned my back on it.'[13] The novel's hero Olkhovsky, who was to become Lenartovich in *August 1914*, was intended to be an idealistic communist; according to Natalya Reshetovskaya, Solzhenitsyn's first wife, the purpose of the novel was to show 'the complete triumph of the Revolution on a global scale'.[14]

Solzhenitsyn soon realized, however, that it was impossible to understand or do justice to the Revolution without appreciating fully the huge significance of the First World War. He started to study some of the war's military campaigns and became increasingly fascinated by the defeat of General Samsonov at the Battle of Tannenberg, in East Prussia. For the first three months of 1937 Solzhenitsyn spent hours in Rostov's libraries studying this particular campaign, an experience he was later to evoke in his poem *Prussian Nights*.

His labours bore fruit in 1937 and 1938 when he drafted the first few chapters of part one of his novel under the provisional title 'Russians in the Advance Guard'. He also sketched in a scene between Olkhovsky and Severtsev (later Vorotyntsev) for a chapter entitled 'Black on Red'. When writing *August 1914* thirty years later, he was able to draw heavily from these initial drafts, taking not only source material but in some cases whole scenes which barely needed any amendment at all.

Solzhenitsyn had now entered the local university where, surprisingly, he elected to take a degree in physics and mathematics rather than in literature. At Rostov University, literature was not taught at faculty level but only at teacher training college where students were prepared for teaching in secondary schools. This was not a prospect that Solzhenitsyn found attractive.

> I had no desire to become a teacher of literature, because I had too many complex ideas of my own, and I simply wasn't interested in retailing crude, simplified nuggets of information to children in school. Teaching mathematics, however, was much more interesting. I didn't have any particular ambitions in the field of science, but I found it came easy to me, very easy, so I decided it would be better for me to become a mathematician and keep literature as a consolation of the spirit. And it was the right thing to do.[15]

It was usual at this time for students to sit an entrance examination before being accepted for a place at university and to submit their social credentials for scrutiny but Solzhenitsyn's superlative record of straight 5s in school meant that he was accepted without an examination. This in turn averted too close a scrutiny of his class origins. In any case he was now becoming adept at avoiding the awkward parts of the endless questionnaires that had become such a feature of Soviet life. He invariably wrote 'office worker' when describing his father's former occupation: 'I could never tell anyone that he had been an officer in the Russian army, because that was considered a disgrace.'[16]

Solzhenitsyn's brilliant academic career continued at university where he received top marks in all his examinations. Simultaneously, finding his course very easy, he found time to develop a new love which was soon vying with literature for his extra-curricular attention. This was the study of Marxism-Leninism. Along with his friends, he had passed with unquestioning ease from the Young Pioneers to the Komsomol in his tenth and final year at school. Then, from the age of seventeen onwards, he threw himself into the study of Party doctrine with an almost religious zeal: 'during my years at the university, I spent a lot of time studying dialectical materialism, not only as part of my courses but in my spare time as well. Then and later ... I read an enormous amount about it and got completely carried away. I was absolutely sincerely enthralled by it over a period of several years.'[17]

As Solzhenitsyn reached manhood it seemed that he was determined to leave his childhood behind in every conceivable sense. He had come to the conclusion that the doubts, fears and confusion of his childhood years were caused by the reactionary errors of his elders who were unfortunately handicapped by their emotional attachment to old and discredited beliefs. With the self-assured audacity of youth, he had rejected old traditions and superstitions in favour of the brave new world presented by the Revolution. He had solved the psychological schism of his boyhood by rejecting the heresies of Russian Orthodoxy and embracing the orthodoxy of Communism. It was all so easy ... 'The Party had become our father and we, the children, obeyed. So when I was leaving school and embarking on my time at university, I made a choice: I banished all my memories, all my childhood misgivings. I was a Communist. The world would be what we made it.'[18]

The banishment of memories must have been made difficult by the occasional reminders that dogged his years at university. In 1937, during his first year, some senior students were arrested and disappeared, and some of the professors were said to have disappeared as well. When Solzhenitsyn heard about this it is hard to believe that the painful vision of Vladimir Fedorovsky's arrest would not have returned to haunt him. Similarly the wretched figure of Professor Trifonov scurrying nervously down the corridors and flinching whenever his name was called must have resurrected unwelcome childhood misgivings. 'We learned later that he had *been inside* and if anybody called out his name in the corridor he thought perhaps the security officers had sent for him.'[19] Is it feasible that the young communist student could have seen this broken wretch of a man without visions of his grandfather, half-maddened by constant persecution, walking the streets with a wooden cross hanging from his neck?

One suspects that the born-again communist nurtured a sneaking admiration for the celebrated mathematician Professor Mordukhai-

Boltovskoi in spite of his anti-Marxist heresies, or perhaps even because of them. On one occasion, according to Solzhenitsyn, the elderly professor was lecturing on Newton when one of the students sent up a note which said, 'Marx wrote that Newton was a materialist, yet you say he was an idealist.' To which the professor replied, 'I can only say that Marx was wrong. Newton believed in God, like every other great scientist.' On another occasion, when his students told him that there was an attack on him in one of the newspapers which were pasted to the walls of the university, he replied with weighted indifference, 'My nanny told me never to read what was written on walls.'[20] Not surprisingly, Mordukhai-Boltovskoi was purged from the university but he was saved from prison by his age, his reputation as a famous mathematician, and allegedly by the personal intervention of Kalinin, chairman of the Central Executive Committee of the USSR, to whom the professor had turned for help. As a result he was reprieved and was merely 'relegated' by being transferred to the teacher training college.

The professor was one of a small and very fortunate minority in being the recipient of state-sponsored leniency at this time. During the 1930s Stalin had instituted a new reign of terror designed principally to eliminate all actual or potential rivals. At the Seventeenth Party Congress, 'the Congress of Victors', in 1934, Stalin had declared that the Party had triumphed over all opposition, promising the Party faithful a glorious and joyful future: 'Life has become better, Comrades. Life has become gayer.' Of the two thousand delegates who applauded on that day, two-thirds were arrested in the course of the next five years. In 1934 Sergei Kirov was murdered in Leningrad and a wave of show trials followed: the trial of Kamenev and Zinoviev in 1935, the Old Bolsheviks trial in 1936, the trial of Pyatakov and Radek in 1937, the trial of Rykov and Bukharin in 1938, and a host of lesser trials. In 1940, having been sentenced to death in his absence, Trotsky was murdered in exile. Yet the new reign of terror was not restricted to the higher echelons of Soviet power. It permeated downwards contaminating every stratum of society with an atmosphere of fear. In Leningrad alone during the spring of 1935 between thirty and forty thousand people were arrested. Over the following three years the total number arrested across the Soviet Union as a whole ran into millions. The purpose of

Stalin's murderous Machiavellianism was summed up succinctly by Michael Scammell: 'Soviet society was turned upside down and re-made in Stalin's image.'[21]

At the height of the Terror it seemed that almost anyone could be arrested at any time. This was illustrated by a grimly absurd episode in Solzhenitsyn's own life. In the mid-1930s he narrowly escaped arrest when standing in a bread queue. The people in the queue were accused of being 'saboteurs' who were 'sowing panic' among the public by suggesting there was a bread shortage. Fortunately for the young and enthusiastic communist, someone interceded on his behalf and he was released without being charged.

There was also a grim irony in the way that socialist intellectuals in the West continued their love affair with the Soviet Union in general and Stalin in particular. When H. G. Wells was granted an audi-ence with Stalin in the autumn of 1934, he told the Soviet leader that 'at the present time there are in the world only two persons to whose opinion, to whose every word, millions are listening – you and Roosevelt'. The incredible gullibility that Wells displayed regu-larly throughout his life was evident when he told his mentor that 'I have already seen the happy faces of healthy men and women and I know that something very considerable is being done here. The contrast with 1920 is astounding.'

'Much more could have been done had we Bolsheviks been clev-erer,' Stalin replied in mock humility. Yet Wells, dazzled by the bril-liance of his hero, would accept no weakness in the Soviet system. If perfection had not been achieved in the socialist utopia, he reasoned, people and not the Party were to blame. 'No,' Wells responded, 'if human beings were cleverer. It would be a good thing to invent a Five Year Plan for the reconstruction of the human brain, which obviously lacks many things needed for a perfect social order.' This riposte met with the Leader's approval and Wells recorded that both men burst out laughing at the wit of his reply.

Wells concluded his meeting with Stalin by mentioning the 'free expression of opinion – even of opposition opinion', adding apolo-getically that 'I do not know if you are prepared yet for that much freedom'. Stalin was quick to reassure him: 'We Bolsheviks call it "self-criticism". It is widely used in the USSR ...' Wells did not record any laughter at this point and Stalin may have managed to keep a straight face, but his own reply, amidst his plans for mass arrests and murder, far exceeded in wit anything Wells had said.

Following Wells' return to England, the transcript of his interview with the Soviet leader was published in *The New Statesman and Nation* on 27 October 1934 under the heading 'A Conversation Between Stalin and Wells'. It was criticized heavily in the subsequent issue, not, as one might expect, for its naïveté, but for being too harsh on Stalin. George Bernard Shaw complained that 'Stalin listens attentively and seriously to Wells, taking in his pleadings exactly, and always hitting the nail precisely on the head in his reply. Wells does not listen to Stalin: he only waits with suffering patience to begin again when Stalin stops. He has not come to be instructed by Stalin, but to instruct him.' Another writer eager to spring to Stalin's defence in the wake of Wells' interview was the German expressionist playwright and poet Ernst Toller who insisted that, compared with fascist countries, intellectual freedom in the USSR was growing.

Within a few years both Wells and Toller had become disillusioned with events in the Soviet Union. Toller committed suicide in New York in 1939 and Wells ended his literary career with the desolate thoughts of *The Mind at the End of its Tether*. Only Shaw remained blissfully oblivious to the many contradictions at the heart of his thinking.

Perhaps one should not be too harsh on those Western intellectuals who had fallen under the spell of Stalin's propaganda machine, especially as many citizens of the Soviet Union were similarly beguiled. During the show trials Soviet newspapers were full of gloating accounts of the defendants' confessions and sycophantic praise of the secret police for their 'eternal vigilance'. The press was full of vituperative rhetoric against the 'enemies of the people' and their constant plots to undermine the good work of the Party through 'ideological and economic sabotage'. Pavlik Morozov became an overnight hero for denouncing his own father to the secret police and was held up as a model for Soviet youth to emulate. All over the country, armies of Party spokesmen were mobilized to lecture the nation's students on why the purges were necessary and to brainwash them into acceptance.

In spite of his near-arrest for daring to queue for bread in a public place, and in spite of the arrests he knew about both in the past and present, Solzhenitsyn accepted the situation as a temporary but necessary phenomenon, crucial to the success of the Revolution. The purges were exactly that, a thorough cleansing of the Party machine so that it could continue the revolutionary struggle in a spirit of purity. Years later, looking back at this period in a spirit of self-critical contrition, Solzhenitsyn grieved over 'the astonishing swinishness of egotistical youth ... We had no sense of living in the midst of a plague, that people were dropping all around us, that a plague was in progress. It's amazing, but we didn't realize it.'[22]

In autumn 1938, during his third year at university and shortly before his twentieth birthday, Solzhenitsyn faced a test, a temptation which, had he succumbed, could have changed his life irrevocably. He was summoned before the District Komsomol Committee and given an application form for entry into one of the training colleges of the NKVD, the government department responsible for the recruitment and training of the secret police. The prospect of joining the secret police must have been tempting. After all, was he not a committed Marxist? A loyal child of the Revolution? Hadn't he learned from all those lectures on historical materialism that the purges were necessary, that 'the struggle against the internal enemy was a crucial battlefront, and to share in it was an honourable task'?[23] Then, of course, apart from such ideological grounds for joining the ranks of the secret police, there were very good material considerations to take into account. Could the provincial university at which he was studying offer him the same opportunities as a career in the NKVD? No, it couldn't. The best he could hope for after graduating was a teaching post at some remote rural school where the pay would be paltry. In comparison the NKVD training college offered the prospect of double or triple pay and the lure of special rations. On the face of it there was no competition. He should join the secret police where he could serve the Party *and* be relatively rich into the bargain. For some reason, however, he hesitated – hesitated and then refused:

> People can shout at you from all sides: 'You must!' And your own head can be saying also: 'You must!' But inside your breast there is a sense of revulsion, repudiation. I don't want to. *It makes me feel sick.* Do what you want without me; I want no part of it.[24]

It was a defining moment and one which would cause Solzhenitsyn much painful heart-searching in years to come: 'if, by the time war broke out, I had already been wearing an NKVD officer's insignia on my blue tabs, what would I have become? ... If my life had turned out differently, might I myself not have become just such an executioner?'[25]

For one so ruthlessly introspective as Solzhenitsyn the issue could not be shirked and the ramifications were chilling: 'It is a dreadful question if one really answers it honestly.'[26]

These, however, were the questions of an old man looking back over a lifetime's suffering. The insight was not available to the young, carefree Solzhenitsyn who was soon able to put the NKVD episode out of his idealistic mind. By day, he and his young communist friends paraded with banners through the streets of Rostov proclaiming the Revolution while, by night, the Black Marias passed unnoticed through the same streets. Ignorance indeed was bliss. 'We twenty-year-olds marched in the column of the October children, and as the Revolution's children, we looked forward to a glittering future.'[27]

The ageing sage saw things differently: 'I was brought up in a Christian spirit but youth in the Soviet period took me away from religion entirely. I now read through some of my letters and my efforts at literature from that period of my youth and I am grasped by a horror of what kind of emptiness awaited me.'[28]

NOTES

1. Quoted in D. M. Thomas, *Alexander Solzhenitsyn: A Century in His Life*, London: Little, Brown and Company, 1998, p. 38.
2. Malcolm Muggeridge, *Chronicles of Wasted Time, Vol. 1: The Green Stick*, London: Fontana, 1975, p. 243.
3. Dimitri Panin, *The Notebooks of Sologdin*, London: Hutchinson, 1976, p. 11.
4. Scammell, *Solzhenitsyn: A Biography*, p. 55.
5. Ibid.
6. Ibid., p. 59.
7. Ibid., pp. 58–9.
8. Ibid., p. 68.
9. Natalya Reshetovskaya, *Sanya: My Life with Alexander Solzhenitsyn*, Indianapolis/New York: Bobbs-Merrill Company, Inc., 1975, p. 19.
10. Scammell, *Solzhenitsyn: A Biography*, p. 83.

11. Alexander Solzhenitsyn, interview with the author, Moscow, 20 July 1998.
12. Ibid.
13. Solzhenitsyn, *The Gulag Archipelago Volume One*, p. 213.
14. Scammell, *Solzhenitsyn: A Biography*, p. 85.
15. Ibid., p. 87.
16. Ibid., p. 85.
17. Ibid., p. 87.
18. Ibid., p. 88.
19. Solzhenitsyn, *The Gulag Archipelago Volume Three*, p. 447.
20. Scammell, *Solzhenitsyn: A Biography*, pp. 88–9.
21. Ibid., p. 89.
22. Ibid., p. 90.
23. Solzhenitsyn, *The Gulag Archipelago Volume One*, p. 161.
24. Ibid.
25. Ibid., pp. 160–1.
26. Ibid., p. 160.
27. Scammell, *Solzhenitsyn: A Biography*, p. 91.
28. Solzhenitsyn, interview with the author.

CHAPTER THREE

MAN AND WIFE

The enormous energy which Solzhenitsyn exuded throughout his life was already evident in his youth. Besides his university studies, his dabblings with literature, his extra-curricular sorties into the intricacies of Marxism-Leninism, and his recreational activities with the close circle of friends with whom he went cycling, he also found time for his first serious romance. Natalya Reshetovskaya records in her memoirs that she first met Solzhenitsyn in 1936, near the beginning of their first year at university. It was during the lunch break and she looked up from the sandwich she was consuming to see 'a tall, lean youth with thick, light hair ... bounding up the stairs two steps at a time'.[1] He spotted two friends and explained in 'a rapid-fire speech' that he was attending some lectures in the chemistry department where Reshetovskaya was studying. 'Everything about him seemed rapid, headlong,' she remembered, adding that he had 'very mobile features'. At the time of his arrival, Natalya was having lunch with Nikolai Vitkevich and Kirill Simonyan, who along with Solzhenitsyn had formed the 'Three Musketeers' at high school. His two friends had both enrolled in the chemistry department and Natalya recalled that Solzhenitsyn's eyes 'darted from one person to the other or focused on me with interest'. The first time his eyes had rested on her, the lower part of her face was masked by 'an enormous apple' which she was munching between bites of her sandwich. When the apple was lowered he saw a full-lipped, chestnut-haired girl who had an air of extrovert exuberance. The three boys began to talk animatedly about their schooldays together and Natalya observed that Solzhenitsyn's energetic mannerisms were merely an outward expression of a lively intellect: 'Their conversation was studded with references to heroic figures from the most varied literary sources imaginable; there were ancient gods, of course, and historical personages galore. They knew everything under the sun, all three of them: that was the way I saw them.'[2]

Little did Natalya realize, as these first impressions sank in, that she and the lively seventeen-year-old had much in common in their family and social backgrounds. Her father had served as a Cossack officer in the First World War and had fought on the side of the Whites in the civil war which followed. In November 1919, with Bolshevik victory imminent, he went into exile with the remnants of the volunteer army. Natalya was only ten months old at the time so, like Solzhenitsyn, had never known her father. Another similarity with Solzhenitsyn was the fact that she was *de facto* an only child. Before her there had been twins but they had been born prematurely and had died in infancy. Her mother had been joined in Rostov by her exiled husband's three unmarried sisters so that, when Solzhenitsyn first set eyes on Natalya, she was living in a flat with four middle-aged ladies, three of them maiden aunts.

Solzhenitsyn's first contact with Natalya's family came on 7 November 1936 when he and the other two 'Musketeers', along with three girl students, were invited by Natalya's mother to visit them. During the course of the evening the group amused themselves by playing forfeits and Natalya, a gifted pianist, entertained her guests with a rendition of Chopin's Fourteenth Etude. Her musicianship impressed Solzhenitsyn immensely and he told her as they were preparing for supper how beautifully she played.[3] Ten days later there was another party, organized by the biology students for the birthday of Liulya Oster, another of Solzhenitsyn's high-school classmates. Solzhenitsyn and Natalya were both present and on this occasion he seems to have been impressed by more than her prowess at the piano. 'Today is exactly twenty years from the day when I considered myself utterly and irrevocably in love with you,' he wrote in a letter to her on 17 November 1956, 'the party at Liulya's; you in a white silk dress and I (playing games, joking, but taking it all quite seriously) on my knees before you. The next day was a holiday – I wandered along Pushkin Boulevard and was out of my mind with love for you.'[4]

If this was indeed the day that Solzhenitsyn fell in love with his future wife, he kept the fact carefully concealed for many months afterwards. One wonders, in fact, whether his letter of twenty years later can be taken as a reliable account of his feelings. It was written at a time when he was once again courting his wife following many years of enforced separation, and one cannot discount the possibility that the words were selected, the memory selective, with this latter-day courtship in mind. Such a view appears to be vindicated by Natalya herself in her observation that Solzhenitsyn conceived his idea for the epic historical novel on the 'very same evening' that he was purportedly out of his mind with love for her. Certainly it appears incongruous that a seventeen-year-old, purportedly in the throes of first love, should spend his evenings mulling over ideas for a literary epic about the Revolution, rather than moping over his new love.

The letter's reliability is further thrown into question by the fact that Solzhenitsyn appears to have shown no outward sign of his love. Perhaps this was mere youthful bashfulness or else the result of loyalty to his friend, Nikolai Vitkevich, who was closer to Natalya than he was. 'That year,' Natalya wrote, she was more Nikolai's friend 'than anyone else's'.[5] It was Nikolai who sat next to Natalya during chemistry lectures and who shared notes with her. It was Nikolai who had taught her to play chess during the winter holidays and it was Nikolai in the summer who had shown her how to ride a bicycle. When Solzhenitsyn, Nikolai and several other friends had embarked on their cycling tour of the Georgian Highway, it was Nikolai and not Solzhenitsyn who had written to her.

It is of course possible that Solzhenitsyn had concealed his feelings as a selfless act of chivalry or in a touching display of loyalty to his old schoolfriend. Yet it is certain that he was outwardly happy during 1937 and that his friendship with Nikolai Vitkevich was as close and as apparently untroubled as ever. Furthermore, he had a whole host of other interests which absorbed both his time and attention and Natalya remained apparently oblivious of any amorous feelings on his part.

It is tempting to conclude that Solzhenitsyn's feelings were not quite as deep in the early days of their friendship as his letter of twenty years later suggested. Far from being 'out of his mind' with love for her, perhaps he felt a mere physical attraction to her in the same way he may have found attractive other young girls of his acquaintance. Possibly she was only one of several for whom his young eyes yearned.

It was not until the winter of 1937, a year after they had first met, that their relationship developed the depth which enabled a full-blown love affair to flourish. Towards the end of the year a course of dancing classes was started at the university and of their closely knit group of friends only Natalya and Solzhenitsyn attended. Predictably enough they became dancing partners and were soon partnering each other beyond the confines of the classes. 'We also started going out together to university parties,' Natalya remembered, 'and we danced only with each other.'⁶ Soon they were also going to the theatre and the cinema together. Solzhenitsyn would pick her up at home and, before leaving, she would play the piano for him. Theirs seemed the ideal student relationship; they were enjoying all the fun and frivolity of undergraduate life without the sacrifice and commitment of a married couple. 'I was happy with things as they were,' wrote Natalya in her memoirs, 'and I did not want any changes at all.' Then, on 2 July 1938, as they sat together in Rostov's Theatrical Park, Solzhenitsyn declared his love for her, explained that he visualized her always at his side and asked whether she was able to give him the same commitment. It was a proposal of marriage and Natalya realized that he was expecting an answer. She was thrown into confusion. What exactly did she feel towards this lively, energetic young man who was seated beside her in the park, waiting expectantly for her reply? 'Was it love – that love for whose sake one is ready to forget everything and everyone and plunge headlong into its abyss? At that time this was the only way I could understand the meaning of true love (I got it out of books, of course). Today, with a lifetime of experience behind me, it is still the only way I know how to understand true love.'⁷

Looking into that abyss, she found herself terrified at the prospect of what true love entailed. She was living such a full and varied life, with many different friends and interests. Solzhenitsyn simply could not take the place of everything, even though he already meant a great deal to her: 'For me the world did not consist of him alone. Nevertheless, it seemed that something had to be decided, something had to be said at once. I turned away, laid my head on the back of the park bench, and began to cry ...'

However, it is doubtful whether Solzhenitsyn had reached the position of 'true love' himself when he made his proposal to

Natalya. At the time, or at least very shortly beforehand, he was seeing another girl, nicknamed 'Little Gipsy', to whom he wrote poems and about whom he later wrote a short story, also called 'Little Gipsy'. Forty years later, he still kept photographs of her in his family album. They show a pretty girl with a smiling face, dark brushed-back hair and brooding eyes. One of the photographs shows him dancing with her at a student picnic to music from a hand-wound gramophone nestling in the grass. This was in April 1938, well after the date when he is supposed to have fallen in love with Natalya. Another shows him with his arm around her as they pose with others for a group picture. It is difficult to discern exactly how serious was Solzhenitsyn's relationship with 'Little Gipsy' but the fact that she inspired him to both poetry and prose suggests something deeper than a mere casual acquaintance. Either way, it does illustrate an ambivalence in his feelings towards Natalya which falls far short of true love.

On 5 July 1938, three days after the failure to receive the desired reply to his proposal, he accompanied Natalya to a concert performance by Tamara Tseretelli, a well-known singer. To her dismay, Natalya felt that his attitude to her had cooled. He was 'reserved, overpolite, taciturn'. Distraught, she feared the worst: 'Did that mean everything was over? Suddenly my full life lost its attractiveness. If only what used to be could have remained that way forever! I could not bear to give up the way things were before. I wanted everything to stay just as it was. Could this be what love was all about?'[8] Many complications, many questions, but precious few answers loomed in front of the naïve nineteen-year-old. Describing herself as 'hitherto always reserved in word and deed', a few days later she wrote Solzhenitsyn a note to say that she loved him. Far from being given freely, her hand had been forced.

Following her surrender Natalya recalled that 'everything did remain as I wanted it to – though not altogether the way it was before. Gradually a great tenderness and affection flowed into our relationship. It was becoming more and more difficult to separate after an evening together, more and more painful not to give in to our desires.'[9] Once again, one suspects that these memories, written more than thirty years afterwards, put a rose-tinted gloss on the reality. Whereas they may have been true for Natalya, it is less likely that

Solzhenitsyn's feelings were quite so intense. During 1938 he was still working on the historical epic, still finding time to write poetry and short stories, and in between was still working diligently at his university studies. In the summer of 1938 he took an extended holiday with Nikolai, cycling through the Ukraine and the Crimea, and at the beginning of 1939 he suggested to Nikolai that they enrol as correspondence students at the MIFLI – the Moscow Institute of Philosophy, Literature and History, the foremost institution in the country for the study of the humanities. Nikolai accepted with enthusiasm and, along with their respective university courses, they embarked on serious study of the 'Oldsters', their nickname for the celebrated philosophers of the past. Solzhenitsyn chose to study literature, Nikolai opted for philosophy, and Kirill, the third 'Musketeer', decided on comparative literature. As external students they would receive their instruction by post, send in their answers to questions also by post, and twice a year, during the winter and summer vacations, were required to travel to Moscow to attend a special course of lectures and be examined on the work of the preceding six months. The content of the courses and the examinations was identical to that for students in residence, and the diploma they received would be of equal academic value. In essence, therefore, the three friends were now embarked on two simultaneous degree courses, one in the sciences and one in the humanities.

Obviously this entailed a considerable extra workload, encroaching still further on the time Solzhenitsyn had available to spend with Natalya. She recalled that his studies had become almost obsessive. Even while waiting for a trolleybus he would flip through a set of small homemade cards on one side of which he had inscribed some historical event or personage and on the other the corresponding dates. Often, before a concert or a film began, she would be called upon to test his memory 'using the same endless cards: When did Marcus Aurelius reign? When was the Edict of Karakol promulgated?' Another set of homemade cards neatly recorded Latin words and phrases. On the days when the courting couple were not planning to go to the cinema or to a concert, Solzhenitsyn would insist that they didn't meet until ten o'clock at night when the reading room closed. He was 'more willing to sacrifice sleep than study time for the sake of his beloved', Natalya complained.[10]

Under these circumstances it was scarcely surprising that Natalya now sought some assurance of her lover's commitment. 'To merge our beings or to part – that was how I began to see our situation.' Increasingly frustrated at Solzhenitsyn's apparent unwillingness to merge his being with hers, she wrote to him suggesting that they take the alternative course. His reply, as uncompromising as ever, could hardly have been what she desired. Although he could not conceive of her as anything but his wife, he feared that marriage might interfere with his main goal in life. For the time being his priority was to complete his course at the MIFLI as quickly as possible after graduating from university. He reminded her that she too was committed to her studies at the conservatory and that this in itself would make rigorous demands on their time. If they were not careful 'time could be placed in jeopardy' by the relative trivia of family life which might ruin their hopes and aspirations. After listing everything else that could possibly rob them of 'the time to spread our wings', he named the final 'pleasant-unpleasant consequence' – a child.[11]

In spite of these reservations, and perhaps rashly given their attitudes, the couple still decided to marry, coming to the decision in early 1939 but agreeing to postpone the event until spring of the following year. 'It was,' writes Michael Scammell, 'as if marriage, for the young Solzhenitsyn, was almost a chore, an inevitable hurdle that somehow had to be taken in one's stride, without causing too much distraction, before resuming one's momentum.'[12]

In the summer of 1939, at the age of twenty, Solzhenitsyn made his first ever visit to Moscow to register at the MIFLI. He and Nikolai had already resolved to take advantage of the journey north to explore uncharted territory and, after registering and attending some introductory lectures, they made their way to Kazan on the river Volga. For the sum of 225 roubles they purchased an ancient *budarka*, a type of primitive dug-out with high boarded gunwales peculiar to that river and region, and proceeded in this cumbersome boat along the Volga on a three-week camping trip. They travelled light, sleeping by night on straw in the bottom of the boat, and rowing or drifting downstream by day, stopping occasionally to cook a meal on a campfire or to visit places of interest. The bulk of their luggage consisted of books and they spent the time either reading these or else locked in passionate discussions about the future prospects of communism, to which both of them remained wholeheartedly committed. Solzhenitsyn was also deeply impressed with the beautiful scenery embracing the banks of the Volga, comparing it favourably with the drab and dusty flatness of his native south. This was Russia's heart, the real Russia which resonated in Russian literature and folklore.

The primeval beauty of the countryside contrasted starkly with the dilapidated state of many of the villages they passed en route. The Russian village, romanticized in many of the classics which the two travellers knew so well, had changed beyond recognition, bearing little resemblance to the healthy self-sufficient communities described by Turgenev, Tolstoy and Chekhov. Instead, as Solzhenitsyn later described in his autobiographical poem *The Way*, the two friends found only decay, desolation and neglect. Loudspeakers blared trite propaganda jingles informing the villagers how good life was under communism while the village consumer co-operative displayed only row upon row of empty shelves. They had arrived in one village looking for food to augment their basic supply of dry biscuits and potatoes but there was none to be found, except for a bucketful of apples which they purchased for a few copecks. The village, like thousands of others throughout Russia, had been devastated by collectivization yet the two young communists, returning disappointed to their boat, were too naïve to understand how the reality before their eyes belied their idealistic discussions of Marxist dogma, the futility of their utopian theorizing.

As the idealists drifted downstream there were other grim reminders that Soviet life was not all that it was purported to be. One evening, while moored by the bank for the night at a place called Krasnaya Glinka, they were suddenly surrounded by a platoon of armed guards and tracker dogs. The guards were searching for a pair of escapees and had evidently mistaken the two terrified students for their quarry. Realizing their error they hurled a string of curses at them, ordered them to move on, and dashed away in pursuit of their prey. On another occasion they passed an open launch crammed with prisoners handcuffed to one another, and near Zhiguli they saw gangs of ragged men with picks and shovels digging foundations for a power station. Later Solzhenitsyn came to understand the significance of these sightings, but only after he had become one of the ragged men himself. For the time being the bewildering visions were cast aside, exorcised from his untroubled mind.

In Kuibyshev, at the end of their voyage, the friends sold their dug-out for 200 roubles, only twenty-five fewer than they had paid for it. Congratulating themselves on a bargain break, they returned by train to Rostov.

Throughout the autumn and winter of 1939 Solzhenitsyn buried himself once more in his studies. Physics and mathematics vied with literature, philosophy and history for his attention and, somewhere in the midst, the courtship with Natalya continued. The spring of 1940 arrived and as prearranged they went ahead with the marriage. The date they chose for the wedding ceremony was 27 April, although as a ceremony it was decidedly unceremonious. It was a warm, windy day and the couple, now both twenty-one, simply went to the city registry office and registered their marriage as the law dictated. They informed no one of the step they were taking, not even their parents. There was only one moment of drama in the otherwise drab affair, and even that was unintended. During the signing of the register, Natalya dipped the ancient quill into the inkwell with a vigorous flourish. As she withdrew it she caught the nib on the side and the pen flew out of her hand, somersaulted in mid-air and landed on Solzhenitsyn's forehead, depositing a large blot. 'It was an omen,' he said, not altogether jokingly, when describing the incident many years later.[13]

In this inauspicious setting the young couple were registered as man and wife. The secular solemnizing of their love seemed to have little in common with the sacramental sacrifice and lavish surroundings of the Russian Orthodox weddings their parents had known. Times had changed and for richer or poorer, better or worse, Alexander Solzhenitsyn and Natalya Reshetovskaya had decided to face the Soviet future together. Yet the doubts remained; as they left the registry office, Solzhenitsyn gave his legally registered wife a photograph of himself with a niggling question inscribed on the back, intended as a plea for the reassurance that even marriage could not give: 'Will you under all circumstances love the man with whom you once united your life?'[14]

NOTES

1. Reshetovskaya, *Sanya*, p. 1.
2. Ibid., p. 2.
3. Ibid., p. 5.
4. Ibid., pp. 5–6.
5. Ibid., p. 6.
6. Ibid.
7. Ibid., pp. 6–7.
8. Ibid., p. 7.
9. Ibid.
10. Ibid., p. 9.
11. Ibid., pp. 7–8.
12. Scammell, *Solzhenitsyn: A Biography*, p. 101.
13. Ibid., p. 102.
14. Reshetovskaya, *Sanya*, p. 9.

CHAPTER FOUR

MAN OF WAR

A few days after their marriage the newlyweds were separated by Natalya's departure for Moscow. She, together with Nikolai and some of the other chemistry students, was to spend the remainder of the academic year at the National Institute for Science and Research. The pair were reunited seven weeks later when Solzhenitsyn arrived in Moscow on 18 June to take his half-yearly MIFLI examinations. Upon his arrival Natalya rushed to meet him and they spent the day strolling through the Park of Rest and Culture and wandering into the Neskuchny Gardens. 'Of course,' Natalya wrote in her memoirs, 'we could not suspect that we would be here again, five years later, and under quite different circumstances. Then we would be separated by barbed wire and would be communicating by sign language, he perched on the third-storey window sill of a house in Kaluzhkaya Plaza, where he was laying parquet floors, and I gazing up at him from these very same Neskuchny Gardens.'[1]

It was from Moscow that Solzhenitsyn finally wrote to his mother, informing her of the marriage. She relayed the news to Solzhenitsyn's two aunts, Irina and Maria, who were shocked at the secrecy surrounding the wedding and, since it had not taken place in church, flatly refused to recognize its validity. Many years later, in an interview with *Stern* magazine in 1971, the ageing Irina still referred to Natalya dismissively as a 'mistress'. Their attitude must have served to alienate Solzhenitsyn still further from his reactionary relatives.

At the end of July, their respective studies completed, the couple rented a modest cabin in the district of Tarusa, a popular country resort about seventy miles south of Moscow. Here, on the very edge of a forest, they spent their honeymoon. In spite of the idyllic surroundings they spent little time exploring the local terrain. Instead they preferred to stretch out comfortably in the shade of the birch trees, while Solzhenitsyn read aloud to his wife from Sergei Esenin's poems or Tolstoy's *War and Peace*. Then, of course, there was the mandatory studying, sometimes together but often separately. Solzhenitsyn was already preparing for the following term's work at the MIFLI, leaving his wife to 'fill up the gaps' in her own education.[2]

One of Solzhenitsyn's principal preoccupations at the time was history, especially the reforms of Peter the Great. Surprisingly perhaps, considering his Marxist education, he found himself vehemently opposed to the 'progress' engendered by Peter's reforms. In his opposition to the former tsar, Solzhenitsyn was aware that he was out of step with the official Party line which fully endorsed Peter's 'progressive' policies. He admitted this in his autobiographical poem *The Way*, when he confessed that his antipathy to Peter meant that 'I'm a heretic'.[3] Perhaps his 'heretical' antipathy was a lasting legacy of his religious childhood; lovers of the old Russian way of life and the traditional forms of the Russian church, such as his own mother and his Aunt Irina, had never forgiven Peter for his brutal persecution of traditionalists.

Apart from this one minor heresy, Solzhenitsyn still prided himself on his orthodox Marxism. As Michael Scammell remarks, Solzhenitsyn 'must be one of the few bridegrooms in history to have taken *Das Kapital* on his honeymoon (and to have read it)'.[4] Awaking in the morning, Natalya would find the space in the bed beside her empty and would discover her husband on the veranda, his head buried in an annotated copy of Marx's masterpiece. In *The Way* Solzhenitsyn evoked his bride's understandable perplexity at his neglect of her, but explained that he was powerless to resist Marx's advances. He was a man possessed. He and his friends were 'apostles ... Bolsheviks ... And I? I believe to the marrow of my bones. I suffer no doubts, no hesitations – life is crystal clear to me.'[5]

Solzhenitsyn and Natalya stayed longer in Tarusa than they had originally intended, extending their honeymoon into the early autumn when the forest was changing colour. The beauty of their holiday hideaway had served to confirm Solzhenitsyn's preference for the landscapes of central Russia over the drabness of the south, first awoken by the journey down the Volga the previous summer.

He now felt that he had been born in the wrong place, but had found himself.

On the rail journey back to Rostov he was confronted with an uncomfortable reminder of the less savoury parts of the previous year's trip down the Volga. Their train halted in a siding next to another that looked somehow odd. It was neither a passenger train like theirs nor a freight train. Peering through the window, Solzhenitsyn caught a glimpse of compartments crowded with shaven-headed troglodytes who looked as if they had come from a different planet. With deep-sunken eyes, distorted faces and sub-human features, the alien creatures gazed back at him. The twenty-one-year-old looked away. A minute or so later the train started again and the aliens disappeared as silently as they had emerged. Little did the naïve newly-wed know it but the trainload of convicts being transported from one labour camp to another were the ghosts of his own future.

Neither did he realize that the grim reality he had glimpsed so fleetingly from a train in the wilderness was also a lot closer to home if only he had eyes to see. One fellow student called Tanya, with whom he had studied side by side at Rostov University for five years, kept hidden the tragedy in her own life at the time. Only fifty years later when Solzhenitsyn returned to Rostov after his years in exile did she reveal it to him. He had asked her nostalgically whether she remembered a particular class photograph being taken. 'How could I not remember?' the old woman replied. 'Just twenty days later, my father was arrested; and three days after that, my uncle ...'[6]

The grim reality confronting many of his colleagues had no place in Solzhenitsyn's own cosseted life during the autumn of 1940. As he began his last year at university, he found himself considerably better off than in previous years and much more prosperous than the vast majority of his fellow students. This was due to his being awarded one of the newly instituted Stalin scholarships for outstanding achievement. Only three of these were granted to the Faculty of Physics and Mathematics and only four more in the entire university. They carried a stipend two and a half times greater than the usual grant and were awarded not only for academic performance but also for social and political activism in the Komsomol. Solzhenitsyn qualified on both counts. He had straight 5s and continued to excel in his studies, but he was also a valued and trusted member of the Komsomol. He was, in fact, a model Soviet citizen.

His most notable achievement as a true son of the Revolution during his last year at university was his editorship of the students' newspaper, which he transformed from a dull unread propaganda sheet, published only twice a year, into a vibrant and widely read weekly journal. This latest success ensured him a place of honour in the local party Komsomol, assuring him an easy transition to full Party membership, with all the privileges that went with it. In every respect he appeared to be on the threshold of a brilliant career.

The improved financial situation meant that Solzhenitsyn and Natalya could afford to take up residence on their own, away from their families. They found a room on Chekhov Lane which Natalya described as 'small but comfortable, even though we had to put up with a cantankerous landlady'.[7] Their new home was conveniently placed with respect to their families and, crucially, to Solzhenitsyn's two favourite reading rooms. Natalya remembered that their first year of married life together, which was also destined to be their last for many years, was 'busy beyond measure'. After an early breakfast they would both depart for the university or, if there were no classes, Solzhenitsyn would leave for the library while Natalya studied at home. They would meet for lunch at three o'clock at the home of one of Natalya's relatives. At Solzhenitsyn's insistence lunch was served punctually so that he would not lose any study time but if for any reason it was delayed he would remove the homemade cards from his pocket and get his wife to test him. Then, lunch consumed, he would hurry off back to the library where he would often stay until it closed at ten o'clock. Returning home he frequently continued to study until two o'clock in the morning before finally collapsing into bed.

Only on Sundays did the couple allow themselves to lie in before going to the home of Solzhenitsyn's mother for lunch. 'She put all her talents, all her love into serving us the most delicious meals possible,' wrote Natalya. 'The energy, the deftness, the speed with which she did everything, despite her illness (she had active tuberculosis), were amazing. Her speech was rapid-fire, just like her son's, only interrupted by brief coughing spells; and she had the same mobile features.'[8]

Somewhere amidst the hectic schedule of his life, Solzhenitsyn managed to continue with his writing. During this period he wrote a politically correct tale entitled 'Mission Abroad', completed in February 1941, whose hero was a Soviet diplomat cunningly outwitting bourgeois statesmen in Western Europe. He continued to write poetry which found its way into the exercise books containing his *Juvenile Verse*. The fruits of his studies at the MIFLI found their way into another exercise book entitled *Remarks on Dialectical Materialism and Art* and all the while he continued to plan his historical epic depicting the glorious triumph of the Revolution.

In spring 1941 he gained a first-class degree in mathematics and physics. In June he travelled to Moscow to take his second-year examinations at the MIFLI, nurturing a desire to move permanently to Russia's capital where he imagined all sorts of opportunities would present themselves. Events in the world at large, however, were destined to lay waste the young man's schemes. On 22 June 1941, the very day that he arrived in Moscow, war was declared between the Soviet Union and Germany. Hitler, too, nurtured a desire for the Russian capital and had launched the might of the Third Reich against his communist foe, unleashing the Wehrmacht across the Soviet border along a two-thousand-mile front.

'What an appalling moment in time this is!' wrote Alan Clark in *Barbarossa*. 'The head-on crash of the two greatest armies, the two most absolute systems, in the world. No battle in history compares with it. Not even that first ponderous heave of August 1914, when all the railway engines in Europe sped the mobilization ... In terms of numbers of men, weight of ammunition, length of front, the desperate crescendo of the fighting, there will never be another day like 22nd June, 1941.'[9]

The Nazi onslaught had thrown the whole of the Soviet Union into turmoil and all thought of examinations at the MIFLI was abandoned. Solzhenitsyn, like most of the other students, rushed to the recruitment office to volunteer on the spot. He was told that as his draft card was in Rostov he must return there in order to enlist. He hurried to the station but found that the railways had been thrown into chaos by the declaration of war. It was several days before he finally succeeded in catching a train south and even then the journey was insufferably slow. For a young man frantic with desire to join the fighting the interminable delays must have been intolerable.

When he eventually arrived in Rostov more disappointment awaited him. His army medical resulted in a classification of 'limited fitness' due to an abdominal disability, the result of a groin disorder in infancy that had gone undetected. The disability was so slight that Solzhenitsyn had barely noticed that he suffered from it; but it was sufficient to disqualify him from military service.

Seething with anger, Solzhenitsyn returned home and was forced to watch helplessly while most of his university friends enlisted and were dispatched for training. The sense of frustration must have been accentuated by his complete commitment to the war effort. Not only was Russia the victim of aggression which would in itself have made it a just war, but she was the standard-bearer of communist truth against the lies and errors of the fascists. Germany had always been Russia's enemy but now, under the tyranny of the Nazi swastika, she was her ideological enemy as well as her historical foe. His Marxist faith left no room for uncertainty about the rights and wrongs of the war, nor about who would be the final victors. The Soviet Union as the champion of the international proletariat would always triumph over her enemies. 'Not for a moment,' he wrote in *The Gulag Archipelago*, 'from the day the war began, did I doubt that we would conquer the Germans.'

A year earlier, on his honeymoon, he had written an ode which bore all the hallmarks of one who relishes the romance of war without having experienced its bloody realities. It was a piece of jingoistic juvenilia, flying defiantly in the face of the 'inexpressible turbulence' of impending war. Invoking Lenin as the inspiration, Solzhenitsyn boasted that his generation, which 'sprang to life' in the 'whirlwind' of the October Revolution, would die willingly so that the Revolution could 'ascend', if necessary 'upon our dead bodies'. His generation, the October generation, 'must make the supreme sacrifice'.[10]

The sacrifice that Solzhenitsyn was in fact called to make in September 1941 was supreme only in its irksome futility. While his friends marched to war, heading for glory, he and Natalya were dispatched to the Cossack settlement of Morozovsk as village schoolteachers. Solzhenitsyn was to teach mathematics and astronomy, while his wife's subjects were chemistry and the foundations of Darwinism. Morozovsk was an isolated community about 180 miles north-east of Rostov and halfway to Stalingrad. It was a dead-end place, or so Solzhenitsyn must have thought in his frustration. Nothing ever happened in Morozovsk. Nevertheless, as he recalled, even there 'anxiety about the German advance was stealing over us like the invisible clouds stealing over the milky sky to smother the small and defenceless moon'.[11] Such feelings were exacerbated by the arrival of trainloads of refugees which stopped at the local station every day before proceeding to Stalingrad. During the break in their journey these refugees would fill the marketplace of Morozovsk with terrible rumours about the disastrous way the war was turning.

The short time that the Solzhenitsyns spent in Morozovsk was relatively tranquil, the calm before the storm. Solzhenitsyn remembered 'quiet, warm, moonlit evenings, not as yet rent by the rumble of planes and by exploding bombs'.[12] He and Natalya had rented lodgings on the same little yard as an older couple, the Bronevitskys. Nikolai Gerasimovich Bronevitsky was a sixty-year-old engineer, described by Solzhenitsyn as 'an intellectual of Chekhovian appearance, very likable, quiet, and clever'. His wife was 'even quieter and gentler than he was – a faded woman with flaxen hair close to her head, twenty-five years younger than her husband, but not at all young in her behaviour'. The two couples struck up a friendship and spent long evenings sitting on the steps of the porch, enjoying the warmth of the fading summer, and talking. The Solzhenitsyns were totally at ease with the Bronevitskys, and Solzhenitsyn remembered that 'we said whatever we thought without noticing the discrepancies between our way of looking at things and theirs'. One discrepancy which Solzhenitsyn did notice was the way that Bronevitsky described those towns which had fallen to the Germans not as having 'surrendered' but as having been 'taken'. Looking back on their friendship, Solzhenitsyn perceived that the older couple probably considered their young counterparts 'two surprising examples of naïvely enthusiastic youth'. Asked what they remembered about 1938 and 1939, the youngsters could only recount the carefree trivia of their student life: 'the university library, examinations, the fun we had on sporting trips, dances, amateur concerts, and of course love affairs – we were at the age for love'. The Bronevitskys listened incredulously to the flippancy of the other couple. But, they asked, hadn't any of their professors been put away at that time? Yes, the Solzhenitsyns replied, two or three of them had been. Their places had been taken by senior lecturers. What about the students – had any of them gone inside? The younger couple did indeed recall that some senior students had been gaoled. Bronevitsky was puzzled:

'And what did you make of it?'

'Nothing; we carried on dancing.'

'And no one near to you was – er – touched?'

'No; no one.'[13]

The reason for Bronevitsky's morbid interest in the darker side of Soviet life soon became apparent. He had been one of the thousands of engineers who had been arrested during the thirties and sent to the newly opened labour camps. He had been in several prisons and camps but spoke with particular passion and disgust about Dzhezkazgan. Recalling the horror of camp life with a lurid disregard for the sheltered sensibilities of his listeners, he described the poisoned water, the poisoned air, the murders, the degradation, and the futility of complaints to Moscow. By the time he had finished, the very syllables 'Dzhez-kaz-gan' made Solzhenitsyn's flesh creep: 'And yet ... did this Dzhezkazgan have the slightest effect on our way of looking at the world? Of course not. It was not very near. It was not happening to us ... It is better not to think about it. Better to forget.'[14]

The Solzhenitsyns' brief friendship with the Bronevitskys came to an end when the younger couple left Morozovsk. Later Natalya learned that Bronevitsky had collaborated with the Germans when they occupied the town the following year. 'Can you imagine it,' she wrote to her husband, 'they say that Bronevitsky acted as burgomaster for the Germans while they were in Morozovsk. How disgusting!' Solzhenitsyn shared his wife's shock at their erstwhile friend's betrayal of the motherland, thinking it a 'filthy thing to do'. Years later his own circumstances would lead him to alter his judgement:

> turning things over in my mind, I remembered Bronevitsky. And I was no longer so schoolboyishly self-righteous. They had unjustly taken his job from him, given him work

that was beneath him, locked him up, tortured him, beaten him, starved him, spat in his face – what was he supposed to do? He was supposed to believe that all this was the price of progress, and that his own life, physical and spiritual, the lives of those dear to him, the anguished lives of our whole people, were of no significance.[15]

Solzhenitsyn was to express a similar view concerning the sense of patriotic duty which Russians were meant to feel towards Stalin's Soviet Union. If our mother has sold us to the gypsies, he asked, or, even worse, thrown us to the dogs, does she still remain our mother? 'If a wife has become a whore, are we really still bound to her in fidelity? A Motherland that betrays its soldiers – is that really a Motherland?'[16]

These sentiments, born of bitter experience, could not have been further from the mind of Solzhenitsyn in 1941. Instead he still longed for the opportunity to fight and if need be die for the Soviet Motherland. In mid-October the war took a further turn for the worse. Moscow was threatened and the German advance seemed irresistible. Under these dire circumstances all classifications of fitness were cast aside as the Soviet authorities scavenged for recruits. In the district of Morozovsk virtually every able-bodied man was summoned to the local recruitment centre. At long last Solzhenitsyn's chance had come. 'How difficult it was to leave home on that day,' he wrote to Natalya many years later, 'but it was only on that day that my life began. We never know at the time what is happening to us.'[17] Later still, as an old man looking back over the salient features of his past, he considered his time in the Soviet army as one of the 'most important and defining moments' in his life. Most interesting of all, he saw it in terms of escape: 'My father died before I was born and so I had lacked upbringing by men. In the army I ran away from that.'[18] What exactly was he running away *from*? Was he looking for a convenient escape from the feminine? His increasingly ill mother? Supercilious aunts, including the three extra aunts and a mother-in-law he had inherited in marrying Natalya? And what of Natalya herself? Was he escaping from her too?

'Solzhenitsyn's military career began as farce and ended in tragedy,' writes Michael Scammell.[19] Certainly it would be fair to say that it began inauspiciously. It was a long time before he finally got to the front and in his first months as a soldier he was often the victim of cruelty at the hands of his more experienced comrades, who took a dislike to the provincial schoolteacher newly arrived in the ranks. 'I did not move in one stride from being a student worn out by mathematics to officer's rank,' he wrote in *The Gulag Archipelago*. 'Before becoming an officer I spent a half-year as a downtrodden soldier. And one might think I would have gotten through my thick skull what it was like always to obey people who were perhaps not worthy of your obedience and to do it on a hungry stomach to boot.'[20]

His experience did not improve once he was accepted for officer training school. He disliked the strict disciplinarian regime, complaining that 'they trained us like young beasts so as to infuriate us to the point where we would later want to take it out on someone else'.[21] Yet however much he hated his time there, his greatest fear, and that of all his fellow candidates, was failure to stick it out until graduation and the receipt of his officer's insignia. The price of failure was immediate posting to the battle for Stalingrad where the casualty rate was so high that being sent there was virtually a death sentence. The threat of Stalingrad receded in October 1942 when Solzhenitsyn was awarded his first lieutenant's stars. Eventually, in June 1944, he was to reach the rank of captain. His experiences ought to have taught him, 'once and for all, the bitterness of service as a rank-and-file soldier'. Yet soon 'they pinned two little stars on my shoulder boards, and then a third, and then a fourth. And I forgot every bit of what it had been like!'[22] He had passed from the rank and file to the rank of officer, from persecuted to persecutor, and only in later years did he realize how he had been brutalized by the experience.

Now that he was an officer Solzhenitsyn hoped he would soon, at long last, be sent to the front. There was to be more disappointment, however, because in early November he was posted to Saransk in central Russia, a town which he described to Natalya as 'three little houses in a flat field'.[23] It was not until 13 February 1943 that his battalion was finally mobilized. Solzhenitsyn was sure that this time they would be heading for the southern front; instead they went in the opposite direction, to the far north, arriving a week or two later in Ostashkov, midway between Rzhev and Novgorod. They then moved slowly westward where they encamped in a forest waiting for orders to advance. Surely now he would see some action. Six weeks passed and nothing happened. Finally, in April, they received further orders and were transferred by train four hundred miles to the south east. At a point just east of Orel they dug in on the river Neruch.

This was an area of Russia unknown to Solzhenitsyn and he was not seeing it at its best. A low-lying, swampy region, dotted with woods, it had never been the most picturesque of landscapes. Now, having been twice fought over in recent months – first during the German advance and then again during their retreat – it was a battle-scarred quagmire. Houses, trees, whole villages, had been flattened by bombs and shells. Roads and fields had been churned into a lumpy soup by thousands of marching feet, exploding shells and the caterpillar tracks of countless tanks. In the distance the *quid pro quo* of both sides' artillery thumped incessant insults at each other. Yet Solzhenitsyn still sensed his nation's soil beneath the desolation. Although it was 'abandoned, wild, overgrown' without crops, vegetable patches or even a grain of rye, it was still 'Turgenev country', and gazing across the war-torn desert, the young soldier 'at last understood that one word – *homeland*'.[24]

At the end of May Solzhenitsyn received the first letter from his mother for many months. Her handwriting had deteriorated and was so weak and spidery that he hardly recognized it. On 12 January, when he was still in Saransk, he had sent her a telegram as soon as he had learned of the German retreat from the Caucasus but it was not until now, four months later, that he finally discovered what had become of her. When the Germans had arrived in Georgievsk, where she had been staying with her relatives, Taissia had returned to Rostov. Upon arrival she had discovered her home in ruins and the furniture destroyed. Now homeless, she was forced to find accommodation in a fourth-floor room without either running water or heating, consequently having to struggle up four floors with buckets of water and firewood. There was little to eat in the ruins of the German-occupied city and, shivering from the intense cold of the winter, she had suffered a severe recurrence of tuberculosis and had been compelled to return to her sister Maria in

Georgievsk. The details of his mother's letter only confirmed what the weakness of her handwriting had hinted. She was now a physically broken woman. One can imagine Solzhenitsyn reflecting on the perverse irony of events. He had been in the army for over eighteen months without so much as a scratch to show for his endeavours; meanwhile the war had crept up from behind and was killing his mother by stealth.

It was while he was encamped on the river Neruch that Solzhenitsyn met up once again with his old friend Nikolai Vitkevich who, as luck would have it, was an infantry officer in a regiment stationed in a neighbouring sector of the front. The two friends had temporarily lost touch with each other but found on being reunited that they had as much in common as ever, both politically and emotionally. They were 'like the two halves of a single walnut'.[25] In the days that followed they enjoyed once more the endless hours of debate and speculation which had been such a joyful part of their adolescent lives. It seemed that nothing had changed. Both men still considered themselves loyal communists and Nikolai, unlike Solzhenitsyn, had actually joined the Party, but there was one important, and ultimately fatal, difference in their thinking from that which had characterized earlier years. Now they had learned to be critical of the Soviet regime, albeit from a Leninist perspective. Rashly they drafted a political manifesto, 'Resolution No. 1', which likened aspects of Stalin's regime to feudalism. Fortunately for the two embryonic dissidents they did not take the suicidal decision to show their 'Resolution' to anyone else but merely promised solemnly to keep a copy of it on their person throughout the war. Their reunion, brief but sweet, was swept away by the eruption of battle.

On 4 July Solzhenitsyn recorded that the Germans had bombed their entrenchment, not with high explosives but with leaflets urging them to surrender before it was too late. 'You have more than once experienced the crushing strength of the German attacks,' the leaflets warned.[26] This was the prelude to the launching of the great German attack on the Kursk salient, the failure of which effectively secured the eventual defeat of the Nazis on the eastern front. In truth, since their defeat at Stalingrad the armies of the Third Reich had been in almost constant retreat. They had been driven out of the Caucasus and Solzhenitsyn's home city of Rostov had been liberated in February. By the time Hitler had launched this last-ditch offensive his forces had been pushed back to a line running from just east of the river Donets in the south to Orel and Kursk in the north. They were far from defeated, however, and no fewer than seventeen panzer divisions and eighteen infantry divisions had been deployed for the Kursk offensive. With such forces at his disposal, Hitler had good reason to be confident that his troops would once again smash their way through the Soviet defences. At last Lieutenant Solzhenitsyn was set to taste the bitterness of war.

The fighting which followed the initial German attack was fierce and intense but the Russians had built up colossal forces of their own in the area and their defensive fortifications stretched back to a depth of sixty miles. The first set-piece tank battle lasted for three weeks but ended in stalemate. In spite of heavy losses on both sides, the Germans had failed in their principal objective, to capture Kursk, and had hardly moved the front forward at all. The last great German offensive in the east had failed but the battle was by no means over. The Nazis still controlled Orel. Solzhenitsyn recalled the morning when the Soviet attack on Orel began and 'thousands of whistles cut through the air above us'.[27]

The battle for Orel lasted a further three weeks of continuous fighting with Solzhenitsyn's unit as part of the central front commanded by General Rokossovsky. On 5 August Solzhenitsyn entered Orel with the victorious Russian army and ten days later he was awarded the Order of the Patriotic War, second class, for his part in the battle. This was the euphoric high-point of his military career, his one, all too brief, taste of glory. Thereafter, the events of the war would increasingly leave him with little more than a rising sense of nausea.

The first bitter blow came in May 1944 when he learned of the death of his mother. 'I am left with all the good she did for me and all the bad I did to her,' he wrote in a letter to Natalya. 'No one wrote to me about her death. A money order came back marked that the addressee was deceased. Apparently she died in March.'[28] His sense of guilt must have been heightened when, some time later, he discovered that she had in fact died on 17 January 1944. There had been no money to pay for a gravedigger and she had been laid in the same grave as his Uncle Roman who had died just two weeks earlier.

There was little time to grieve. Within a month Solzhenitsyn had been promoted to the rank of captain and found himself once more in the middle of some of the bloodiest battles on the eastern front. In June the Soviet assault on Belorussia began and Solzhenitsyn's battery of sixty men was in the thick of the fighting. From almost as far north as Minsk, then westward across Belorussia, the Soviet army advanced inexorably until its triumphant crossing of the Polish border. Amidst the mayhem Solzhenitsyn still found time to sketch ideas for a novel on the war in the notebook he always carried with him. In particular he was fascinated by the figure of their political commissar, Major Arseny Pashkin, who fought as courageously as the military men around him and who had subordinated his political function to the urgent demands of the military campaign. Observing the actions of this man closely, Solzhenitsyn made plans to include him in the design for his novel. 'I'm sketching in more and more new details of Pashkin,' he wrote excitedly in a letter to Natalya, 'oh, when will I be able to sit down to write *The Sixth Course*? I will write it so magnificently! Especially now, when the battle of Orel-Kursk stands out in such bold relief and can be seen so vividly through the prism of the year 1944.'[29]

Another source of inspiration was the distant figure of Bronevitsky, whose collaboration with the Germans in Morozovsk held a morbid fascination for Solzhenitsyn. It was a fascination born of emotional contrasts. He had been genuinely fond of the old man and his younger wife, holding both of them in affection, yet their support for the German invader was utterly incomprehensible and ultimately unforgivable. What made the old man do it? It was a conundrum which Solzhenitsyn was determined to solve. He planned to get to grips with the whole issue in a story about Bronevitsky entitled 'In the Town of M'. To assist him in the writing of this story he made a point of going into as many small towns as he could, as the Soviet army continued its westward march, to find out what life had been like under German occupation. He became increasingly fascinated by the phenomenon of occupation and the psychological reaction to it. He strove to understand the feelings of the people in the occupied territories, and especially of the collaborators among them. Their treachery still repelled him but the very repulsion acted as an attraction. Perhaps he felt the same repulsive attraction that many people feel towards understanding the minds of murderers or serial killers. Without any desire to commit acts of treachery himself, he still needed to know why people did it.

And what of those Russians who actually fought in the German army? What motivated them to take up arms against the Motherland and to kill their compatriots? Such treason was almost beyond comprehension. When Solzhenitsyn had first seen a German propaganda leaflet reporting the creation of the 'Russian Liberation Army' he had frankly disbelieved it, dismissing it as the lies of the enemy. Then came the battle of Orel and a rude awakening:

> We soon discovered that there really were Russians fighting against us and that they fought harder than any SS men. In July, 1943, for example, near Orel, a platoon of Russians in German uniform defended Sobakinskiye Vyselki. They fought with the desperation that might have been expected if they had built the place themselves. One of them was driven into a root cellar. They threw hand grenades in after him and he fell silent. But they had no more than stuck their heads in than he let them have another volley from his automatic pistol. Only when they lobbed in an anti-tank grenade did they find out that, within the root cellar, he had another foxhole in which he had taken shelter from the infantry grenades. Just try to imagine the degree of shock, deafness, and hopelessness in which he had kept on fighting.[30]

Other stories abounded about the bravery of these enemy Russians. They defended the Dnieper bridgehead south of Tursk so fiercely that for two weeks the Soviet units with whom Solzhenitsyn was deployed made little progress in spite of continuous fighting. Then there was the tragi-comic tale which Solzhenitsyn recounted about the fierce battles which raged near Malye Kozlovichi in December 1943:

> Through many long days both we and they went through the extreme trials of winter, fighting in winter camouflage cloaks that covered our overcoats and caps ... As the

soldiers dashed back and forth among the pines, things got confused, and two soldiers lay down next to one another. No longer very accurately oriented, they kept shooting at someone, somewhere over there. Both had Soviet automatic pistols. They shared their cartridges, praised one another, and together swore at the grease freezing on their automatic pistols. Finally, their pistols stopped firing altogether, and they decided to take a break and light up. They pulled back their white hoods – and at the same instant each saw the other's cap ... the eagle and the star. They jumped up! Their automatic pistols still refused to fire! Grabbing them by the barrel and swinging them like clubs, they began to go at each other. This, if you will, was not politics and not the Motherland, but just sheer caveman distrust: If I take pity on him, he is going to kill me.[31]

The reason for the reluctance of these enemy Russians to surrender was clear. What awaited them at the hands of Stalin's secret police would be worse than death. Better to die than surrender. This harsh reality was experienced by Solzhenitsyn when he arrived in Bobruisk at the start of the Belorussian offensive. He was walking along the highway, in the midst of the wreckage of battle, when he heard a desperate cry for help from a fellow Russian. 'Captain, sir! Captain, sir!' Looking in the direction of the cries, he saw a Russian, naked from the waist up but wearing German breeches. He had blood all over his face, chest, shoulders and back, and was being driven along by a mounted security sergeant who was whipping him continuously and spurring his horse into him. 'He kept lashing that naked back up and down with the whip, without letting him turn around, without letting him ask for help. He drove him along, beating and beating him, raising new crimson welts on his skin.'

Solzhenitsyn recalled the incident with shame, in a spirit of self-recrimination and contrition, lamenting that 'any officer, possessing any authority, in any army on earth ought to have stopped that senseless torture'. Yet the Soviet army was different from any other army on earth, and Captain Solzhenitsyn had learned to fear the consequences of questioning the rising tide of brutality he was witnessing. 'I was afraid ... I said nothing and I did nothing. I passed him by as if I could not hear him ...'[32] And all the time a metamorphosis was taking place as a direct result of the suffering he saw around him. The questions he was too afraid to ask out loud were formulating themselves all the more forcefully inside him. Slowly, almost indiscernibly, the naïve young communist was fading away, being erased by experience, making way for someone much stronger.

NOTES

1. Reshetovskaya, *Sanya*, pp. 9–10.
2. Ibid., p. 10.
3. Scammell, *Solzhenitsyn: A Biography*, p. 104.
4. Ibid.
5. Ibid., pp. 104–5.
6. Thomas, *Solzhenitsyn: A Century in His Life*, pp. 75–6.
7. Reshetovskaya, *Sanya*, p. 11.
8. Ibid., pp. 11–12.
9. Alan Clark, *Barbarossa*, London: Weidenfeld & Nicolson, 1995, p. 46.
10. Scammell, *Solzhenitsyn: A Biography*, pp. 109–10.
11. Solzhenitsyn, *The Gulag Archipelago Volume Three*, p. 20.
12. Ibid.
13. Ibid., pp. 20–1.
14. Ibid., pp. 21–2.
15. Ibid., p. 22.
16. Solzhenitsyn, *The Gulag Archipelago Volume One*, pp. 219–20.
17. Reshetovskaya, *Sanya*, p. 21.
18. Solzhenitsyn, interview with the author.
19. Scammell, *Solzhenitsyn: A Biography*, p. 112.
20. Solzhenitsyn, *The Gulag Archipelago Volume One*, p. 162.
21. Ibid.
22. Ibid.
23. Scammell, *Solzhenitsyn: A Biography*, p. 119.
24. Ibid., p. 121.
25. Ibid., p. 122.
26. Solzhenitsyn, *The Gulag Archipelago Volume Two*, p. 290.
27. Ibid., p. 291.
28. Reshetovskaya, *Sanya*, p. 50.
29. Ibid., p. 55.
30. Solzhenitsyn, *The Gulag Archipelago Volume One*, p. 254.
31. Ibid., pp. 254–5.
32. Ibid., p. 256.

CHAPTER FIVE

ARRESTED DEVELOPMENT

By the end of 1944 Soviet forces had crossed the border into Poland. Final victory over the Nazi enemy was in sight.

Solzhenitsyn and his battery, encamped on the river Narev southeast of Belostock, waited expectantly for the order to advance on Germany itself. It arrived in the second week of January 1945 when Captain Solzhenitsyn received a bundle of leaflets for distribution to the troops under his command. The leaflet contained Marshal Rokossovsky's famous message: 'Soldiers, sergeants, officers, and generals! Today at 5 a.m. we commence our great last offensive. Germany lies before us! One more blow and the enemy will collapse, and immortal victory will crown our divisions!' A more ominous message had already reached the troops from Stalin himself. He had announced that 'everything was allowed' once Soviet forces entered Germany. In a hate-filled address he solemnly ordered the countless troops about to be unleashed on German soil to wreak vengeance for all that Russia had suffered during the war. An eye for an eye and a tooth for a tooth. Rape, pillage and plunder. Nothing was forbidden.

Repelled by this naked incitement to greed and cruelty, Solzhenitsyn lectured his battery on the need to exercise moderation and restraint. Looking back on the moment, he composed an imaginary speech to his men which he incorporated in *The Way*, calling for Russian soldiers to keep their heads, take a responsible stand, and 'act the proud sons of a magnanimous land'.[1]

Magnanimity was not on the mind of the Soviet army as it marched into Germany. Solzhenitsyn's words fell on deaf and defiant ears. As the Red Army descended on the dying embers of the Third Reich it was Stalin's vision, not Solzhenitsyn's, that became reality.

As it advanced through Poland, Solzhenitsyn's regiment met little or no resistance from a retreating German army and within days it had swung north into East Prussia. To his delight Solzhenitsyn found himself following in the footsteps of General Samsonov, whose disastrous campaign in the First World War had inspired the young Solzhenitsyn to pore over maps in reading rooms, researching his epic. The maps were coming to life before his eyes and he found himself in the very region where Samsonov had been defeated thirty years earlier, passing through some of the towns and villages he had attempted to describe in 1936 in his planned series of novels. The poignancy was accentuated by the knowledge that this was also where his own father had been during the previous war. Like Samsonov, Solzhenitsyn entered the town of Niedenburg when it was in flame, set ablaze by rampaging Russian troops. 'Am tramping through East Prussia for the second day,' he wrote to Natalya, 'a hell of a lot of impressions.'[2]

The impressions were destined to come to dramatic fruition in the battle scenes of *August 1914* but also, and with added power, in his great narrative poem *Prussian Nights*. Having reached Neidenburg (now Nidzica) on 20 January, his unit reached Allenstein (now Olsztyn) on 22 January, and finally the Baltic – cutting off the German armies to the east – on 26 January. Although the poem is not autobiography in the strict sense, the verse narrative conveys Solzhenitsyn's impressions and experiences of those fateful days far more evocatively than a mere dry rendition of the facts could achieve.

At the beginning of *Prussian Nights* the jingoistic praise of Russia's glorious advance is soon overshadowed as the fiery fingers groping for revenge claw across the 'foul witch' of Germany. The narrative sweeps and sways almost drunkenly as Solzhenitsyn describes the wanton destruction of villages, churches, farms and farm animals. It is an 'exultant chaos'. Amid the flames, the narrator almost unwillingly begins to perceive something metaphysically infernal in the physical inferno all about him. It is 'portentous, evil, temptingly, work of a devil'.[3] As Stalin's edict is carried out with gusto, the narrator stands aloof. He has no vengeance in his heart but, 'like Pilate when he washed his hands', will do nothing to quench the flames.

Prussian Nights also recounts a scene of inhumanity which exceeds in its shocking precision anything achieved by Owen or

Sassoon in their poetic accounts of the First World War. The narrator comes across a house which has 'not been burned, just looted, rifled' where he hears 'a moaning, by the walls half-muffled'. Inside he finds a mother and her little daughter. The mother is wounded but still alive. The daughter is dead, having suffered beforehand a fate worse than death. She lies lifeless on a mattress, the victim of a mass rape, and the narrator wonders how many Russian soldiers had lain on top of the girl's battered body before she died. 'A platoon, a company, perhaps?' – 'A girl's been turned into a woman, a woman turned into a corpse'.[4] The mother, her eyes 'hazy and bloodshot', has been blinded in the vain struggle to save herself and her daughter. She has nothing to live for and begs the narrator, a soldier she can hear but not see, to kill her. Neither is this the only sickening account of mass rape depicted in the narrative. A few pages later the anarchic invaders come across 'a rich house, full of German virgins', ignoring the desperate pleas of the women that they are not Germans but Polish.[5] There is a description of the cold-blooded murder of an elderly woman and her bedridden husband. The poem concludes with the narrator finally succumbing to the temptations all around him. He rapes a woman compliant from fear who, when the ordeal is over, begs him not to shoot her. Sickened with remorse, and knowing that it is too late to rectify the wrong he has done, he feels the burden of another's soul weighing heavily on his own. The climactic evil he has perpetrated has left him unfulfilled, unsatisfied. All that remains is an anticlimax of guilt, intensified into futility.

Of course, it is impossible to discern which parts of this epic verse are autobiographical, which are the result of conversations with fellow veterans such as his prison-camp friend Lev Kopelev, and which are simply the work of poetic licence. Nonetheless, as a description of the terrible days of January 1945 they are invaluably evocative, as well as graphically displaying Solzhenitsyn's great sense of guilt for the part he played in those heady and hellish weeks. Perhaps his feelings were most accurately expressed through the medium of Gleb Nerzhin, the most autobiographically inspired of all the characters in his novel *The First Circle*:

it's not that I consider myself a good man. In fact I'm very bad – when I remember what I did during the war in Germany, what we all did … But I picked up a lot of it in a corrupt world. What was wrong didn't seem wrong to me, but something normal, even praiseworthy. But the lower I sank in that inhumanly ruthless world, in some strange way the more I listened to those few who, even then, spoke to my conscience.[6]

In addition to the atrocities perpetrated by Russians on his own side, Solzhenitsyn continued to come across Russians who were fighting for the Germans. His last contact with these enemy compatriots, deep in the heart of East Prussia at the end of January, almost cost him his life. Finding themselves surrounded on all sides by advancing Soviets, the enemy Russians attempted to break through the position occupied by Solzhenitsyn's unit. This they did in silence, without artillery preparation, under cover of darkness. As there was no firmly delineated front they succeeded in penetrating deep into Soviet territory. Just before dawn Solzhenitsyn saw them 'as they suddenly rose from the snow where they'd dug in, wearing their winter camouflage cloaks' and 'hurled themselves with a cheer' on the battery of a 152-millimetre gun battalion, knocking out twelve heavy cannon with hand grenades before they could fire a shot. Pursued by their tracer bullets, the remnants of Solzhenitsyn's group ran almost two miles in fresh snow, fleeing for their lives, until they reached the bridge across the Passarge River. Here, hopelessly outgunned and outnumbered, the surviving enemy Russians were forced to surrender.[7] 'They knew they would never have the faintest glimpse of mercy,' wrote Solzhenitsyn. 'When we captured them, we shot them as soon as the first intelligible Russian word came from their mouths.' Whether this was common practice, it was not always what happened. Sometimes Russians in enemy uniform were taken prisoner to await their fate in the Soviet Union. This, for many, was considered worse than death itself. Solzhenitsyn records an occasion when three captured enemy Russians were being marched along the roadside a few steps away from him. All of a sudden, one of them twisted around and threw himself under a T-34 tank. The tank veered to avoid him but the edge of its track crushed him nevertheless. 'The broken man lay writhing, bloody foam coming from his mouth. And one could certainly understand him! He preferred a soldier's death to being hanged in a dungeon.'[8]

Even amidst the chaos of the Russian rampage through a near-defeated Germany, Solzhenitsyn was able to write to his friends and to Natalya. Now, however, things were different between husband and wife. It seemed that much more separated them than the hundreds of miles between them, or the hundreds of days since they had last seen each other. Much had changed and perhaps it was Solzhenitsyn himself who had changed most of all. His experiences as a front-line soldier, stretching back over eighteen months and culminating in the horrific vision of these Prussian nights, had killed off the carefree youth who had married his student girlfriend nearly five years earlier. The boy had become a man, and the man saw things very differently from the boy. He also saw things very differently from the woman he had married who was unable to comprehend the changes in her husband's attitude towards her. 'The very last letter my husband wrote me from the front again heaped a mountain of suffering upon me. With one hand he seemed to push me away, and with the other he drew me even closer, even tighter to himself.'

Natalya described the letter as 'an irritated sermon', which perhaps it was, but it is clear from Natalya's own response that, for her part, she considered it not only irritated but irritating, an annoyance. The truth was that she was as irritated by her husband as he was by her. In essence the letter castigated Natalya for the 'egotistical' nature of her love:

> You imagine our future as an uninterrupted life together, with accumulating furniture, with a cozy apartment, with regular visits from guests, evenings at the theatre ... It is quite probable that none of this will transpire. Ours may be a restless life. Moving from apartment to apartment. Things will accumulate but they will have to be just as easily discarded.
>
> Everything depends upon you. I love you, I love nobody else. But just as a train cannot move off the rails for a single millimetre without crashing, so is it with me – I must not swerve from my path at any point. For now, you

love only me, which means, in the final analysis, you love only for yourself, for the satisfaction of your own needs.[9]

The letter concluded with a plea that his wife rise above her 'completely understandable, completely human' but 'egotistical' plans for their future. If she could do this, he suggested, real harmony would reign.

All that reigned when Natalya read her husband's words was a sense of confusion born out of incomprehension. This gave way to 'worry, fear, despair, and finally a sense of hopelessness'.

Perhaps it was not surprising that Solzhenitsyn's words should have been incomprehensible to his wife. They were a conundrum, but contained the key to understanding the man, at least as he was in January 1945. At the simplest level the letter appears unreasonable. It seems that it is Solzhenitsyn, not Natalya, whose love is egotistical. It is he, not she, who is demanding that the marriage should progress according to pre-set criteria. It is he, not she, who 'must not swerve' from the path at any point; he, not she, who is unprepared to compromise. Yet on a deeper level the unreasonableness was an expression of something more important to the maturing soldier. He was beginning to perceive that a spirit of sacrifice was at the heart of marriage, and of life, and that the selfish pursuit of needlessly created wants was an obstacle to true happiness. Real harmony could reign only when the desire for material possessions was subjugated to higher goals. For Solzhenitsyn the higher goal was his art, from which he 'must not swerve'. Even his marriage to Natalya was of secondary importance when compared with his literary aspirations. What he needed from her, and demanded from her, was an acceptance that she must be prepared to sacrifice herself to this higher goal. She must love him not because she wanted him or needed him or sought to possess him, but by giving herself heart and soul to him, selflessly sacrificing herself on the altar of his art. He, on the other hand, could not be expected to sacrifice his art for her, or indeed for anything else. Either she must sacrifice herself for their marriage or he would sacrifice their marriage for his art. It was an ultimatum.

Years later Solzhenitsyn sought to explain these feelings. 'I was so wound up – my path was like that of a piston ... Everything's important, yes, every side of life has its importance, but at the same time I would have lost my momentum and my kinetic energy.'[10]

The wartime delay in the postal system meant that Solzhenitsyn's letters to his wife usually took a month to arrive. She received the letter containing his confusing ultimatum in early March. About a week later, instead of his next letter, her own postcard to him was returned. It bore the notation: 'The addressee has left the unit.' Natalya panicked and wrote to anyone and everyone who might know her husband's whereabouts.

Recalling this troubled time in her memoirs, Natalya chose to quote from one of her husband's novels, letting the autobiographical element in the fiction speak for itself:

> It is always difficult to wait for a husband to come home from war. But the last months before war's end are most difficult of all: shrapnel and bullets take no account of how long a man has been fighting.
>
> It was precisely at this point that letters from Gleb stopped arriving.
>
> Nadya would run outside to look for the mailman. She wrote her husband, she wrote his friends, she wrote to his superiors. Everyone maintained a silence, as though enchanted.
>
> In the spring of 1945 hardly an evening went by without salutes blasting the skies. One city after another was taken! Taken! Taken! – Königsberg, Frankfurt, Berlin, Prague.
>
> But there were no letters. The world dimmed. Apathy set in. But she must not let go of herself. What if he is alive and returns? ... And she consumed herself with long-extended days of work – nights alone were reserved for tears.[11]

Little did Natalya know that even as she worried and wept at home her husband was languishing in a Soviet gaol. In a grim twist of fate, or a providential adjustment of divine symmetry, Solzhenitsyn found himself being sacrificed to a 'higher goal'. As he had sought Natalya's sacrifice on the altar of art, so he was now being sacrificed on the altar of Stalin's all-powerful State.

A few days after his self-assured letter to his wife insisting that his life could not move one millimetre from the tracks on which he had set it, the crushing apparatus of the Soviet state brought all his plans, his schemes, his ambitions, his life itself, to a grinding halt. He was plucked helpless from his path, and placed in an alien environment where the road ahead could not be seen, if indeed any such road existed.

The catastrophic turn in his fortunes commenced with a telephone call from brigade headquarters on 9 February 1945. He was to report at once to Brigadier-General Travkin. As he entered the brigadier-general's office he noticed a group of officers standing in a corner of the room, of whom he recognized only one, the brigade's political commissar. Travkin ordered Solzhenitsyn to step forward and hand over his revolver. Puzzled, he obeyed, handing the weapon to Travkin who slowly wound the leather strap round and round the butt before placing it in his desk drawer. Then in a low voice Travkin said:

'All right, you must go now.'

Solzhenitsyn did not understand and remained awkwardly where he was.

'Yes, yes,' repeated Travkin in the uneasy silence, 'it is time for you to go somewhere.'

Instantly two officers stepped forward from among the group in the corner and told Solzhenitsyn he was under arrest. 'Me?' he gasped in reply. 'What for?'

Without bothering to explain further the two officers ripped his epaulettes from his shoulders and the star from his cap, removed his belt, snatched the map-case from his hands and began to march him from the room.

'Wait a moment!' ordered Travkin.

The two counter-intelligence officers released their grip momentarily and Solzhenitsyn turned to face the brigadier-general.

'Have you,' Travkin asked meaningfully, 'a friend on the First Ukrainian Front?'

'That's against regulations!' the two arresting officers shouted angrily. 'You have no right!'[12]

Travkin could say no more but Solzhenitsyn knew instantly that this was a reference to his old friend Nikolai Vitkevich and that it was intended as a warning. Evidently his arrest had something to do with his correspondence with Nikolai, or perhaps with their 'Resolution No. 1'. Later he was to consider both the correspondence and the Resolution 'a piece of childish stupidity'.[13] He and Nikolai knew that censorship was in place and that their letters would be read but this had not prevented them making derogatory comments about Stalin in their correspondence. They were, with the wisdom of hindsight, extremely foolish. Solzhenitsyn wrote that their naïveté 'aroused only laughter and astonishment' when he discussed their case with fellow prisoners. 'Other prisoners told me that two more such stupid jackasses couldn't exist. And I became convinced of it myself.'[14]

As he spent his first day as a prisoner, desolate and bemused, he must have groped in desperation for some last straw of hope. There must have been a mistake. Yes, that was it. There had been a mistake and soon he would receive an apology. He would be released and everything would be all right. Yet as he spent the next three days in the counter-intelligence prison at the headquarters of the front, he heard the disquieting voices of his fellow cellmates. They spoke of the deceptions practised by the interrogators, their threats and beatings. They told him that once a person was arrested he was never released. No one was ever released. Hope as he might, there had been no mistake. The system didn't make mistakes. He was told by his fellow prisoners that he would get a 'tenner', a ten-year sentence. In fact they would all get tenners. Everyone got tenners. As he listened to these voices his hopes, the only light on the horizon, faded away. The future was black, too black to see. An abyss. A nightmare, but no dream. Reality.

In time the harsh realities of prison life would become the only reality he knew, eclipsing his previous memories. Two years later he even saw his time in the army as belonging to a different, distant world: 'The war had licked away four of my years. I no longer believed that it had all actually happened and I didn't want to remember it. Two years *here*, two years in the Archipelago, had dimmed in my mind all the roads of the front, all the comradeship of the front line, had totally darkened them.'[15]

Many years later, having passed through the suffering of the prison system, he would see how important the arrest and imprisonment had been to the subsequent development of his life and personality. He even learned to be grateful to the Gulag, confessing that, along with his time in the army, the most important event 'would be the arrest'. He went so far as to describe it as the second 'defining moment' of his life, crucial 'because it allowed me to understand Soviet reality in its entirety and not merely the one-sided view I had of it previous to the arrest'.[16] He then reiterated what had been taken away from him by his youth in the Soviet Union, most notably the 'Christian spirit' of his childhood. If he had not been arrested, he could only imagine with 'horror ... what kind of emptiness awaited me. The gaol returned all that to me.'[17]

Solzhenitsyn's military career, as Scammell wrote, had begun as farce and ended in tragedy. Yet the tragic end was really only the beginning. It was the crucifixion preceding the resurrection, labour pains preceding birth. The arrest was the real beginning of the Passion Play of Solzhenitsyn's life, in which the pride and selfishness of his former self were stripped away like unwanted garments.

NOTES

1. Scammell, *Solzhenitsyn: A Biography*, p. 138.
2. Reshetovskaya, *Sanya*, p. 63.
3. Alexander Solzhenitsyn, *Prussian Nights*, London: Collins & Harvill Press, 1977, p. 23.
4. Ibid., p. 41.
5. Ibid., pp. 51–3.
6. Alexander Solzhenitsyn, *The First Circle*, London: Collins & Harvill Press, 1968, pp. 518–19.
7. Solzhenitsyn, *The Gulag Archipelago Volume One*, p. 260.
8. Ibid., p. 255.
9. Reshetovskaya, *Sanya*, pp. 63–4.
10. Scammell, *Solzhenitsyn: A Biography*, p. 142.
11. Solzhenitsyn, *The First Circle*, quoted in Reshetovskaya, *Sanya*, pp. 64–5.
12. Scammell, *Solzhenitsyn: A Biography*, pp. 142–3; Reshetovskaya, *Sanya*, pp. 70–1.
13. Solzhenitsyn, *The Gulag Archipelago Volume One*, p. 134.
14. Ibid.
15. Ibid., p. 594.
16. Solzhenitsyn, interview with the author.
17. Ibid.

CHAPTER SIX

HELL INTO PURGATORY

In sooth I had not been so courteous
  While I was living, for the great desire
  Of excellence, on which my heart was bent.

Here of such pride is paid the forfeiture;
  And yet I should not be here, were it not
  That, having power to sin, I turned to God.
    – Dante, Purgatorio, *Canto XI*

After the privileges that Solzhenitsyn had enjoyed as an officer in the Soviet army, life as a prisoner must have seemed unbearable. During the first days in the counter-intelligence prison he had slept on rotten straw beside the latrine bucket, had witnessed the pathetic sight of beaten and sleepless men, had tasted with disgust the prison gruel, and had listened in horror as his fellow prisoners detailed the lurid and hopeless future that awaited him. All his ambitions, which had seemed to stretch out before him on reassuringly immovable tracks, had been derailed. His world, so meticulously planned and worked out in advance, had fallen apart.

Nevertheless, although he was technically no longer a soldier, still less an officer, Solzhenitsyn continued to feel himself superior to those of subordinate rank around him. The prejudice and snobbery he had learned at officer training school were deeply ingrained and he fumed with indignation whenever a non-commissioned officer barked an order at him. This attitude of superiority was exhibited at its worst when he and seven other prisoners were marched the forty-five miles from Osterode, on the front, to Brodnica, where the counter-intelligence headquarters was located. All the prisoners were Russians with the exception of one German civilian who, dressed in a black three-piece suit, black overcoat and black hat, stood out from the rest, his white face 'nurtured on gentleman's food'.[1] The German knew no Russian and it is doubtful whether the Russians would have spoken to the hated enemy even if he had been fluent in their language.

Before they set out on the march to Brodnica, which would take two days in cold, changeable weather, the chief of the convoy, a sergeant, ordered Solzhenitsyn to pick up the sealed suitcase which contained his officer's equipment as well as the papers which had been seized as evidence when he was arrested. Solzhenitsyn was incensed. A mere sergeant was ordering an officer to carry a large, heavy suitcase. The impudence! Besides, were there not six men from the ranks in their convoy, all empty-handed? And what about the German? 'I am an officer,' Solzhenitsyn responded truculently. 'Let the German carry it.' Recalling this incident later, Solzhenitsyn remembered with shame the astonished look he received from the Russian prisoner beside him, and was relieved that the German could not understand what he had said. The German was ordered to carry the suitcase and did so until he nearly collapsed with exhaustion. At that point the Russian who was walking beside him, a former prisoner of war, took the suitcase of his own free will and commenced carrying it. After that all the other Russian POWs took turns in carrying Solzhenitsyn's case, all without being ordered to do so, only returning it to the German when it was once again his turn. All carried the case except its owner who, walking at the back of the convoy, witnessed the selflessness of his colleagues with a growing sense of humiliation.

After three days at Brodnica he was escorted to the railway station destined, he was told, for Moscow. The first part of the journey, to Bialystok and the Soviet border, was made on the platform of a flat railway wagon, totally exposed to the icy winds and snow of February. Three-quarters of the train consisted of similar wagons packed tight with Russian women and girls who had been rounded up in the occupied territories for alleged collaboration with the enemy. Crossing the Soviet border, Solzhenitsyn, escorted by three counter-intelligence officers, was transferred to a passenger train to Minsk, where they caught the Minsk–Moscow Express. Arriving in the Russian capital on 20 February 1945, he was taken via the metro to the famous and feared Lubyanka prison. His experiences upon arrival have been documented in the closing pages of *The First Circle* which, he informed Michael Scammell, were an accurate description of his own ordeal. Thus, in the fictional setting of Innokenti Volodin's arrest and arrival at the Lubyanka in Solzhenitsyn's novel, the brutality and inhumanity of the author's first hours in a Russian gaol are relived. They began with a period in a tiny windowless cell, so small that it was impossible to lie down in it. A solitary table and stool filled almost the entire floor space. When seated on the stool it was impossible to straighten one's legs. At regular intervals the silent monotony was broken by the sound of the shutter on the peep-hole being slid back so that a solitary eye could peer in at him.

Eventually the door was unlocked and he was ordered to go to another room. Here he was strip-searched. Having removed all his clothes, Solzhenitsyn stood passively while a man in a grey overall explored every orifice of his body. He thrust his fingers in the prisoner's mouth, his ears, pulled down his lower eyelids, and jerked Solzhenitsyn's head back to look into his nostrils. The humiliated prisoner was then ordered to take hold of his penis, turn the foreskin back and lift it to the left and right. Finally he was told to spread his legs as far apart as they would go, bend over, take his buttocks in each hand and pull them apart so that the last remaining orifice could be inspected.

The strip search completed, Solzhenitsyn was told to sit naked on a stool, teeth chattering from the cold, while the man in the grey overall commenced a thorough search of his clothes. Beginning with underpants, vest and socks, he pinched all the seams and folds before throwing them at the prisoner's feet and telling him to put them on. Taking out a jack-knife, the man thrust it between the soles of Solzhenitsyn's boots and pierced the heels with a marlinspike. Next came Solzhenitsyn's beloved captain's tunic. The former officer watched in horror as the man meticulously tore off all the gold braid and piping, cut off the buttons and button-loops, and ripped open the lining to feel inside. His trousers and tailored greatcoat received the same scrupulous attention. Buttons were removed and the knife once again went to work slicing through the lining.

At last, an hour or so after he had arrived, the man in the grey overall scooped up the ripped-off braid and piping and departed without a word. Solzhenitsyn, left alone with only the tattered trappings of his former life, was beginning to realize that he was no longer an officer in the Soviet army. Instead, though he did not know it at the time, he had joined another desolate and ragged army numbering millions throughout the victorious Soviet Union. He was among the ranks of Stalin's slaves.

No sooner had the new recruit to this other army recovered from the first ordeal than another began. A warder, this time in an off-white overall, ordered him once again to remove all his clothes and sit naked on the stool. He felt an iron grip on his neck as the warder shaved first his head, then his armpits and finally his pubic hair. Shortly after this warder had departed another arrived. Now the purpose was a medical examination, for which the prisoner was obliged to strip once more. The 'examination' consisted principally of a series of questions about venereal disease, syphilis, leprosy, and other contagions.

The 'processing' of the prisoner continued with the instruction to undress again, this time in order to take a shower, before he was escorted to another room where his photograph and fingerprints were taken.

By the time these formalities had been completed it was late at night. Solzhenitsyn was again confined in the tiny windowless cell in which he had originally been placed and to which he had intermittently been returned between one or other of the various humiliating episodes. He was utterly exhausted and, in spite of the cramped conditions, sought to get to sleep by curling up on the floor. The shutter of the peep-hole slid back, the solitary eye peered in, the door was opened and a warder ordered the prisoner to stay awake. Sleeping was against regulations. Again, oblivious to regulations, Solzhenitsyn sought to sleep by leaning his head on the table. Again, obeying regulations, the warder opened the door and demanded that the prisoner stay awake. Sleep was impossible.

Eventually he was told to put on his clothes and was once more taken from the cell. He was led along corridors, into a yard, down some steps and into another wing of the prison. Ascending to the fourth floor in a lift, he was placed in another cell, almost identical to the previous one. This, he assumed, was his new 'home'. Soon he was again on the move, this time to a slightly bigger cell, about ten feet by five, which had a wooden bench fastened to the wall as well as the customary stool and table. Compared with his previous home, this new cell was a luxury. He almost, unwillingly and unconsciously, felt grateful. After all, the bench was long enough to stretch out on full-length, long enough to sleep on. Already Solzhenitsyn was adapting himself to the survivalist psychology of the long-term prisoner. The unconscious gratitude was accentuated a few moments later when the door opened and, instead of being called out for a further bout of humiliation, he was handed a mattress, a sheet, a pillow, pillowslip and blanket. He was being allowed to sleep! Almost as soon as his eyes were closed, the door burst open and a warder stormed in. He was supposed to sleep with his arms outside the blanket. Regulations. This was easier said than done. His arms grew cold as the night wore on and he was unable to pull the blankets up to cover his shoulders. In this unnatural position and with a powerful 200-watt bulb glaring overhead, he had a restless night, sleeping only fitfully.

Having been 'processed', Solzhenitsyn was now ready for interrogation. He was led to the office of Captain I. I. Ezepov where a thirteen-foot-high, full-length portrait of Stalin gazed down menacingly from the wall, piercing the accused with his larger-than-life eyes. He was informed that he was being charged under Article 58, paragraph 10, of the criminal code for committing anti-Soviet propaganda, and under Article 58, paragraph 11, for founding a hostile organization. Solzhenitsyn soon learned that his interrogator possessed copies of all correspondence between Solzhenitsyn, Nikolai, Natalya, Kirill and Lydia from April 1944 to February 1945. He also possessed a copy of 'Resolution No. 1' which Solzhenitsyn had kept in his map-case. The letters contained numerous thinly veiled attacks on Stalin, while the Resolution stated unequivocally the intention of Nikolai and Solzhenitsyn to organize a new party. This was more than enough evidence for the experienced interrogator to build a case that Solzhenitsyn was part of a sinister conspiracy to overthrow the Soviet regime.

After four days of interrogation Captain Ezepov was sufficiently confident about securing a conviction that he gave permission for Solzhenitsyn to be transferred from solitary confinement to a normal investigation cell. Here he would be sharing with three other prisoners, three other human beings in the same pathetic predicament as himself. He would have someone to talk to, someone with whom he could share experiences. After the days of nightmarish seclusion and uncertainty, he would now have human contact, mutual support, companionship. He again felt the involuntary gratitude that had swept over him when he first arrived in the 'luxury' cell four days earlier. In *The Gulag Archipelago* Solzhenitsyn wrote that he was so happy when the cell door opened and he saw 'those three unshaven, crumpled, pale faces ... so human, so dear' that he stood hugging his mattress and smiling with happiness. 'Out of all the cells you've been in,' Solzhenitsyn recalled, 'your first cell is a very special one, the place where you first encountered others like yourself, doomed to the same fate. All your life you will remember it with an emotion that you otherwise experience only in remembering your first love.'[2]

There was another parallel with first love. In his contact with these three prisoners he was about to be introduced to new horizons, new insights into life, new perspectives which had been invisible to him in his previous blinkered existence. His eyes were opening to a whole new world.

First there was Anatoly Ilyich Fastenko, the oldest of the prisoners. Fastenko was an Old Bolshevik, one of that revered elite of revolutionaries who had been members of the Bolshevik Party before the Revolution. At this stage Solzhenitsyn still considered himself a good and loyal Marxist. His only complaint was with Stalin, not with Marxism-Leninism, and this Old Bolshevik was an object of reverence in the young communist's eyes. Solzhenitsyn listened wide-eyed as Fastenko recounted his life story. He had been arrested under the tsarist regime as long ago as 1904 and had participated in the revolution of 1905. He served eight years' hard labour, followed by internal exile, and fled abroad to Canada and the United States, only returning to Russia after the October Revolution. Most interesting of all, in Solzhenitsyn's eyes, was the fact that this Old Bolshevik had actually known Lenin personally. Pressing Fastenko for anecdotes and impressions of the great man, who was still for Solzhenitsyn an object of idolization, he was shocked to find that the Old Bolshevik was ready to criticize Lenin as well as Stalin. It was tantamount to blasphemy as far as Solzhenitsyn was concerned.

Stalin may indeed have betrayed the Revolution but Lenin could do no wrong. As Solzhenitsyn insisted on Lenin's infallibility, a slight coolness developed between the old man and the young Marxist. 'Thou shalt not make unto thee any graven image,' Fastenko responded.

The second prisoner in the interrogation cell was a middle-aged Estonian lawyer named Arnold Susi. Whereas Solzhenitsyn could relate readily to the Old Bolshevik's life story, steeped as it was in the revolutionary traditions which had been instilled in Solzhenitsyn as an integral part of his Soviet education, the Estonian was of a type quite new to him. Not only was Susi an educated European who spoke fluent Russian, German and English, as well as his native Estonian, he was, politically speaking, both an Estonian nationalist and a democrat. 'Although I had never expected to become interested in Estonia, much less bourgeois democracy', Solzhenitsyn wrote, he found himself fascinated by Susi's 'loving stories' about his country's struggle for national self-determination. As he listened, Solzhenitsyn grew to love 'that modest, work-loving, small nation of big men' and became interested in the democratic principles of the Estonian constitution, 'which had been borrowed from the best of European experience ... And, though the *why* of it wasn't clear, I began to like it all and store it all away in my experience.'[3]

The third cellmate was Georgi Kramarenko, a man for whom Solzhenitsyn developed an almost instant dislike. There was 'something alien', something not quite right about him. Neither was it very long before Solzhenitsyn learned that his initial suspicions were justified. He had never come across the word *nasedka* – 'stool-pigeon' – but he realized quickly that Kramarenko was betraying their private conversations to the prison authorities.

In these three prisoners, and with the incisive grasp of human personality that was to characterize his books, Solzhenitsyn began to see everything more clearly. The Old Bolshevik who criticized Lenin; the cultured Estonian who loved democracy and the smallness of his own nation; and the 'stool-pigeon' who had sold his soul, betrayed his companions and prostituted himself to the prison system. Three very different people in one small cell. But what of the fourth prisoner in the cell, Solzhenitsyn himself? Arnold Susi later recalled that Solzhenitsyn emerged in their conversations about

Estonia and democracy as 'a strange mixture of Marxist and democrat', an observation which Solzhenitsyn thought was accurate: 'Yes, things were wildly mixed up inside me at that time.'[4]

As his worldly ambitions had crumbled so had his ideological and political preconceptions. From atop the rubble of his former ideas he was slowly, meticulously, observing the world through fresh and unprejudiced eyes. 'For the first time in my life I was learning to look at things through a magnifying glass.'

All this time Solzhenitsyn was still being interrogated and trying desperately not to incriminate anyone else in the process. After all, his interrogator had letters from his wife and university friends. And all the time, beyond the walls of the Lubyanka and the claustrophobic world it enclosed, major events were unfolding in the world at large.

At the end of April the blackout shade on the window of the cell was removed, the only perceptible signal the prisoners received that the war was almost over. On 1 May the Lubyanka was quieter than ever. All the interrogators were out in Moscow celebrating and no one was taken for questioning. The silence was broken by someone protesting across the corridor. The unknown, unseen prisoner was bundled into one of the windowless cells that had greeted Solzhenitsyn on his arrival in the Lubyanka ten weeks earlier. The door to the tiny cell was left open while the warders beat the prisoner for what seemed like hours. 'In the suspended silence,' wrote Solzhenitsyn, 'every blow on his soft and choking mouth could be heard clearly.'[5]

On the following day a thirty-gun salute roared out across Moscow. Hearing it, the prisoners guessed that it signified the capture of another European capital. Only two had not yet fallen – Berlin and Prague – and the occupants of the cell tried to guess whether it was the German or Czech capital that had succumbed. In fact, it was Berlin, amongst the ruins of which the suicide of Hitler had signified the death of the Third Reich. A week later, on 9 May, there was another thirty-gun salute. Prague had fallen. This was followed on the same day by a forty-gun salute announcing the end of the war in Europe, final victory for the Soviet army. Again the Lubyanka was thrown into a deathly silence by the absence of warders and interrogators who had gone to join the thousands of revellers thronging the streets of Moscow.

Blissfully oblivious to the darker secrets sealed behind the walls of the Lubyanka, one Western observer witnessed the joy in the Russian capital on the day victory was announced:

> May 9 was an unforgettable day in Moscow. The spontaneous joy of the two or three million people who thronged the Red Square that evening – and the Moscow River embankments, and Gorki Street, all the way up to the Belorussian Station – was of a quality and depth I had never yet seen in Moscow before. They danced and sang in the streets; every soldier and officer was hugged and kissed; outside the US Embassy the crowds shouted 'Hurray for Roosevelt!' (Even though he had died a month before) ... Nothing like *this* had ever happened in Moscow before. For once, Moscow had thrown all reserve and restraint to the winds. The fireworks display that evening was the most spectacular I have ever seen.[6]

The contrast between the hush of the cells and the celebrations on the streets could not have been more marked. Solzhenitsyn and his desolate colleagues observed the fireworks lighting the heavens through the window of their private hell. 'Above the muzzle of our window, and from all the other cells of the Lubyanka, and from all the windows of all the Moscow prisons, we, too, former prisoners of war and former front-line soldiers, watched the Moscow heavens, patterned with fireworks and crisscrossed by the beams of searchlights.'[7]

There was no rejoicing in the cells and no hugs and kisses for the soldiers. 'That victory was not for us ...'

In June, after his interrogator had informed him that the investigation was now completed, Solzhenitsyn was transferred to Butyrki, another Moscow prison, to await his fate. Arriving in his new cell, he could hear through the windows further reminders of the world beyond the walls. Every morning and evening the prisoners stood by the windows and listened to the sound of brass bands playing marches in the streets below. This seemed to confirm the rumour that had filtered through even to the prisoners that preparations were under way for a huge Victory parade in Red Square on 22 June – the fourth anniversary of the beginning of the war between Russia and Germany. One wonders what thoughts passed through Solzhenitsyn's mind as the anniversary arrived. Four years earlier, fresh from university, he had arrived in Moscow full of hopes and dreams of the future, the world seemingly at his feet. Now that world had fallen away beneath him, disappearing from view so that it was not four years but an eternity away.

With the iron resilience that would serve him so well in the years ahead, Solzhenitsyn was already adapting to his new world, the world of the Gulag. His education continued in the cell at Butyrki where he heard nightmare stories from returning prisoners of war who had survived the Nazi death camps. After all they had suffered, they were returning home not to the hero's welcome being rehearsed in the streets below but to the fate awaiting 'traitors of the Motherland'. Having endured Hitler's concentration camps they were now to experience Stalin's concentration camps. Such, Solzhenitsyn concluded, was the nature of Soviet justice.

In the summer of 1945 Solzhenitsyn, still only twenty-six years old, was about to receive some valued lessons from an even younger generation of dissident Russians, the most notable of whom was Boris Gammerov. Solzhenitsyn's first impressions of this young man, four years his junior, were graphic. He was 'a pale, yellowish youth, with a Jewish tenderness of face, wrapped, despite the summer, in a threadbare soldier's overcoat shot full of holes: he was chilled'.[8] Yet, though feeble and anaemic-looking, Gammerov held a reserve of spiritual strength which belied his physical frailty. He had served as a sergeant in an anti-tank unit on the front and had been invalided out with shrapnel wounds in a lung. The wound had not healed, causing his poor physical condition. Almost as soon as they met, Solzhenitsyn and Gammerov began a long conversation, principally on politics. Somewhere in the course of the dialogue Solzhenitsyn had recalled one of the favourite prayers of the late President Roosevelt, which had been published in one of the Soviet newspapers following Roosevelt's death two months earlier. Having quoted the prayer, Solzhenitsyn expressed what he assumed was a self-evident evaluation of it: 'Well, that's hypocrisy, of course.' To his surprise, Gammerov frowned in obvious disagreement. 'Why?' the youth asked pointedly. 'Why do you not admit the possibility that a political leader might sincerely believe in God?'

Solzhenitsyn was completely taken aback by the nature of Gammerov's reply. If the words had been spoken by someone of his parents' generation he could have dismissed them as superstitious nonsense. After all, this was 1945 and Soviet society had progressed beyond irrational belief in a God of any description. Yet the riposte to his self-assured atheism had not come from an elderly Russian tied to the traditions of the Old Believers, but from a twenty-two-year-old New Believer not even born when the Revolution had swept religion aside, allegedly for ever. Forced to reappraise his own self-assured certainty, Solzhenitsyn suddenly realized that his condemnation of Roosevelt's prayer had been spoken not out of conviction but as the result of a Pavlovian response instilled by Soviet education. For once he was lost for words and found himself unable to answer Gammerov's question. Instead he asked meekly whether Gammerov believed in God. 'Of course,' was the simple and calm response. Again, Solzhenitsyn was dumbstruck.

Although Gammerov's words had given him food for thought, as had so many other words he had heard since his imprisonment began, Solzhenitsyn was still a long way from any faith in the existence of God. He did, however, share a faith with the majority of other prisoners in something far more tangible – a general amnesty. It was simply inconceivable that all these people, thousands upon thousands of them, could be kept in prison for much longer, especially as so many appeared to have committed no crime other than being taken prisoner by the Germans. Explaining prisoners' hopes at the time, Solzhenitsyn wrote that 'it just couldn't be that so many people were to remain in prison after the greatest victory in the world. It was just to frighten us that they were holding us for the time being: so that we might remember and take heed. Of course, there would soon be a total amnesty and all of us would be released.'[9] Their hopes were fuelled by the various rumours that were rife at the time. Someone had even sworn that he had read in a newspaper that Stalin, replying to some American correspondent, had promised an amnesty after the war the likes of which the world had never seen. Desperate to believe anything that would offer a glimmer of light at the end of their tunnels of fear and misery, the prisoners convinced themselves that it was no longer a question of *whether* there was going to be an amnesty but *when* it was going to be. They were placing all their faith and hope in Comrade Stalin's charity.

As the rumours circulated, faith in the impending amnesty became obsessive. Every new prisoner was asked, the moment he entered the cell, what he had heard of the amnesty. If two or three prisoners were taken from their cells *with their things* it was immediately assumed that they were being taken out to be released. Perhaps it had begun! Every prisoner was on the lookout for signs and one day, early in July, a sign was given. Written infallibly in soap on a glazed lavender slab in the Butyrki baths were the words of prophecy: 'Hurrah!! Amnesty on July 17!' There were celebrations throughout the prison as the inmates prepared joyfully for their imminent release.

The seventeenth of July came and went but hopes remained high nonetheless. There had been a slight miscalculation perhaps, but the infallibility of the soapy message was still in no doubt. Then, after morning tea on 27 July, Solzhenitsyn and another prisoner were summoned from their cell. Their cellmates saw them off with boisterous good wishes and they were assured that they were on their way to freedom. At long last the amnesty had arrived. Perhaps they had misread the message in the baths. Perhaps it had said 'July 27' and not 'July 17'. After all, it was not easy to write clearly in soap.

Solzhenitsyn soon discovered that he was one of twenty prisoners summoned from various cells throughout the prison. For three hours they waited, hoping from the depths of their being that the prophecy of the baths was true. Were they on the point of freedom? After what seemed an eternity, the door opened and one of their number was summoned. The tension was beyond bearing. The door opened again. Another was summoned and the first man returned. He was a changed man. The life had drained from his face and his glazed expression struck fear into the hearts of his colleagues. 'Well?' they asked him, already sensing the worst. 'Five years,' he replied, crestfallen. At that point the second man returned and a third was summoned. 'Well?' they asked, crowding round the returning man in the forlorn hope that the first result was an aberration. 'Fifteen years,' was the hope-shattering reply.

Not since the arrest itself had Solzhenitsyn's hopes for the future collapsed so forcefully, nosediving to new depths of despair. He waited in dread for his turn to come.

When he was finally ushered in to hear his sentence he had already become accustomed to the inevitable. He was brought before a bored, black-haired NKVD major who informed him that he had been sentenced to eight years. Without further ado he was given the relevant documentation to sign so that he could be shepherded out to make way for the next victim. 'It was all so everyday and routine,' Solzhenitsyn recalled. 'Could this really be my sentence – the turning point of my life?'[10] He refused to sign the document until he had read it and, having done so, looked expectantly at the major for some further clarification. None was forthcoming. Instead the major gestured to the gaoler to get the next prisoner ready. 'But, really, this is terrible,' Solzhenitsyn objected in a half-hearted and futile plea for some sort of explanation. 'Eight years! What for?'

'Right there.' The major pointed to where the prisoner was expected to sign.

Defeated and deflated, Solzhenitsyn signed, mumbling about the injustice of the sentence and his right to appeal.

'Let's move along,' commanded the gaoler, ushering him from the room.

His sentence had begun.

Even after the sentence was pronounced, Solzhenitsyn, like most other prisoners, still nurtured hopes of an amnesty. In his first prison letter to Natalya, which she received six months after his last letter to her from the front, he expressed his confidence that he would not have to serve the full eight years. He told Natalya that he was pinning his hopes on an amnesty, about which there were many rumours. In the letter he also wrote that, should the amnesty not materialize, he felt duty-bound to grant her 'complete personal freedom' for the entire term of the sentence. He assured her of the depth of his love for his 'beautiful woman' whose youth had been spent waiting in vain for a long-promised future. This was a milder, gentler Solzhenitsyn whose plans for the future seemed much more subdued and less ambitious than his previous, pre-prison self would have contemplated. In the army he had dreamed that he and Natalya would set up home in the hustle and bustle of Moscow or Leningrad. Now he saw things differently. After his return to freedom, he informed her, he would like them to live in a 'remote, but thriving, well-provisioned, and picturesque village'. This ideal village would need to be far from the nearest railway, perhaps in Siberia or in Kuban, or along the Volga, or even on the Don. They could both become high-school teachers and could spend the summer vacations travelling. Their new life together would be contented, peaceful, close to nature, and safe from such 'accidents' as the one that had befallen him on 9 February 1945. Once again, however, his vision of the future was out of focus with Natalya's own desires. Now she had her heart and ambition set on her 'future professorship' and didn't relish the prospect of teaching in a remote village school.[11] Not for the first time, husband and wife were separated by more than miles, time or prison walls.

Throughout his letters to his wife, Solzhenitsyn continued to express his hopes for an amnesty. After he was transferred to the New Jerusalem prison in August 1945, he wrote of his 'basic hope ... for an amnesty for those convicted under Article 58', adding that 'I still think that this will happen'. The hope was that the amnesty would come in November but when it, too, failed to materialize, Solzhenitsyn's faith began to falter. It was revived again in March 1946 when he wrote to Natalya that 'I am 100 per cent sure and still convinced beyond doubt that the amnesty was prepared long ago, in the autumn of 1945, and that it was approved in substance by our government. But then, for some reason, it was postponed.'[12] Months passed and new hopes were voiced in almost every letter. On the first anniversary of the victory over the Germans, hopes were particularly high: 'Today we were waiting very hard. Although the rumours were conflicting about the ninth, still, from the ninth on, we are giving it another week or two of time. Such a weariness has descended upon us all, it's as though the newspapers had promised the amnesty for this day, today.'[13] It was only after he had been in prison for eighteen months that he finally confessed resignedly to Natalya that 'whenever they start talking of amnesty – I smile crookedly and go off to one side'.[14]

As the months passed, a spiritual chasm was beginning to separate Natalya from her husband and she failed to recognize the full significance of the changes he was undergoing. The eventual rejection of the false hopes and false faith in an imaginary amnesty was part of the spiritual metamorphosis at the heart of Solzhenitsyn's being. Its significance was expressed in the third volume of *The Gulag Archipelago*: 'Dismayed by the hopeless length of my sentence, stunned by my first acquaintance with the world of Gulag, I could never have believed at the beginning of my time there that my spirit would recover by degrees from its dejection: that as the years went by, I should ascend, so gradually that I was hardly aware of it myself ...'[15]

In the midst of hell, Solzhenitsyn had passed into purgatory.

NOTES

1. Solzhenitsyn, *The Gulag Archipelago Volume One*, p. 165.
2. Ibid., p. 180.
3. Ibid., p. 213.
4. Ibid.
5. Ibid., p. 235.
6. Alexander Werth, *Russia at War: 1941–1945*, New York, 1964, p. 969, quoted in Scammell, *Solzhenitsyn: A Biography*, p. 169.
7. Solzhenitsyn, *The Gulag Archipelago Volume One*, p. 235.
8. Ibid., p. 611.
9. Ibid., pp. 270–1.
10. Ibid., pp. 277–8.
11. Reshetovskaya, *Sanya*, p. 93.
12. Ibid., p. 100.
13. Ibid., p. 101.
14. Ibid.
15. Solzhenitsyn, *The Gulag Archipelago Volume Three*, p. 37.

CHAPTER SEVEN

PROFIT FROM LOSS

On the day he was sentenced, Solzhenitsyn, numbed by the prospect of eight years in Soviet labour camps, stared blindly into the abyss before him. The cellmate who had been sentenced with him, seeking to come to terms with his own fate and possibly seeking to reassure both himself and Solzhenitsyn at the same time, tried to remain positive. They were still young, he asserted, and they would live for a long time to come. The most important thing was not to upset the authorities still further. They would serve out their sentence as model prisoners, working hard and keeping their mouths shut. They would conform and utter no words of dissent.

Solzhenitsyn listened in silence as his friend spoke, but words of dissent were already forming inside him: 'One wanted to agree with him, to serve out the term cozily, and then expunge from one's head what one had lived through. But I had begun to sense a truth inside myself: if in order to live it is necessary *not to live*, then what's it all for?'[1]

To be or not to be, that was the question. It was the beginning of an ardent and arduous search for truth which was to preoccupy Solzhenitsyn throughout the long years and drudgery of the labour camps. Even at this early stage of his sentence, he was beginning to discern that a man's spirit was not determined by his material circumstances but could rise above them. Much later in the sentence, at the beginning of his fourth spell in this same Butyrki Prison, he heard for the thousandth time the same endless catchphrase of the Gulag: 'Last name? Given name and patronymic? Year of birth?' He muttered the same time-honoured response but inside he was giving a different answer: 'My name? I am the Interstellar Wanderer! They have tightly bound my body, but my soul is beyond their power.'[2]

In early August, only days after sentence had been passed, Solzhenitsyn was transferred to the Krasnaya Presnya transit prison in another part of Moscow. This prison, close to the Novokhoroshevo Highway in the heart of Russia's capital, was also at the heart of the Soviet prison system. It was a teeming hive of activity, always bursting at the seams with prisoners en route to some labour camp or other. In the same way that the entire Soviet railway system converged on Moscow, so the prison system converged on Krasnaya Presnya. It was the main terminus; Gulag Junction.

The overcrowding at this prison must have been hard to bear at the best of times but in the heat of August it was intolerable. Solzhenitsyn speaks of bedbugs and flies biting all night long as the prisoners lay 'naked and sweaty under the bright lights'. During the day, the inmates streamed with sweat every time they moved and 'it simply poured out' when they ate. There were a hundred to a cell, and since the cells were no larger than an average-sized room the prisoners were packed in so tightly that there was no floor space even to put one's feet. Two little windows on one wall were blocked with 'muzzles' made of steel sheets which not only stopped the air from circulating but got very hot from the sun, radiating an intense heat that turned the cell into an oven.[3]

The overcrowding and high turnover of prisoners, the sheer weight of numbers at Krasnaya Presnya, had turned it into a factory farm, a people processing plant. The bread rations were piled high on wheelbarrows and the steaming gruel was served from buckets.

There was one other important respect in which Krasnaya Presnya differed from the Butyrki Prison which Solzhenitsyn had just left. At Butyrki all the inmates were political prisoners but now, for the first time, Solzhenitsyn found himself amongst hardened criminals, devoid of all civilized standards of behaviour. He was about to undergo a brutal baptism.

Armed only with the valued food parcel that Natalya had sent him, he was placed in his first cell at Krasnaya Presnya. Apart from the overcrowding, the heat and the stench, the first thing he noticed upon arrival was that there were no spare bunks. The upper tier of bunks was occupied by the criminals. Their leaders, the top dogs, had the bunks by the window. The lower tier was occupied by 'a neutral grey mass', mostly former prisoners of war. There was, however, plenty of space under the bunks. Having no option Solzhenitsyn slid along the asphalt floor on his belly, inching himself under one of the bunks. A few moments later, in the semi-darkness, he heard 'a word-less rustling' and noticed juveniles, some as young as twelve, creeping up on all fours 'like big rats'. They jumped on him from all sides and, in total silence, 'with only the sound of sinister sniffing', he felt several pairs of hands searching for his precious bundle of bacon, sugar and bread. He was totally powerless to resist, trapped beneath the bunk and unable to get up or move. Then, as swiftly and silently as they had arrived, they were gone. Solzhenitsyn was left feeling stupid and hu-miliated. Creeping out awkwardly, rear end first, he got up from under the bunk. Rising, he noticed the cell's godfather seated on his throne, an upper-tier bunk beside the window. In front of him were the contents of Solzhenitsyn's food parcel, displayed as trophies. The godfather's face 'sagged crookedly and loosely, with a low forehead, a savage scar, and modern steel crowns on the front teeth. His little eyes were exactly large enough to see all familiar objects and yet not take delight in the beauties of the world.' He looked at Solzhenitsyn 'as a boar looks at a deer, knowing he could always knock me off my feet'.[4]

It was then that Solzhenitsyn acted in a way which would torment his conscience for many years afterwards. In a display of mean-spirited selfishness similar to that of the episode with the suit-case soon after his arrest, he complained indignantly that since the godfather had taken his food he might at least be granted a place on one of the bunks. The godfather agreed and ordered a former pris-oner of war to vacate his bunk by the window. The POW obeyed submissively and crawled under one of the other bunks. It was not until nightfall that Solzhenitsyn heard the reproachful whispers of his neighbours. How could he kowtow to the thieves by driving one *of his own people* under the bunks in his place? The whispers struck a raw nerve. Yes, they were his own people, imprisoned under 58-1b, the POWs. They were his own brothers-in-loss and he had be-trayed them. 'And only then did awareness of my own meanness prick my conscience and make me blush. (And for many years thereafter I blushed every time I remembered it.)'[5]

The feelings of guilt rushing through Solzhenitsyn's body as he felt the reproachful glare of his own people engendered a spell of intense introspection. What sort of person was he? A traitor?

A Judas? A coward? Surely not a coward. Hadn't he pushed his way into the heat of a bombing in the open steppe? Hadn't he driven bravely through a minefield? Hadn't he remained cool-headed when he had led his battery out of encirclement in East Prussia and hadn't he even gone back into the midst of the danger zone to salvage a damaged command car? No, surely he was not a coward. Why, then, had he submitted so cravenly to the theft of his food? Why had he not smashed his fist into the godfather's ugly face? Perhaps, after all, he *was* a coward. Certainly it seemed harder to be brave in the sickening heat of this prison cell than it had been in the gory heat of battle. And, in any case, even if he was no coward, he was a traitor, a Judas betraying his friends not with a kiss but with a craven plea to a craven crook. And all because of a few rashers of bacon.

The introspection sent ideas whirling round and round in the prisoner's conscience until it fastened on the thought of food parcels. Were they not more trouble than they were worth? Did they not consume much more than they were consumed? Had they not already consumed the soul of the godfather? Were they not too cruel a temptation?

> Foolish relatives! They dash about in freedom, borrow money ... and send you foodstuffs and things – the widow's last mite, but also a poisoned gift, because it transforms you from a free though hungry person into one who is anxious and cowardly, and it deprives you of that newly dawning enlightenment, that toughening resolve, which are all you need for your descent into the abyss. Oh, wise Gospel saying about the camel and the eye of a needle! These material things will keep you from entering the heavenly kingdom of the liberated spirit.[6]

Slowly the introspection began to heal his troubled mind. He had come to accept the loss of the food parcel and, in the very act of doing so, had profited from the loss. Profit from loss – a purgatorial paradox, pointing to paradise. He had learned a valuable lesson at Krasnaya Presnya: 'And thus it is that we have to keep getting banged on flank and snout again and again so as to become, in time at least, human beings, yes, human beings.'[7]

Having learned the lesson, Solzhenitsyn did not have to tolerate the cramped and criminal environment of Krasnaya Presnya for very long. On 14 August 1945 he and sixty other political prisoners were transferred to Novy Ierusalim – 'New Jerusalem' – a somewhat inapt name for a corrective labour camp situated thirty miles west of Moscow in the buildings of a former monastery of the same name. They were transported in two open lorries but were ordered to squat on the floor so as not to be visible to inquisitive onlookers on Moscow's streets. The streets themselves were bedecked with flags. It was VJ Day, the day of final victory over Japan. The Second World War, which Solzhenitsyn had greeted with such jingoistic delight when the Soviet motherland had entered the fray four years earlier, had finally come to an end. With the irony of these reflections in his mind one wonders what Solzhenitsyn thought when he arrived at New Jerusalem for the first time to be greeted with cries that 'the Fascists have arrived!' Many of the prisoners arriving for the first time with him had suffered terribly as prisoners of war in Nazi death camps and such cries of derision added insult to injury. None of this mattered amidst the unsubtle stereotypes which governed thought in the Soviet Union. All political prisoners were 'fascists' and were considered worse than their 'criminal' counterparts.

It was at New Jerusalem that Solzhenitsyn got his first bitter taste of forced labour. He was put to work in the digging brigades in the clay-pits and for the first time felt the crushing force of his physical limitations. 'The work-loads of an unskilled labourer are beyond my strength,' he wrote to Natalya. 'I curse my physical underdevelopment.'[8] In fact he had told Natalya only half the story, less than half the story.

At long last there had been an amnesty, but it applied only to those who, in Solzhenitsyn's words, were 'habitual criminals and nonpolitical offenders'.[9] Not only were the political prisoners, the 'fascists', excluded from the amnesty, they were expected to work even harder because of it. All over the camp, giant slogans appeared: 'For this broad amnesty let us thank our dear Party and government by doubling productivity'. The production target for each worker in the clay-pits was raised to six wagons of clay per shift, far beyond the capabilities of anyone unaccustomed to physical labour, and Solzhenitsyn worked himself into the ground struggling to fill half that number. The squelch and squalor of those dismal days in the clay-pits at New Jerusalem were described graphically in *The Gulag Archipelago*:

> And the next day that fine drizzle kept falling and falling. The clay pit had got drenched, and we were stuck in it for good. No matter how much clay you took on your spade, and no matter how much you banged it on the side of the truck, the clay would not drop off. And each time we had to reach over and push the clay off the spade into the car. And then we realized that we had been merely doing extra work. We put aside the spades and began simply to gather up the squelching clay from under our feet and toss it into the car.[10]

Solzhenitsyn's work partner during those days in the pit was Boris Gammerov, the young man whose candid confession of faith back in Butyrki Prison had forced Solzhenitsyn to confront the shallowness of his own implicit atheism. The two men tried to keep their spirits up by discussing the importance of Vladimir Solovyev, the Russian poet, philosopher and Christian mystic, or endeavoured to make light of their labours by telling jokes. When they became too exhausted to talk, Gammerov would gain consolation by composing poetry in his head. Solzhenitsyn looked upon his friend, who was still only twenty-two, with a mixture of admiration and fear. He admired his spiritual strength and dogged resilience, but feared for his physical health. The fragment of a German tank shell was still lodged immovably in his lungs and he was visibly weakening, his face becoming skeletal in appearance.

The young poet did not survive his first winter in the camps, dying a few months later of tuberculosis and exhaustion. 'I revere in him a poet who was never even allowed to peep,' wrote Solzhenitsyn. 'His spiritual image was lofty, and his verses seemed to me very powerful at the time. But I did not memorize even one of them, and I can find them nowhere now, so as to be able at least to make him a gravestone from those little stones.'[11]

Solzhenitsyn escaped from the exhausting labour, the sludge and the reddish-grey monotony of the clay-pits quite unexpectedly on

9 September 1945. New Jerusalem was to become a camp for German prisoners of war and, in order to make way for them, all the current prisoners at the camp were to be transferred elsewhere. Solzhenitsyn was being returned to Moscow, this time to Kaluga Gate on the south side of the city. As he made the return journey his spirits lifted. He had enjoyed the outward journey, only three weeks earlier, as 'one of the supreme hours' of his life and there is no reason to believe that his feelings on escaping the infernal pits of New Jerusalem were any less exhilarating. He now seemed to see the beauties of life for the first time. Once he had been free to enjoy them whenever he chose but had been too blind to see; now, deprived of them except on rare moments such as these journeys between camps, the whole of creation came to glorious life. As the prison transport sped through the Russian countryside heading for Moscow, 'a whirlwind of scents of new-mown hay and of the early evening freshness of the meadows swirled around our shaven heads. This meadow breeze – who could breathe it more greedily than prisoners? Real genuine green blinded our eyes, grown used to grey and more grey ... all the air, the speed, the colours were ours. Oh, forgotten brightness of the world!'[12] For the first time he was enjoying what G. K. Chesterton called 'the glorious gift of the senses and the sensational experience of sensation'.[13] He was fully alive. As the prison transport arrived in Moscow, he wondered whether the teeming thousands of free people in the city streets were as fully alive as he was. 'The streetcars were red, the trolley-buses sky-blue, the crowd in white and many-coloured. Do they themselves see these colours as they crowd onto the buses?'[14] Could they see, or were they as blind to the beauty around them as they were to the suffering of their compatriots in the camps?

Solzhenitsyn was destined to spend ten months at Kaluga Gate until, in the early afternoon of 18 July 1946, he was transferred the short distance across the city to Butyrki, where he had spent a month the preceding summer. In the year that had elapsed since he was last there, the prison had become busier and more crowded. It took eleven hours for Solzhenitsyn to be processed in the now familiar way: search – endless minutes alone in a windowless cell – bath – endless minutes alone in a windowless cell – fumigation – endless minutes alone in a windowless cell ... All punctuated at regular intervals with the endless repetition of the catchphrase: name, date of birth, place of birth, charge, and sentence.

It was not until three o'clock the following morning that Solzhenitsyn finally arrived at Cell 75, his new home. The overcrowded and stuffy conditions in the hot July air, the buzz of tireless flies flitting from sleeper to sleeper, making them twitch, must have reminded him of the criminal-infested cell at Krasnaya Presnya. This time eighty men had been squeezed into a cell designed for twenty-five and Solzhenitsyn found a space of unoccupied floor beneath the lowest tier of bunks, next to the latrine tank. Throughout the night, prisoners needing to use the latrine tank would step across Solzhenitsyn's fitfully sleeping body, and the acrid stench of the tank itself, putrefying in the heat, bore on his nostrils as mercilessly as the two bright electric bulbs bore on his eyelids, and the incessant flies bore on his skin. Yet such was the horror of life in the labour camps that this was luxury in comparison.

> I was happy! There, on the asphalt floor, under the bunks, in a dog's den, with dust and crumbs from the bunks falling in our eyes, I was absolutely happy, without any qualifications. Epicurus spoke truly: Even the absence of variety can be sensed as satisfaction when a variety of dissatisfactions has preceded it. After camp, which had already seemed endless, and after a ten-hour workday, after cold, rain, and aching back, oh, what happiness it was to lie there for whole days on end, to sleep, and nevertheless receive a pound and a half of bread and two hot meals a day – made from cattle feed, or from dolphin's flesh.[15]

After the ordeal of forced labour at New Jerusalem and Kaluga Gate, sleep was particularly welcome. During his two months in the cell he slept enough 'to make up for the past year and the year ahead'. Nevertheless his second spell at Butyrki was not all spent in sleep and he developed many friendships with fellow prisoners. There were discussion groups, games of chess, a limited number of books to read and all the while his education at the hands of others was continuing. He listened intently as émigrés spoke of their experiences in various parts of the world, and soaked up the lectures by others on a host of subjects ranging from Gogol and Le Corbusier to the habits of bees.

He was not shy of getting involved himself when the occasion arose. When an Orthodox priest, Evgeny Divnich, strayed from discussions of theology to denunciations of Marxism, Solzhenitsyn felt duty-bound to spring to its defence. He was, after all, still a Marxist, wasn't he? Battle was joined between the Orthodox believer and the loyal child of the Revolution. Divnich condemned Marxism and claimed that, as a political philosophy, it was a spent force and that nobody in Europe had taken it seriously for years. Solzhenitsyn did his best to counter the arguments with all the well-rehearsed and well-worn ripostes but somehow his responses sounded hollow and less convincing than they had done in the past. 'Even a year ago I would have confidently demolished him with quotations; how disparagingly I would have mocked him!'[16] Now, however, a year in prison had left its mark and he was no longer so sure of the correctness of his former beliefs. He hesitated, fumbled, conceded points that he never would have done previously. Almost imperceptibly, he had changed over the past twelve months, and it was only when he was called upon to defend his old ideas in open debate that he realized the change which had taken place. 'My whole line of reasoning began to weaken, and so they could beat me in our arguments without half-trying.'[17]

A more tangible ghost from Solzhenitsyn's past than that of his youthful Marxism returned to haunt him during his brief stay at Butyrki in the summer of 1946. To his embarrassment he bumped into the elderly German civilian whom he had obliged to carry his suitcase on the long march to Brodnica almost eighteen months earlier. Solzhenitsyn blushed apologetically at the recollection of his ignoble actions, but the German appeared to have wholly forgiven him and to be genuinely pleased by their meeting. Having exercised forgiveness, exorcising the ghost of Solzhenitsyn's guilt in the process, the German informed his erstwhile persecutor that he had been sentenced to ten years' hard labour. Looking on the elderly man's worn and weary features, Solzhenitsyn knew that he would not live to see Germany again.

Solzhenitsyn's reprieve from the harshness of the labour camps was due to his re-categorization as a 'special-assignment prisoner' bound for one of the special prison institutes for scientific research, known as *sharashkas*. These were fully equipped with laboratories, research apparatus, workshops and sometimes whole factories, and were run by prisoners capable of producing results in their specialist fields. Solzhenitsyn had been saved from the hardship and drudgery of the camps, and possibly from death itself, by his degree in mathematics and physics from Rostov University.

The first *sharashka* to which Solzhenitsyn was consigned, in September 1946, was at Rybinsk on the upper reaches of the Volga, where jet engines were being designed and constructed. After five months he was moved to another *sharashka*, in Zagorsk, but was informed that he was there only in transit and that his final destination was yet another *sharashka* which was to be opened shortly. This was Marfino, otherwise known as 'Special Prison No. 16', on the northern outskirts of Moscow, to which Solzhenitsyn was dispatched on 9 July 1947. It became the inspiration and the setting for almost the whole of his novel *The First Circle*, in which Marfino is renamed 'Mavrino'. Life at the Special Prison is described in the novel as better than life in the camps: 'There was meat for dinner and butter for breakfast. You didn't have to work till the skin came off your hands and your fingers froze. You didn't have to flop down at night half dead, in your filthy rope sandals, on the wooden boards of a bunk. At Mavrino you slept sweetly under a nice clean sheet.'[18]

Three months after Solzhenitsyn's own arrival at Marfino, a new prisoner arrived at the *sharashka*. He was Dimitri Panin.

In his memoirs Panin described his first meeting with Solzhenitsyn on the morning after his arrival in October 1947. Panin recalled seeing 'an impressive figure of a man in an officer's greatcoat' coming down the stairs and took 'an immediate liking to the candid face, the bold blue eyes, the splendid light brown hair, the aquiline nose'.[19] For his part, Solzhenitsyn appeared to be equally taken by Panin. The character of Dimitri Sologdin in *The First Circle* was so closely based on Panin that Panin described him as 'my literary double'. Panin also considered *The First Circle* a vivid and honest record of their time in Marfino, in which the inmates are brilliantly described, and that in the novel's principal character, Gleb Nerzhin, Solzhenitsyn 'gives an extraordinarily truthful and accurate picture of himself'.[20] This being so, it seems legitimate to draw extensively from

The First Circle in order to throw light on Solzhenitsyn's relationship with Panin.

Physically, Sologdin/Panin is described in the novel as though he was the very image of an idealized knight of Christendom. He had a high, straight forehead, regular features, penetrating blue eyes, blond moustache and beard, muscular physique, and upright bearing. This striking physical image was complemented by a mind of equal stature, diamond-sharp in both science and philosophy. If not the epitome of a Nietzschean superman, he was certainly an icon of medieval Christian chivalry.

Panin was six years older than Solzhenitsyn and could remember scenes from the Revolution and civil war that the latter had been too young to experience directly. From childhood onwards he had remained hostile to the communist regime. As a child, Panin could remember anti-Soviet intellectuals among the small circles of friends and acquaintances of his parents and enjoyed the benefit of their candid, accurate appraisals of past events. He had the same experience of Soviet indoctrination at school as had Solzhenitsyn but, being older, appears to have been largely immune to its effects: 'they pumped us full of political propaganda and other sickening rubbish, all this in an atmosphere of mutual denunciation and constant spying'.[21] He appears to have been similarly immune to the anti-Christian nature of Soviet education: 'Next, there was the brutal uprooting of religion. Horrible persecutions were started against the church. By these means, the authorities encouraged many believers to break away. And then the active propagation of atheism began. Religious literature, as well as philosophical works unpalatable to the regime, were destroyed wholesale. Furnaces burned entire libraries down to ashes.'[22]

Panin graduated from a technical school in 1928, a resolute if quietly resigned Christian in a revolutionary and atheist world. He remembered the 'frightful year' of his graduation when he witnessed the systematic destruction of hundreds of churches in Moscow. In 1931 the magnificent Cathedral of Christ the Saviour, erected in thanksgiving for Russia's deliverance from Napoleon in 1812, was demolished. In spite of this there were no public protests. 'The Russian people, deformed by the weight of dictatorship, were being reduced to abject compliance.' Only once did he witness the pain that such persecution was causing beneath the seemingly calm surface of Soviet society. With secret admiration he had observed an elderly woman on her knees in the rubble of a demolished cathedral, praying fervently and making the sign of the cross, oblivious to the danger she was bringing upon herself. He was told that her husband, a fervent believer, had died in prison.

Although Panin detested the communist regime, harbouring a secret nostalgia for pre-revolutionary Russia and a secret sympathy for the Whites in the civil war who 'had tried to save Russia – and the rest of the world as well – from impending disaster',[23] he was himself being browbeaten into submission by the system he despised. In 1930 a massive campaign was started in factories throughout the Soviet Union to induce the workforces into membership of the Communist Party. The factory just outside Moscow in which Panin worked as an engineer was included in this campaign and, reluctantly, the closet anti-communist joined the Komsomol, remaining a member 'in name only'. Almost immediately he regretted his decision to join but found that he was trapped in the communist net: 'I could not resign – an open break would have carried the threat of prison. I had to sweat it out until they considered me old enough to be crossed off the rolls officially. All the time I was a member I had a feeling of shameful complicity.'[24]

Panin found himself living a precarious life, engaged in double-think for much of the time. At work he made the right noises because to make the wrong ones was perilous. At home and with trusted friends, and in the privacy of his own thoughts, he maintained a staunch antipathy to the Soviet regime. He likened this period to 'a walk over a tightrope stretched above a horrible, evil-smelling quicksand bog'.[25] Trying desperately to keep his balance he knew that one slip would mean disaster.

Unfortunately, this precarious state of affairs led Panin to find allies in various unsavoury guises. Almost anyone was a friend as long as they were an enemy of Stalin, even 'untouchables' like Hitler and Mussolini. Endeavouring to explain this youthful error in his autobiography, he saw it in terms of the vacuum created by an insufficient understanding of Christianity: 'A godless dictatorship both sullies and disfigures a man. Only a deep religious faith can provide him with stout armour. When the church is destroyed and people are left on their own, it is easy for them to fall in with evil schemes.'[26]

From 1932 onwards articles abusive of the Nazis began appearing in Soviet newspapers. The Nazis in Germany and the Fascists in Italy were depicted by Soviet propaganda much as a Christian might depict the Antichrist. Hitler and Mussolini were the ultimate embodiment of evil. Meanwhile, of course, in Germany and Italy the very opposite was being preached. National Socialism and Fascism would save the world from the horrors of communism, it was claimed, and only strong men like Hitler and Mussolini could stave off the impending world revolution. The Antichrist, as far as fascist propaganda was concerned, was Stalin.

Perhaps Panin's analysis was correct and it was easy for whole peoples to fall in with evil schemes without the stout armour provided by religious faith. Throughout the world, anti-communists became fascist sympathizers, and anti-fascists found themselves fellow-travellers with the communists. The world, it seemed, was heading for Armageddon, after which either one extreme or the other would emerge triumphant. Amidst this madness the Catholic Church emerged, not for the first time in her history, as a guardian of sanity. The Church continued to condemn both the atheism of the communists and the paganism of the Nazis, considering the two creeds nothing more than opposite sides of the same pernicious coin. 'Totalitarianism,' wrote Pope Pius XII, 'extends the civil power beyond due limits; it determines and fixes, both in substance and form, every field of activity, and thus compresses all legitimate manifestation of life – personal, local and professional – into a mechanical unity of collectivity under the stamp of nation, race, or class.'[27] Earlier, the same Pope had pointed to the futility of all materialistic creeds: 'The wound of our individualistic and materialistic society will not be healed, the deep chasm will not be bridged, by no matter what system, if the system itself is materialistic in principle and mechanical in practice.'[28]

This teaching, fully comprehended by Panin and Solzhenitsyn alike in later years, was beyond their grasp in the years leading up to the Second World War. Solzhenitsyn was convinced of the correctness of Marxism-Leninism, hating fascism as an 'enemy of the people'; Panin took the opposite view, though obviously in secret, that the rise of the Nazis in Germany offered the prospect of Russia's liberation from communism. Panin's heart leapt with hope, if not with joy, on hearing of the Nazis' rise to power in 1933. 'The Nazis' theory of racial superiority and the aggression that it generated naturally provoked our sharp disapproval,' he wrote in his autobiography. 'I never met a single man in the Soviet Union who made excuses for them. Nonetheless, Hitler's promise of a war against Stalin gave the hope, strength, and patience we needed for enduring a terrible existence while we awaited the hour of our opportunity. Russians in all walks of life expected there would be a war of liberation; it made no difference to them who triggered it off. Our constant dream was that war would start very soon.'[29]

War seemed to be edging ever closer in 1936 with the eruption of a civil war in Spain which looked like a dress rehearsal for the future world conflict between communism and fascism. The Soviet Union was openly backing the communist forces in Spain, supplying weapons, equipment, even pilots. Communist parties throughout the world aided their Spanish comrades by supplying volunteers in the international brigades. At the same time the Germans and the Italians were backing Franco's fascists. Thus the Spanish Civil War, over-subscribed with weapons of mass destruction on both sides and fomented by the ideological hatreds which divided the combatants, raged for three years until the final victory of Franco.

The war in Spain coincided with the worst excesses of the Stalinist terror in the Soviet Union, making all discussion of the rights and wrongs of the Spanish war totally impossible, at least in public. In private, however, Panin was wholly on the side of Franco, an act of anti-communist heresy guaranteed to lead to his arrest if discovered. 'At the time,' he wrote, 'we were not at all interested in how much the Franco regime differed from the Western democracies – as slaves under a dictatorship, we could not afford the luxury of such fine distinctions; therefore we gave Spain's indomitable anticommunists our approval and support.'[30]

It was inevitable that one so heretical to communist orthodoxy as Dimitri Panin could not survive at liberty for long in the inquisitorial atmosphere of Stalinist Russia. Eventually he spoke too freely in the presence of unsympathetic ears and was denounced to the authorities by a work colleague. This led, in July 1940, to a sentence of five years in the labour camps. In 1943, while still serving his first sentence in various camps in the Arctic north, he was given a second sentence, this time for a period of ten years, for 'defeatist propaganda'. Thus, when Solzhenitsyn first met Panin in Marfino he had already served seven years, suffering unimaginable hardships which had in turn hardened his hatred of the Stalinist regime still further.

A month after Panin's arrival at Marfino another prisoner appeared on the scene who, in many respects, was the diametrical and dialectical opposite of Panin. This was Lev Kopelev, who, as a deeply committed Marxist, loyal Party member, and staunch supporter of the Soviet regime, seemed to represent everything that Panin despised. Surprisingly, however, the two men were best of friends as well as best of enemies, having met previously in Butyrki before their respective transfers reunited them at the *sharashka*.

In spite of their differences, Panin had befriended Kopelev in Butyrki. Unlike Panin, Kopelev was still a relative novice in the camps, still receiving food parcels from his family. To Panin's great surprise, Kopelev broke a loaf of white bread in two and handed him half. After seven years in the labour camps of the Arctic, Panin had forgotten how white bread tasted. 'If Lev had given me only a tiny bit of it, I would have been rapturously happy. But here was half a loaf! His grand gesture affected me ... A generous nature and a nobility of spirit distinguished Lev from ordinary men.'[31]

In fact, Kopelev's generous nature and nobility of spirit, both dangerous virtues in Stalinist Russia, had eventually caused his imprisonment. During the latter stages of the war he had reached the rank of major and, being fluent in German, was responsible for organizing anti-Nazi propaganda behind the enemy lines. His downfall came when he opposed the looting, rape and terror carried out by the advancing Soviet army under the slogan 'Blood for blood, death for death'. Accused of being 'soft on the Germans', he was arrested in the same area of the Prussian front as Solzhenitsyn and narrowly escaped a charge of treason.

Solzhenitsyn's friendship with Kopelev, like that of Panin, was to be hugely influential and was also immortalized in *The First Circle*, where Kopelev became the inspiration for the character of Lev Rubin. Solzhenitsyn, Panin and Kopelev, reinvented in *The First Circle* as respectively Nerzhin, Sologdin and Rubin, formed a triumvirate of truth-seekers whose interminable arguments never became quarrels. For Solzhenitsyn, positioned midway between the two dialectically opposed combatants, the experience was pivotal to his own development, enabling him to weigh up each thesis and antithesis carefully before forming a new synthesis of his own from the clash of ideas. The benefits accrued were considerable and came to creative fruition in one of his finest novels which at its highest level is a hymn of praise to the pursuit of philosophical truth in the midst of tribulation. 'Time to sort yourself out,' Sologdin tells Nerzhin, 'to understand the part of good and evil in human life. Where could you do this better than in prison?' Nerzhin sighs, caught between a scepticism he is uncomfortable with and a faith beyond his reach. 'All we know is that we don't know anything,' he replies dejectedly. Yet to himself, Nerzhin ponders with gratitude the insight his friendship with this believing Christian has conferred on him: 'it was Sologdin who had first prompted him to reflect that prison was not only a curse but also a blessing'.[32]

'Thank God for prison!' Nerzhin exclaims to Rubin on another occasion. 'It has given me the chance to think things out. To understand the nature of happiness we first have to know what it means to eat one's fill.' He reminds Rubin of the foul prison food they had been given during their interrogation at the Lubyanka:

> Can you say you *ate* it? No. It was like Holy Communion, you took it like the sacraments, like the *prana* of the yogis. You ate it slowly, from the tip of a wooden spoon, entirely absorbed in the process of eating, in thinking about eating – and it spread through your body like nectar. You quivered from the exquisite feeling you got from those sodden little grains and the muddy slops in which they floated ... Can you compare that with the way people wolf down steaks? ... So miserable wretches like ourselves really do know from bitter experience what it means to eat one's fill. It's not a matter of *how much* you eat, but of the *way* you eat. It's the same with happiness – it doesn't depend on the actual number of blessings we manage to snatch from life, but only on our attitude towards them...

'You've certainly worked it all out,' Rubin replies sceptically, asking with suspicion whether Sologdin had put Nerzhin up to it.

'Perhaps he has,' Nerzhin concedes. 'For you I suppose it's just idealism and metaphysics. But listen! The happiness that comes from easy victories, from the total fulfilment of desire, from success, from feeling completely gorged – *that* is suffering! That is spiritual death, a kind of unending moral indigestion ... people don't know what they are striving for. They exhaust themselves in the senseless pursuit of material things and die without realizing their spiritual wealth ...'[33]

Looking back over the spiritual wealth he has accrued in the half-century since he first received these revelations, Solzhenitsyn states with simplicity 'I am deeply convinced that God participates in every life.'[34] Similarly, in his autobiography *The Oak and the Calf* he hints at the role of providence in his life and work. In 1948, however, Solzhenitsyn did not have this spiritual wealth to draw on. Nor did he know that providence was about to offer further opportunities to make spiritual profit from material loss.

NOTES

1. Solzhenitsyn, *The Gulag Archipelago Volume One*, p. 280.
2. Ibid., pp. 594–5.
3. Ibid., pp. 537–8.
4. Ibid., pp. 547–8.
5. Ibid., pp. 548–9.
6. Ibid., p. 546.
7. Ibid., p. 549.
8. Reshetovskaya, *Sanya*, p. 95.
9. Ibid., p. 190.
10. Ibid., p. 194.
11. Ibid., p. 195.
12. Ibid., p. 168.
13. G. K. Chesterton, *Autobiography*, London: Hutchinson, 1936, p. 343.
14. Solzhenitsyn, *The Gulag Archipelago Volume Two*, p. 168.
15. Solzhenitsyn, *The Gulag Archipelago Volume One*, p. 601.
16. Ibid., p. 602.
17. Ibid.
18. Solzhenitsyn, *The First Circle*, p. 47.
19. Panin, *The Notebooks of Sologdin*, p. 262.

20. Ibid., pp. xiii, 262–3.
21. Ibid., p. 6.
22. Ibid.
23. Ibid.
24. Ibid., p. 12.
25. Ibid.
26. Ibid.
27. Robert C. Pollock (ed.), *The Mind of Pius XII*, London: Fireside Press/W. Foulsham & Co. Ltd, 1955, p. 52.
28. Ibid., p. 33.
29. Panin, *The Notebooks of Sologdin*, pp. 12–13.
30. Ibid., p. 13.
31. Ibid., p. 259.
32. Solzhenitsyn, *The First Circle*, pp. 139–40.
33. Ibid., pp. 38–9.
34. Solzhenitsyn, interview with the author.

CHAPTER EIGHT

LIFE AND DEATH

The depth of the spiritual and intellectual discussions held between
Solzhenitsyn, Panin and Kopelev at Marfino contrasted starkly with
the vacuity of the books in the prison library. Through the character
of Khorobrov in *The First Circle* Solzhenitsyn expressed his contempt for the state of Soviet literature in 1948. He poured scorn on
one book in particular, a hack novel called *Far from Moscow* by
Vasiley Azhayev which topped the bestseller lists in 1948. It describes in glowingly romantic terms the heroic feat of building an oil
pipeline in Siberia without ever mentioning that the back-breaking
work was done by prison labour. Instead Azhayev's novel portrayed
the workers as 'happy young members of the Komsomol, well-fed,
well-shod and bursting with enthusiasm'. There was no mention
of half-starved skeletal shadows being literally worked to death.
Khorobrov had tried reading the novel but found that it 'turned his
stomach'. He could sense that the author knew the truth. Perhaps he
had even been a security officer in one of the Siberian death camps.
He knew but he 'was cold-bloodedly lying'.[1]

Khorobrov had then tried a volume of the selected writings of
Galakhov, whose literary reputation was at its height. Again he was
disappointed and put the book down without finishing it. 'Even
Galakhov, who could write so prettily about love, had been stricken
with mental paralysis and was going down the drain with the ever-
swelling crowd of writers who wrote, if not for children, then for
morons who had seen and known nothing of life and were only too
delighted to be amused with any rubbish.'

Soviet literature was truly in a sorry state, Khorobrov mused.
'Everything that really moves the human heart was absent ... There
was nothing to read.'[2]

Pondering the state of Soviet literature during the idle hours on his prison bunk in Marfino, Solzhenitsyn's own literary vocation began to take shape. With an iron determination, he was resolved to tell the truth – the full, unexpurgated truth – about life in Stalin's camps. He would, single-handedly if necessary, break the conspiracy of silence.

Even as he pondered dejectedly in his prison cell, several key literary figures in England were speaking out against the evils of Stalinism in the forthright terms that Solzhenitsyn was to use himself in later years. In early June 1948, during a radio broadcast for the BBC, Malcolm Muggeridge criticized the dynamic duo of Fabian socialism, Beatrice and Sidney Webb, for their naïve eulogizing of the Soviet regime. Muggeridge attributed to Beatrice Webb the statement 'Old people take to pets, and mine is the USSR'. With the sardonic humour for which he was famous, Muggeridge added that a tabby or a pekinese 'might have been easier to handle and certainly better house-trained'. He concluded his talk by comparing Beatrice Webb to Don Quixote: 'she finished up enmeshed in her own self-deception, adulating a regime which bore as little relation to the Fabian Good Life as Dulcinea del Toboso to the Mistress of Don Quixote's dreams'.[3]

Having witnessed the horrors of Stalinism as a correspondent in Moscow before the war, Muggeridge was appalled by the continuing gullibility of Western intellectuals. He could not understand the obstinate support for Stalin of Shaw and the Webbs, and was amazed at the sermons in support of the 'glorious social experiment taking place in the Soviet Union' given by leading Christians such as the Reverend Hewlett Johnson, the 'Red Dean of Canterbury'. 'As a symbol, from the Communists' point of view, the Dean is incomparable,' Muggeridge wrote. 'All their ridicule of Christianity, all their confidence that its day is done, seems to come true in his very person. Moscow newspapers, in their cartoons, present the Christian Church in just such a guise: gaiters, cross, white locks, and seeming venerability, adorning absurdity.'[4]

As he witnessed the descent of the Iron Curtain across Europe, Muggeridge considered with dismay the Soviet policy of Clement Attlee's government. Labour policy towards the Soviet Union was based on the belief that Britain would benefit because 'Left would speak to Left'. Such a view, Muggeridge claimed, was the epitome of self-delusion: 'As far as Stalin was concerned, the Leftism of Mr Attlee and his colleagues was about as congenial as ginger beer to a congenital drunkard.'⁵

Such comments, had he been able to read them, would have warmed the prisoner's heart as he lay in Marfino lamenting the state of affairs in his own country. Doubtless also, his heart would have leapt and his despondency would have been dispersed somewhat, had he known that George Orwell was in the midst of writing *Nineteen Eighty-Four*, a novel which, perhaps, would be more important than any other in turning people away from totalitarianism. Still less could the prisoner have guessed that he was destined as a writer to become more influential even than Orwell in the fight against political dictatorships. Orwell's classic was published the following year, 1949, complementing *Animal Farm*, his earlier satirical fable attacking communism, which had been published in 1945.

Years later Solzhenitsyn acknowledged the importance of both Muggeridge and Orwell in heightening awareness of the dangers of communism in the West. Orwell's books, he believed, had come as a shock to certain intellectuals: 'In the west of course many stubbornly resisted and did not want to understand. Understanding, comprehension, tends to project emotion ahead so that some did not want to know. Bernard Shaw for instance did not want to know, and so Orwell was received with difficulty.'⁶ In the Soviet Union, on the other hand, although 'it was difficult to get hold of', *Nineteen Eighty-Four* was greeted with 'admiration' by those who managed, illegally, to obtain a copy because it was 'precisely accurate'.⁷ Meanwhile Muggeridge was worthy of respect because 'he was able to travel that difficult path of freeing himself from socialist lies and attaining spiritual heights'.⁸

Solzhenitsyn, of course, was travelling the same path as Muggeridge but in more difficult circumstances. One particular difficulty, coming to crisis point during his time at Marfino, was the state of his marriage. Again, the autobiographical elements in *The First Circle* shed some light on his own feelings as he sensed the tension in his precarious relationship with Natalya. In the novel Gleb Nerzhin mulls over the words of Nadya, his wife, who has written 'when you come back ...' in a letter to him. 'But the horror was that there was no going back. To *return* was impossible. After four years in the army and a ten-year prison sentence there would probably not be a single cell of his body which was the same. Although the man who came back would have the same surname as her husband, he would be a different person and she would realize that her one and only, for whom she had waited fourteen lonely years, was not this man at all – he no longer existed.'[9]

Ironically, the result of Solzhenitsyn's spiritual development, the fruit of his endless discussions with Panin and Kopelev, was that he was growing ever more divorced from the aspirations he had once nurtured and those his wife continued to nurture in his absence. He was trapped by circumstances. If other married couples sometimes grew apart even when they had lived together for years, what hope had he and Natalya after all the years of enforced separation? Yet however hopeless the situation seemed, he still nurtured the belief that perhaps, in spite of all the odds, they might still survive the experience. Again, Solzhenitsyn uses the character of Gleb Nerzhin to express the emotions he was feeling in 1948:

> He could not understand how Nadya could have waited so long for him. How could she move among those bustling, insatiable crowds, constantly feeling men's eyes on her – and not waver in her love for him? Gleb imagined that if it had been the other way round – if she were imprisoned and he were free – he would not have held out for as much as a year. Before, he would never have believed his frail little wife to be capable of such rocklike constancy and for a long time he had doubted her, but now he had a feeling that Nadya did not find waiting too difficult.[10]

Then, on 19 December 1948 during a rare prison visit, Natalya informed Solzhenitsyn that she would have to obtain a formal divorce from him or she would lose her job. She told him that security was being tightened at the laboratory where she worked and that if she declared her marriage to a political prisoner on the forms she was required to fill in, she would certainly not be retained as an employee. Outwardly Solzhenitsyn put on a brave face and agreed that, under the circumstances, Natalya had no choice but to divorce him. In a letter to Natalya's mother a couple of weeks later he wrote that her decision was 'correct, the sober thing to do; it should have been done three years ago'.[11] Inwardly, however, he was devastated, shaken to the core, and confessed later that after the visit he was left in the darkest despair.[12] In reality Natalya had already filed court papers declaring the dissolution of their marriage a couple of months before she informed her husband of the fact. As a result she was able to declare him as a former husband on the form she had to fill out for her job, an act made all the easier by her decision to retain her own surname, rather than take Solzhenitsyn's, at the time of their marriage eight years earlier.

Although Natalya had assured him during the visit that the divorce was a mere formality and that she would still wait for him, he found himself troubled by doubts. If the divorce was not the end of their marriage, surely it was the beginning of the end...

> What a pity that he had not made up his mind to kiss her at the very beginning of the visit. Now, that kiss was gone for ever. His wife's lips had looked different, they seemed to have weakened and forgotten how to kiss. How weary she had been, what a hunted look there had been in her eyes when she had talked of divorce ... she would get a divorce in order to avoid the persecution inseparable from being a political prisoner's wife and having done so, before she knew where she was, she would have married again. Somehow, as he had watched her give a last wave of her ringless hand he had felt a stab of premonition that they were saying goodbye to each other for the last time ...[13]

Throughout 1949 there was a slow but discernible estrangement between Solzhenitsyn and Natalya, a creeping paralysis in their relations with each other. Towards the end of the year, Solzhenitsyn wrote to Natalya urging her to complete the severance between them and give up writing to him. Her own well-being was more important to him than 'this illusion of family relations that long ago ceased to exist'.[14] He was aware that she was becoming more and more involved in her busy new life as a lecturer and that in the evenings she was kept fully occupied playing the piano at various concerts. On the one hand he saw more clearly than ever that he was casting an unwelcome shadow on her life, while on the other he was developing a stoic calmness about his own fate. He was also beginning to suspect that his prison term would be followed by a period in 'perpetual exile', effectively ending all hope that he and Natalya would ever be reunited. Natalya ignored Solzhenitsyn's suggestion and the couple continued to correspond, though not on the same terms as before. As they were supposed to be no longer married, the tone of the correspondence, particularly on Natalya's part, was more circumspect, dampening any expressions of affection in their letters. Meanwhile, in her professional life, Natalya continued to prosper and in March 1950 she was appointed head of the chemistry department at the research institute. In the same month there was another of the rare visits to Solzhenitsyn. Their meeting, though subdued, was touched by genuine warmth. Natalya informed Solzhenitsyn that she still loved him and had no intention of leaving him. For his part Solzhenitsyn confessed that his advice that she end their relationship had come from his head but his heart 'had shrunk from fear' that it could possibly come to pass.[15] Solzhenitsyn also confessed that he now regretted they had never had children, a reversal of his pre-prison view that children would merely interfere with his literary aspirations. In those days it was Natalya, not Solzhenitsyn, who had wanted desperately to start a family but now she was not so sure. In any case, she told him, it was probably too late to think of such things now.

According to Natalya, Solzhenitsyn was very pensive throughout the meeting. He had much to be pensive about. Their relationship, it seemed, was held together by a thread.

A couple of months later, on 19 May 1950, Solzhenitsyn was transferred, along with several other prisoners, from the relative 'luxury' of Marfino to an unknown destination. His feelings, and those of his fellow prisoners, were described at the conclusion of *The First Circle*:

> They all knew well enough that what awaited them was incomparably worse than Mavrino. They all knew that when they were in their labour camps they would dream nostalgically of Mavrino as of a golden age. For the moment,

however, to bolster their morale they felt a need to curse the special prison so that none of them might actually feel any regrets about it or blame himself for whatever action had led to his transfer ... The prospects that awaited them were the taiga and the tundra, the Cold Pole at Oi-Myakoi and the copper mines of Jezkazgan, kicking and shoving, starvation rations, soggy bread, hospital, death. No fate on earth could possibly be worse. Yet they were at peace within themselves. They were as fearless as men are who have lost everything they ever had – a fearlessness hard to attain but enduring once it is reached.[16]

After yet another short spell at Butyrki, Solzhenitsyn began a long and insufferable journey across the Soviet Union which took two exhausting months to complete. He eventually arrived at his destination, Ekibastuz labour camp, deep in the semi-arid steppes of Kazakhstan in Soviet central Asia, in the third week of August. The first sight of his new 'home' confirmed that Solzhenitsyn was now more securely clasped within the jaws of the Soviet prison system than ever before. The 'special camp' in which he found himself was enclosed by double fences of barbed wire, between which Alsatian dogs prowled menacingly, overlooked by armed guards. A strip of ploughed land encircled the perimeter to reveal the footprints of anyone attempting to escape, and sharp-pointed stakes were set in the ground at forty-five-degree angles, designed to impale would-be escapees before they had the opportunity to leave their footprints on the ploughed strip beyond. Thoughts of escape were futile and, beyond the perimeter, hundreds upon hundreds of miles separated the new arrival from the world he had once known. The thin thread between Solzhenitsyn and Natalya, his only remaining link with his old life, was about to snap.

For Natalya, who had lived a life of heroic exile from her husband for almost a decade, it was too much to bear. Until his transfer to the labour camp she had still clung to the last lingering hopes that some day she and Solzhenitsyn would embrace again in freedom. 'But when the first letter came from faraway Ekibastuz, I learned that now we were not to see each other at all. Now there would be no meetings, and letters would arrive only twice a year. Now we were separated not only by time but by distance.'[17]

The distance separating them went beyond the merely geographical. Gradually, to her dismay – or perhaps, if she was looking for an excuse to escape, to her relief – she sensed another remoteness. In his infrequent letters he was 'expressing moods entirely different from those I had known'. They appeared to be written by a Solzhenitsyn who was completely new to her. Instead of his impetuous and impatient will and his worldly ambition, there was now a 'passive waiting ... resignation ... submission to destiny'. 'Perhaps,' he wrote in one of the rare letters he was permitted to send, 'this faith in destiny is the beginning of religiosity? I don't know. It seems to me I'm still far from having reached the point of believing in a god.' Such a discussion of 'god' was itself an example of the remoteness that so alienated Natalya. Neither of them had ever taken religion seriously, both having absorbed the atheism of the Soviet education system, so Natalya viewed this rising religiosity with an element of alarm. 'Although the word "god" was still not capitalized,' she wrote, 'it nevertheless began to crop up with increasing frequency.' She then quotes a letter of December 1950, in which reference to the divine is indeed frequently made: 'Haven't been ill here yet, thank god, and may god grant that no illness befall me in the future.' Natalya's memoirs display her continuing irritation with this further example of what she calls one of Solzhenitsyn's 'precious ideas'.[18]

During 1951 Natalya no longer perceived Solzhenitsyn 'as a living person, in flesh and blood. He was an illusion.'[19] The end was nigh and was hastened by the arrival of a new admirer in Natalya's life, the flesh and blood she needed to exorcise Solzhenitsyn's ghost. This was Vsevolod Somov, a scientific colleague, who began courting her in earnest in the spring, encouraged by Natalya's mother who was understandably anxious about her daughter's uncertain future.

Natalya was still going through the motions of corresponding with Solzhenitsyn but by July he detected from the tone of her letters that something was amiss. 'It seems as though you had to force yourself to begin the letter,' he wrote. 'A kind of reticence fettered your tongue, and after a few lines you broke off.'[20] Soon she stopped writing altogether, except for a solitary birthday greeting in December wishing him happiness in life.

In the spring of 1952 Natalya decided to restructure her life in its entirety. She moved in with Vsevolod Somov without any formal marriage ceremony, declaring to her friends that they should now be considered man and wife. 'I shall neither justify nor blame myself,' Natalya wrote in her memoirs. 'After all the years of trials, I could no longer sustain my "saintliness". I began to live a real life.'[21]

Natalya admitted that she lacked the courage to write to her former husband, and Solzhenitsyn was forced to write repeatedly to Natalya's Aunt Nina requesting that she clear up the uncertainty. Feeling that she could say nothing without her niece's consent, she did not reply until, at Natalya's request, she finally wrote a short note in September 1952: 'Natasha has asked me to tell you that you may arrange your life independently of her.'[22] Not surprisingly, Solzhenitsyn was more confused than ever by the vagueness and terseness of the note and wrote to Natalya directly, urging a full explanation of 'such an insignificant, enigmatic phrase'. 'No matter what you've done during the past two years,' he wrote, 'you will not be guilty in my eyes. I shall not criticize or reproach you either in my thoughts or my words. Neither by my former behaviour nor my luckless life, which has ruined and withered your youth, have I justified that rare, that great love that you once felt for me and that I don't believe is exhausted now. The only guilty one is me. I have brought you so little joy, I shall be forever in your debt.'[23] Natalya responded by informing him of her 'marriage' to another man, ending their careworn sixteen-year relationship with a finality that confirmed Solzhenitsyn's fears.

However, Solzhenitsyn had other fears to contend with during this period of uncertainty. In December 1951, at around the time Natalya had sent him the birthday card wishing him happiness in life, his own luckless life was thrown into further anxiety by the discovery of a small swelling on his right groin. At first he tried to ignore it but gradually it grew to the size of a lemon and was becoming increasingly painful. On 30 January 1952 he was diagnosed as having cancer and was admitted to the camp hospital. Having survived the first gruelling winter at Ekibastuz, the sufferings of which became the inspiration for *One Day in the Life of Ivan Denisovich*, he had been struck down with a potentially fatal disease. He had survived all the cruelty and bullying, the starvation rations, the manual labour in icy winds which slashed knife-like across the flat defenceless steppe at forty below zero, only to succumb to something worse. He had passed from the desperation of the labour camp to the desolation of his death bed, from bare existence on the edge of death to the final triumph of death itself. Such must have been the thoughts whirling endlessly through Solzhenitsyn's mind as he waited two long weeks in the camp hospital for an operation which the doctors had recommended should be carried out at once. It was eventually performed on 12 February under a local anaesthetic. For a while after the operation he ran a high fever and was in considerable pain.

But he was soon making a good recovery. Once more he had proved to be a survivor and once more he would profit from the threat of loss. In facing death he had gained an immeasurably greater understanding of life. It was the eternal paradox, at the very heart of life and death, which is encapsulated in the Gospels: 'He who loses his life shall find it.'

As he recovered physically in the camp hospital, his spirits were simultaneously being healed. The spiritual healing could not be seen as readily as the scar on his right groin, but it was as real: more real, in fact. The former atheist had ceased seeing life in terms of dialectical materialism and was beginning to perceive it in the light of theological mysticism. This was the change, accelerated by his arrival at Ekibastuz, that had so alienated his wife. In one of his letters to her he had described the change at the very core of his being: 'Years go by, yes, but if the heart grows warmer from the misfortunes suffered, if it is cleansed therein – the years are not going by in vain.'[24] This, which to Solzhenitsyn was the source of his inner strength, was to Natalya a sign of outward weakness. For her, but not for him, resignation was merely the absence of determination, a failure of the will; for her, but not for him, inner peace was really only an abject surrender to circumstance. They were no longer speaking the same language.

At this time, however, Solzhenitsyn's experience of strength through suffering was not seen in specifically Christian terms. The way of mortification was not necessarily the way of the Cross; or, returning to his letters to Natalya, God was still 'god' and not 'God'. All this was to change in the days following his operation as he lay in the surgical ward of the camp hospital. He was hot and feverish, unable to move, but his thoughts were alive and not prone to dissolve into delirium. In his incapacitated condition he was grateful for the company of Dr Boris Nikolayevich Kornfeld who sat beside his bed talking to him. Alone in the ward together in the evening, with the light turned out so as not to hurt the patient's eyes, Kornfeld told Solzhenitsyn the long story of his conversion from Judaism to Christianity. As he listened, Solzhenitsyn was astonished at the conviction of the new convert, the ardour of his words:

> 'And on the whole, do you know, I have become convinced that there is no punishment that comes to us in this life on earth which is undeserved. Superficially it can have nothing to do with what we are guilty of in actual fact, but if you go over your life with a fine-tooth comb and ponder it deeply, you will always be able to hunt down that transgression of yours for which you have now received this blow.'[25]

Thus Kornfeld ended the account of his conversion experience and Solzhenitsyn shuddered at the mystical knowledge in his voice. Solzhenitsyn must have shuddered again the following morning when he was awoken by the sound of running about and tramping in the corridor. The orderlies were carrying Kornfeld's body to the operating room. He had been dealt eight blows to the skull with a plasterer's mallet while he slept, and died on the operating table without regaining consciousness: 'And so it happened that Kornfeld's prophetic words were his last words on earth. And, directed to me, they lay upon me as an inheritance. You cannot brush off that kind of inheritance by shrugging your shoulders.'[26]

Many commentators have suggested that this poignant meeting with Kornfeld, on the eve of his death, was pivotal to Solzhenitsyn's final embrace of Christianity. This may be so but its importance should not be overstated. The war, the camps, the cancer had all prepared the ground before they met. By February 1952 Solzhenitsyn was ripe for conversion. After all, had he not just looked death squarely in the face and lived? The story of Kornfeld's conversion may perhaps have been the final catalyst but when the light came on Solzhenitsyn's own road to Damascus, it was at least half-expected. As Solzhenitsyn remarked concerning his fateful meeting with

Kornfeld: 'by that time I myself had matured to similar thoughts'.[27]

In fact he had matured sufficiently to see through and beyond Kornfeld's 'universal law of life'. The truth, Solzhenitsyn reasoned, went deeper than Kornfeld realized. To accept Kornfeld's thesis at face value one would have to admit that those who suffer most are in some way more evil than those who are relatively free from pain. Did that mean that he and the millions of other prisoners in Stalin's camps were more evil than those who had escaped their miserable fate? Did it mean that those who suffered an even worse fate, such as tortuously slow death, were the most evil people of all? Worse, did it mean that those who committed the torture were less evil than their victims? And what of those who prospered rather than suffered? What of the malicious criminals he had met in various camps over the years? What of the camp guards? Worst of all, what of Stalin himself? Did it mean that Stalin was less evil than the millions of innocents he had slaughtered? Surely not. What of the torturers, Solzhenitsyn asked: 'Why does not fate punish *them*? Why do they prosper?'

> And the only solution to this would be that the meaning of earthly existence lies not, as we have grown used to thinking, in prospering, but ... in the development of the soul. From *that* point of view our torturers have been punished most horribly of all: they are turning into swine, they are departing downward from humanity. From that point of view punishment is inflicted on those whose development *... holds out hope.*[28]

Having passed beyond Kornfeld's theory, Solzhenitsyn could look back at it from the other side. From this new angle, he saw that for individuals in their one-to-one relationship with the Creator, the theory actually held true: 'But there was something in Kornfeld's last words that touched a sensitive chord, and that I accept quite completely *for myself*. And many will accept the same for themselves.'[29]

All alone in the recovery room in the camp hospital from which Kornfeld had gone to his death, Solzhenitsyn passed long sleepless nights pondering with astonishment his own life and the turns it had taken. For the first time he seemed fully awake, fully alive, to the sublime realities at the root of his personal experiences. At last, all the doubts, all the shadows, seemed to disappear and everything appeared resolved, crystal clear. Slowly, as the interminable minutes passed, he set down his thoughts in rhymed verses:

When did I so utterly, totally,
Strew the good grain like chaff to the winds
And shun those same temples where all through my youth
I was lulled by Your radiant hymns?

My dazzling book-garnered wisdom proved more than
This arrogant brain could withstand.
The world with its secrets spread open before me
And Fate was but wax in my hands.

Each new surge of blood as it pounded within me
Lured me on with its shimmering hues,
While the faith in my heart, like a building deserted,
Crumbled, soundless, and slipped into ruin.

But picking my way between life and extinction,
Now falling, now scrambling back,
I gaze through new eyes at the life I once followed
And gazing, I shudder with thanks.

It was not my own intellect, not my desiring
That illumined each twist in my path
But the still, even light of a Higher design,
That only with time I could grasp.

And now, as I sip with new-found moderation
From the lifegiving waters – I see
That my faith is restored, O Lord of Creation!
I renounced You, but You stood by me.[30]

NOTES

1. Solzhenitsyn, *The First Circle*, p. 168.
2. Ibid., pp. 168–9.
3. Quoted in Gregory Wolfe, *Malcolm Muggeridge: A Biography*, London: Hodder & Stoughton, 1995, p. 243.
4. *Daily Telegraph*, 9 September 1951.
5. Ibid.
6. Solzhenitsyn, interview with the author.
7. Ibid.
8. Ibid.
9. Solzhenitsyn, *The First Circle*, pp. 200–1.
10. Ibid., p. 201.
11. Reshetovskaya, *Sanya*, p. 132.
12. Ibid., p. 136.
13. Solzhenitsyn, *The First Circle*, p. 253.
14. Reshetovskaya, *Sanya*, p. 148.
15. Ibid.
16. Solzhenitsyn, *The First Circle*, p. 581.
17. Reshetovskaya, *Sanya*, p. 152.
18. Ibid.
19. Ibid., p. 162.
20. Ibid.
21. Ibid., p. 169.
22. Ibid.
23. Scammell, *Solzhenitsyn: A Biography*, p. 309.
24. Reshetovskaya, *Sanya*, p. 115.
25. Solzhenitsyn, *The Gulag Archipelago Volume Two*, p. 612.
26. Ibid., p. 613.
27. Ibid.
28. Ibid.
29. Ibid.
30. Solzhenitsyn, *The Gulag Archipelago Volume Two*, 'Ascent'; translated by Michael A. Nicholson.

CHAPTER NINE

BEAUTIFUL EXILE

Solzhenitsyn would always consider his close encounter with death at the Ekibastuz labour camp as the third and final of the 'most important and defining moments' in his life, following his experiences as a front-line soldier and his subsequent arrest.[1] 'When at the end of gaol, on top of everything else, I was placed with cancer, then I was fully cleansed and came back to a deep awareness of God and a deep understanding of life. From that time I was formed essentially into who I am now. After that it was mostly evolution, there were no abrupt turns, no breaking directions.'[2] The process, culminating in religious conversion, was summed up succinctly in an interview Solzhenitsyn gave to Georges Suffert in 1976: 'first comes the fight for survival, then the discovery of life, then God'.[3]

One is drawn to parallels between Solzhenitsyn's experience and those of his great literary predecessor Fyodor Dostoyevsky, who also felt that his life had been transformed by his sufferings as a prisoner in Siberia. 'It was a good school,' he wrote. 'It strengthened my faith and awakened my love for those who bear all their suffering with patience. It also strengthened my love for Russia and opened my eyes to the great qualities of the Russian people.'[4] The kinship is further illustrated in Dostoyevsky's appraisal of the importance of suffering to his development as a writer: 'I have been through a lot and will see and experience even more – you shall see how much I will have to write about.'[5]

Having embraced Christianity, Solzhenitsyn began to sympathize more than ever with those who had been persecuted for their religious faith. At Ekibastuz he rubbed shoulders with many devout men who had been imprisoned for their beliefs and began to feel a deep affinity with them. The Old Believers, the traditionalist recusants of the Orthodox church, were no longer the strange anachronism they had

118

seemed to Solzhenitsyn in his days as a Marxist. Now they were the 'eternally persecuted, eternal exiles', the ones who three centuries earlier had 'divined the ruthlessness at the heart of Authority'.[6] He heard with a sense of growing admiration about the struggle of these Old Believers to retain their faith and way of life in the hostile environment of Stalin's Russia. In *The Gulag Archipelago* he recounts the story of the Yaruyevo Old Believers who had fled from the oppression of Soviet collectivization. A whole village had literally uprooted itself and disappeared deep into the remoteness of the Russian wilderness. For twenty years these uncompromising Christians had lived a self-sufficient existence in the vast basin of the Podkamennaya Tunguska, living in secluded isolation from the prying eyes of the outside world. The end came in 1950 when the previously unknown settlement was spotted from a plane and its position reported to the authorities. When Soviet troops arrived they found a small but thriving community that had enjoyed 'twenty years of life as free human beings among the wild beasts, instead of twenty years of ... misery'. They were all wearing homespun garments and homemade knee boots, and they were all 'exceptionally sturdy'.[7] The whole village was arrested on a charge of 'anti-Soviet agitation' and for constituting a hostile organization and found themselves in the same labour camps as Solzhenitsyn.

In 1946, four years before the Yaruyevo Old Believers were discovered, another group of Old Believers was arrested in a forgotten monastery somewhere in the backwoods. They were then floated on rafts down the Yenisei river bound for the camps. 'Prisoners still, and still indomitable – the same under Stalin as they had been under Peter! – they jumped from the rafts into the waters of the Yenisei, where our Tommy-gunners finished them off.'[8]

Solzhenitsyn heard these stories and consigned them carefully to memory. He was determined that one day the world should know the full truth, the ugly secrets lurking in the murky depths of Soviet society. In order to do this he had his own secrets to keep. He was now writing more than ever before, scrawling lines of verse on scraps of paper which were burnt as soon as he had memorized the words. If his thoughts were discovered on paper he would certainly receive a further sentence of imprisonment and he was determined not to make the same naïve mistakes which had led to his initial

arrest more than seven years earlier. At Ekibastuz his writing became almost obsessive, pressing on his consciousness at all hours of
the day. 'In the interval between two barrowloads of mortar I would
put my bit of paper on the bricks and (without letting my neighbours see what I was doing) write down with a pencil stub the verses
which had rushed into my head while I was slapping on the last
hodful.'⁹ According to his own account of this period of intensive
writing at Ekibastuz in 1952, he lived in a dream for much of the
time and sat in the mess hall over the ritual gruel 'deaf to those
around me – feeling my way about my verses and trimming them to
fit like bricks in a wall'.¹⁰

> I realized that I was not the only one, that I was party to a
> great secret, a secret maturing in other lonely breasts like
> mine on the scattered islands of the Archipelago, to reveal
> itself in years to come, perhaps when we were dead, and to
> merge into the Russian literature of the future ...
>
> How many of us were there? Many more, I think, than
> have come to the surface in the intervening years. Not all
> of them were to survive. Some buried manuscripts in bot-
> tles, without telling anyone where. Some put their work in
> careless or, on the contrary, in excessively cautious hands
> for safekeeping. Some could not write their work down in
> time.
>
> Even on the isle of Ekibastuz, could we really get to
> know each other? encourage each other? support each
> other? Like wolves, we hid from everyone, and that meant
> from each other, too. Yet even so I was to discover a few
> others in Ekibastuz.¹¹

The most important of Solzhenitsyn's fellow literary conspirators at
Ekibastuz was the religious poet Anatoly Vasilyevich Silin. Solzhenitsyn had met him initially through their mutual friendship with the
Baptist prisoners at the camp. He was over forty, about ten years
Solzhenitsyn's senior, and Solzhenitsyn described him as 'meek and
gentle with everyone, but reserved'. During their long conversations, strolling round the camp on their Sundays off, the younger
prisoner discovered in the older man a kindred spirit. Silin had been

a homeless child, brought up as an atheist in a children's home, but had come across some religious books in a German prisoner-of-war camp and been totally carried away by them. From that time he had become not only a fervent believer but also a gifted philosopher and theologian. Since he had spent the entire period since his conversion in prisons of one sort or another he had never had the benefit of further spiritual reading. Instead he gleaned the truth through his own perceptions, expressed in verse. According to Solzhenitsyn, Silin knew some twenty thousand lines of verse by heart at the time they met, reciting many of them to his younger fellow poet. Like Solzhenitsyn, Silin looked upon his verse as 'a way of remembering and of transmitting thoughts'.[12]

For *The Gulag Archipelago* Solzhenitsyn gleaned a few precious memories of their time together in the camp. He recalled Silin bending over one of the rare blades of grass growing in the barren camp. 'How beautiful are the grasses of the earth,' he exclaimed. 'But even these the Creator has given to man for a carpet under his feet. How much more beautiful, then, must we be than they!' Silin's theological mysticism was distinctly unpuritanical, and he asserted to Solzhenitsyn that 'even earthly, carnal love is a manifestation of a lofty aspiration to Union'. On another occasion he had answered the refusal of atheists to believe that spirit could beget matter: 'Why don't they ask themselves how crude matter could beget spirit? That way round, it would surely be a miracle. Yes, a still greater miracle!' Yet it was in his belief in the necessity of suffering that he had most in common with Solzhenitsyn. Silin declared that the soul must suffer before it was able to know the 'perfect bliss of paradise', and that 'by grief alone is love perfected'. This law, though harsh, was the only way that weak men could 'win eternal peace'.[13]

Solzhenitsyn wrote of Silin that this 'doomed and exhausted slave, with four number patches on his clothes ... had more in his heart to say to living human beings than the whole tribe of hacks firmly established in journals, in publishing houses, in radio – and of no use to anyone except themselves'.[14]

If the twenty thousand lines of poetry that Silin had memorized was an awesome achievement, Solzhenitsyn's own powers of retention were scarcely less remarkable. By the time he was released he had consigned twelve thousand lines of his own work to memory.

He had been helped in this by the use of a rosary which had been made for him by some Catholic Lithuanian prisoners. Each bead, made of small pieces of wet bread, represented a line of verse, and Solzhenitsyn could often be seen fingering the beads, apparently in prayer, but actually memorizing his poetry.

Most of the poetry Solzhenitsyn wrote at Ekibastuz, collectively entitled *The Way*, was broadly autobiographical. He later rejected much of it as unworthy of publication but *Prussian Nights*, the epic poem based on his experiences in Prussia in January 1945, was an exception, being born from *The Way* but taking on a full and vibrant life of its own. Also composed at Ekibastuz were *A Feast of Conquerors* (published in English in 1981 under the title *Victory Celebrations*), which was a play written entirely in rhymed verse, and a longer play entitled *Prisoners*.

Many critics have highlighted the flaws in these plays and Solzhenitsyn concedes that 'they are inferior to my other work in the sense that I was using them for the expression of ideas and I was not as demanding perhaps in terms of dramaturgical requirements'.[15]

In *A Feast of Conquerors* the idea Solzhenitsyn was seeking to convey found expression in the contrasting characters of Gridnev and Galina. In many respects these two characters are an incarnation of the warring spirits at the core of all Solzhenitsyn's art. Gridnev takes the path of least resistance, becoming utterly corrupted by his desire to find the most comfortable route through life; Galina, on the other hand, takes the path of sacrifice, embodying the alternative vision of nobility and heroism in the face of adversity, the way of the Cross. Yet the eternal verities incarnated in these two characters are also rooted in a specific historical context. *A Feast of Conquerors* is set in an East Prussian country house and depicts a scene similar to one experienced by Solzhenitsyn himself during the Soviet advance in January 1945. Like *Prussian Nights* it is infused with autobiographical detail. For this reason Solzhenitsyn insists that the conflict between Galina and Gridnev should be seen on several different levels, physical as well as metaphysical:

> This conflict represents not even their personal tragedy but the tragedy of the Russian people as a whole under the oppression of the communists, the bolsheviks. The people

wanted to be free but it was impossible until the war. They believed that the Germans were bringing freedom to us and looked towards the Germans believing that they would help, or at least would not hinder, the liberation from communism. But the world powers were already aligned in such a way that the Allies – the US, the UK – did not want to tolerate any more fighting against the communists because the communists were their allies. And so these people were trapped between the Russian Soviets, the Germans, and the Americans and English, all of whom considered them as traitors. This affected many millions. Millions. Several millions retreated with the Germans.[16]

Prisoners shares many of the themes which were at the centre of *A Feast of Conquerors*. The moral dilemma of those fighting in the anti-communist Russian Liberation Army is addressed. Having signed up with the Nazi devil these 'liberators' were swallowed up by the deep red sea of the Soviet advance. The other *leitmotif* in *Prisoners* resonant of *A Feast of Conquerors* is that depicting the triumph of unconquerable spirit over physical adversity. Throughout both plays there is a recurrent anger at the injustice at the heart of the Soviet regime, an anger which became the energy, the motive force, behind Solzhenitsyn's future work. The quiet prisoner saying his 'prayers' with the crude rosary at Ekibastuz was preparing a literary time-bomb, primed to explode at an unknown date in the future.

As the months of 1952 passed slowly away, another future date was pressing ever more insistently on Solzhenitsyn's mind. The date of his release. Officially his sentence ended on 9 February 1953 and as the golden day approached he dreamed of the exile that awaited him. He knew that he would not be allowed to return to normal life and that, in all probability, perpetual exile was all he could expect, but after the ordeal of the camps even 'exile' sounded like Eden or Paradise to his freedom-starved heart. 'The dream of exile burns like a secret light in the prisoner's mind,' Solzhenitsyn wrote, 'a flickering iridescent mirage, and the wasted breasts of prisoners on their dark bunks heave in sighs of longing: "If only they would sentence me to exile!"'[17] Solzhenitsyn was not immune to such longing. As long ago as the infernal clay-pits at New Jerusalem which had killed his friend Boris Gammerov, he had listened to the cocks crowing in the nearby village and had dreamed of exile.

His dream came true on 13 February 1953 when, four days after the official end of his sentence, he was led out of the main camp gates with a group of other released prisoners and marched under armed guard to the railway station. Almost exactly a year earlier he had been operated on for cancer yet now, fit and well, he was finally on the verge of freedom. Perhaps, at long last, his luckless life was about to change for the better. There followed one of the customary interminable journeys to an unknown destination and an unknown future. Several days later Solzhenitsyn and the other prisoners arrived in Dzhambul, midway between Alma-Ata and Tashkent in Kazakhstan, where they were informed that they were being exiled 'in perpetuity' to the district of Kok-Terek, on the southern fringe of Kazakhstan's vast desert of Bet-Pak-Dala. He finally arrived at his new home on the edge of the arid wastelands of Kazakhstan on 3 March 1953, eighteen days after leaving Ekibastuz. His eight-year sentence of imprisonment had ended; his perpetual sentence of exile had begun.

For the first few days of his new life Solzhenitsyn was drunk with freedom. On the first night he was unable to sleep and walked and walked in the moonlight. 'The donkeys sing their song. The camels sing. Every fibre in me sings: I am free! I am free!' In the end, overtaken by tiredness he spread out on a bed of hay in a barn, listening to the horses a few yards away, standing at their mangers munching hay. He could imagine 'no sweeter, no more friendly sound' on this his first night of freedom: 'Champ away, you mild, inoffensive creatures!'[18] The following day he managed to find private lodgings in a tiny hut, with a single window and a roof so low that it was impossible to stand upright. The floor was earthen but he managed to obtain two wooden boxes which served as a makeshift bed. He didn't own the hut and even the boxes were borrowed, but he felt richer than he had ever been in his life. 'What more could I desire? ...'

Then, on 6 March, as he woke on his third morning of freedom, he heard the news that surpassed all his desires. His elderly landlady, herself an exile from Novgorod, whispered that he should go to the town square and listen to the announcements on the radio. She dared not repeat the news she had just heard. Intrigued, he made his way to the square where a crowd of about two hundred people had gathered round the loudspeaker. For the most part the crowd were clearly grief-stricken. Even before he heard the news confirmed by the announcer on the radio, he had guessed what had happened. Stalin was dead.

Throughout the Soviet Union there was a phenomenal outpouring of largely genuine grief. In the days that followed, countless mourners would be crushed to death outside the House of Unions where the body of the 'Wise Father of all the Peoples' lay in state, in the very Columned Hall where he had ordered the infamous show trials in the 1930s which had consigned so many thousands of his countrymen to the labour camps.

In *The First Circle*, Solzhenitsyn allowed himself the liberty of imagining Stalin's last days, locked up in his room, distrustful of everyone he knew, fearing assassination. Stalin, the great dictator who had exiled millions of Russians to the far-flung corners of the Soviet empire, was himself an exile in his own palace, an exile of his own paranoia. The irony was not lost on the happy exile in Kok-Terek.

> They were all like that, in all the ministries – every one of them was trying to hoodwink their Leader. How could he possibly trust them. He had no choice but to work at nights.
>
> He suddenly staggered into a chair ... He felt as though some weight was forcing the left half of his head downwards. He lost hold of his train of thought and stared with blurred gaze round the room, unable to make out whether the walls were near or far.
>
> He was an old man without any friends. Nobody loved him, he believed in nothing and he wanted nothing. He no longer even had any need of his daughter, once his favourite but now only admitted on rare holidays. Helpless fear overcame him as he sensed the dwindling memory, the failing mind. Loneliness crept over him like a paralysis.

> Death had already laid its hand on him, but he would
> not believe it.[19]

Needless to say, Solzhenitsyn's feelings as he heard the news of
Stalin's death were anything but grief-stricken:

> This was the moment my friends and I had looked forward
> to ... The moment for which every zek in Gulag (except
> the orthodox communists) had prayed! He's dead, the Asi-
> atic dictator is dead! The villain has curled up and died!
> What unconcealed rejoicing there would be back home in
> the Special Camp! But where I was, Russian girls, school-
> teachers, stood sobbing their hearts out ... They had lost a
> beloved parent ... I could have howled with joy there by
> the loudspeaker; I could even have danced a wild jig! But
> alas, the rivers of history flow slowly. My face, trained to
> meet all occasions, assumed a frown of mournful attention.
> For the present I must pretend, go on pretending as before.[20]

He returned to his hut to spend the remainder of the day writing a
poem, 'The Fifth of March', to commemorate the occasion. Certainly his life in exile had begun magnificently.

In April Solzhenitsyn was finally accepted as a teacher of maths
and physics in a local school, having been rejected when he had initially applied a month earlier. He was overjoyed. 'Shall I describe the
happiness it gave me to go into the classroom and pick up the chalk?
This was really the day of my release, the restoration of my citizenship ...'[21]

At last, or so it must have seemed as he began life as a village
schoolteacher, Solzhenitsyn's future could be faced with optimism.
His circumstances, which had already improved beyond measure
since the misery of the camps, could only get better. He was still
only thirty-four years old. He had many good years of life ahead of
him. Then, like a death knell tolling his doom across the barren
steppe, the spectre of his cancer returned. As the year rolled on, the
deadly disease tormented him more and more, 'as though it was in
league with my gaolers'.[22] Intermittently, but with ever greater frequency, he was struck by excruciating pains in the abdominal area.

During the day he could barely stand up in front of his class and at night he slept very little. He had no appetite for food and was visibly weakening with every week that passed. At first he had not wanted to believe that the cause of his illness was a return of the cancer that had nearly claimed his life in Ekibastuz. His hopes were raised, albeit falsely, by the inability of the medical authorities in Kok-Terek to diagnose his condition. They thought it might be an ulcer, or perhaps gastritis. Yet as the year drew to a close, Solzhenitsyn began to fear the worst. Perhaps his own life was also drawing to a close. Hurriedly he wrote down all that he had previously written in the camp and stored in his memory, and all that he had composed in exile since his release, and buried it in the ground in the forlorn hope that someone, some day, might dig it up by accident and read it.

Since his condition continued to baffle the local doctors, it was decided that he needed the attention of specialists. He was granted permission to leave for Dzhambul, the administrative centre of the region, for further tests on his abdomen. An X-ray revealed exactly what Solzhenitsyn had feared. The cause of his pain was not an ulcer, but a tumour the size of a big fist, which had grown from the back wall of the abdominal cavity. It was entirely possible, he was informed, that the tumour was malignant.

Solzhenitsyn returned to Kok-Terek in early December, knowing he would have to report to the Oncological Health Centre in Tashkent a few weeks later. Once again he was staring death in the face, gaining a few priceless morsels of consolation from the belief that death would not be the end of life. Yet even his faith could not totally eclipse the bitterness he felt at what appeared to be the futility of his life. 'I remember clearly that night before I left for Tashkent, the last night of 1953: it seemed as though for me life, and literature, was ending right there. I felt cheated.'[23]

Solzhenitsyn was admitted to Ward 13 of the Tashkent Medical Institute on 4 January 1954. The following day a drawing was made on his stomach, dividing it into four squares, and each square was irradiated in turn. Over the next month and a half, he had fifty-five sessions of radiotherapy during which the tumour was bombarded with 12,000 roentgens of radiation.

Solzhenitsyn's experiences in the Tashkent Medical Institute during January and February 1954 became the background to, and the inspiration for, his novel *Cancer Ward*. This novel, like *The First Circle* and so much of his other work, is infused throughout with autobiographical fragments. In the character of Kostoglotov, the most autobiographically sketched of the characters in *Cancer Ward*, there is much to be gleaned about Solzhenitsyn's own feelings as a cancer patient. Kostoglotov tells Zoya, one of the nurses, that during the last month he hasn't been able to lie, sit down or stand without it hurting, and has been sleeping only a few minutes a day. As a result he has done plenty of thinking:

> This autumn I learned from experience that a man can cross the threshold of death even when his body is not dead. Your blood still circulates and your stomach digests, while you yourself have gone through the whole psychological preparation for death – and lived through death itself. Everything around you, you see as from the grave. And although you've never counted yourself a Christian, indeed the very opposite sometimes, all of a sudden you find you've forgiven all those who trespassed against you and bear no ill-will towards those who persecuted you.[24]

This transcendental approach to life's ultimate realities is contrasted with the inability of other characters in the novel to come to terms with their terminal illness. For these people, corrupted by the transient material comforts of life, the prospect of death is unthinkable, unmentionable. 'Modern man is helpless when confronted with death,' another character muses, 'he has no weapon to meet it with.'[25] The angst at the very core of modern man is analysed in the relationships of the various cancer patients in the novel, not only with each other but with themselves as they struggle to deal with the abyss lying before them. In one particularly poignant passage Kostoglotov, in the midst of an argument on the validity of Marxism, suddenly perceives the pettiness and futility of politics in the face of higher truths:

> Was it weariness or illness that gave him this urge to yawn? Or was it because these arguments, counter-arguments, technical terms, bitter, angry glances suddenly seemed so

much squelching in a swamp? None of this was to be compared with the disease that afflicted them or with death, which loomed before them. He yearned for the touch of something different, something pure and unshakable. But where he would find that Oleg had no idea.[26]

This passage from *Cancer Ward* encapsulates much of Solzhenitsyn's central message to the modern world. The ultimate subsistence of politics within a higher moral and ultimately religious truth; the transcendent nature of pain and death and the immensity of both in relation to transient circumstantial comforts; and, perhaps most important of all, the inarticulate yearning of agnostic man for the sublime depths of theological truth, a return to religious faith. Commenting on this particular passage, Solzhenitsyn agreed that he was attempting to grapple with the way people struggled with eternal verities in the absence of religion: 'I am describing Soviet people who are devoid of religion. Therefore there's a feeling for some sort of other form, some ersatz. They're groping, they're trying to clamber upwards.'[27]

There were, however, other motivations behind the writing of *Cancer Ward*. One was the desire to explore 'the relationship between the corporeal and the spiritual aspects of love'.

> Then we have the theme of life and death. And it is not by accident that the teaching of Bacon on idols is resurrected to show that several centuries back people used to worship the same idols. And of course there were the undercurrents of the current political events of spring 1955. I was depicting them. I cannot do without doing that, precisely what was going on in those days, during those weeks. It was the first beginnings, hints of freedom from Stalin's claw. And this political theme is also linked with the image at the end of the book with the mangled monkey, where they threw the tobacco in the monkey's eyes, a metaphor for what was done to the people.[28]

Solzhenitsyn was discharged from the cancer ward in Tashkent in mid-March. When he arrived two months earlier, he had been given only a one-in-three chance of survival. He had responded well to treatment and had made a remarkable recovery. The tumour had shrunk to only half its previous size. But he was still not out of danger and was told that he would have to return in June for a further course of treatment.

Before returning to exile at Kok-Terek, Solzhenitsyn took the opportunity to wander round the city and was astonished to find a church that was actually open. For the first time since attending requiem Mass as a child with his mother, he entered a real, living church and gave thanks for having survived to see another spring.

In June he returned to Tashkent where radiotherapy was resumed. As he lay once more in the cancer ward, with thoughts of the future novel floating in his head, the horrors of the Gulag he had left less than eighteen months earlier were carrying on without him. During that same June, at Kengir Camp in Kazakhstan, eight thousand political prisoners had staged a mutiny and taken over the camp. Religious services were held, and men and women who had previously corresponded secretly from their separate stockades met and consummated their love. Then, on 25 June, the Soviet tanks rolled in, crushing everyone in their way. One prisoner remembered the corner of a hut collapsing 'as if in a nightmare', and the tank rolling over the wreckage and over living bodies. Prisoners were bayoneted in cold blood; women, desperately trying to shield their men from the cold steel, were bayoneted first. One young couple, unprepared to be separated again so soon after they had been united, threw themselves under a tank clasped in each other's arms, choosing to die together rather than live apart. By the time the rebellion was crushed some three hundred prisoners had been killed.[29]

Almost simultaneously Jean-Paul Sartre, in an act of wilful ignorance reminiscent of that shown by Wells, Shaw and the Webbs in the thirties, was eulogizing the Soviet regime in the pages of *Libération*. Having recently visited the Soviet Union he assured his interviewer that 'Soviet citizens criticize their government much more and more effectively than we do. There is total freedom of criticism in the USSR.'[30] Furthermore, Sartre assured *Libération*'s readers, the only reason that Soviet citizens did not travel abroad was not that they were in any way prevented from doing so but that they had no desire to leave their marvellous country.

Meanwhile, in his marvellous country, Solzhenitsyn was discharged from hospital, totally cured of the cancer, and returned to the tiny village on the edge of the desert where he was condemned to live in perpetuity, prevented even from travelling to other parts of the Soviet Union, let alone abroad.

Back in Kok-Terek Solzhenitsyn threw himself into his writing. He wrote another play, initially called 'The Republic of Labour' but eventually published under the title *The Love Girl and the Innocent*, and in the following year, 1955, he began work on his first novel. This was *The First Circle*, based on his experiences at the Marfino *sharashka*. He must have been helped in this by a renewal of his acquaintance with Dimitri Panin and Lev Kopelev, his old intellectual sparring partners at Marfino. Of course they couldn't possibly meet in the flesh – Panin, like Solzhenitsyn, was still in exile, while Kopelev was living in Moscow – but, after Panin's wife had succeeded in tracking her husband's friends down, they began to correspond regularly.

In many respects Solzhenitsyn later looked on these months in Kok-Terek as amongst the happiest in his life. In *The Gulag Archipelago* he referred to the period as 'my two years of truly Beautiful Exile', evoking with delight the contentment that reigned within him:

> all my days were lived in a state of constant blissfully heightened awareness, and I felt no constraint on my freedom. At school I could give as many lessons as I wanted, in both shifts – and every lesson brought a throbbing happiness, never weariness or boredom. And every day I had a little time left for writing – and there was never any need for me to attune my thoughts: as soon as I sat down the lines raced from under my pen.[31]

Regular employment as a schoolteacher had improved his financial circumstances. He bought a little clay house and a firm table to write on but still eschewed other material comforts, choosing to continue sleeping on the same bare wooden boxes. He did, however, invest in a short-wave radio set, listening surreptitiously for any forbidden news from the West, holding his ear close to the speaker in an effort to make out what he could through 'the cascading crash of jam-ming'. Yet for all his efforts he heard little to inspire him: 'We were so worn out by decades of lying nonsense, we yearned for any scrap of truth, however tattered – and yet this work was not worth the time I wasted on it: the infantile West had no riches of wisdom or courage to bestow on those of us who were nurtured by the Archi-pelago.'³²

As with his time in the Archipelago, Solzhenitsyn 'was fully con-scious that exile was a blessing', cherishing the 'purer vision' it gave. He was utterly content and fully resigned to living in Kok-Terek if not in perpetuity, then at least for twenty years or so. Events in the Soviet Union were on the move, however, even if the isolated exile was not fully aware of the changes afoot. Soon, much sooner than he expected, he would be catapulted back into the centre of the storm.

Following Stalin's death a power struggle had ensued within the Soviet leadership as warring factions fought for supremacy. The first victim was Lavrenty Beria, the hated chief of the secret police, who was arrested and executed in July 1953. Georgi Malenkov, who had succeeded Stalin in 1953, was forced from office in February 1955 and in July 1957 was accused with Molotov and Kaganovich of set-ting up an 'anti-party group'. In one of the many ironies of fate in the twisted history of the Soviet Union, Malenkov was dismissed from all senior party positions and exiled to Kazakhstan as manager of a hydroelectric plant. Molotov, meanwhile, was exiled to Outer Mongolia where he served as ambassador until 1960. Kaganovich would soon disappear without trace but was last heard of in August 1957, in 'a position of considerable responsibility' in a Siberian cement works. One doubts whether these erstwhile heroes of the Soviet Union would have agreed with Solzhenitsyn that exile could be a blessing.

The man who emerged triumphant from this bout of internecine feuding and bloodletting was Nikita Khrushchev who, in 1956, broke the taboo by giving a 'Secret Speech' to the Twentieth Party Congress in which Stalin was criticized openly for the first time. Khrushchev officially implicated the 'Wise Father of all the Peoples' in Kirov's murder and held him responsible for the sufferings of mil-lions during the Terror. The unspeakable had been uttered and many delegates to the Congress were said to have been traumatized by the revelations. Not that Khrushchev was himself blameless. During the Terror he had been so ruthless in the execution of Stalin's orders that he had earned the nickname 'Butcher of the Ukraine'. Indeed, in the very year in which he made the Secret Speech, he earned another nickname as the 'Butcher of Budapest', ordering Soviet tanks into Hungary to put down brutally the anti-communist uprising there. Later he was to oversee the building of the Berlin Wall and take the world to the brink of nuclear war during the Cuban Missile Crisis. Nonetheless, Khrushchev's policy of de-Stalinization came as a great relief to millions of persecuted Soviet citizens. During 1956 thousands of political prisoners were rehabilitated and returned from the camps or from exile, and Solzhenitsyn was destined to be one tiny but scarcely insignificant drop in that returning ocean.

Solzhenitsyn's rehabilitation came following a session of the Military Collegium of the Supreme Court of the USSR on 6 February 1956. During the course of the session the Chief Military Prosecutor called for all charges against Solzhenitsyn to be dropped on the grounds that there was an 'absence of proof of a crime'. The reasons given were as follows:

> It is clear from the evidence in this case that Solzhenitsyn, in his diary and letters to a friend, N. D. Vitkevich, although speaking of the correctness of Marxism-Leninism, the progressiveness of the socialist revolution in our country and the inevitability of its victory throughout the world, also spoke out against the personality of Stalin and wrote of the artistic and ideological shortcomings of the works of many Soviet authors and the air of unreality that pervades many of them. He also wrote that our works of art fail to give readers of the bourgeois world a sufficiently comprehensive and versatile explanation of the inevitability of the victory of the Soviet army and people, and that our literary works are no match for the adroitly fashioned slanders of the bourgeois world against our country.[33]

'These statements by Solzhenitsyn,' the Chief Military Prosecutor asserted, 'do not constitute proof of a crime.'

The Collegium then questioned a number of people, including Natalya, to whom Solzhenitsyn was alleged to have made anti-Soviet allegations, all of whom 'characterized Solzhenitsyn as a Soviet patriot and denied that he had conducted anti-Soviet conversations'. The Collegium also examined Solzhenitsyn's military record and a report by Captain Melnikov with whom he had served. From these the Collegium concluded that Solzhenitsyn had 'fought courageously for his homeland, more than once displayed personal heroism and inspired the devotion of the section he commanded'. Furthermore, 'Solzhenitsyn's section was the best in the unit for discipline and battle effectiveness.'

Having examined all the evidence the Collegium ruled that 'Solzhenitsyn's actions do not constitute a crime and his case should be closed for lack of proof.'

The decision to drop all charges had come a decade too late, after the man who was now declared innocent had already served eight years in prison and three in exile. One wonders whether Solzhenitsyn still managed to raise a wry smile when reading the Supreme Court document. He had, almost overnight, been transformed from a hated enemy of the people, a pariah, to a war hero and wise critic of Stalin's deficiencies. Now, presumably, he was supposed to go home quietly, like a good and loyal Soviet citizen, and say nothing of the horrors he had seen and experienced.

Little did the Chief Military Prosecutor know it, but he had plucked this ticking time-bomb from the relative safety of a village in Kazakhstan and placed it carefully at the heart of Soviet society. Solzhenitsyn, strengthened and purified by his time in prison and exile, was primed and ready to explode on an unsuspecting literary world.

NOTES

1. Solzhenitsyn, interview with the author.
2. Ibid.
3. Alexander Solzhenitsyn, interview published in *Encounter*, April 1976, quoted in John B. Dunlop, Richard S. Haugh, Michael Nicholson (eds.), *Solzhenitsyn In Exile: Critical Essays and Documentary Materials*, Stanford, California: Hoover Institute Press, 1985, p. 262.
4. Quoted in D. M. Thomas, *Solzhenitsyn: A Century in His Life*, p. 194.

5. Ibid.
6. Solzhenitsyn, *The Gulag Archipelago Volume Three*, p. 366.
7. Ibid., pp. 366–7.
8. Ibid., p. 367.
9. Ibid., p. 104.
10. Ibid.
11. Ibid., pp. 104–5.
12. Ibid., p. 106.
13. Ibid., pp. 106–7.
14. Ibid., p. 107.
15. Solzhenitsyn, interview with the author.
16. Ibid.
17. Solzhenitsyn, *The Gulag Archipelago Volume Three*, p. 406.
18. Ibid., p. 420.
19. Solzhenitsyn, *The First Circle*, p. 120.
20. Solzhenitsyn, *The Gulag Archipelago Volume Three*, pp. 421–2.
21. Ibid., p. 428.
22. Ibid., p. 440.
23. Ibid.
24. Alexander Solzhenitsyn, *Cancer Ward*, London: Book Club Associates by arrangement with The Bodley Head Ltd, 1975, pp. 37–8.
25. Ibid., p. 522.
26. Ibid., p. 478.
27. Solzhenitsyn, interview with the author.
28. Ibid.
29. Solzhenitsyn, *The Gulag Archipelago Volume Three*, p. 328.
30. Paul Johnson, *Intellectuals*, London: Weidenfeld, 1988, p. 244.
31. Solzhenitsyn, *The Gulag Archipelago Volume Three*, p. 440.
32. Ibid.
33. Supreme Court of the USSR Decision no. 4n-083/56, published in Leopold Labedz (ed.), *Solzhenitsyn: A Documentary Record*, Harmondsworth, Middlesex: Penguin Books, 2nd edn., 1974, p. 26.

CHAPTER TEN

IVAN THE TERRIBLE

In April 1956, several weeks after learning of his rehabilitation, Solzhenitsyn wrote to Natalya informing her that he had been freed from exile and that his previous convictions had been officially expunged from the record. He now wished to settle in some relatively remote region and hoped that Natalya could make inquiries in the Ryazan Region, where she was currently living, to see whether there were any vacancies in the field of physics or mathematics. At the same time he sought to assure her that, should he take up residence in Ryazan, there would be 'no shadow cast upon your life'. In reply, Natalya informed him that there was a surplus of mathematicians and physicists in the Ryazan area and that he should try to settle in a city.[1]

Meanwhile Solzhenitsyn remained at Kok-Terek until he had fulfilled his obligations as a schoolteacher. It was not until he had marked the final examinations at the end of the school year that he was finally free to leave. On 20 June 1956 he caught the train to Moscow, a journey taking four days. For the first two days the train travelled through the hot, dusty steppes of central Asia, his home as prisoner and exile for the previous six years. On the third the train crossed the Volga and, as it did so, Solzhenitsyn found himself overwhelmed emotionally by the sense of return to the central Russian heartland. He walked along the corridor until he found a platform where the upper half of the door was open, and stood there seemingly for an eternity, staring out at the Russian countryside. The wind rushed into his face and the tears streamed from his eyes.[2] He was coming home.

On 24 June Solzhenitsyn was met at the Kazan station in Moscow by both Panin and Kopelev, the former having been released from exile in January. Paradoxically, his arrival home had found him with nowhere to live and he moved in with the Kopelevs for a while. Shortly afterwards he resided for a time with some cousins whom he had not seen since childhood, before finding temporary accommodation with the Panins.

It was while staying with the Panins that Solzhenitsyn had a wholly unexpected meeting with Natalya. She was on a trip to Moscow and decided to call on Panin's wife. When she arrived she found Solzhenitsyn and Panin seated at a table drinking tea. The Panins contrived to leave Solzhenitsyn and Natalya alone together and Solzhenitsyn told her of his plans for the future. He hated the hustle and bustle of the city, the noise, the hurry, the crowds, and was determined to escape to a quieter existence in the provinces. He hoped to settle in Vladimir Region about a hundred miles from Moscow.

Eventually, the subject of their own troubled relationship was broached and Solzhenitsyn questioned her earnestly, endeavouring to understand how Natalya's final separation from him had come about. 'I was created to love you alone,' she replied, 'but fate decreed otherwise.'[3] When they parted, Solzhenitsyn handed her a sheaf of poems that he had written to or about her throughout the years of separation. That night she read them and discovered that they had 'opened up old scars in my soul'. Returning to Ryazan, Natalya found herself continually reading and rereading the poems, turning them over and over in her mind, twisting a knife in the old wound. It was not long before Somov, her second 'husband', began to detect that something was wrong. Although Natalya had told him of her meeting with Solzhenitsyn she had assured him that 'nothing had changed as a result – everything would remain as it was'. He could see, however, that everything was not as it had been and he did everything in his power to win her back from the ghost of her past. He took her on a boat trip along the Oka in their own motor boat and on a holiday to Solotcha during August. It was a difficult and painful time; Somov was distressed to find that nothing he did could amuse his wife or distract her from her thoughts about the other man. Then the other man sent a letter: 'If you have the inclination and should you find it possible – you can write me. My address, as of 21 August, is ... Vladimir Region.'[4]

Correspondence commenced and Solzhenitsyn wrote that he believed a new happiness was possible for them. He suggested they meet and Natalya agreed, waiting for the opportunity to escape from her husband. That opportunity arose in October when Somov went to Odessa to attend a celebration in honour of a scientific colleague. While he was away, Natalya informed her mother that she had been summoned to Moscow in connection with Solzhenitsyn's rehabilitation. In fact she had no intention of going to Moscow but, on 19 October, bought a ticket to Torfprodukt, Vladimir Region.

The next three days were like a second honeymoon, exorcising any remaining doubts Natalya may have had about where her future lay. For his part, Solzhenitsyn felt compelled to inform her that he was still gravely ill and was doomed to a short life, possibly only another year or two. 'I need you in every way,' Natalya replied, 'alive or dying.'[5]

'As we discussed our joint plans,' Natalya wrote, '... I was quite aware even then that I was causing enormous sorrow to good people, but only now, looking back, do I comprehend the enormity of it. Was there anything that could have stopped me? Probably not.'[6] Among her friends and colleagues, as well as among friends of her second husband, 'there were many, very many, who censured me'.

In November Natalya and Somov separated.

Solzhenitsyn made his first visit to Ryazan on 30 December 1956 and on the following day they went to the Registry Office to register their marriage for a second time. No complications were caused by Natalya's former 'marriage' to Somov because they had never been officially wed, merely cohabiting as man and wife, but the re-registry was frustrated by the fact that Solzhenitsyn's passport contained no record of a divorce. This necessitated a trip to Moscow, which the couple undertook a few days later, to retrieve Solzhenitsyn's notification of divorce from the archives at the City Court. Now they could prove to the satisfaction of the bureaucrats that they had been legitimately divorced, they would be allowed to remarry.

Throughout the following months it gradually became apparent that the chasm which existed between them in the months before their separation had not been bridged by their physical reunion. Solzhenitsyn now preached a gospel of self-limitation, seeking to live as simply as possible without the glitter and glamour of modern diversions. He insisted that they should not visit the cinema more than twice a month, nor go to concerts or the theatre more than once every two months. This conscious rationing scarcely constituted a monastic existence but the restrictions proved irksome to Natalya, who had grown accustomed to a life of relative opulence with her second husband. For Solzhenitsyn their lifestyle was one of voluntary poverty leading to an improved quality of life freed from the clutter of needlessly created wants; for Natalya it amounted to the imposition of involuntary poverty, the denial of her right to legitimate pleasures, 'about going or not going to the movies; about buying or not buying books; about winning or not winning a bond on a lottery ticket'.[7]

The intensity and depth of Solzhenitsyn's own views at the time can be gauged from the fact that this was the period during which he was most deeply involved in the writing of *The First Circle*. From the summer of 1957 through to the spring of 1958, his life and Natalya's were spent in the shadow of the *sharashka* as he relived the long discussions with Panin and Kopelev in Marfino, charting its importance to his own spiritual and intellectual development. 'It's not a matter of *how much* you eat,' Nerzhin had told Rubin, 'but of the *way* you eat. It's the same with happiness – it doesn't depend on the actual number of blessings we manage to snatch from life, but only on our attitude towards them ...' One can imagine Solzhenitsyn repeating such sermons to his wife whenever she complained about the relative austerity of their life together: 'But listen! The happiness that comes from easy victories, from the total fulfilment of desire, from success, from feeling completely gorged – *that* is suffering! That is spiritual death, a kind of unending moral indigestion ...'[8]

Unfortunately, this perception of the eternal conflict between the material and spiritual aspects of life, gained by Solzhenitsyn in the passion and crucifixion of the camps, was seemingly unattainable to Natalya who continued to resent her husband's strictures and restrictions. Their own marriage was becoming a physical incarnation of the metaphysical struggle Solzhenitsyn was attempting to explore in *The First Circle*. This can be seen in Natalya's own incomprehension of her husband's words. Solzhenitsyn had written to her from prison that 'if the heart grows warmer from the misfortunes suffered, if it is cleansed therein – the years are not going by in vain'. In her memoirs Natalya immediately followed this quote with another from her husband's letters: 'Perhaps, if it should happen some day that I start living happily, I will become heartless again? Although it's hard to believe, still, anything can happen.' She then appends her own comments: 'How I wish that Solzhenitsyn's own apprehensions had never been confirmed! That he had not also turned in for incineration, along with his prison garb, the highest, noblest impulses of his soul!'[9] Leaving aside the rights and wrongs of Natalya's own version of events, Solzhenitsyn was clearly concerned never to lose sight of the truths he had learned in the camps, never to allow the comforts of life to corrupt him from the purity of the vision he believed he had acquired there. It was precisely 'the highest, noblest impulses of the soul' that he felt he had discovered in prison and precisely those impulses that he was determined the material pleasures of life should not obscure. Natalya's failure to grasp this central aspect of her husband's psyche illustrates the absence of empathy in their relationship.

Similar conflicts were apparent in Dimitri Panin's marriage. Panin had found his Christian faith intensified by the experience of prison with the result that, following his release, he had found his wife's lack of faith difficult to cope with. She in turn had found her husband's intense Christianity an insurmountable obstacle to their satisfactory reconciliation. By the time Panin came to stay with the Solzhenitsyns at the beginning of 1958 he and his wife had separated. Natalya found herself in complete sympathy with Panin's wife, possibly sensing parallels with her own situation: 'A sinful man had returned to a sinless wife. But he made up for it by becoming a believer. Now both she and her son were supposed to become believers too. There followed persuasions, attempts to convince, demands, ultimatums.'[10]

During his stay Panin read through the manuscript of *The First Circle*. He informed Solzhenitsyn of his utmost approval of the novel and the two friends discussed the means by which the philosophical dimension could best be expressed.

In the spring Natalya departed for Moscow for several days to attend a scientific conference on catalysis, rejoicing in the realization that her own work had not been forgotten by her former colleagues. Several eminent contributors to the conference referred to her research and she was pleased to see that the title page of her own dissertation was displayed prominently at the Kobozev Laboratory. 'Perhaps everything could have been different,' she pondered wistfully.[11] At around the same time, her husband suffered a relapse and was admitted to hospital for a course of chemotherapy. Natalya and Solzhenitsyn were both gravely concerned. The previous year he had urged her to go to the Lenin Library to read everything she could about cancer and malignant tumours, with the result that they both believed he had only about four years to live. As Solzhenitsyn entered the hospital, the thought must have crossed their minds that they had miscalculated and the end was coming sooner. In the event the chemotherapy proved successful and he was discharged after only two weeks, continuing his treatment as an outpatient. By the end of the treatment, the tumour had subsided and was no longer causing discomfort. He felt fitter than he had done for years and threw himself with added gusto into his work.

'The favourite work is always the one on which you are currently working,' Solzhenitsyn stated forty years later. 'When I wrote *The First Circle* it was alive with intrigue, with philosophical underpinnings, and I was absorbed in it.'[12] Much of the rest of the year was taken up with completing a third draft of his novel and only when he was satisfied with it, for the time being at least, could he put his mind to other projects.

The next major project was born on 18 May 1959, with the idea that he should write a novel about one day in the life of a labour camp prisoner in Ekibastuz. This would come to fruition as one of the most influential books ever written in terms of its socio-political impact on the world. In its power to undermine the very foundations of the Soviet system *Ivan Denisovich* would become a literary Ivan the Terrible.

Although the book owed its portentous birth to that moment of inspiration in May 1959, its gestation period in the womb of Solzhenitsyn's imagination stretched back seven years. It had first been conceived while he was working as a bricklayer at Ekibastuz in 1952:

> It was an ordinary camp day – hard, as usual, and I was working. I was helping to carry a hand-barrow full of mortar, and I thought that this was the way to describe the whole world of the camps. Of course, I could have described

my whole ten years there, I could have done the whole history of the camps that way, but it was sufficient to gather everything into one day, all the different fragments ... and to describe just one day in the life of an average and in no way remarkable prisoner from morning till night.[13]

Once Solzhenitsyn had found the inspiration to put the long-standing idea into practice it was probably, of all his vast output, one of the easiest books to write. Looking back on its creation, his words interspersed with infectious chuckling and his eyes aglint with pleasure at the memory, Solzhenitsyn recounted with amusement the easy flow of the creative process:

> The book by which most people came to know of me, both in the Soviet Union and in America, *One Day in the Life of Ivan Denisovich*, came out of me in one breath, in one flow. I wrote it in forty days. In fact, I was surrounded by so much material, so much material surrounded me at that moment, that I was not in a position of a writer wondering what to put in. There was so much material that, on the contrary, I was saying I won't take this, I won't take that, I don't really need this, I won't take that. It was like the whole life of the camps fitted into one day of one person's life.[14]

One of the principal reasons for the surge of creativity was the choice of subject matter. The overriding desire to tell the world the full and horrific truth about life in the camps was the passionate pulse at the heart of Solzhenitsyn's literary vocation. More than anything else he desired to tell this truth to anyone who would listen. In *One Day in the Life of Ivan Denisovich* he had done this in a condensed and concentrated form with potentially explosive results. 'It seemed to me that the most interesting and important thing to do was to depict the fate of Russia. Of all the drama that Russia has lived through, the deepest was the tragedy of the Ivan Denisoviches. I wanted to set the record straight concerning the false rumours about the camps.'[15]

In spite of its relative brevity compared with the weighty volumes on the subject that Solzhenitsyn was to write in later years, *One Day in the Life of Ivan Denisovich* contains many of the *leitmotifs* which recur throughout his work. All the poignant features of camp life discussed in great detail in the three volumes of *The Gulag Archipelago* found expression with microscopic intensity in *One Day in the Life*: the loss and recovery of human dignity; the injustice at the heart of Soviet 'justice'; ennoblement versus decay; self-limitation versus selfishness; hints of divine providence; hunger and the description of meals as a pseudo-religious ritual; and, last but not least, the Christian response to the prisoner's sense of hopelessness and the temptation to despair.

Apart from Ivan Denisovich himself, the principal hero to emerge from the pages of *One Day in the Life* is Alyosha the Baptist. He is principal because he is principled, rising above the horror of daily life in the camps through the triumph of belief over adversity. Towards the end of the novel, Solzhenitsyn puts into the words of Alyosha the core of his own belief in self-limitation: 'Ivan Denisovich, you shouldn't pray to get parcels or for extra skilly, not for that. Things that man puts a high price on are vile in the eyes of Our Lord. We must pray about things of the spirit – that the Lord Jesus should remove the scum of anger from our hearts ...'[16]

Having written *One Day in the Life* in a flood of inspiration in May and June 1959, Solzhenitsyn consigned it to his growing pile of unpublished manuscripts, doubting whether it would ever see the light of day. He wrote later that he was convinced he would never see a single line of his work in print in his own lifetime. Such was his fear of Soviet persecution that he scarcely dared allow any of his close acquaintances to read anything he had written for fear that it would become known.[17]

In the summer of 1959, during a visit to Rostov, Solzhenitsyn took the opportunity to meet up with some old friends, most notably Nikolai Vitkevich, the closest friend of his school and university years who had been his partner in crime in the criticism of Stalin during the war. Like Solzhenitsyn, Nikolai had been sentenced to forced labour for his part in the correspondence and the drafting of 'Resolution No. 1'. Unlike Solzhenitsyn, the experience had crushed him emotionally and spiritually. They had met briefly at Marfino during their term of imprisonment, where Solzhenitsyn had been disappointed to find his friend broken in spirit and uninterested in philosophical or ideological debate. Whereas Solzhenitsyn was finding himself in vigorous, furious but ultimately friendly arguments with Panin and Kopelev, Nikolai had not wished to join in and desired only to forget about the past and lead an untroubled life in the future. His response to the struggle for survival in the camps had been psychological surrender.

Any hopes nurtured by Solzhenitsyn that his friend would have regained his old fighting spirit along with his freedom were soon to be dashed. By the summer of 1959 Nikolai had married and was busy completing his PhD dissertation. He was entirely concerned with his own life and career and had lost all interest in wider issues. This became apparent when Solzhenitsyn sought to discuss the Pasternak case. Boris Pasternak had been awarded the Nobel Prize for Literature for *Doctor Zhivago* the previous October, causing a storm of controversy in the Soviet Union. Solzhenitsyn sought Nikolai's opinions but was surprised to find him totally indifferent, being more concerned about the internal politics of the chemistry department at Rostov University, where he now worked, and about his prospects of promotion. The two friends, so inseparable in their youth, had become strangers.

In contrast to Nikolai's agnostic indifference and apathy, Solzhenitsyn shared Pasternak's passion for the higher purpose of both life and literature. In an interview with a Swedish critic the previous year, Pasternak had decoded the meaning of *Doctor Zhivago* as a novel-parable concerned with the need of the human soul to strive for higher sources of spiritual wealth. 'During the short period of time that we live in this world,' Pasternak explained, 'we have to understand our attitude toward existence, our place in the universe. Otherwise, life is meaningless. This, as I understand it, means a rejection of the nineteenth century materialistic world view, means a resurrection of our interior life, a resurrection of religion.'[18]

This was a view with which Solzhenitsyn concurred completely and, furthermore, was one of the main motive forces behind many of his own literary endeavours.

In the autumn of 1960 Solzhenitsyn returned to a story he had started some time earlier about an elderly woman, Matryona Zakharova, with whom he had lodged four years earlier during his first weeks of freedom at Torfprodukt in the Vladimir Region. '*Matryona's House* was something that was very, very emotional for me,' Solzhenitsyn recalls, 'and was dedicated to the memory of a holy Russian woman.'[19]

> She was a poor housekeeper. In other words she refused to strain herself to buy gadgets and possessions and then to guard them and care for them more than for her own life.
>
> She never cared for smart clothes, the garments that embellish the ugly and disguise the wicked.
>
> Misunderstood and rejected by her husband, a stranger to her own family despite her happy, amiable temperament, comical, so foolish that she worked for others for no reward, this woman ... had stored up no earthly goods. Nothing but a dirty white goat, a lame cat and a row of fig-plants.
>
> None of us who lived close to her perceived that she was that one righteous person without whom, as the saying goes, no city can stand.
>
> Nor the world.[20]

A few weeks after the completion of *Matryona's House*, Solzhenitsyn started work on *Candle in the Wind*, arguably his best play. Also known as *The Light Within You*, the play's central theme, as both titles suggest, is the need to protect one's soul, the light of life which burns within everyone, from the worldly winds which threaten to snub it out. The extent to which the various characters in the play succeed or fail in salvaging the light within is explored as the plot unfolds.

In the character of Aunt Christine the ghost of Matryona is resurrected as the one righteous person in the midst of the ethical confusion which permeates the rest of the play. In her extreme poverty and contented unworldliness is encapsulated the profound relationship between asceticism and spirituality. Although her physical presence does not play a major role in the dramatic development of the plot, her spiritual presence is crucial. At one key moment, impelled it seems by nothing but mystical intuition, the significantly named Christine appears at Maurice's death bed, carrying a candle and invoking the Christian moral which was Solzhenitsyn's overriding theme: 'Take heed therefore that the light which is within thee be not darkness.'

Taking this theme as his motivation for writing *Candle in the Wind*, Solzhenitsyn explored its relevance to the play's protagonists. As always, and as in the character of Aunt Christine, Solzhenitsyn drew heavily from autobiographical experience in delineating his characters. There is little doubt that the character of Philip is a loosely sketched pen portrait of Nikolai Vitkevich. Like Alex, the character in the play most closely based on Solzhenitsyn himself, Philip was sentenced to ten years' imprisonment as the result of a legal error. Now, however, he has concealed his past and, as a respected scientist, has become a career-oriented opportunist, hell-bent on success in his chosen field of bio-cybernetics. Perhaps the parallel was a little unfair, or at least uncharitable, but the fact that Philip is a caricature of Nikolai is beyond doubt. Natalya confirmed that her husband had 'Nikolai Vitkevich in mind when he created the character of Philip', but stressed that the character was 'enormously exaggerated'.[21] In another example of the lack of empathy which existed between husband and wife, Natalya appeared to prefer the character of Philip to that of Alex – Vitkevich to Solzhenitsyn. If Philip's purpose in life was misguided, Natalya complained, 'that of his antipode Alex – the "positive hero" – was wholly negative: I reject this, I don't want that!'[22]

Natalya betrayed further lack of understanding about her husband in her analysis of *Candle in the Wind*, this time in her failure to grasp one of his secondary intentions in writing the play. 'The only thing I found unconvincing and superfluous,' she complained, 'was the desire of Alex, the author's stand-in, to put a stop to the development of science.'[23] With a firm grasp of scientific principles himself, Solzhenitsyn had no desire that the development of science should stop. One of the purposes of the play was to point out that science, like every other field of human activity, was subject to ethical considerations. The abuse of technology, in this case bio-cybernetics, was always likely, indeed inevitable, if science refused to be restrained by ethics.

The nature of scientific abuse in *Candle in the Wind* centres on the use of Alda, a lovable but over-sensitive and neurotic woman, as a guinea pig in experiments in 'neurostabilization'. The result of this 'brain-scrambling' is that Alda changes from being hyper-sensitive to insensitive, from painfully alive to comfortably numb. She escapes from suffering only by becoming less alive: the end result, as Solzhenitsyn was eager to stress, of 'technological interference in the complex psychology of human beings. It is almost a discussion of a worldwide process, not so much an experiment on her. The rush, the onward push of technology destroys the human psyche.'[24] Does this mean that Alda can be seen as an archetype of the modern world itself? 'Yes, yes,' Solzhenitsyn stresses emphatically, 'the modern world in the capacity as victim: the vulnerable part of modernity and the modern world.'[25]

What then would have been the solution to Alda's, and the world's, neurosis? Did Alda need love not mechanisms? 'Yes,' Solzhenitsyn replies, 'the solution would have been spiritual.'

A spiritual solution. Whatever one may feel about Solzhenitsyn's spiritual alternative to intrusive technology it is not, contrary to Natalya's claims, 'wholly negative'.

If Natalya's views on *Candle in the Wind* illumine the gulf separating her own aspirations from those of her husband, Solzhenitsyn's descriptions of his 'fictional' wife in the play are even more evocative of the sense of alienation in their marriage. Alex tells Alda that he was happy with few possessions and a tiny clay house before his wife appeared on the scene. 'She was absolutely tireless and she was ashamed of our hut! She was ambitious as well and demanded that I erect a palace with a slate roof! She demanded that I earn more too. And that I take her to the city and the big stores.' He laments that his wife is typical of those who 'think only of how best to grab and buy things and impress their neighbours' and attempts to explain why he is incapable of living that way: 'To have to please someone, worry about someone, and let that determine my philosophy. I live only once and I want to act in accordance with absolute truth.' Accepting that as a husband he could never live up to materialist expectations, he adds: 'My wife did a wise thing: she immediately found herself another husband who made good money ...'

Apart from the undercurrents of bickering, Solzhenitsyn's purpose in writing the play was always that higher goal espoused by Pasternak two years earlier. Its principal concern is the meaning of life itself, the preservation of the light within which is diminished by hedonistic materialism, nihilism and the lust for life which is really a living death. Against this hell-bound path of least resistance are contraposed suffering, described by Alex as 'a lever for the growth of the soul',[26] and poverty: 'It's not a question of how much you earn, it's a question of how little you spend.'[27]

Perhaps the play is summarized most succinctly by Keith Armes in the introduction to his translation of the English edition: 'Solzhenitsyn attempts to persuade a reluctant world of the dangers of materialism and of the worship of science. In doing so he proclaims that Christian faith which was later to inspire the *Easter Procession* and the *Lenten Letter*.'[28]

In spite of the suppression of Pasternak's *Doctor Zhivago*, the much-heralded cultural thaw in the Soviet Union following Khrushchev's accession to power gave Solzhenitsyn hope that at last he could emerge from the shadows and his literature would see the light of day. 'Finally, at the age of forty-two,' he wrote, 'this secret authorship began to wear me down. The most difficult thing of all to bear was that I could not get my works judged by people with literary training. In 1961, after the twenty-second Congress of the USSR Communist Party and Tvardovsky's speech at this, I decided to emerge and to offer *One Day in the Life of Ivan Denisovich*.'[29]

In his speech to the Congress, Tvardovsky, editor of the literary journal *Novy Mir*, had spoken of the need to 'show the labours and ordeals of our people in a manner that is totally truthful to life',[30] and even Khrushchev himself, in an attack on Stalin, had promised to erect a monument in Moscow 'to the memory of the comrades who fell victims to arbitrary power'.

'Comrades!' Khrushchev had implored. 'Our duty is to investigate carefully such abuses of power in all their aspects. Time passes and we shall die, since all of us are mortal, but as long as we have the strength to work we must clear up many things and tell the truth to the Party and our people.'[31]

Solzhenitsyn did not trust Khrushchev, still believing that his own emergence from the shadows would be very risky and 'might lead to the loss of my manuscripts and to my own destruction',[32] but Tvardovsky's words offered hope and he decided to present the manuscript of *One Day in the Life* to Tvardovsky for possible publication in *Novy Mir*.

On 11 December 1961, his forty-third birthday, Solzhenitsyn received a telegram from Tvardovsky inviting him to Moscow at *Novy Mir*'s expense. The dryness of the telegram concealed the delight with which Tvardovsky had read the manuscript. He had sat up all night reading it and declared to several friends the following day that a great writer had just been born. One friend recalled that he had never seen *Novy Mir*'s editor so enthusiastic as he was that day, insisting that he would do everything in his power to ensure Solzhenitsyn's novel was published: 'They say that Russian literature's been killed. Damn and blast it! It's in this folder with the ribbons. But who is he? Nobody's seen him yet. We've sent a telegram ... We'll take him under our wing, help him, and push his book through.' He told the novelist Vera Panova that 'believe it or not, I've got a manuscript from a new Gogol'.[33]

A year later Solzhenitsyn expressed his gratitude to Tvardovsky: 'The greatest happiness that "recognition" has given me I experienced in December last year, when you found *Denisovich* worth a sleepless night. None of the praise that came afterwards could outstrip that.'[34]

At the conclusion of their meeting in Moscow, Tvardovsky insisted on drawing up a contract, stipulating the payment of an advance of 300 roubles to the author on signature, a sum equivalent to more than twice his annual salary as a schoolteacher. Solzhenitsyn had made his first major breakthrough as a writer.

Natalya could not believe her eyes when she saw the terms of the contract and burst into tears. Meanwhile, in a spirit of euphoria, Solzhenitsyn wrote to friends that the reception of his manuscript had 'exceeded my wildest expectations' and that 'the whole thing has knocked me sideways'.[35]

An unwelcome reminder that he was still walking on a knife-edge came at the beginning of 1962 when he returned to the offices of *Novy Mir* to hear the verdict on *Matryona's House*. Although Tvardovsky liked the story he feared that it was 'a bit too Christian' for a Soviet journal. It was too subversive and he dared not publish it. Nonetheless, he assured Solzhenitsyn that he *wanted* to publish it and stressed that he had no wish to browbeat his new-found prodigy into political submission. 'Please don't become ideologically reliable,' he quipped at the end of the meeting. 'Don't write anything that my staff could pass without my having to know about it.'[36] It was clear that Tvardovsky and Solzhenitsyn were on dangerous ground and both men realized that the courage of their convictions was being put to the test. As if to emphasize the point, Tvardovsky assured Solzhenitsyn that he was determined to publish *One Day in the Life of Ivan Denisovich* and would do everything he could to overcome any opposition he might meet along the way.

Tvardovsky's efforts to secure publication involved a complete circumvention of the normal channels which would, if followed, have resulted in the manuscript's rejection. Instead he sought the support of leading literary figures, eliciting favourable reports from them about the manuscript's merits. He then showed these to some of his political friends in the hope of persuading them that *One Day in the Life* could be used to bolster Khrushchev's policy of debunking Stalinism. Solzhenitsyn was becoming a player in a dangerous game of power politics.

On 23 July 1962 Solzhenitsyn raised the tension and the stakes by refusing to agree to various cuts which would have made the book more politically acceptable. These included a number of alleged insults to Soviet art and the discussions about religion centred on Alyosha the Baptist.

Such were the waves that Solzhenitsyn's manuscript was causing in the higher echelons of Soviet society that by September it had come to the notice of Khrushchev himself. He demanded to see it and, to everyone's relief, liked it. He could see no reason why *One Day in the Life of Ivan Denisovich* could not be published. The news was greeted ecstatically at the offices of *Novy Mir* and on 16 September the glad tidings were dispatched to Solzhenitsyn in a letter: 'Now we can say that *Ivan D* is on the very threshold. We are expecting news any day.'[37] With Khrushchev's approval it was surely a mere formality; the Central Committee would simply rubber-stamp the decision. Yet the days passed and there was still no official go-ahead. Tvardovsky was on tenterhooks and is said to have threatened to resign if permission was refused. Finally, at midday on 21 September, the long-awaited phone call was received. It was not, however, what Tvardovsky had either hoped or feared. Permission was neither granted nor refused but merely deferred. Instead Khrushchev ordered twenty-three copies to be delivered by the following morning.

Tvardovsky was thrown into a panic. He did not possess twenty-three copies and it would be impossible to get that number typed up in a single night. The only option was a limited printing of the necessary copies. He rang the head of the printing department at the leading national newspaper *Izvestia*, explained the urgency of the situation, and arranged to have four machines set aside from printing *Izvestia* that night and reserved for printing twenty-five copies of *Ivan Denisovich*.

The copies were duly delivered next morning and Khrushchev ordered that they be distributed to members of the Party Presidium. What transpired at the next meeting of the Presidium is not known for certain and has become a source of legend. It is clear, however, that Khrushchev met considerable opposition from hard-liners in the government who were strongly against publication. 'How can we fight against the remnants of the personality cult if Stalinists of this type are still among us?' Khrushchev is alleged to have said.[38] Another source reported Khrushchev as saying that 'there's a Stalinist in each of you; there's even some of the Stalinist in me. We must root out this evil.'[39] There were, in fact, more Stalinists at the meeting than Khrushchev cared or dared to admit, each looking for the opportunity to bring about his downfall. One by one, Khrushchev was alienating the powerful interest groups which dominated Soviet politics. His de-Stalinization was unpopular with all hard-line communists and particularly with the KGB; his emphasis on nuclear rather than conventional weapons had lost him the support of the military; and his administrative reforms had struck at the bureaucratic heart of the Party apparatus. Too much was changing too quickly for many sectional interests in the Soviet hierarchy and it was only a matter of time before they struck back at the man responsible. Like Solzhenitsyn, Khrushchev was walking on a knife-edge. Two years later, in October 1964, he would be toppled in a bloodless coup and presented with his own resignation 'for reasons of health'. For now, however, he still had a firm grip on power and forced through the publication of *One Day in the Life*, proposing the motion which authorized it himself.

Having won this small though significant victory at home, Khrushchev was faced down on the world stage by President Kennedy, being induced to remove Soviet missiles from Cuba in

October 1962 at the culmination of an international crisis which had brought the world to the brink of nuclear war. Meanwhile Solzhenitsyn, still not even a published author, had gained many powerful enemies among the Soviet leadership, while enjoying the support of a Soviet president who was living on borrowed time. He was making his literary debut in dangerous circumstances.

NOTES

1. Reshetovskaya, *Sanya*, pp. 185–6.
2. Scammell, *Solzhenitsyn: A Biography*, p. 355.
3. Reshetovskaya, *Sanya*, p. 187.
4. Ibid., p. 188.
5. Ibid., p. 191.
6. Ibid., p. 192.
7. Ibid., p. 200.
8. Solzhenitsyn, *The First Circle*, pp. 38–9.
9. Reshetovskaya, *Sanya*, p. 115.
10. Ibid., p. 206.
11. Ibid., p. 207.
12. Solzhenitsyn, interview with the author.
13. Alexander Solzhenitsyn, *Warning to the Western World*, transcript of interview on *Panorama*, BBC Television, London, 1 March 1976, London: The Bodley Head & BBC, p. 5.
14. Solzhenitsyn, interview with the author.
15. Scammell, *Solzhenitsyn: A Biography*, p. 382.
16. Alexander Solzhenitsyn, *One Day in the Life of Ivan Denisovich*, Harmondsworth, Middlesex: Penguin Books, 1963, p. 139.
17. Labedz, *Solzhenitsyn: A Documentary Record*, p. 31.
18. Quoted in Leonid Rzhevsky, *Solzhenitsyn: Creator and Heroic Deed*, University of Alabama Press, 1978, p. 17.
19. Solzhenitsyn, interview with the author.
20. Alexander Solzhenitsyn, *Stories and Prose Poems*, London: The Bodley Head, 1971, p. 54.
21. Reshetovskaya, *Sanya*, p. 214.
22. Ibid., p. 215.
23. Ibid., p. 214.
24. Solzhenitsyn, interview with the author.
25. Ibid.
26. Alexander Solzhenitsyn, *Candle in the Wind*, London: The Bodley Head and Oxford University Press, 1973, p. 119.
27. Ibid., p. 133.
28. Ibid., p. 17.
29. Labedz, *Solzhenitsyn: A Documentary Record*, p. 31.
30. Scammell, *Solzhenitsyn: A Biography*, p. 408.

31. Ibid., pp. 406–7.
32. Labedz, *Solzhenitsyn: A Documentary Record*, p. 31.
33. Scammell, *Solzhenitsyn: A Biography*, p. 414.
34. Ibid., p. 415.
35. Ibid., p. 418.
36. Ibid., p. 421.
37. Ibid., p. 434.
38. Michel Tatu, *Power in the Kremlin*, New York, 1967, p. 248.
39. Max Hayward and Edward L. Crowley (eds.), *Soviet Literature in the Sixties*, London, 1965, p. 191.

CHAPTER ELEVEN

TOO HOT TO HANDLE

On Sunday 21 October 1962, without a word of explanation, *Pravda*, the Communist Party daily newspaper, published 'The Heirs of Stalin', an anti-Stalinist poem by Evgeni Evtushenko, in which he warned against those Stalinists in positions of power who wanted to turn back the clock. It was a timely reminder that the winds of change were themselves inconstant; but the fact that *Pravda* had chosen to publish Evtushenko's poem indicated that, for the time being at least, the winds were blowing in favour of the reformers.

In the favourable atmosphere of de-Stalinization *One Day in the Life of Ivan Denisovich* made its first public appearance. It was an instant success. Tvardovsky informed Solzhenitsyn that several thousand copies of the November issue of *Novy Mir* containing Solzhenitsyn's novel had been diverted to the bookstalls set up in the Kremlin for delegates to the plenary session of the Central Committee. Khrushchev had announced from the platform that *One Day in the Life of Ivan Denisovich* was an extremely important work which every delegate should read. Dutifully they had all trooped off to the bookstalls to acquire a copy. Elsewhere in Moscow it had sold out completely, despite the printing of several thousand extra copies, and was already a collector's item.

Solzhenitsyn's popular success was accompanied by critical acclaim. Either the Soviet press genuinely shared the public's enthusiasm for *One Day in the Life*, or else the reviewers were merely intent on following the current party line. Whatever the reason, reviews were universally positive. Konstantin Simonov, writing in *Izvestia* on 18 November 1962, declared that '*One Day in the Life of Ivan Denisovich* is written with the sure hand of a mature, unique master. A powerful talent has come into our literature. I personally have no doubts on that score.' Although Solzhenitsyn would doubt-less have been flattered by such praise he must have found some of Simonov's other observations a little difficult to swallow. Worst of all was Simonov's assertion that Solzhenitsyn 'has shown himself a true helper of the Party'. Admittedly Simonov had made the asser-tion in relation to the role that *One Day in the Life* was playing in 'the struggle against the cult of personality and its consequences', but, regardless of the context, Solzhenitsyn must have balked at any suggestion that he was helping to perpetuate the Party he had grown to despise.

The incongruity of Solzhenitsyn's position as a true helper of the Party was hammered home even more forcefully five days later when a review of his novel appeared in *Pravda*. The review was written by Vladimir Ermilov, a communist time-server who epito-mized everything Solzhenitsyn detested. During the Stalinist purges Ermilov had been a secret-police informer who had denounced many writers and intellectuals, consigning them to the very camps that Solzhenitsyn was describing. Now that the tide had turned against Stalin, Ermilov had turned with it, determined to remain in favour. Stalin was now the 'enemy of the people' while Solzhenitsyn was a newly discovered hero, 'a writer gifted with a rare talent, and, as befits a real artist, he has told us a truth that cannot be forgotten, and must not be forgotten, a truth that is staring us in the face'.

Whatever his attitude to official praise of his work, Solzhenitsyn surely received a degree of genuine consolation from the letters he began to receive from former prisoners. 'You have taken a picture of quite a day ... Reading your story and comparing it with the camp, it is impossible to distinguish one from another. They are alike as two peas – the arrangement of the compound, the punishment block, and the attitude to the prisoners ...' 'I could not sit still. I kept leaping up, walking about and imagined all those scenes as taking place in the camp I was in ...' 'When I read it, I literally felt the blast of cold as one leaves the hut for inspection ...'

Another former prisoner, after declaring that his own life was described exactly in the novel, recounted his riposte to 'a loudly dressed lady with a gold ring' who had said that she didn't like Solzhenitsyn's novel because it was too depressing: 'It's better to have a bitter truth than a sweet lie,' he had replied.

'After reading it,' wrote a woman whose husband had perished in the camps, 'the only thing left to do is to knock a nail into the wall, tie a knot and hang oneself.' A young female student who had lost both her grandparents in the camps could not even bear to read it, writing to Solzhenitsyn that she had flicked through it before being forced to put it down. Another woman, the wife of one who had died, expressed the grief more eloquently:

> I see, I hear this crowd of hungry, freezing creatures, half people, half animals, and amongst them is my husband ... Continue to write, write the truth, even though they won't print it now! Our floods of tears were not shed in vain – the truth will rise to the surface in this river of tears ... My husband wrote to me from Taishet that one of his companions in misfortune would come to me some day and tell me about him, and give me a ring that he made for me there, in his place of torment. But nobody came to me, and now will never come ...[1]

There were other letters too, not sent to Solzhenitsyn but published in the press. These were not from former political prisoners but from those who had never experienced 'one day in the life of Ivan Denisovich'. Many of these were either blissfully ignorant of the realities depicted in Solzhenitsyn's novel or else were guards or former guards who held the prisoners in contempt. 'These submen with their shabby little souls were dealt with too leniently by the courts ...' 'Why give a lot of food to those who do not work? Their energy remains unexpended ... I say the criminal world is being treated far too gently ...' 'Where rations are concerned we shouldn't forget one thing – that they are not in a holiday resort. They must atone for their guilt with honest toil ...' 'Solzhenitsyn's story should be withdrawn immediately from all libraries and reading rooms ...' 'This book should not have been published, the material should have been handed over to the Organs of the KGB instead ...'[2]

There was one letter which Solzhenitsyn found grimly amusing for its woeful lack of scriptural knowledge. 'I've never before had to swallow such trash ... And this is not just my opinion. Many of us feel the same, our name is Legion.'

'Quite right,' Solzhenitsyn replied, 'their name is Legion. Only they were in too much of a hurry to check their reference to the Gospel. It was of course a Legion of devils.'[3]

Clearly *One Day in the Life of Ivan Denisovich* had touched a raw nerve. As its impact resounded throughout the Soviet Union, from the grandeur of the Kremlin to the humble homes of former prisoners, Solzhenitsyn contemplated the power his novel had unleashed. 'If the first tiny droplet of truth has exploded like a psychological bomb, what then will happen in our country when whole waterfalls of Truth burst forth?'[4] Solzhenitsyn was not the only person asking this question. There were many who had a vested interest in keeping the truth hidden and these people, the hard-line Stalinists, were already preparing their response.

However, it was Khrushchev himself who had planted the psychological bomb at the highest level of Soviet life and had given it his blessing. Encouraged by this, Tvardovsky felt confident enough to overcome his initial misgivings and publish *Matryona's House*, along with another short story by Solzhenitsyn entitled *An Incident at Krechetovka Station*, in the January 1963 edition of *Novy Mir*. In many ways *Matryona's House* is one of the most important of Solzhenitsyn's works, a spiritual bomb just as *One Day in the Life* was a psychological bomb. According to the dissident historian Grigori Pomerants, Christianity began for a million Russians with the reading of *Matryona's House*. 'A million people (if not more) took the first step towards the light with Solzhenitsyn.'[5]

Yet where some saw the light others saw only darkness. *Matryona's House* was condemned at a meeting of Moscow writers in March for failing to educate youth by positive examples. It was the task of Soviet writers to lead the youth 'to a bright future, to communism': 'When you read this story you get the impression that the peasant's psychology has remained the same as it was sixty years ago. But this is not true! We need works which are historically truthful, and tell of the enormous revolutionary changes that have taken place in the Soviet village.'[6]

A few days later, Sergei Pavlov, First Secretary of the Young Communist League, attacked Solzhenitsyn and other writers in *Novy Mir* for failing 'to speak of lofty ideas, of communism ... under the pretext of the struggle against the consequences of the cult of the individual and dogmatism'. *Matryona's House* was 'immersed in a narrow little world of philistine problems' and breathed 'such pessimism, mustiness, hopelessness'.[7]

Against the crescendo of resentment, Khrushchev's words a week or so earlier sounded ominously isolated: 'The party gives its backing to artistic creations which are really truthful, whatever negative aspects of life they may deal with, so long as they help the people in their effort to build a new society.'[8]

The last thing the Stalinists desired was a new society with all the unwelcome changes which would inevitably accompany it. Sensing that the winds of change were once more blowing in their direction they ceased fighting a rearguard action and moved on to the offensive.

The publication of Solzhenitsyn's *For the Good of the Cause* in the July 1963 edition of *Novy Mir* heralded a major debate between the two schools of thought vying for supremacy in the Soviet Union, the Stalinists and those fighting for a de-Stalinized new society. *For the Good of the Cause*, as the ironic title suggested, was Solzhenitsyn's boldest attack yet on the corruption and injustice endemic in the communist regime. As such it was bound to provoke a hostile response.

The first shots were fired by Yuri Barabash, a well-known literary critic and champion of the old guard, who considered Solzhenitsyn's description of a corrupt bureaucracy at the heart of Soviet life to be a fantasy invented by the author: 'we are presented with an artificially constructed, imaginary world, where honest, decent, but weak-willed champions of justice are found to be helpless ... in the face of some indifferent, unfeeling force, which can be sensed behind the faceless, nameless representatives of unnamed institutions'. These were serious defects in the very conception of Solzhenitsyn's story which adversely affected its literary qualities, rendering it a failure.

Barabash also scoffed at the moral tone in Solzhenitsyn's work, derisively dismissing the concept of the righteous woman in *Matryona's House* and the fruitless efforts to discuss right and wrong in terms other than those dictated by dialectical materialism. Furthermore, Solzhenitsyn's insistence on such an unprogressive moral outlook illustrated that his 'view of life and his attitude towards it will be seen to have remained just as unmodern, and in many respects as archaic, as they were in *Matryona's House*'.[9]

The case for the defence was put by the Leningrad novelist Danil Granin who replied to Barabash's original article in the leading literary journal *Literaturnaya Gazeta*. Granin wrote that Solzhenitsyn in *For the Good of the Cause* was demanding justice and asking some very important questions about life in Soviet society.[10] An irate reader, R. L. Seliverstov, replying to Granin, was incensed at the very suggestion that the Soviet system was unjust: 'Genuine justice, fought for and won by the Party and our whole people – and not "abstract" justice – runs through our life today and is triumphant! A writer who takes it upon himself to deal with an important contemporary theme cannot fail to take all this into account.'[11] Seliverstov's remarks were accompanied by a statement from the editors of the *Literaturnaya Gazeta*: 'It seems to the editors that R. N. Seliverstov makes valid comments on Solzhenitsyn's story and Granin's article.' Furthermore, they insisted that Barabash's original criticisms of *For the Good of the Cause* were well founded. The editors chastised Solzhenitsyn for employing the universal approach to concepts of justice rather than the class approach, reminding him that 'a socialist-realist artist handles themes from the standpoint of the communist view of the world'.

At this stage the editors of *Novy Mir* became embroiled in a bitter feud with their rivals at the *Literaturnaya Gazeta* which would keep the debate over *For the Good of the Cause* in the forefront of both publications for the rest of the year.

Towards the end of the year the editors of *Novy Mir* controversially nominated Solzhenitsyn for the coveted Lenin Prize for Literature for *One Day in the Life of Ivan Denisovich*. It was a bold gesture but had no real chance of success. The prize was awarded by a jury which consisted overwhelmingly of reliable members of the old guard who would never contemplate awarding someone so heretical as Solzhenitsyn such an accolade. On 11 April 1964 an article in *Pravda* quoted extracts from letters which the editors had allegedly received from a number of readers whose addresses were not given. 'They all come to the same conclusion,' the article stated, 'Solzhenitsyn's short novel deserves a positive assessment but it cannot be placed among such outstanding works which are worthy of the Lenin Prize.'

While the controversy surrounding his previous work raged in the pages of the Soviet press, Solzhenitsyn was putting the finishing touches to his next book. This was *The First Circle*, the novel based on his experiences and discussions at Marfino special prison. Not only was it his most ambitious work to date, it was easily his most audacious, going far beyond his other work in its fundamental questioning of Soviet preconceptions. Having read the attacks that his work had provoked already he must have had serious concerns about its reception and, more to the point, serious doubts about its chances of ever being published.

The First Circle has been described by the critic Leonid Rzhevsky as 'a ruthless rejection of Stalinism'.[12] By early 1964 the ruthless rejection of Stalinism was not as safe as it had been two years previously. It now seemed, in the rapidly changing political climate, that the more ruthless the rejection of Stalinism the more ruthless would be the consequences.

Nevertheless Solzhenitsyn put his doubts and fears to one side, inviting Tvardovsky to his home in Ryazan on 2 May 1964 to read the finished manuscript of *The First Circle*. Tvardovsky was still Solzhenitsyn's most valued and influential champion. Not only had he nominated *One Day in the Life* for the Lenin Prize, he had been more upset than Solzhenitsyn when it failed to win. If anyone would appreciate the literary merit of *The First Circle* it was Tvardovsky, and if anyone could get it published he could.

Natalya accompanied her husband to the station to meet their distinguished guest. Surprisingly it was the first time she had ever met Tvardovsky, even though her husband had worked closely with him for nearly two and a half years, an indication of how far she had been marginalized during Solzhenitsyn's rise to fame. The next day, when Tvardovsky was enchanted by Natalya's piano playing, he found Solzhenitsyn more interested in a BBC broadcast on the radio. Husband and wife had drifted apart since the days of courtship many years before when Solzhenitsyn himself had been enchanted by her playing.

As Tvardovsky sat down to read *The First Circle* he found himself becoming more and more enthusiastic. 'Great stuff! ... So far, so far: I promise nothing!' Increasingly intoxicated by both the book and the bottle of cognac he was consuming while reading it, he even became flippant about the dangers that the book presented to all concerned: 'This is great, as good as Tolstoy and Dostoyevsky. So far, so far! When you're inside I'll bring you parcels! You'll even get the odd bottle of cognac.' Through the drunken numbness he endeavoured to inject a word of caution, urging Solzhenitsyn to tone down the Stalin pages, but ultimately a heady mixture of undiluted praise and undiluted alcohol prevailed: 'This is wonderful, Alexander Isayevich – not a superfluous line! ... *I shall be put inside for publishing it!* Even though it's basically optimistic.'[13]

It was a far more sombre and sober Tvardovsky who presided over the editorial meeting to discuss the manuscript of *The First Circle* on 11 June. 'By the normal standards,' he began, 'this novel should be scuttled and the author arrested. But what sort of people are we?' Tvardovsky's colleagues on the editorial board of *Novy Mir* were thrown into confusion. One, with a show of indecision which nevertheless put the problem in a nutshell, remarked that it was impossible to publish, and morally impossible not to. Another procrastinated, requesting a second reading, while a third, clearly disturbed by the issues raised in the novel, said that the writing was tremendous but 'the novel plunges us into doubt and dismay'. Only the youngest member of the group, the bright-eyed head of the criticism section, argued warmly and unequivocally for acceptance. He would clearly go far ... perhaps all the way to Siberia.

In spite of the initial reluctance a contract was drawn up within days. Yet the greatest obstacle, state censorship, still remained. Tvardovsky decided to try a similar approach to the one he had employed to circumvent the censors in the case of *One Day in the Life*. He sent the first quarter of the manuscript to Vladimir Lebedev, Khrushchev's private secretary, who had been crucial to the successful publication of Solzhenitsyn's earlier novel. Yet much had changed since the heady days of 1962. The reply, and the advice, was blunt: 'Bury it!'

'But Khrushchev ...'

'... Is no longer enamoured of *Ivan Denisovich*; he thinks [Ivan's] brought him a lot of trouble.'[14]

The doom-laden truth dawned on a crestfallen Tvardovsky. If even Khrushchev found Solzhenitsyn too hot to handle, what hope was there for *Novy Mir*? The author of *One Day in the Life of Ivan*

Denisovich had passed from being an enemy of the people to being a hero of the people and back to an enemy of the people – all in the space of a couple of years. A surprise beneficiary of de-Stalinization, he had become a casualty of re-Stalinization.

Within months Khrushchev was himself a casualty, being deposed by the bloodless coup in October. Thereafter the former president became something of a dissident himself, listening to the BBC World Service and Voice of America, criticizing the persecution of dissidents and opposing the Soviet invasion of Czechoslovakia in 1968. Shortly after Khrushchev's downfall, Lebedev, his faithful secretary, died. No one from the hierarchy attended his funeral except Tvardovsky, an isolated figure who must have seen his hopes for the future being lowered with the coffin. 'In my mind's eye,' wrote Solzhenitsyn, 'I can see that sturdy, broad-backed figure bending sadly over little Lebedev's coffin.'[15]

Solzhenitsyn sensed that the accession of Brezhnev signalled the end of his own brief honeymoon period with the Soviet regime. He was once again a pariah whose work would never get past the state censorship system. Abandoning all hope of expressing himself in official publications, he allowed his work to be published more and more frequently in the underground literature of *samizdat*, literally 'self publishing house'. *Samizdat* consisted of dissident literature reproduced mainly in typewritten form and circulated clandestinely among the reading public. Each typescript was copied often and, much like a chain letter, gained additional circulation as a result. Throughout the sixties, *samizdat* became increasingly organized and by 1968 there was a regular *samizdat* periodical called *Chronicle of Current Events* which documented instances of state repression and the spirited resistance of the 'democratic opposition'. Increasingly, *samizdat* became the battlefront for the literary underground and the means by which Solzhenitsyn and other dissident writers could be heard.

Even before Khrushchev's demise Solzhenitsyn had released his prose poems into *samizdat* where they were circulating widely. In the month of the coup which brought Brezhnev to power they were published in the West in the émigré magazine *Grani*. Having at last been heard, Solzhenitsyn was determined not to be silenced.

The changed circumstances required a more circumspect approach to his writing, and much more caution. He began to work away from home, a choice dictated by the need for greater security but also, perhaps, made desirable by the increasing estrangement in his marriage. Often he left Natalya at home while he worked away at the houses of friends, or at the home of Agafya, an old peasant woman, in Solotcha, a village about thirty miles from Ryazan. The cautious approach was also due to his work on a detailed history of the Soviet prison system, discovery of which might be perilous. It would, of course, be published many years later as *The Gulag Archipelago*. His work on this was at its most intensive in 1965, in the period of heightened repression under Brezhnev, so he had to proceed in deepest secrecy. He concealed the source material from prying eyes as far as possible, dispersing it in various places. 'I even had to camouflage the time I spent on the book with what looked like work on other things.' The magnitude of the task before him and the immensity of the risk attached to it, led to thoughts of abandoning it altogether amidst doubts about whether he had the stamina for its completion. 'But when, in addition to what I had collected, prisoners' letters converged on me from all over the country, I realized that since all this had been given to me, I had a duty.'[16]

'I must explain,' Solzhenitsyn added, 'that *never once* did this whole book, in all its parts, lie on the same desk at the same time.'

The wisdom of this precaution was highlighted in September 1965 when Solzhenitsyn learned that the KGB had raided the home of one of his friends and confiscated all three copies of *The First Circle*. He had foolishly sent the only other copy to a literary critic at *Pravda* in the naïve hope that, even in the neo-Stalinist atmosphere of Brezhnev's presidency, it might be considered fairly. Worse news was to follow. The KGB had also discovered and confiscated the archive which contained, among other things, his verse play *A Feast of Conquerors*, which was far more anti-Soviet than any of his other work. He had only dared show it to his most trusted friends, knowing that it was far too inflammatory and politically incorrect to see the light of day. Now it was in the hands of the KGB. He feared the worst and visions of the Gulag flitted like a *danse macabre* through his mind. Perhaps as an enemy of the people he was about to become a prisoner of the people once again.

His fears were well founded. Three days prior to the confiscation of his own material, the KGB had arrested the literary critic Andrei

Sinyavsky for smuggling stories to the West. It looked very much like the signal for a general purge of literary dissidents, in which case Solzhenitsyn, as one of the most prominent, would surely suffer more than most.

It was not, however, the sense of fear that was paramount in the days following the confiscation of his works. Any fear was eclipsed by a sense of loss, a deep mourning for the months of creative labour which had seemingly disappeared, lost for ever in the destructive machine of Soviet repression. For some months after 'the catastrophe of September 1965' Solzhenitsyn felt the loss 'as though it were a real, unhealing physical wound – a javelin wound right through the breast, with the tip so firmly lodged that it could not be pulled out. The slightest stirring within me (perhaps the memory of some line or other from my impounded archive) caused a stab of pain ...'[17]

For about three months after the KGB raid he suffered intermittent bouts of hopelessness which, at their most extreme, bordered on despair. It was during this period, possibly the unhappiest in his life, that he contemplated suicide for the first and last time. He woke up every day in the expectation that it would be his last day of freedom. Arrest was inevitable, he thought, and could come at any moment. Desperately and hastily, Solzhenitsyn dispersed his notes and unfinished drafts of *The Gulag Archipelago* to secret locations and wrote to the editor of *Pravda* requesting the return of the only copy of *The First Circle* not in the hands of the KGB. To his great relief his novel was returned to him but he was disappointed to learn that Tvardovsky was no longer prepared to consider it for *Novy Mir*. Solzhenitsyn was now unpublishable; any association with him could carry the risk of arrest. Even Tvardovsky, his greatest ally, was careful to keep him at arm's length.

The pressures of persecution were also having a detrimental effect on Solzhenitsyn's marriage which was once again nearing breaking point. For some time Natalya had resented Solzhenitsyn's long absences at the various hiding places where he worked in secrecy and in constant fear of discovery. Solzhenitsyn wrote that his wife had come to hate *The Gulag Archipelago*, blaming it as the cause of their problems, the bane of their marriage. 'She would not have been afraid of typing it if she had been with me, but if I departed for its sake and could not even write home, then it could go to hell, this

Archipelago!'[18] Natalya's frustrations came to a head in a bitter row during which she told her husband that she would rather see him arrested than hiding away and deliberately neglecting her. 'From that instant,' Solzhenitsyn wrote, 'I knew I could no longer depend on her. What was worse, I would have to keep up the arrangements that she was party to, while at the same time establishing a whole new secret system that would have to be kept hidden from her as from a hostile outsider.'[19]

After almost thirty years, their crisis-bound tragedy of a romance was fading to an ignominious conclusion. Over the next few years the marriage stalled and stuttered to a halt, before sputtering into a series of claims and counter-claims concerning who was ultimately responsible for the breakdown. 'I could not have imagined into whose clutches our divorce would drive my wife,' Solzhenitsyn wrote in 1974, 'nor that she was on the verge of becoming (or had already become) more dangerous to me than any spy, both because she was ready to collaborate with anyone against me and because she knew so many of my secret allies.'[20]

Such an accusation might have appeared unreasonable. No one other than Solzhenitsyn himself had suffered more for his art than his wife. Yet she was unable to appreciate the importance of her husband's work, either to the world or to Solzhenitsyn himself, and could not share in the sense of mission that motivated him. Particularly in the later stages of their marriage, every sacrifice she was called upon to make on the altar of her husband's art became irksome, breeding resentment. Solzhenitsyn was not prepared to compromise. He approached his work with a vocational zeal compared with which his very life, and that of his wife, were of little importance. He was a man possessed and, as such, could not and would not be possessed by his wife.

Yet Solzhenitsyn's accusation is not as unreasonable as it seems. Natalya's memoir of her life with him, published in the West in 1975, contained many bitter distortions of the truth designed apparently to cause her former husband as much harm and hurt as possible. Solzhenitsyn became convinced that she was working in league with the Soviet authorities, with the KGB itself. It is tempting to treat such a view with incredulity; it seems too much like the seedy scenario for a Cold War espionage novel. The spurned woman manipulated by the unscrupulous secret police. 'The spy who loved me.'

Natalya did her utmost to refute Solzhenitsyn's published accusations of her treachery. She wrote an open letter to him in 1980, denying that she had collaborated with the KGB, and stating that she had been outraged by the way the original text of her memoirs had been cut by a quarter and grossly distorted. It was only in 1996, when she was seriously ill, that the full and secret truth emerged. On being transferred from one hospital to another, she was told that the new hospital required her internal passport. She asked a female relative to collect it for her and the woman was astounded to discover that the document listed Natalya as the widow of Konstantin Semyonov, the journalist assigned by the publishers to edit her first memoir. She had been married to him from 1974 until his death in 1981. Since Semyonov was the KGB agent responsible for the gross distortions she had complained of in her open letter, it was surprising to discover that she had been married to him at the time the letter was written. Understandably Natalya had done everything in her power to keep the marriage secret and was thunderstruck when she realized that her secret was out: 'Is that known about? That's – my secret, my secret marriage.' She was horrified at the prospect of Solzhenitsyn discovering the truth and pleaded in mitigation that marriage to Semyonov had saved her after Solzhenitsyn's exile. 'I was without a job, without everything. Marrying him allowed me to live in Moscow. He was my closest friend ... All that time we concealed our marriage. I was never a KGB agent, I swear it!'[21]

This confession was Natalya's last public comment on her long and tragic relationship with Solzhenitsyn. It was the final bitter twist in a complicated tale. Perhaps the closing words should belong to Solzhenitsyn:

> As always, every family story is incredibly complicated and confused. Each side can marshal a thousand arguments, and each person is unavoidably guilty – it's always that way. That's why it is the sort of thing that doesn't allow of a simple solution or a simple paraphrase. All that can be said in the most general terms, when you take a bird's-eye view of it ... is that we were both wrong to get

married, especially the second time; we should never have done it twice ... But of course, so many feelings and memories are invested in any joint life together. And it's terribly painful when it breaks up ...[22]

NOTES

1. Labedz, *Solzhenitsyn: A Documentary Record*, pp. 48–53.
2. Solzhenitsyn, *The Gulag Archipelago Volume Three*, pp. 473–4.
3. Ibid., p. 474.
4. Solzhenitsyn, *The Gulag Archipelago Volume One*, p. 298.
5. Scammell, *Solzhenitsyn: A Biography*, p. 930.
6. *Literaturnaya Gazeta*, 19 March 1963.
7. *Komsomolskaya Pravda*, 22 March 1963.
8. *Literaturnaya Gazeta*, 12 March 1963.
9. Ibid., 31 August 1963.
10. Ibid., 15 October 1963.
11. Ibid., 19 October 1963.
12. Rzhevsky, *Solzhenitsyn: Creator and Heroic Deed*, p. 68.
13. Solzhenitsyn, *The Oak and the Calf*, pp. 73–6.
14. Ibid.
15. Ibid., p. 87.
16. Solzhenitsyn, *The Gulag Archipelago Volume Three*, p. 526.
17. Solzhenitsyn, *The Oak and the Calf*, p. 103.
18. Alexander Solzhenitsyn, *Invisible Allies*, Washington, DC: Counterpoint, 1995, p. 59.
19. Ibid., p. 116.
20. Ibid., pp. 20–1.
21. Thomas, *Solzhenitsyn: A Century in His Life*, p. 533.
22. Scammell, *Solzhenitsyn: A Biography*, pp. 990–1.

CHAPTER TWELVE

OLD ENEMIES AND NEW FRIENDS

In spring 1966 Solzhenitsyn was working away from home at the dacha of his friend Kornei Chukovsky in Peredelkino, the writers' colony just outside Moscow, where he was putting the finishing touches to his novel *Cancer Ward*. On Easter Day, 10 April, he wandered down to the patriarchal Church of the Transfiguration to watch the Easter procession. What he observed upon his arrival inspired one of his most evocative essays. Instead of pious groups of believers he was greeted outside the church by rowdy youths dressed in the latest fashions who, oblivious to the fact that they were on consecrated ground, were shrieking and cavorting to the sound of pop music from transistor radios. 'About one in four has been drinking, one in ten is drunk, and half of them are smoking – in that repulsive way with the cigarette stuck to the lower lip. There is no incense yet, but instead of it swathes of grey-blue cigarette smoke rise towards the Easter sky under the electric light of the churchyard in dense, hovering clouds.' Solzhenitsyn looked on in disgust as the youths spat on the asphalt path, whistled loudly and shouted obscenities at each other. The boys kissed their girlfriends, who were then pulled from one boy to another.

> These youths are not breaking the law; although they are doing violence, it is bloodless. Their lips twisted into a gangsterish leer, their brazen talk, their loud laughter, their flirting and snide jokes, their smoking and spitting – it all amounts to an insult to the Passion of Christ, which is being celebrated a few yards away from them. It is expressed in the arrogant, derisory look worn by these snotty hooligans as they come to watch how the old folk still practise the rites of their forefathers.

This behaviour was in marked contrast to that of the participants in the procession. Some were clearly intimidated by the contemptuous attitude of the onlookers, huddling close together for mutual comfort, but a group of ten women, walking in pairs and holding thick lighted candles, offered a vision of heroic virtue: 'elderly women with faces set in an unworldly gaze, prepared for death if they are attacked'.

> Two out of the ten are young girls of the same age as those crowding round with the boys, yet how pure and bright their faces are. The ten women, walking in close formation, are singing and looking as solemn as though the people around them were crossing themselves, praying and falling to their knees in repentance. They do not breathe the cigarette smoke; their ears are deaf to the vile language; the soles of their feet do not feel how the churchyard has been turned into a dance-floor.

Gripped with the poignancy of the moment, Solzhenitsyn prophetically transformed this insignificant incident so that the characters became archetypes of the future, turning the Easter procession at Peredelkino into a parable:

> These millions we have bred and reared – what will become of them? Where have the enlightened efforts and the inspiring visions of great thinkers led us? What good can we expect of our future generations?
> The truth is that one day they will turn and trample on us all. And as for those who urged them on to this, they will trample on them too.[1]

Back in his creative hideaway, Solzhenitsyn wrote the essay describing the vision he had just witnessed. Having done so, he returned to work on the final chapters of *Cancer Ward*, completing a preliminary draft a few weeks later. As soon as it was ready, he dispatched the novel to *Novy Mir* where it was discussed at the editorial meeting on 18 June. Opinions were divided, as they had been during the earlier discussion on *The First Circle*, some being strongly in favour of its publication and others as strongly opposed. At first Tvardovsky spoke vehemently in the novel's defence, declaring that 'art does not exist in this world to be a weapon in the class struggle'. Furthermore, it was 'topical in that it presents a moral reckoning on behalf of a newly awakened people'. He assured Solzhenitsyn that he wanted to publish and that 'we will launch it and fight for it to the limit of our powers'.[2]

Although initially encouraged by this positive response, Solzhenitsyn soon became irritated by what seemed to be a change of heart, or mind, on Tvardovsky's part. *Novy Mir*'s editor appeared to be less enthusiastic, demanded many cuts and alterations, and started to equivocate over his plans for publication. Angered by the straitjacket of censorship with which Tvardovsky was now attempting to constrain him, and frustrated by the uncertainty surrounding prospects for publication, Solzhenitsyn decided to allow *Cancer Ward* to circulate in *samizdat*. He still recalled with pain and bitterness the farcical failure of *Novy Mir* to publish *The First Circle* and he was determined that the same fate should not meet his latest offering. Tvardovsky was furious when he learned that copies of the novel were circulating in *samizdat* and the ensuing disagreement led to a temporary parting of the ways between Solzhenitsyn and *Novy Mir*.

Determined to do everything in his power to get *Cancer Ward* published, Solzhenitsyn managed to arrange a discussion of his novel at a meeting of the Central Writers' Club in Moscow on 17 November 1966. News of the debate spread rapidly in literary circles and tickets for the event soon became hard to come by. The attendance was far higher than normal for meetings of the club with fifty-two writers present. Debate was largely sympathetic and constructive, though it became heated when Zoya Kedrina stood up to address the meeting. Kedrina had gained notoriety during the recent show trial of the dissident writers Andrei Sinyavsky and Yuli Daniel for her role as 'social accuser' on behalf of the Soviet prosecutors. During her speech to the meeting, she was heckled angrily and some sections of the audience staged a walk-out in protest. Overall, however, Solzhenitsyn's novel was praised by his peers and compared favourably with several key works of Russian literature, most notably Tolstoy's *The Death of Ivan Ilyich*. At the meeting's conclusion, Solzhenitsyn expressed his gratitude for the hearing he had been given and must have been delighted by the passing of a resolution that the club would take steps to bring about the publication of *Cancer Ward*. As the first step it was proposed by Lev Kopelev that a transcript of their discussion be sent to *Zvesda* and *Prostor*, two reviews to which Solzhenitsyn had submitted the manuscript of *Cancer Ward* following its formal rejection by *Novy Mir*. The meeting had been a personal and practical triumph for Solzhenitsyn, ending on an appropriately optimistic note as the poet Bella Akhmadulina rushed up to the platform and, turning to Solzhenitsyn, shouted: 'Wonderful man! Let us pray to God to grant good health to Alexander Solzhenitsyn!'[3]

Encouraged by his success at this meeting, Solzhenitsyn began a tactical war of nerves with the Soviet authorities. Contrary to all regulations, he granted an interview in November 1966 to a Japanese news correspondent, in the course of which he mentioned the existence of *The First Circle*, stated that its publication had been blocked, and referred to his two unpublished plays, *The Love Girl and the Innocent* and *Candle in the Wind*. As the world was gripped in the clutches of the Cold War, it was common for interviewers to ask writers to offer their views on 'the writer's duties in defence of peace'. Solzhenitsyn, however, did not offer the Japanese journalist the usual trite response:

> I shall broaden the scope of this question. The fight for peace is only part of the writer's duties to society. Not one little bit less important is the fight for social justice and for the strengthening of spiritual values in his contemporaries. This, and nowhere else, is where the effective defence of peace must begin – with the defence of spiritual values in the soul of every human being. I was brought up in the traditions of Russian literature, and I cannot imagine myself working as a writer without such aims.[4]

Within days of his unauthorized interview with the Japanese journalist, Solzhenitsyn accepted an invitation to speak at the Kurchatov Institute of Physics in Moscow. Six hundred people were present and his readings from *Cancer Ward*, *Candle in the Wind* and the ostensibly 'forbidden' *The First Circle* were received with warmth and enthusiasm. News of his appearance spread quickly and he was inundated with similar invitations from all over Moscow. He accepted as many as he could, nine in all, but at the last moment each lecture was mysteriously cancelled. At the Karpov Institute, Solzhenitsyn actually arrived in the car that had been sent for him only to find a notice pinned to the door: 'Cancelled owing to the author's indisposition'.[5] The reason for these cancellations soon became apparent. The Moscow City Party Committee had telephoned the organizers of each of the meetings, threatening reprisals if they went ahead. In spite of this, Solzhenitsyn was invited to speak at the Lazarev Institute of Oriental Studies on 30 November, although whether this was in open defiance of the Party's ban or merely because the less than omniscient Party had failed to detect that one particular meeting is not clear.

Five hundred people listened intently as Solzhenitsyn read two chapters from *Cancer Ward* but they were not prepared for the open show of defiance that followed. In response to a question from the audience Solzhenitsyn openly declared war on the power of the Party, boldly testing its alleged omnipotence. 'I must explain why, although I used to refuse to talk to reporters or make public appearances, I have now started giving interviews and am standing here before you.' Explaining that circumstances had dictated the necessity that he defend himself, he launched into an outright attack on the KGB:

> There is a certain *organization* that has no obvious claim to tutelage over the arts, that you may think has no business at all supervising literature – but that does these things. This organization took away my novel and my archive ... Even so, I said nothing, but went on working quietly. However, they then made use of excerpts from my papers, taken out of context, to launch a campaign of defamation against me ... What can I do about it? Only defend myself! So here I am![6]

The audience was at first stunned by the apparently suicidal courage of the speaker in front of them. It was unheard of for anyone to attack the KGB in such terms from a public platform in the Soviet

Union. It simply wasn't done. It was courage beyond the call of duty and beyond the bounds of safety, courage which the faint-hearted would call foolhardy. Yet Solzhenitsyn had just said these words in front of their disbelieving ears. With a growing sense of exhilaration, the audience listened as Solzhenitsyn began to read from *The First Circle*, the 'forbidden' novel that the KGB had confiscated. This time, unlike the readings from the novel he had given at the Kurchatov Institute which had been tame by comparison, he deliberately read the most provocative chapters, the most political ones. Solzhenitsyn was intoxicated by the freedom of expression and would always look back with pleasure to 'that hour of free speech from a platform with an audience of five hundred people, also intoxicated with freedom'.[7]

Within days the five hundred people had set off a chain reaction of gossip around Moscow that set the city buzzing with the news of Solzhenitsyn's daring defiance of the KGB. The legend of Solzhenitsyn was being born.

Yet at the beginning of December, even as his escapades were being discussed in countless homes around Russia's capital, Solzhenitsyn shaved off his beard so that he would be more difficult to recognize and slipped out of the city to one of his hideaways to continue work on *The Gulag Archipelago*. Commenting on the legend which was beginning to surround Solzhenitsyn, Michael Scammell writes that he was 'not so much a musketeer as a pimpernel' who was 'beginning to live a life ... that far surpassed, in excitement and danger, the lives of his fictional heroes'.[8]

Between December 1966 and February 1967 Solzhenitsyn worked on the second draft of the first six parts of *The Gulag Archipelago*, revising and retyping over fifteen hundred pages in only two and a half months. To achieve this superhuman task he worked sixteen hours a day in two eight-hour shifts and completed the work on 22 February. On that day he penned the afterword which appeared at the end of the third volume of the published edition in which he expressed his surprise that he had managed to finish it safely: 'I have several times thought they would not let me.' Indeed, if the communist authorities had realized he was working on such a devastating exposé of the Soviet prison system, it is certain they would not have let him. As it was, the fact that he had completed the work safely was a tribute to his own cautious and secretive endeavour and that of the small handful of people who had helped him. 'I am finishing it,' Solzhenitsyn wrote, 'in the year of a double anniversary (and the two anniversaries are connected): it is fifty years since the revolution which created Gulag, and a hundred since the invention of barbed wire (1867). This second anniversary will no doubt pass unnoticed.'[9]

Having completed work on *The Gulag Archipelago* Solzhenitsyn moved back on to the offensive in his struggle against Soviet repression. On 16 May he wrote an open letter to the Fourth Soviet Writers' Congress, ensuring that copies were sent to the editors of literary newspapers and magazines. The target of his ire was 'the no longer tolerable oppression, in the form of censorship, which our literature has endured for decades'. This censorship 'imposes a yoke on our literature and gives people unversed in literature arbitrary control over writers ... Works that might express the mature thinking of the people, that might have a timely and salutary influence on the realm of the spirit or on the development of a social conscience, are proscribed or distorted by censorship on the basis of considerations that are petty, egotistical, and – from the national point of view – shortsighted.'[10]

After giving a full exposition of the case against censorship in principle, Solzhenitsyn proceeded to examine the cases of various writers who had suffered censorship and persecution at the hands of the Soviet regime in previous decades. He concluded with an examination of his own case, detailing the plight of each of his works which had been 'smothered, gagged, and slandered' at the hands of the censors. 'In view of such flagrant infringements ... will the Fourth Congress defend me – yes or no? It seems to me that the choice is also not without importance for the literary future of several of the delegates.' He ended on a note of defiance: 'I am of course confident that I will fulfil my duty as a writer in all circumstances ... No one can bar the road to truth, and to advance its cause I am prepared to accept even death. But may it be that repeated lessons will finally teach us not to stop the writer's pen during his lifetime? At no time has this ennobled our history.'[11]

Solzhenitsyn's calculated gamble in going public with his protestations to the Writers' Union appeared to have paid off. Within days a letter of support signed by eighty members of the Writers' Union was sent to the Presidium of the Fourth All-Union Soviet Writers' Congress. This stated that Solzhenitsyn's letter confronted the Writers' Union and each one of its members with questions of vital importance. It was impossible to pretend that the letter did not exist and simply take refuge in silence. To keep silent 'would inevitably do grave damage to the authority of our literature and the dignity of our society'. The eighty writers insisted that only a full and open discussion of Solzhenitsyn's letter could serve as a guarantee for the healthy future of literature, which had been called upon to be the conscience of the people. This was not the only expression of support for Solzhenitsyn's open letter. A number of other writers sent letters or telegrams to the Presidium of the Writers' Congress calling for a full discussion of the issues raised.

In a crass disregard for its members' wishes, the Presidium proceeded with the congress without even mentioning Solzhenitsyn's letter, and only one delegate had the courage to challenge the leadership's conspicuous silence on the matter. A writer named Vera Ketlinskaya complained that it was intolerable to ignore someone completely and pretend they did not exist, as the speakers had done with regard to Solzhenitsyn. She was greeted with loud applause but apart from this one embarrassing moment, the powers that be succeeded in conducting the entire congress without any reference to the open letter.

On 12 June Solzhenitsyn heard from Tvardovsky of an apparent climbdown by the union's leadership and, along with Tvardovsky himself, he was invited to a meeting with four members of the union's secretariat. Solzhenitsyn was surprised to find that his erstwhile adversaries were both polite and conciliatory. The secretariat members were concerned about the number of copies of *Cancer Ward* circulating in *samizdat*; there were rumours that copies might even have found their way to the West. Solzhenitsyn simply stated that if this was so he was not to blame. At this point Tvardovsky seized the opportunity to extract concessions. 'That's just why I say that *Cancer Ward* must be published immediately. That will put a stop to all the hullaboo in the West and prevent its publication there. We must put excerpts in the *Literaturnaya Gazeta* two days from now, with a note that the story will be published in full.'[12] To

Solzhenitsyn's astonishment, the members of the secretariat agreed and he left the meeting with a feeling of elation that he had at last beaten the ban on his work.

The elation was premature. No statement from the Writers' Union appeared in the *Literaturnaya Gazeta*, nor did the promised extract from *Cancer Ward*. The proposal had been vetoed by the cultural department of the Central Committee.

Three months later, on 12 September 1967, Solzhenitsyn resumed his offensive, writing a letter to all members of the secretariat of the Writers' Union. He complained that his open letter had still neither been published nor answered even though supported by more than a hundred writers. His principal purpose, however, was to complain at the persistent stalling tactics being employed to prevent publication of *Cancer Ward*. His novel had been in the same equivocal state – no direct prohibition, no direct permission – for over a year, since the summer of 1966. He reiterated the desire of *Novy Mir* to publish the story even though it still lacked permission to do so. 'Does the Secretariat believe that my novel will silently disappear as a result of these endless delays, that I will cease to exist ... ? While this is going on, the book is being read avidly everywhere. At the behest of the readers, it has already appeared in hundreds of typewritten copies.' He reminded the members of the secretariat of their discussion on 12 June and the concerns expressed that *Cancer Ward* might be published in the West if the censorship persisted in the Soviet Union. Then, in a brilliant *coup de grâce* intended to raise the stakes and step up the pressure, he suggested that publication in the West 'will clearly be the fault (or perhaps the wish?)' of the secretariat who were ultimately responsible for the senseless delay of many months in gaining the permission required for Soviet publication. 'I insist that my story be published without delay.'[13]

The letter had the desired effect. Ten days later Solzhenitsyn attended a meeting of the secretariat, at which some thirty secretaries of the Writers' Union were present, along with a representative of the cultural department of the Central Committee.

From the outset the meeting was highly charged. The chairman commenced proceedings plaintively, stating that Solzhenitsyn's recent letter had been an insult to the collective and that it contained something in the nature of a threat. It was offensive, 'like a slap in the face', suggesting that members of the secretariat were 'reprobates and not representatives of the creative intelligentsia'. Another member demanded to know how the contents of Solzhenitsyn's first letter had been broadcast over the radio in the West and asked why he had not dissociated himself from this 'licentious bourgeois propaganda'. Solzhenitsyn responded that he was not a schoolboy who was required to jump up obediently to answer every question. Later he responded to the complaint of some members of the secretariat that his recent letter amounted to an ultimatum: either print the story or it would be printed in the West. 'It isn't *I* who presents this ultimatum to the secretariat,' he replied, 'life presents this ultimatum to you and me both.' Hundreds of typewritten copies of *Cancer Ward* were now circulating around Russia, he explained, and it was only a matter of time before some of these copies made their way to the West. Whether he liked it or not, there was nothing he could do to stop this from happening. Neither was he impressed by the complaints that his letter had failed to treat the members of the secretariat as 'brothers in writing and labour'. 'Well, the fact of the matter is that these brothers in writing and labour have for two and a half years calmly watched me being oppressed, persecuted, and slandered ... and newspaper editors, also like brothers, contribute to the web of falsehood that is woven around me by not publishing my denials.'

The enmity between the 'brothers' became increasingly apparent as the meeting progressed, or rather regressed into the rut of entrenched positions. Utterly unconcerned by Solzhenitsyn's libellous treatment at the hands of the Soviet press, one of the secretaries demanded that he speak out publicly against Western propaganda. Another stated that *Cancer Ward* must not be published because it would be used against the Soviet regime: 'the works of Solzhenitsyn are more dangerous to us than those of Pasternak: Pasternak was a man divorced from life, while Solzhenitsyn, with his animated, militant, ideological temperament, is a man of principle'.

Finding himself hopelessly isolated in the midst of a hostile audience, several members of which had already called for his expulsion from the union, Solzhenitsyn, the dangerous man of principle, struck back:

I absolutely do not understand why *Cancer Ward* is accused of being anti-humanitarian. Quite the reverse is true – life conquers death ... By my very nature, were this not the case, I would not have undertaken to write it. But I do not believe that it is the task of literature, with respect to either society or the individual, to conceal the truth or to tone it down ... The task of the writer is to select ... universal and eternal questions, the secrets of the human heart and conscience, the confrontation between life and death, the triumph over spiritual sorrow, the laws in the history of mankind that were born in the depths of time immemorial and that will cease to exist only when the sun ceases to shine.[14]

Solzhenitsyn's restatement of eternal verities fell on deaf ears. His audience believed that the laws governing the history of mankind had only been discovered a hundred years earlier by a German émigré living in London. Now it had fallen to the Communist Party of the Soviet Union to be the infallible guardians of that absolute truth. To the secretaries of the Writers' Union Solzhenitsyn was simply a heretic who must be silenced. The meeting ended acrimoniously with the secretaries demanding that Solzhenitsyn renounce his role as leader of the political opposition, 'the role they ascribe to you in the West', to which Solzhenitsyn replied that his role as a writer was above politics. Solzhenitsyn left the meeting in the knowledge that his lonely battle with totalitarianism had entered a new and dangerous phase.

Towards the end of the meeting Solzhenitsyn had remarked defiantly that although he was unable to reply to the slander that was being spread about him, especially if the Writers' Union refused to help him refute the false allegations, he derived comfort from the knowledge that he would never suffer from such slander because he had been strengthened in the Stalinist camps. Painfully aware that he lacked allies and that his enemies were preparing the next stage of their war on him, he braced himself for another wave of slander. It came on 5 October in a vicious attack by Mikhail Zimyanin, the editor of *Pravda*, during a speech at the Press House in Leningrad. 'At the moment,' Zimyanin began, 'Solzhenitsyn occupies an important

As a schoolboy. Rostov-on-the-Don, 1933.

As an artillery school student. Kostroma, 1942.

Working on a manuscript in a dug-out on the First Belorussian front, February 1944.

Lieutenant Solzhenitsyn (left) with artillery battalion commander Captain Pshechenko on the North-western front, early 1943.

The Marfino *sharashka* (prison), setting of
The First Circle. Prisoner Solzhenitsyn
worked at the *sharashka* from 1947 to 1950.

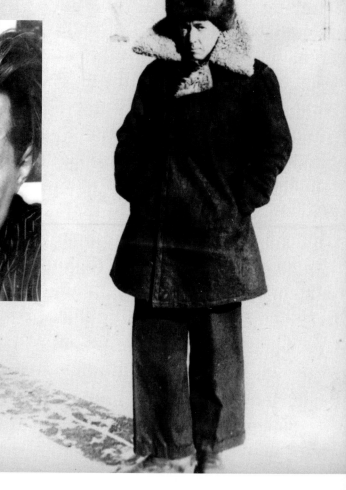

In internal exile.
Kok-Terok, 1954.

Recovering from cancer, with a colt. Cancer Ward, Tashkent, 1954.

Leading students into the steppe for a land-surveying lesson. Kok-Terek, 1955.

With the tenth-grade (graduating) Kazakh class at the Kirov secondary school. Kok-Terek, 1955.

Matryona's House in the village of Miltsevo, Vladimir *oblast*. Solzhenitsyn lived and taught in Miltsevo from August 1956 to June 1957.

In a yard at a self-made table, on which *One Day in the Life of Ivan Denisovich* was written. Ryazan, 1958.

With Natalya Reshetovskaya, summer 1962.

The *Novy Mir* Editorial Board, February 1970. Tvardovsky is seated, third from left.

At the funeral of Tvardovsky with Maria Illarionovna Tvardovskaya, the poet's widow. Moscow, December 1971.

At the church of Artemy the Righteous, near the village of Verkola, Arkhangelsk *oblast*, July 1969.

below: With his son, Yermolai during the last summer in Russia before his exile. Firsanovka, 1973.

right: With his sons in Cavendish, Vermont, 1976.

above: Natalya Dmitrievna Solzhenitsyn, 1974.

right: With his sons on a self-made bench (from left to right): Ignat, Yermolai, Stephan. Cavendish, 1978.

Solzhenitsyn receives the Templeton Prize in London, May 1983. (*PA News Photo Library*)

top: With his wife, Yermolai and Ignat. Cavendish, 1988.

middle: In his Vermont home with his wife and sons, 1990.

left: Travelling round the country with his wife. Tver, September 1996.

place in the propaganda of capitalist countries. He ... is a psychologically unbalanced person, a schizophrenic ... Solzhenitsyn's works are aimed at the Soviet regime in which he finds only sores and cancerous tumours. He doesn't see anything positive in our society ... Obviously we cannot publish his works. Solzhenitsyn's demands that we do so cannot be met. If he writes stories which correspond to the interests of our society, then his works will be published.'[15]

In the same month that Zimyanin was making these unjust attacks on him, Solzhenitsyn wrote a letter on the subject of justice to three students who had visited him previously. He equated justice with conscience, stating that there was nothing relative about justice, as there is nothing relative about conscience. Indeed, justice *is* conscience, not a personal conscience but the conscience of the whole of humanity. Those who clearly recognize the voice of their own conscience usually recognize also the voice of justice. The obverse was equally true, that those sufficiently corrupted that they have ceased following the dictates of conscience are those most susceptible to the perpetration of acts of injustice. 'Convictions based on conscience are as infallible as the internal rhythm of the heart (and one knows that in private life it is the voice of conscience which we often try to suppress).'[16]

Solzhenitsyn's own private life was about to undergo major changes during the coming year. To one who listened as attentively to his conscience as he did, they were to cause pain, introspection and guilt before resolving themselves in a way which was certainly best for him, though arguably not so for Natalya.

On 26 August 1968 he met a twenty-eight-year-old mathematician working for her doctorate, called Natalya Svetlova. He was immediately taken with this 'intense young woman, her dark hair swept forward above her hazel eyes! No trace of affectation in her manner of dress.' He would soon discover that she thought with electronic rapidity and shared his views on Soviet society. She was to become a highly efficient helper in his struggles with authority.

Alya, as Svetlova liked to be called, was born in Moscow in 1939. Like so many others she was raised in the shadow of the Gulag. Her maternal grandfather had been arrested the year before her birth and subsequently perished in the camps. Her father had been killed at the front in December 1941. In 1956 she finished high school in

Moscow with a gold medal for outstanding academic achievement. (According to Ignat Solzhenitsyn this was the equivalent of receiving straight A's or 5s throughout the ten years of her schooling.)[17] Feeling herself drawn towards history and literature but disgusted by the ideological censorship then omnipresent in the humanities, she decided to enrol in the famous *mekhmat*, the 'mechanic-mathematics' department of Moscow University, where she studied under Professor Kolmogorov. After graduating she was invited to work in his laboratory of mathematical statistics.

While still at school, and then during her years at university, Alya was active at several sports. She twice won the USSR rowing championship and later took a vigorous interest in mountain climbing, river expeditions and serious rock-climbing. At university she married an algebra student at the *mekhmat*, Andrei Tyurin, and in 1962 their son Dimitri was born. In 1964 Alya and Tyurin divorced, although a warm relationship with him, and later with his second family, have been maintained right up to the present day. (Today Tyurin lives in Moscow, and is a Corresponding Member of the Russian Academy of Sciences.)

When Alya first met Solzhenitsyn she had already been an active participant in the social and cultural life of Moscow for several years, and was acquainted with many of the leading figures in the city's literary and musical circles. She was a frequent guest in the home of Nadezhda Yakovlevna Mandelstam, one of barely half a dozen writers whose names stand out as possibly having world-class literary talent in post-war Russia.[18] It was chez Mandelstam that Alya had met and become friendly with Natalya Stolyarova, secretary to the writer Ilya Ehrenburg. Stolyarova was a great admirer of Solzhenitsyn and, having herself served a sentence in the labour camps after her voluntary return to the Soviet Union from Paris, had supplied him with much valuable information for *The Gulag Archipelago*. It was Stolyarova who introduced Alya to Solzhenitsyn.[19]

Following their first meeting Alya became one of Solzhenitsyn's most trusted and efficient allies. She agreed to type out the complete version of *The First Circle*, doing so diligently for a couple of hours each evening after putting her young son to bed. 'The fourth or fifth time we met,' Solzhenitsyn recalled, 'I put my hands on her shoulders as one does when expressing gratitude and confidence to a friend. And this gesture instantly turned our lives upside down: from now on she was Alya, my second wife ...'[20]

There was of course still the awkward question of the first wife. In spite of their many differences and the fact that Solzhenitsyn was away from home for ever longer periods, Natalya still felt possessive towards him and jealous of the greater part of his life he spent apart from her. The awkwardness remained for a further four years until their divorce allowed Solzhenitsyn to marry Alya. In the interim one can only guess to what degree Solzhenitsyn fought to suppress the voice of conscience. There is, however, little doubt that he had finally found his partner in life. In Alya, a mutual friend reflected, Solzhenitsyn found what he needed most. 'She was educated, intelligent, witty, with a great many friends; she was small, shapely, and moved with grace.' She worked conscientiously for him, and he could trust her absolutely with any secret. Although she was strong-willed and independent-minded, no mere echo of Solzhenitsyn, she was nevertheless of one mind with him in essence. 'She is a rare woman, and one in whom there has never been any vainglory.'[21]

For years, Solzhenitsyn wrote, he had dreamed in vain of finding a male friend whose ideas would be so close to his own. At last, when he had all but given up hope, he had met his soul-mate, someone who shared not only his political outlook but, far more importantly, his spiritual outlook also. Although she was Jewish on her maternal side, Alya was an Orthodox Christian in belief and deeply, patriotically Russian at the core of her being. She possessed 'a deep-rooted spiritual affinity with everything quintessentially Russian, as well as an unusual concern and affection for the Russian language. This, together with her vibrant energy, made me want to see her more often.'[22] For her part, Alya told a friend that, much as she had admired and respected her first husband, she had not known what love was until she met Solzhenitsyn.[23]

Her love would cost her dearly. Following their marriage she bore him three children, all sons, in quick succession. Then, with three infants, she followed her husband into exile, coping heroically with the omnipresent publicity and the trials of starting life anew, first in Switzerland and then in the United States. Through it all she proved a tower of resilience, bringing up the children and selflessly supporting her husband in all his endeavours. Solzhenitsyn, in late middle age, had found his greatest ally.

A few months after his first meeting with Alya, Solzhenitsyn found himself with a host of new friends from much farther afield. In the autumn, *Cancer Ward* and *The First Circle* were published in Britain and the United States, having been published already in Milan, Frankfurt and Paris. Unlike his old enemies at home, his new friends in the West had nothing but praise for Solzhenitsyn's work. Reviews for *The First Circle* were particularly laudatory. Thomas Lask in the *New York Times* wrote that it was 'at once classic and contemporary ... future generations will read it with wonder and awe'. Richard Hingley in the *Spectator* described it as 'arguably the greatest Russian novel of the twentieth century'. Julian Symons of the *Sunday Times* called it 'a majestic work of genius'.

How different this reception was from the one he had received from his brothers in the Writers' Union. More to the point, what could he expect from those brothers now that the bourgeois forces in the West had declared themselves his friends? Whatever new friends he may have gained, Solzhenitsyn was only too aware that his old enemies were the same as they had always been. He did not need reminding of what awaited him. Even as his books were being published in the West, Soviet tanks were rolling into Czechoslovakia, crushing free speech in the time-honoured way pioneered by Stalin.

Solzhenitsyn, with Alya Svetlova for spiritual succour and support, waited expectantly, bracing himself for the impending storm.

NOTES

1. Solzhenitsyn, 'Easter Procession', *Stories and Prose Poems*, pp. 121–6.
2. Solzhenitsyn, *The Oak and the Calf*, p. 135.
3. Labedz, *Solzhenitsyn: A Documentary Record*, pp. 87–109.
4. Solzhenitsyn, *The Oak and the Calf*, p. 458.
5. Ibid., pp. 142–5.
6. Ibid., pp. 144–5.
7. Ibid.
8. Scammell, *Solzhenitsyn: A Biography*, p. 575.
9. Solzhenitsyn, *The Gulag Archipelago Volume Three*, p. 527.
10. Labedz, *Solzhenitsyn: A Documentary Record*, pp. 110–11.

11. Ibid., p. 116.
12. Solzhenitsyn, *The Oak and the Calf*, pp. 169–74.
13. Labedz, *Solzhenitsyn: A Documentary Record*, pp. 130–1.
14. Ibid., pp. 132–54.
15. Ibid., pp. 156–7.
16. Ibid., pp. 155–6.
17. Ignat Solzhenitsyn, note appended to Natalya Solzhenitsyn's answers to the author, October 1998.
18. Scammell, *Solzhenitsyn: A Biography*, p. 484.
19. The foregoing biographical information was given by Natalya Solzhenitsyn in answer to questions from the author.
20. Solzhenitsyn, *Invisible Allies*, pp. 198–200.
21. Thomas, *Solzhenitsyn: A Century in His Life*, p. 340.
22. Solzhenitsyn, *Invisible Allies*, pp. 198–9.
23. Scammell, *Solzhenitsyn: A Biography*, p. 661.

CHAPTER THIRTEEN

'I FEEL SORRY FOR RUSSIA'

During 1969 the West continued to court Solzhenitsyn. His books were selling strongly in Europe and America and Western publishers were clamouring and competing for new translations of his work. Two of his plays, *Candle in the Wind* and *The Love Girl and the Innocent*, were published in Frankfurt and London respectively. Scarcely did the liberal intelligentsia in the West suspect that Solzhenitsyn, far from being a champion of Western values, was as little enamoured of capitalist consumerism as he was of communist totalitarianism.

His own views were still developing at this time, but they sprang from Russian tradition and had little in common with the materialism which was in the ascendancy in Europe and the United States. Rooted in the spiritual struggles in the camps, Solzhenitsyn's central belief was in selfless self-limitation as opposed to the selfish gratification of needless wants. As he watched Russians gorging themselves on gadgets and other consumer goods, taking their lead from the West, he felt a sense of nausea. This was not what life was about.

It was only a matter of time before his views brought him into conflict not only with his old enemies in the communist hierarchy but with his old friends among the liberal dissidents. The conflict came to a head in September 1969 when Solzhenitsyn's differences with the editors of *Novy Mir* were made public. The cause of the dispute was a polemical debate that *Novy Mir* had been conducting with the monthly magazine *Molodaya Gvardia* (Young Guard). The disagreement arose from two articles by the literary critic Victor Chalmayev, published the previous year in *Molodaya Gvardia*. Chalmayev's views were dubbed 'National Bolshevik' by his opponents and were essentially a reactionary mishmash of garbled Marxism and Russian patriotism, a confusion of mutually contradictory premises. Chalmayev had denounced the West as being hopelessly corrupt and degenerate, 'choking on a surfeit of hate' and the fount of all evil. Attempting to build bridges with it by importing its technology or, even worse, its consumer goods or its culture would be both wrong and dangerous. The only result would be that the West's poison would spread to the East. Compared with the corrupt decadence of the West, the traditions of Russia were pure and ethical, fed by a 'sacred spring'. In recent years this Russian spirit had degenerated under the trivializing impact of Western imports such as television, cinema and the mass media, but it could be revitalized by returning to its roots, drawing inspiration from the Russian village, the moral and spiritual values of the Russian people, and the pure idioms of popular speech. Chalmayev referred mystically to the sacramental power of the native soil and even invoked Holy Russia with her 'saints and just men born of a yearning for miracles and loving kindness'. All this, Chalmayev asserted in a bizarre leap of logic, had culminated in the glorious Russian Revolution, that 'sacramental act' which was the finest expression and the crowning moment in a thousand years of Russian history. It was not that Solzhenitsyn agreed with Chalmayev's articles *per se* – indeed there were aspects of them which he found abhorrent – but he disagreed with *Novy Mir*'s grounds for attacking them.

Amidst the outcry and controversy that followed publication of Chalmayev's articles, *Novy Mir* published its own response to his views in the June 1969 issue. The author of *Novy Mir*'s riposte, Alexander Dementyev, poured scorn on Chalmayev's patriotism and his extraordinary 'un-Leninist' genuflections to church history. Chalmayev's slavophilism was reactionary and his praise of a Russian rural idyll unrealistic. Worst of all was his hostility to technological modernization. Such hostility was not Marxism-Leninism, Dementyev wrote, but a 'dogmatic perversion'. Marxism-Leninism was internationalist, progressive, and in favour of modernization.

When Solzhenitsyn paid a visit to the offices of *Novy Mir* in September it was assumed that he would agree wholeheartedly with Dementyev's liberal Marxist critique of Chalmayev's article. Yet Solzhenitsyn was neither a liberal nor a Marxist and felt that Dementyev had attacked Chalmayev for all the wrong reasons. The parts of Chalmayev's articles with which he had disagreed most were the eulogizing references to the Revolution and the absurd assertion that Marxism, itself a decadent import from the West, had anything to do with the noble aspects of Russian history. Certainly he shared *Novy Mir*'s disgust with Chalmayev's bombastic and bigoted tone, his cheap, jingoistic rhetoric, and his extreme xenophobia. Nevertheless he was encouraged to find in the article certain positive and healthy themes and ideas which, to the best of his knowledge, were appearing in an official Soviet publication for the first time. He was pleased by Chalmayev's appeal to Russian, as opposed to Soviet, patriotism; was delighted by his praise for the early Russian church and Russian saints, and the appreciation of Russian village life and folk culture; and shared Chalmayev's reverence for the uniqueness of Russian national tradition.

The gulf between Solzhenitsyn and the liberal Marxists of *Novy Mir* could hardly have been more apparent. Whereas they had rejected Russian national tradition in the name of the Revolution, he had arrived at the diametrically opposite view – that it was necessary to reject the Revolution in the name of national tradition. This, of course, was a dangerous heresy in the Soviet Union and would have been too much even for the ears of the tolerant liberals at *Novy Mir*. Choosing the path of reticence, he avoided dispraising the Revolution and even refrained from mentioning that he shared with Chalmayev many of his criticisms of the West, while making it clear that he disagreed with the nature of Dementyev's reply.

Increasingly alienated from some of his allies, Solzhenitsyn prepared himself for the next wave of persecution by his enemies. It was not long in coming. On 4 November 1969, he attended a meeting of the Ryazan writers' organization, of which he was a member. The meeting opened with a report about the measures being taken by the Writers' Union to intensify ideological-educational work among writers. As part of this campaign charges had been laid against several members of the Moscow section, including Lev Kopelev, and against one member of their own section in Ryazan, namely Solzhenitsyn. One of the members, Vasily Matushkin, reminded the meeting that the Writers' Union existed to bring together people who shared the same views – who built up communism, gave it all their creative work and followed the path of socialist realism. 'Accordingly, there is no room for Solzhenitsyn in a writers' organization; let him work on his own. Bitter though it is, I am bound to say, A. I., that our paths differ from yours and we will have to part company.' Another member complained that the ideological quality of Solzhenitsyn's writings did not help in building a communist society and cast slurs on the Soviet Union's glowing future. One by one, the members of the group condemned Solzhenitsyn and called for his expulsion. Solzhenitsyn's defence was as defiant as ever: 'No! it will not be possible indefinitely to keep silent about Stalin's crimes or go against the truth. There were millions of people who suffered from the crimes and they demand exposure. It would be a good idea, too, to reflect: what moral effect will the silence on these crimes have on the younger generation – it will mean the *corruption* of still more millions.'

With the members unmoved by Solzhenitsyn's words, a previously prepared draft resolution was read out: 'The meeting considers that Solzhenitsyn's conduct is anti-social in character and is radically in conflict with the aims and purposes of the USSR Union of Writers. In view of his anti-social behaviour ... the writer Solzhenitsyn is hereby expelled from the USSR Union of Writers. We request that the Secretariat endorse this decision.' In the vote that followed only one member voted against.[1]

The decision to expel Solzhenitsyn from the Writers' Union was duly endorsed by the Secretariat and was reported in the *Literaturnaya Gazeta* on 12 November. The *Gazeta* reminded its readers that Solzhenitsyn's works had been actively used by hostile bourgeois propaganda for a campaign of slander against his country and that Solzhenitsyn's own actions and statements had substantially helped to fan the flames of anti-Soviet sensationalism around his name.

Solzhenitsyn's letter of protest, sent to the Secretariat of the Writers' Union, was a masterpiece of invective, venting his spleen on his would-be silencers:

> Blow the dust off the clock. Your watches are behind the times. Throw open the heavy curtains which are so dear to you – you do not even suspect that the day has already dawned outside. It is no longer that stifling, that sombre, irrevocable time when you expelled Akhmatova in the same servile manner. It is not even that timid, frosty period when you expelled Pasternak, whining abuse at him. Was

this shame not enough for you? Do you want to make it greater? But the time is near when each of you will seek to erase his signature from today's resolution.

There followed an attack on the blind tribalism of the Cold War and a warning about the environmental disasters it could bring:

> You could not live without 'enemies'; hatred, a hatred no better than racial hatred, has become your sterile atmosphere. But in this way a sense of our single, common humanity is lost and its doom is accelerated. Should the antarctic ice melt tomorrow, we would all become a sea of drowning humanity, and into whose heads would you then be drilling your concepts of 'class struggle'? Not to speak of the time when the few surviving bipeds will be wandering over radioactive earth, dying.

Solzhenitsyn reminded his persecutors that they belonged first and foremost to humanity, that what was required was freedom of thought and freedom of speech: 'Openness, honest and complete openness – that is the first condition of health in all societies, including our own. And he who does not want this openness for our country cares nothing for his fatherland and thinks only of his own interest. He who does not wish this openness for his fatherland does not want to purify it of its diseases, but only to drive them inwards, there to fester.'[2]

Solzhenitsyn's expulsion caused a storm of protest from the West. David Carver and Pierre Emmanuel, in their respective capacities as Secretary and President of the International PEN Club, sent a telegram to Konstantin Fedin, chairman of the Soviet Writers' Union, on 18 November stating that they were appalled and shocked at the expulsion of the 'great and universally respected writer'. Carver and Emmanuel called on Fedin to intervene personally to restore Solzhenitsyn's membership. By doing so he would be helping to combat the 'much deplored prolonged persecution' of one of 'our most eminent colleagues'. Fedin's reply was terse in the extreme, calling Carver's and Emmanuel's telegram an unprecedented interference in the internal affairs of the Writers' Union of the USSR. In response Carver and Emmanuel expressed their regret at the tone and content of Fedin's telegram, reiterating their view that a writer of Solzhenitsyn's calibre would be welcome anywhere and that the Soviet Writers' Union should feel honoured to have him as a member.[3]

More worrying for the Soviet authorities must have been the strong criticism from socialist fellow-travellers in the West who would normally be sympathetic to Soviet policy. Typical of the outrage on the Left in the wake of Solzhenitsyn's expulsion was a statement by the French National Writers' Committee. Signed by sixteen prominent French writers including Louis Aragon, Michel Butor and Jean-Paul Sartre, the statement expressed concern that Solzhenitsyn's expulsion 'constitutes in the eyes of the whole world a monumental mistake which not only does harm to the Soviet Union but helps confirm the view of socialism as propagated by its enemies'. Despite this 'mistake' the writers remained confident of the essential political correctness of the Soviet regime, stating that 'we still wish to believe that ... there will be found in the high councils of the nation, to whom we owe the Dawn of October and the defeat of Hitlerian fascism, men capable of realizing the wrong that has been done and of putting it right'. The statement was signed in the name of 'the common cause for which we live, fight and die'.[4]

More impressive still was a letter addressed to Konstantin Fedin on 3 December from a group of prominent international figures. 'We reject the conception that an artist's refusal humbly to accept state censorship is in any sense criminal in a civilized society, or that publication by foreigners of his books is ground for persecuting him ... We sign our names as men of peace declaring our solidarity with Alexander Solzhenitsyn's defence of those fundamental rights of the human spirit which unite civilized people everywhere.' It was signed by Arthur Miller, Charles Bracelen Flood, Harrison Salisbury, John Updike, John Cheever, Truman Capote, Richard Wilbur, Jean-Paul Sartre, Carlos Fuentes, Yukio Mishima, Igor Stravinsky, Gunter Grass, Friedrich Dürrenmatt, Heinrich Böll, Kurt Vonnegut and Mitchell Wilson.[5]

On 16 December *The Times* published a letter signed by thirty well-known writers, condemning the silencing of a writer of Solzhenitsyn's stature as a crime against civilization. Among the signatories were W. H. Auden, A. J. Ayer, Brian Glanville, Gunter Grass, Graham Greene, Julian Huxley, Rosamond Lehmann, Arthur Miller, Mary McCarthy, Muriel Spark, Philip Toynbee and Bernard Wall.

As the world's literati lined up to denounce the Soviet Union as an enemy of civilization, it must have been clear to all but the most blind of Soviet officials that the efforts to crush Solzhenitsyn through the crude expedient of expulsion from the Writers' Union had been a woeful error of judgement. He had become an international *cause célèbre*, a living symbol of the struggle for human rights in the face of state censorship. If there was any doubt remaining about Solzhenitsyn's triumphant emergence from this latest bout of persecution, it was dispelled on 8 October 1970 when he was awarded the Nobel Prize for Literature 'for the ethical force with which he has pursued the indispensable traditions of Russian literature'.

Predictably, the official Soviet reaction to the award of the world's most prestigious literary prize to Solzhenitsyn was one of outrage. On 10 October *Izvestia*, after claiming that Solzhenitsyn's expulsion from the Writers' Union had been actively supported by the entire public of the country, declared that the award was a further example of Solzhenitsyn's work being used by reactionary circles in the West for anti-Soviet purposes. On 14 October, the neo-Stalinist newspaper *Sovetskaya Rossiya* described it as a purely political act which was in its essence a provocation and another international act of an anti-Soviet character. On the same day the *Literaturnaya Gazeta* accused the Nobel committee of succumbing to anti-Soviet trends. *Soviet Weekly*, on 17 October, derided the award by stating that it was 'not a real literary award, but a maliciously prepared sensation'. Having dismissed the award, the paper dismissed Solzhenitsyn himself as a run-of-the-mill writer: 'he must surely realize himself that his literary gifts are not only below those of the giants of the past, but also inferior to many of his Soviet contemporaries – writers the West choose to ignore because they find the impact of the truth in their writing most unpalatable'.

On the same day that *Soviet Weekly* dismissed both Solzhenitsyn and the Nobel Prize with such contempt, *Komsomolskaya Pravda* went one better, describing the awarding of the prize to Solzhenitsyn as sacrilege. Moreover, the journal continued, Solzhenitsyn was lacking in both civic feelings and generally accepted principles of morality so that he had 'forgone his conscience and stooped to lies'.

Others saw it differently. A message smuggled out of a Soviet labour camp at Potma in Mordovia and signed by a group of political prisoners including Yuri Galanskov, the young Russian poet sentenced in 1968 to seven years' hard labour for editing the *samizdat* journal *Phoenix*, offered Solzhenitsyn heartfelt congratulations: 'Barbed wire and automatic weapons prevent us from expressing to you personally the depth of our admiration for your courageous creative work, upholding the sense of human dignity and exposing the trampling down of the human soul and the destruction of human values.'[6]

The Soviet authorities might not have been too concerned about the views of these political prisoners, mere enemies of the people, but they must have been worried at the support Solzhenitsyn was being given by French and Italian communists, their comrades in the West. A writer in the French communist newspaper *Humanité* applauded the awarding of the Nobel Prize to Solzhenitsyn who was a 'real writer, faithful to his vocation to speak the truth as he sees it, which is an essential part of his responsibility to society'.[7] Meanwhile *L'Unità*, a journal of the Italian communists, considered it 'a question of freedom of expression and of dissent in a socialist country, of its legitimacy, and even of its value'.[8]

The question of freedom of expression and dissent was uppermost in the minds of many Soviet citizens in the wake of the Nobel award. Thirty-seven prominent Soviet intellectuals signed a letter congratulating Solzhenitsyn on 10 October and three weeks later the celebrated cellist and composer Mstislav Rostropovich sent an open letter to the editors of *Pravda, Izvestia, Literaturnaya Gazeta* and the cultural journal *Sovetskaya Kultura*. Rostropovich and Solzhenitsyn were good friends, and Solzhenitsyn was a frequent guest at Rostropovich's house near Moscow. At the time that Solzhenitsyn had been expelled from the Writers' Union he had been working on his novel *August 1914* while staying with Rostropovich. He was also staying with him, putting the finishing touches to the same novel, on the day he heard the news that he had been awarded the Nobel Prize. Now, in the wake of the hostile campaign against his friend in the Soviet press, Rostropovich had been provoked into entering the fray. 'I know that after my letter there will undoubtedly be an "opinion" about me, but I am not afraid of it. I openly say what I think ... I know many of the works of Solzhenitsyn. I like them. I consider he seeks the right through his suffering to write the truth as he saw it and I see no reason to hide my attitude toward him at a time when a campaign is being launched against him.'

Needless to say, Rostropovich's letter was not published in any of the journals to which it was addressed, but it caused a considerable stir when it appeared in the *New York Times* on 16 November. His bravery in going public was an embodiment of the growing number of dissident voices prepared to be heard in the face of Soviet repression. Solzhenitsyn's courage was clearly contagious and was spreading to parts of Soviet society that the authorities had hoped it would never reach.

In the shadow of the hostile reaction in official circles, Solzhenitsyn decided against travelling to Sweden to receive the award. Writing to the Swedish Academy on 27 November he explained that any trip abroad would be used to cut him off from his native land. He would be prevented from returning home.[9] He now perceived that the Soviet government considered him a liability and that they would very much like to get rid of him. He could see them squirming and had no intention of letting them off the hook so easily. Besides, he had no desire to leave his Russian homeland for a life of exile in the West. Whatever the future held he wanted to face it on his native soil.

At the conclusion of his letter to the Swedish Academy, Solzhenitsyn stated his intention of providing a written text for the Nobel Lecture which his absence from the official ceremony would prevent him from giving in person. When this was finally published over a year later it became another powerful weapon in the battle for civil liberties in the Soviet Union. It was also, however, an incisively perceptive exposition of the nature and purpose of art. 'The task of the artist,' Solzhenitsyn asserted,

> is to sense more keenly than others the harmony of the
> world, the beauty and the outrage of what man has done to
> it, and poignantly to let people know ... By means of art

we are sometimes sent – dimly, briefly – revelations unattainable by reason. Like that little mirror in the fairy tales – look into it, and you will see not yourself but, for a moment, that which passeth understanding, a realm to which no man can ride or fly. And for which the soul begins to ache ...[10]

The fact that such a view is rooted in Solzhenitsyn's Christianity is emphasized by Richard Haugh in the essay 'The Philosophical Foundations of Solzhenitsyn's Vision of Art':

Solzhenitsyn's vision of the source of art and value is ultimately rooted in his belief in the Absolute. In an unambiguous text from his Nobel Lecture Solzhenitsyn states that the artist has not 'created this world, nor does he control it: *there can be no doubts about its foundations.*' For Solzhenitsyn the world is a created world. It is a world which might not have existed at all and hence it points beyond itself to its spiritual source. The world, for Solzhenitsyn, is necessarily dependent and participatory, deriving its value and meaning from the uncreated and eternal.[11]

Art was, or should be, a key to the treasures of mystical experience, a means of expressing through sub-creation man's unity with the primary Creation of which he is part. It could also, in its highest form, be an expression of the homesickness of the soul in spiritual exile, a longing for that eternal realm for which the soul begins to ache.

In the historical sphere art was invaluable as the custodian of cultural tradition. 'Literature transmits condensed and irrefutable human experience in still another priceless way: from generation to generation. It thus becomes the living memory of a nation. What has faded into history it thus keeps warm and preserves in a form that defies distortion and falsehood. Thus literature, together with language, preserves and protects a nation's soul.'[12]

This conception of the nation's soul was a cornerstone of Solzhenitsyn's whole view of the world. As culture was essentially spiritual it must, in some mystical sense, possess a soul. Furthermore, since individual native cultures have something unique to offer the world they must also possess a mystical soul unique to themselves. The Russian soul was distinct from, say, the English or the French soul. 'I am deeply convinced,' Solzhenitsyn would say in 1998, 'that God is present both in the lives of every person and also in the lives of entire nations.'[13] These sentiments were expressed with eloquence in his Nobel Lecture:

> It has become fashionable in recent times to talk of the levelling of nations, and of various peoples disappearing into the melting pot of contemporary civilization. I disagree with this, but that is another matter; all that should be said here is that the disappearance of whole nations would impoverish us no less than if all the people were to become identical, with the same character and the same face. Nations are the wealth of humanity, its generalized personalities. The least among them has its own special colours, and harbours within itself a special aspect of God's design.[14]

The sense of a mystical providence at the heart of a nation's life was at the forefront of Solzhenitsyn's mind as he was writing his historical novel *August 1914*, which was completed at around the time that the Nobel Prize was awarded. Published in the West on 11 June 1971, the sweeping historical panorama invited comparisons with *War and Peace* and many of the themes which had been preoccupying Solzhenitsyn found powerful expression. In the novel, youthful self-centredness and the snobbery of modern secular values were contrasted with the perennial wisdom of the peasants who express their view of the world proverbially. It was no coincidence that Solzhenitsyn had chosen to conclude his Nobel Lecture with an old Russian proverb: 'One word of truth outweighs the world.' Solzhenitsyn was also becoming much more daring in his anti-communist allusions. Whereas in earlier works he had remained circumspect in his criticisms, carefully differentiating between Stalinism and the 'pure' Marxism of the Revolution, in *August 1914* he pulled no punches. All Marxism was evil, pure or otherwise. This oppositional attitude found its most potent expression in Varya's rape at the hands of the young revolutionary, a thinly veiled allegory of the communist rape of Russia.

Equally poignant, and perhaps the point of the novel itself, were the words of Sanya as he prepares to enlist in the army at the outbreak of war. At the conclusion of the first chapter of the novel he is unable to answer Varya's objections to his decision to enlist, replying sadly that 'I feel sorry for Russia'. When, in 1998, Solzhenitsyn was asked what he meant by this sad, solitary phrase, he stared intently at the interviewer, pausing momentarily before answering: 'that character which you ask about is a depiction of my father. At the time amongst that generation there was a pretty wide feeling of care, of feeling sorry for the country, and feeling concerned about what was going to happen to it. Today, unfortunately, much of this is lost. There are very few people left like this. They certainly are a small minority. In this lies one of the reasons for our current troubles.'[15]

As Solzhenitsyn answered the question, his old but penetrating eyes seemed to repeat the refrain that his father had uttered over eighty years earlier: 'I feel sorry for Russia.'

NOTES

1. Labedz, *Solzhenitsyn: A Documentary Record*, pp. 209–21.
2. Ibid., pp. 222–4.
3. Ibid., p. 225.
4. Ibid., pp. 226–7.
5. Ibid., p. 227.
6. Ibid., p. 248.
7. *Humanité*, 9 October 1970.
8. *L'Unità*, 9 October 1970.
9. *New York Times*, 1 December 1970.
10. Alexander Solzhenitsyn, *Nobel Lecture*, New York, 1972, pp. 5–6.
11. Quoted in Niels C. Nielsen, *Solzhenitsyn's Religion*, London: Mowbray, 1976, p. 135.
12. Solzhenitsyn, *Nobel Lecture*, p. 19.
13. Solzhenitsyn, interview with the author.
14. Solzhenitsyn, *Nobel Lecture*, p. 19.
15. Solzhenitsyn, interview with the author.

CHAPTER FOURTEEN

OUT IN THE COLD

For all Solzhenitsyn's differences with the liberals at *Novy Mir* he was conscious that they remained allies in the struggle against Soviet repression. This was more evident than ever in February 1970 when his old friend Alexander Tvardovsky was removed from his post as *Novy Mir*'s editor after sixteen years at the helm. Tvardovsky was devastated by his dismissal and never recovered from the blow. Within six months his health had collapsed and he died a year afterwards on 18 December 1971.

Solzhenitsyn's presence at the funeral three days later caused a considerable stir. Although the high-ranking officials of the Writers' Union who were officially responsible for organizing the ceremony had sought to keep him away, he had attended at the insistence of Tvardovsky's widow, sitting beside her in the front row. Watched by the world's media, Solzhenitsyn stepped forward at the end of the ceremony and made the sign of the cross over the open coffin. 'There are many ways of killing a poet,' Solzhenitsyn wrote in his eulogy to his friend published a week later, 'the method chosen for Tvardovsky was to take away his offspring, his passion, his journal.' Having blamed Tvardovsky's death on his dismissal from *Novy Mir*, Solzhenitsyn rounded on his friend's persecutors who had brazenly sought to hijack the funeral: 'And now the whole gang from the Writers' Union has flopped on to the scene. The guard of honour comprises that same flabby crowd that hunted him down with unholy shrieks and cries. Yes, it's an old, old custom of ours, it was the same with Pushkin: it is precisely into the hands of his enemies that the dead poet falls. And they hastily dispose of the body, covering up with glib speeches.'[1]

The Soviet authorities may have succeeded in silencing Tvardovsky but they were still singularly failing in all efforts to silence

Solzhenitsyn. In the months following his friend's funeral, Solzhen-itsyn's voice reached more people throughout the world than ever before. During 1972 his work was translated into thirty-five lan-guages.[2] This was also the year in which he went public with an open confession of Christianity by means of a *Lenten Letter to the Patri-arch of All Russia*. Until the publication of this open letter most peo-ple were unaware of Solzhenitsyn's Christianity, principally because the need for discretion had dictated that he either avoid or tone down overt references to his religious faith in his books. The Christ-ian aspects of his work had been expressed by way of sympathetic characterization or allegorical allusion, with little else to suggest that Solzhenitsyn was anything more than a dispassionate observer of religious issues. Certainly few people realized that he considered himself an Orthodox believer.

The inspiration for writing the letter to Patriarch Pimen, who had been elected head of the Russian church the previous year, was the Patriarch's pastoral letter which was read out on a Western radio sta-tion during the broadcast of a religious service on Christmas Eve 1971, only three days after Tvardovsky's funeral. 'At once I was fired with a desire to write to him. I had no choice but to write! And this meant new troubles, new burdens, new complicating factors.'[3]

One complication was the hostility his open expression of Chris-tianity caused among many of his erstwhile allies. His *Lenten Letter* urged the Patriarch to act with greater courage in the face of the atheism of the Soviet regime. Yet many of his liberal-minded friends considered Orthodoxy an archaic irrelevance and were surprised and antagonized by Solzhenitsyn's stance. For the first time Liusha Chukovskaya, one of his most devoted helpers, rebelled against him and adamantly refused to type the *Letter*. 'After more than six years of working together,' Solzhenitsyn recalled, 'it became apparent that we did not think alike.'[4]

There is no doubt that many others began to detect in the emer-gence of Solzhenitsyn's traditional Christianity a spirit to which they were not akin, although Solzhenitsyn himself insists that the break with many of his former allies dated from the publication of *August 1914* the previous year. This, he believed, was the origin of the schism among his readers, the steady loss of supporters, with more leaving than remained behind.

I was received with 'hurrahs' as long as I appeared to be against Stalinist abuses only ... In my first works I was concealing my features from the police censorship – but, by the same token, from the public at large. With each subsequent step I inevitably revealed more and more of myself: the time had come to speak more precisely, to go even deeper. And in doing so I should inevitably lose the reading public, lose my contemporaries in the hope of winning posterity. It was painful, though, to lose support even among those closest to me.[5]

Even if the origins of the schism were slightly earlier, Solzhenitsyn was still surprised by the hostility his *Lenten Letter* aroused. He had intended the letter to be low-key, releasing it only to the limited circulation of the narrow ecclesiastical *samizdat* network, with the idea that it would gradually find its way to all those whom it really concerned. Inevitably, however, considering his controversial international reputation, it was published almost immediately in the West and provoked a flood of interest in the Western media. He learned that the letter and the coverage it had received in the West had left the KGB spluttering with rage – a rage more violent than that excited by most of his actions before or since. There was no mystery here, he added. 'Atheism is the core of the whole Communist system.' Yet if the anger of the KGB was scarcely surprising, he was not prepared for the hostility of normally sympathetic circles, observing that the move had aroused disapproval and even disgust among the intelligentsia too: 'How narrow, blind and limited I must be, thought some, to concern myself with such problems as that of the Church.' Yet regardless of the opposition and the consequent loss of powerful allies, Solzhenitsyn remained defiant: 'Though many people condemned me, I have never regretted this step: if our spiritual fathers need not be the first to set us an example of spiritual freedom from the lie, where are we to look for it?'[6]

In the *Lenten Letter* Solzhenitsyn had berated the Patriarch for addressing his pious words only to the world's Russian émigrés, ignoring the needs of the beleaguered believers in Russia itself: 'Yes, Christ bade us to go seek the hundredth lost sheep, but only after ninety-nine are safe. But when the ninety-nine who should be at hand are lost – should *they* not be our first concern?'[7] There followed a plea for the Church to speak out against the persecution of religious practice in the Soviet Union, before he concluded with a call to sacrifice. External fetters, he insisted, were not so strong as the spirit which was capable of overcoming all persecution. 'It was no easier at the time of the birth of Christianity, but nevertheless Christianity withstood everything and flourished. And it showed us the way: the way of sacrifice. He who is deprived of all material strength will finally always be triumphant through sacrifice. Within our memory our priests and fellow-believers have undergone just such a martyrdom worthy of the first centuries of Christianity.'[8]

For all the hostility it caused in irreligious circles, Solzhenitsyn's public acknowledgement of his Christianity was greeted with joy and admiration among Christians in both East and West. One admirer was Father Alexander Schmemann, dean of St Vladimir's Orthodox Theological Seminary in New York State, who had read the *Lenten Letter* as soon as it was published in the West. He was deeply impressed by its elevated style and biblical rhythms and detected in Solzhenitsyn's words the mark of prophecy. Father Schmemann was a regular broadcaster of religious programmes to the Soviet Union and he made Solzhenitsyn's letter the subject of his Easter sermon, broadcast by Radio Liberty:

> In the Old Testament, in the history of the ancient chosen people, there was the astonishing phenomenon of the *prophets*. Strange and extraordinary men who could not experience peace and self-satisfaction, who swam, as they say, against the tide, told the truth, proclaimed the heavenly judgement over all untruth, weakness and hypocrisy ... And now this forgotten spirit of prophecy has suddenly awakened in the heart of Christianity. We hear the ringing voice of a lone man who has said in the hearing of all that everything that is going on – concessions, submission, the eternal world of the church compromising with the world and political power – all this is evil. And this man is Solzhenitsyn.[9]

Solzhenitsyn heard the broadcast and was much encouraged. Father Schmemann was someone whose judgement he respected, not least because the priest had been one of the first to discern the Christianity at the heart of his own work. As early as 1970 Father Schmemann had written that Solzhenitsyn's books were explicable in terms of the 'triune intuition of creation, fall, and redemption'. Although at the time Schmemann was unaware whether Solzhenitsyn accepted or rejected Christian dogma, ecclesiastical ritual, or the Church herself, he nevertheless insisted that here was a Christian writer who had 'a deep and all-embracing, although possibly unconscious perception of the world, man, and life, which, historically, was born and grew from Biblical and Christian revelation, and only from it'.[10] Solzhenitsyn had read Father Schmemann's article and wrote that it was 'very valuable to me ... it explained me to myself ... it also formulated important traits of Christianity which I could not have formulated myself'.[11]

It is clear, therefore, that Solzhenitsyn already held Father Schmemann in high regard and was particularly pleased that such a figure had spoken so seriously about his *Letter to the Patriarch*. A few months later he recalled how profoundly he had been moved to hear that his favourite preacher had given his approval and how he felt that 'this in itself was my spiritual reward for the letter, and for me, conclusive confirmation that I was right'.[12]

Another by-product of Solzhenitsyn's public profession of faith would be as vociferously negative as Father Schmemann's broadcast had been positive. Solzhenitsyn's religious 'regression', coupled with what was perceived as his reactionary revisionism in *August 1914*, ensured that the communist press in the West now fell in with the official Moscow line. Solzhenitsyn was no longer the persecuted writer unjustly expelled from the Writers' Union, he was now a dangerous renegade seeking to rewrite and blacken the glorious history of the Revolution. Communist journals in the West queued up to condemn *August 1914* and their negative reviews were reprinted gleefully in the Soviet media.

Solzhenitsyn's treatment at the hands of Western communists during this period prompted a bitter response in his autobiography where he complained that 'under the laws of leftist topsy-turvydom, *red* sinners are always forgiven, *red* sins are soon forgotten. As

Orwell writes, those very same Western public figures who were outraged by individual executions anywhere else on earth applauded when Stalin shot hundreds of thousands; they grieved for starving India, but the devastating famine in the Ukraine went unnoticed.'[13] By the early seventies the red sins carried out by the Soviet government may not have been as brutal as those perpetrated under Stalin's murderous regime but the red sinners of the KGB were still as active as ever. On 12 August 1971 Alexander Gorlov, a friend of Solzhenitsyn, was beaten brutally when he surprised a group of KGB officers in the process of searching Solzhenitsyn's country cottage at Rozhdestvo. Finding the plain-clothed intruders in the house Gorlov had demanded their identification, to which the intruders had responded by knocking him to the ground, tying him up and dragging him face down into the woods where he was viciously assaulted. Gorlov, his face mutilated and his suit torn to ribbons, was then bundled into a car and driven off to the local police station. The KGB officers demanded that he sign an oath of secrecy but Gorlov adamantly refused. 'If Solzhenitsyn finds out what took place at the dacha,' he was told, 'it's all over with you. Your official career will go no further ... This will affect your family and children, and, if necessary, we will put you in prison.' In defiance of all these threats, Gorlov informed Solzhenitsyn of all that had happened as soon as he was released. The next day Solzhenitsyn wrote an open letter to Yuri Andropov, the head of the KGB.

> For many years, I have borne in silence the lawlessness of your employees: the inspection of all my correspondence, the confiscation of half of it, the search of my correspondents' homes, and their official and administrative persecution, the spying around my house, the shadowing of visitors, the tapping of telephone conversations, the drilling of holes in ceilings, the placing of recording apparatuses in my city apartment and at my garden cottage, and a persistent slander campaign against me from speakers' platforms when they are offered to employees of your Ministry. But after the raid yesterday, I will no longer be silent.

After detailing the brutal nature of Gorlov's treatment and the threats made against him, Solzhenitsyn demanded that Andropov publicly identify the intruders, oversee their punishment as criminals and offer an explanation of why the incident had occurred. 'Otherwise,' Solzhenitsyn concluded, 'I can only believe that you sent them.'[14] Solzhenitsyn sent a copy of the letter to Alexei Kosygin, chairman of the Council of Ministers, stating that he considered Andropov 'personally responsible for all the illegalities mentioned' and that if the government wished to distance itself from such actions it should conduct an investigation into the matter.

Far from distancing itself, the government awarded Andropov with a place on the Politburo two years later. This was the beginning of his rise to supreme power within the Soviet Union. On the death of Brezhnev in 1982 he became General Secretary of the Communist Party, consolidating his power in June of the following year with his election to the presidency. Thus the head of the hated KGB became the head of state.

On 23 August 1973 Solzhenitsyn gave an interview to the Associated Press news agency and *Le Monde* in which he detailed death threats he had received. He was convinced that these were the work of the KGB. He had also heard from sources allegedly within the KGB that there had been a plan to kill him in a car accident. Even as he was speaking to these Western journalists, the KGB was being implicated in the death of Elizaveta Voronyanskaya, a frail sixty-seven-year-old woman who was one of Solzhenitsyn's most devoted supporters. Over the years she had typed up many of his works and was known to be one of his confidantes. She was arrested by the KGB and broke down under interrogation, divulging the whereabouts of a hidden copy of *The Gulag Archipelago*. Racked with guilt she returned home on 23 August and apparently committed suicide by hanging herself, though there were rumours that the KGB had a direct hand in her death. Such rumours were fuelled by the fact that her body was taken to the Leningrad morgue in strictest secrecy and was not shown even to the family before being sealed in a coffin for burial. There seems to be no doubt that the KGB was at least indirectly responsible for the death of this elderly woman.

Solzhenitsyn had done everything in his power to keep the existence of *The Gulag Archipelago* a secret from the authorities. Now that they had a copy in their possession he had no choice but to order publication in the West as soon as possible. He announced the existence of the book, and his decision to publish it, to Western correspondents in Moscow. If the cat was out of the bag, the whole world and not just the KGB ought to know about it.

A few weeks later, on 24 September, there was an enigmatic meeting between Solzhenitsyn and Natalya on a station platform which seemed to bear all the hallmarks of KGB involvement. The unhappily married couple, who for several years had not lived as man and wife in anything but pretence, had finally divorced six months earlier and Solzhenitsyn had married Alya soon afterwards. Relations between Natalya and her former husband had been strained and Solzhenitsyn was surprised when she phoned to arrange the meeting. He deduced from the tone of her voice that her motives were not merely personal and he reluctantly agreed to meet up with her at the neutral location of the Kazan station. Natalya told him that she had been speaking to 'certain people' and had come to discuss the publication of some of Solzhenitsyn's suppressed works, particularly *Cancer Ward*. The prospect of finally having *Cancer Ward* published in the Soviet Union was certainly alluring but there was something in the nature of his former wife's offer that aroused his suspicions. She told him that he was wrong to keep attacking the security organs. It was the Central Committee that was persecuting him, not the KGB. She announced that she had recently made many new and influential friends in high places, and that they were far cleverer than Solzhenitsyn realized. If these people had been searching for his manuscripts, Solzhenitsyn had only himself to blame: 'You tell the world that your most important works are still to come, that the flow will continue even if you die, and that way you force them to come looking.' It was then that Natalya had mentioned what these certain people evidently wanted her to convey, no doubt with the threatened publication of *The Gulag Archipelago* in mind. 'Why don't you make a declaration that all your works are in your exclusive possession and that you won't publish anything for twenty years?'[15] So that was it. If he agreed to block publication of *The Gulag Archipelago* in the West, Natalya's influential friends would agree to the publication of *Cancer Ward* in the Soviet Union. Insisting that her only aim was to help him, Natalya asked cautiously whether he would agree to talk to someone a little higher up. Solzhenitsyn replied that he would speak only to the Politburo and 'only about the nation's destiny, not my own'.[16]

In fact, although he conveyed no details to Natalya, Solzhenitsyn had taken steps only weeks earlier to do just as he said. On 5 September he had written a letter of constructive criticism to the leaders of the Soviet Union in the hope of evoking some sort of positive response from them about the nation's destiny. As a sign of good faith he had not treated it as an open letter and did not release it to his friends or to the press. On the contrary he had endeavoured to keep its very existence a secret, dispatching individual copies to leading figures in the Soviet government. It was a genuine attempt at dialogue.

Solzhenitsyn's *Letter to Soviet Leaders* was in many respects a visionary document, detailing the way in which civilization in both the East and the West was in peril – the peril of 'progress'.

> How fond our progressive publicists were, both before and after the revolution, of ridiculing those *retrogrades* ... who called upon us to cherish and have pity on our past, even on the most god-forsaken hamlet with a couple of hovels ... who called upon us to keep horses even after the advent of the motor car, not to abandon small factories for enormous plants and combines, not to discard organic manure in favour of chemical fertilizers, not to mass by the million in cities, not to clamber on top of one another in multi-storey blocks.[17]

The world had been 'dragged along the whole of the Western bourgeois-industrial and Marxist path' only to discover

> what any village greybeard in the Ukraine or Russia had understood from time immemorial ... that a dozen maggots can't go on and on gnawing the same apple *forever*; that if the earth is a *finite* object, then its expanses and resources are finite also, and the *endless, infinite* progress dinned into our heads by the dreamers of the Enlightenment cannot be accomplished on it ... All that 'endless progress' turned out to be an insane, ill-considered, furious dash into a blind

alley. A civilization greedy for 'perpetual progress' has now choked and is on its last legs.[18]

Solzhenitsyn's visionary rhetoric was not aimed solely at condemning past crimes but was an urgent effort to convince the Soviet government of its responsibility as the guardian of the future: 'We have squandered our resources foolishly without so much as a backward glance, sapped our soil ... and contaminated belts of waste land around our industrial centres – but for the moment, at least, far more still remains untainted by us, which we haven't had time to touch. So let us come to our senses in time, let us change our course!'[19]

To secure the future and create a land of clean air and clean water for our children it was necessary to overcome the dictatorship of short-term economic considerations and to renounce many forms of industrial production which result in toxic waste.[20]

Amidst the political polemics, the text of the *Letter to Soviet Leaders* was enlivened by the aesthetic ruminations of a literary master. Thus a discourse on the need for disarmament concluded with a plea for peace – not the peace of the politician but the peace of the poet:

> In reducing our military forces we shall also deliver our skies from the sickening roar of aerial armadas – day and night, all the hours that God made, they perform their interminable flights and exercises over our broad lands, breaking the sound barrier, roaring and booming, shattering the daily life, rest, sleep and nerves of hundreds of thousands of people, effectively addling their brains by screeching overhead ... and all this has been going on for decades and has nothing to do with saving the country – it is a futile waste of energy. Give the country back a healthy *silence*, without which you cannot begin to have a healthy people.[21]

A similar observation offered an alternative to the utterly unnatural life which people were forced to endure in modern cities. Against the huge industrial conurbations Solzhenitsyn contraposed life in the 'old towns – towns made for people, horses, dogs ... towns which were humane, friendly, cosy places, where the air was always clean, which were snow-clad in winter and in spring redolent with garden aromas streaming through the fences into the streets ... An economy of *non*-giantism with small-scale though highly developed technology will not only allow for but will necessitate the building of *new* towns of the *old* type.'[22]

At the conclusion of his heartfelt address Solzhenitsyn pleaded for equally fair treatment for all ideological and moral currents, in particular between all religions. He stated that personally he considered Christianity the only living spiritual force capable of undertaking the spiritual healing of Russia but proposed no special privileges for it, simply that it should be treated fairly and not suppressed. Besides the freedom to worship, he called for 'a free art and literature ... allow us philosophical, ethical, economic and social studies, and you will see what a rich harvest it brings and how it bears fruit – for the good of Russia'.[23]

Although Solzhenitsyn's *Letter to Soviet Leaders* was written specifically from a Russian perspective there were remarkable parallels between its central message and that of the radical economist E. F. Schumacher's *Small is Beautiful*, which was being published almost simultaneously in the West. Schumacher's book was destined to have a dramatic impact on Western thought; its publication served to bolster the environmentalist lobby and launch the 'green' movement. Schumacher's call for sustainable development, eco-friendly economics and human-scale enterprises echoed Solzhenitsyn's own thoughts. 'I came to the same conclusions in parallel with him but independently,' Solzhenitsyn stated. 'If you have read my *Letter to Soviet Leaders* you will see that I say much the same thing as he did at about the same sort of time.'[24]

There were other parallels with Schumacher. Like Solzhenitsyn, Schumacher believed that economic activity subsisted within a higher moral, and ultimately religious, framework. Like Solzhenitsyn he had made his first public profession of faith the previous year, in his case with his reception into the Roman Catholic Church. There was, however, one notable difference. Whereas Schumacher was lauded and applauded by Western leaders, including American President Jimmy Carter, Solzhenitsyn received nothing but a wall of silence in response to his *Letter to Soviet Leaders*. In 1974

Schumacher was awarded the CBE by the British government for his services to economics. In the same year Solzhenitsyn was exiled by the Soviet government as a traitor.

In the last quarter of 1973, Solzhenitsyn remained preoccupied with the subject of Russia's reconstruction along the lines he had outlined in his *Letter to Soviet Leaders*. Specifically, he was in the process of editing a collection of eleven essays, later to be published as *From Under the Rubble*, which was intended to stir debate on matters of fundamental principle concerning the contemporary state of Russian life. Each essay sought to shed light both on the present evils and on possible future long-term solutions. Solzhenitsyn wrote three essays for the collection, the first of which, entitled 'As Breathing and Consciousness Return', included a reiteration of the thoughts on nationhood which he had elucidated in his Nobel Lecture: 'In spite of Marxism, the twentieth century has revealed to us the inexhaustible strength and vitality of national feelings and impels us to think more deeply about this riddle: why is the nation a no less sharply defined and irreducible human entity than the individual? Does not national variety enrich mankind as faceting increases the value of a jewel? Should it be destroyed? And can it be destroyed?'[25] Having stated his own belief in the enriching variety of nations, he compared it with the desire of Andrei Sakharov for an intellectual world leadership, for world government. Such a government, Solzhenitsyn maintained, would be impossible under democracy 'for given universal franchise, when and where would an intellectual elite be elected to govern?' Consequently, any world government would need to be imposed because it would never be elected. It would constitute authoritarian rule. 'Whether such a government proved very bad or excellent, the means of creating it, the principles of its formation and operation, can have nothing in common with modern democracy.'[26]

In October 1973 Solzhenitsyn wrote a postscript to his original essay in which he asked fundamental questions about the nature and meaning of 'happiness' and 'freedom'. The current conception that both were linked to material considerations, such as the absence of poverty or increasing disposable income, was inadequate. At their deepest and most meaningful level happiness and freedom both found their fulfilment on a transcendent spiritual plane. To illustrate the point he gave the example of the desire of the peasants for land in pre-revolutionary Russia: 'The peasant masses longed for *land* and if this in a certain sense means freedom and wealth, in another (and more important) sense it means obligation, in yet another (and its highest) sense it means a mystical tie with the world and a feeling of personal worth.'[27]

Solzhenitsyn used this practical example of natural peasant yearnings as a springboard into a deeper discussion of metaphysical reality:

> Can external freedom for its own sake be the goal of conscious living beings? Or is it only a framework within which other and higher aims can be realized? We are creatures born with inner freedom of will, freedom of choice – the most important freedom of all is a gift to us at birth. External, or social, freedom is very desirable for the sake of undistorted growth, but is no more than a condition, a medium, and to regard it as the object of our existence is nonsense. We can firmly assert our inner freedom even in external conditions of unfreedom ... In an unfree environment we do not lose the possibility of progress toward moral goals (that for instance of leaving this earth better men than our hereditary endowment has made us). The need to struggle against our surroundings rewards our efforts with greater inner success.[28]

On the other hand, a surfeit of comfort, which some mistake as freedom, leads to corruption. For this reason the materially affluent Western democracies were in a state of spiritual confusion. The moral health of civilization had been preserved by past generations who had never known the modern conveniences of technological society: 'a level of moral health incomparably higher than that expressed today in simian radio music, pop songs and insulting advertisements: could a listener from outer space imagine that our planet had already known and left behind it Bach, Rembrandt and Dante?'[29]

If the essay displayed Solzhenitsyn's contempt for the moral bankruptcy of Western materialism, he still saved his fiercest scorn for the immoral totalitarianism of the Soviet system:

Our present system is unique in world history, because over and above its physical and economic constraints, it demands of us total surrender of our souls, continuous and active participation in the general, conscious *lie*. To this putrefaction of the soul, this spiritual enslavement, human beings who wish to be human cannot consent. When Caesar, having exacted what is Caesar's, demands still more insistently that we render unto him what is God's – that is a sacrifice we dare not make![30]

In November Solzhenitsyn wrote another essay for inclusion in *From Under the Rubble*, entitled 'Repentance and Self-Limitation'. A quarter of a century later he would still consider this one of his more important articles, expressing one of his key thoughts.[31] In one important respect it was his own considered reply to the issue of 'National Bolshevism' which had caused such acrimony with the liberal critics of *Novy Mir*. Although he had disagreed strongly with the nature of their critique of National Bolshevism, feeling that they were attacking it for the wrong reasons, Solzhenitsyn was opposed to the xenophobic chauvinism and jingoism of the National Bolsheviks. In 'Repentance and Self-Limitation' he sought to dissect the essence of National Bolshevism, which made communism and patriotism inseparable, praised the Revolution and the subsequent history of the Soviet Union as a triumph of the Russian spirit, and believed that blood alone determined whether one was Russian or non-Russian. As for things spiritual, Solzhenitsyn wrote, all trends are admissible to the National Bolshevik. 'Orthodoxy is not the least bit more Russian than Marxism, atheism, the scientific outlook, or, shall we say, Hinduism. God need not be written with a capital letter, but Government must be.'[32]

Against such triumphalist pseudo-fascism, dressed up in Marxist clothes, Solzhenitsyn placed his own view of love for one's country:

As we understand it patriotism means unqualified and un-wavering love for the nation, which implies not uncritical eagerness to serve, not support for unjust claims, but frank assessment of its vices and sins, and penitence for them. We ought to get used to the idea that no people is eternally

great or eternally noble ... that the greatness of a people is
to be sought not in the blare of trumpets – physical might
is purchased at a spiritual price beyond our means – but in
the level of its *inner* development, in its breadth of soul ...'

Like a latter-day John the Baptist calling on his fellow-countrymen
to repent, Solzhenitsyn reminded them that 'we Russians are not tra-
versing the heavens in a blaze of glory but sitting forlornly on a heap
of spiritual cinders ... And unless we recover the gift of repentance,
our country will perish and will drag down the whole world with it.
Only through the repentance of a multitude of people can the air
and the soil of Russia be cleansed so that a new, healthy national
life can grow up. We cannot raise a clean crop on a false, unsound,
obdurate soil.'[33]

The concept of repentance and self-limitation was not applicable
to nations only. It was equally applicable to individuals, in fact more
so, because any national repentance could only start in the hearts
and minds of individuals. 'We are always anxiously on the lookout
for ways of curbing the inordinate greed of the *other man*, but no
one is heard renouncing his *own* inordinate greed.' It was this selfishness, this pride, at the very heart of man which lay at the root of
society's problems.

After the Western ideal of unlimited freedom, after the
Marxist concept of freedom as acceptance of the yoke of
necessity – here is the true Christian definition of freedom.
Freedom is *self-restriction*! Restriction of the self for the
sake of others!

...this principle diverts us – as individuals, in all forms
of human association, societies and nations – from *outward* to *inward* development, thereby giving us greater
spiritual depth.

The turn toward *inward* development, the triumph of
inwardness over outwardness, if it ever happens, will be a
great turning point in the history of mankind, comparable
to the transition from the Middle Ages to the Renaissance
...If in some places this is destined to be a revolutionary
process, these revolutions will not be like earlier ones –

physical, bloody and never beneficial – but will be *moral revolutions*, requiring both courage and sacrifice, though not cruelty – a new phenomenon in human history ...[34]

A quarter of a century later, Solzhenitsyn had succumbed to more than a trace of scepticism: 'I believe that if people knew how to self-limit they would be morally much higher. Unfortunately, the idea of self-limitation is not successful if you try to propagandize it. It does not resonate. Mostly, I think, only highly religious people are willing to accept this idea. For instance, if you try to propagandize the idea of self-limitation to governments or states and say that they should learn not to grab what belongs to others, this does not have an effect.'[35]

Solzhenitsyn's third and final essay for *From Under the Rubble* was entitled 'The Smatterers', combining a pessimistic appraisal of the recent past, a plaintive cry against present trends, and a defiant optimism about the future. He finished it in January 1974 and passed it to Liusha Chukovskaya, the trusted friend who had helped him for the previous eight years. He requested that she type it, along with the other two essays destined for *From Under the Rubble*, but was surprised when she returned a few days later and launched into a raging tirade against him, against which her previous disquiet over the *Lenten Letter* paled into insignificance. She had been horrified by the content of the essays and thrust a sheaf of notes listing her disagreements into his hands. Her anger was heightened by the confirmation that for all those years she had helped a man with whom she now knew she disagreed on fundamentals.

Chukovskaya was not alone in her apprehensions about the direction that Solzhenitsyn seemed to be taking. Another helper, Mirra Petrova, disliked what she perceived as a reactionary drift in Solzhenitsyn's work, particularly in *August 1914* and *October 1916*, and despised every mention of religion. Solzhenitsyn also alienated his old friend Lev Kopelev who was very critical of the contents of the *Letter to Soviet Leaders*. For his part, Solzhenitsyn thought that Kopelev had reverted to his earlier communist sympathies, feeling that his old ally had become a fierce and abiding foe.

Solzhenitsyn grieved at the cooling or loss of previous friendships, understanding the apprehensions of erstwhile allies but finally unable to accept their disagreements. It must have seemed as though he was losing the warmth of many of those closest to him, finding himself out in the cold in the grimmest heat of battle. Yet he still had the indomitable strength of Alya to lean on. She had just given him their third son in as many years and he knew that, in her at least, he had an ally who agreed with all he was doing and saying. She was his rock, standing firm amid the storms which his own efforts were unleashing upon both of them. Nevertheless the joys of fatherhood and family life could not dispel entirely the sorrows incurred through the sacrifice of old friendships. In a moment of melancholy in December 1973 he had asked himself 'when will the din of battle cease? If only I could go away from it all, go away for many years to the back of beyond with nothing but fields and open skies and woods and horses in sight, nothing to do but write my novel at my own pace ...'[36]

Little could he know that within two months his prayer would be answered, although scarcely in the way he had envisaged. He was about to find himself thrust out in the cold by his enemies as well as his friends. Out in the cold and a long way from home.

NOTES

1. Labedz, *Solzhenitsyn: A Documentary Record*, pp. 270–1.
2. *The Times*, 5 March 1976.
3. Solzhenitsyn, *The Oak and the Calf*, p. 327.
4. Solzhenitsyn, *Invisible Allies*, p. 130.
5. Solzhenitsyn, *The Oak and the Calf*, p. 327.
6. Ibid., p. 330.
7. Alexander Solzhenitsyn, *A Lenten Letter to Pimen, Patriarch of All Russia*, Minneapolis, Minnesota: Burgess Publishing Company, 1972, p. 5.
8. Ibid., p. 8.
9. Quoted in Scammell, *Solzhenitsyn: A Biography*, pp. 768–9.
10. Quoted in Edward E. Ericson Jr., *Solzhenitsyn: The Moral Vision*, Grand Rapids, Michigan: William B. Eerdmans, 1980, p. 4.
11. Ibid.
12. Scammell, *Solzhenitsyn: A Biography*, p. 769.
13. Solzhenitsyn, *The Oak and the Calf*, p. 332.
14. Labedz, *Solzhenitsyn: A Documentary Record*, pp. 267–8.
15. Solzhenitsyn, *The Oak and the Calf*, pp. 363–6.
16. Scammell, *Solzhenitsyn: A Biography*, p. 819.

17. Alexander Solzhenitsyn, *Letter to Soviet Leaders*, London: Index on Censorship, 1974, p. 20.
18. Ibid., p. 21.
19. Ibid., p. 26.
20. Ibid., p. 35.
21. Ibid., p. 37.
22. Ibid. pp. 37–8.
23. Ibid., pp. 56–7.
24. Solzhenitsyn, interview with the author.
25. Alexander Solzhenitsyn *et al.*, *From Under the Rubble*, Boston, Massachusetts: Little, Brown, 1975, p. 15.
26. Ibid., p. 19.
27. Ibid., p. 21.
28. Ibid., pp. 21–2.
29. Ibid., p. 23.
30. Ibid., pp. 24–5.
31. Solzhenitsyn, interview with the author.
32. Solzhenitsyn *et al.*, *From Under the Rubble*, p. 120.
33. Ibid., pp. 120–1.
34. Ibid., pp. 136–7.
35. Solzhenitsyn, interview with the author.
36. Solzhenitsyn, *The Oak and the Calf*, p. 379.

CHAPTER FIFTEEN

COLD-SHOULDERED

The publication of the first volume of *The Gulag Archipelago* in Paris in December 1973 provoked the full fury of the Soviet authorities. Typical of their splenetic response was an article in *Pravda* on 14 January 1974 entitled 'The Path of Treason' in which *The Gulag Archipelago* was described as 'another slanderous book by A. Solzhenitsyn'. It was clearly designed to fool and cheat gullible people with all kinds of fabrications about the Soviet Union, and Solzhenitsyn was literally choking with pathological hatred for the country where he was born and grew up, for the socialist system, for the Soviet people. *The Gulag Archipelago* contained nothing but 'the outpourings of a deranged imagination' and was 'stuffed with cynical falsifications concocted to serve the forces of imperial reaction'. Its author was seeing the Soviet system through the eyes of those who were shooting and hanging communists, revolutionary workers and peasants, while they were defending the black cause of counter-revolution. Solzhenitsyn was guilty of moral degradation, spiritual poverty and, perhaps worst of all, was 'playing the role of a Christian fool'. The history of the labour camps documented in the book was nothing but a vicious fabrication and, anyway, was unnecessary be-cause the Communist Party of the Soviet Union had already subjected abuses of the Soviet legal system in the days of the personality cult to unqualified criticism. The article concluded with an ominous threat: 'Solzhenitsyn deserves the merit for which he has so zealously strived – the fate of a traitor from whom all Soviet working people, and every honest man on earth, cannot but turn away in anger and disgust.'

Four days after the appearance of the *Pravda* article Solzhenitsyn issued a statement in his own defence, complaining that the furious press campaign had concealed the book's purpose from the Soviet reader:

Pravda lies when it says that the author 'sees with the eyes of those who hanged revolutionary workers and peasants'. No! with the eyes of those who were shot and tortured by the NKVD. *Pravda* asserts that in our country there is 'unqualified criticism' of the pre-1956 period. So let them just give us a sample of their unqualified criticism. I have provided them with the richest factual material for it.[1]

Several leading dissidents sprang to Solzhenitsyn's defence, putting themselves at considerable risk as the campaign against him became ever more vociferous and hysterical. Andrei Sakharov and four other dissidents put their name to a letter in which they expressed their deep concern about the 'new threats to Alexander Solzhenitsyn' contained in a recent statement by TASS, the Soviet news agency.

TASS declares that Solzhenitsyn is a traitor to the fatherland and that he is slandering its past. But how can one believe that 'past errors' have been condemned and corrected and at the same time consider slanderous an honest effort to collect and publish people's historical testimonies about a part of those crimes which are on our collective conscience? It is impossible to deny that there were mass arrests, inhuman conditions, forced labour, deliberate annihilation of millions of people in the camps. There was the abolition of the *kulaks*, the persecution and destruction of hundreds of thousands of religious believers, deportations of whole peoples, anti-worker and anti-peasant laws, persecution of former prisoners of war. There were other crimes, appalling in their ruthlessness, cowardice and cynicism.[2]

Responding to this letter by Sakharov and others, the American writer Saul Bellow added his voice to those seeking to protect Solzhenitsyn from further persecution. Writing in the *New York Times*, Bellow declared that the word 'hero', long in disrepute, had been redeemed by Solzhenitsyn. In a counter-threat to the Soviet authorities Bellow warned that further persecution of Solzhenitsyn – deportation, confinement in a madhouse or exile – would be taken as final evidence of the complete moral degeneracy of the Soviet regime.[3]

In the event, the Soviet regime displayed its moral degeneracy just three weeks later. Solzhenitsyn was arrested at his Moscow home on 12 February 1974 and taken to Lefortovo prison where he was charged with treason. On the following day, having been stripped of his Soviet citizenship, he was expelled from his homeland as a traitor. There is little doubt that under Stalin he would have been executed, an indication that the Soviet system had modified its methods if not its intolerant credo. The subtle shift of approach had not been lost on the dissident L. L. Regelson, who wrote an open letter to the Soviet government on 17 February protesting at Solzhenitsyn's banishment:

> You have, it seems, gradually begun to understand that in a spiritual battle an opponent slain is more dangerous than an opponent still living ... But ... you have still not realized that with the appearance of *The Gulag Archipelago*, that hour in history has struck which will be fatal to you ... that tens of murdered millions have risen up against you ... They have long been knocking for entrance into our lives, but there was none to open the door ... *The Gulag Archipelago* is the indictment with which your trial at the hands of the human race begins ... May the paralysis with which God punished your first leader serve as a prophetic prefiguring of the spiritual paralysis which is now inexorably advancing upon you.
>
> ...Perhaps some of you may begin to ask yourself: And is there One over us all who will demand a full reckoning?
>
> Never doubt it – there is.
>
> He will demand a reckoning. And you will answer.
>
> ...Take Russia out of the hands of Cain, and give her back to God.[4]

Six weeks after Solzhenitsyn's expulsion, his family were allowed to leave for Switzerland to join him in his new life in exile. On 27 March, two days before their final departure, Alya had organized a farewell gathering of friends. Many well-known dissidents were in attendance, including Lev Kopelev, Yuli Daniel and Alexander Ginsburg, as well as a number of Western correspondents. In the true spirit of her husband, and in keeping with her own resilient charac- ter, Alya made a fiery and defiant statement to those assembled. 'It is painful to part from Russia,' she said, 'painful that our children are condemned to a life without a homeland, painful and difficult to leave friends who are not protected.' Concerning her husband's ex- pulsion, she stressed that 'they can separate a Russian writer from his native land, but no one has the power and strength to sever his spiritual link with it, to tear Solzhenitsyn away from it. And even if his books are now set ablaze on bonfires, their existence in his homeland is indestructible, just as Solzhenitsyn's love for Russia is indestructible.' In conclusion she echoed the words of the wives of the Decembrists – the rebel aristocrats who had defied the Tsar in December 1825 – who had followed their husbands into exile a cen- tury and a half earlier. 'My place is beside him, but leaving Russia is excruciatingly painful.'[5]

His wife and family now safely with him, Solzhenitsyn began to come to terms with his new life. Throughout all the years of struggle against Soviet censorship, he had never sought to defect to the West. On the contrary, his love for Russia was such that he had earnestly desired to remain on Soviet soil whatever the cost. Nevertheless there was no denying the sense of liberation that accompanied his arrival in Zurich. For the next two years he would enjoy the free- dom to write and say exactly what he wanted without the threat of imprisonment.

Before the end of his first year in exile he completed work on his autobiography *The Oak and the Calf*, published in 1975. Shortly af- terwards he finished a supplement to this entitled *Invisible Allies*, which was not published for a further twenty years for fear of in- criminating his friends and allies still resident in the Soviet Union. The first year of exile also saw the publication of *Prussian Nights*, Solzhenitsyn's poetic account of his memories of front-line service in the Second World War. Meanwhile he was working on *Lenin in Zurich*, his indictment of Lenin's collaboration with Russia's ene- mies during the previous war. Such a revisionist approach to Lenin's shady business deals and to the role of the Germans and big business in the bankrolling of the Bolshevik Revolution would have been tantamount to blasphemy in the Soviet Union. Although Stalin had been dethroned and attacked for nurturing a personality cult, the cult surrounding Lenin was still sacrosanct. He was still the ultimate stainless communist icon, and *Lenin in Zurich* was seen by the Soviets as an act of unforgivable iconoclasm.

Solzhenitsyn had been helped considerably in his research for *Lenin in Zurich* by several historical studies which had been published in the West but were not available in the Soviet Union. Unwittingly, by expelling Solzhenitsyn to the West, his enemies in Russia had opened up a whole new world of research to him, placing powerful new weapons at his disposal. In the author's note at the end of *Lenin in Zurich* Solzhenitsyn expressed gratitude to the writers of these historical studies 'for their close attention to events which determined the course of the twentieth century, but which have been carefully concealed from history, and which because of the direction taken by the development of the West have received little attention'.[6] Questioned about this cryptic conclusion to his study of Lenin, Solzhenitsyn reiterated that the four authors explicitly named and to whom he was particularly indebted in his research for the book were moving against the wind of the century: 'Both the meaning and the facts which they relayed were cast in doubt and certainly most people asked the question "why do we need this?" Specifically, one of the books which had concentrated on Lenin's ties with Germany was simply rejected even though there were stacks of documents to verify its claims and people just continued to deny that these things had ever happened.'[7]

In this defence of unfashionable Western historians, Solzhenitsyn was firing his first warning shots to the governments of the West. Within months of his arrival he had begun to rock the boat, starting to side with Western dissidents as vociferously as he had sided with dissidents in the East. It was clear that, in spite of the claims of the Soviet press, Solzhenitsyn was no mere mouthpiece for the liberal humanists who ruled in the West. He had hinted as much in Volume One of *The Gulag Archipelago*, stating that 'I do not like these "left" and "right" classifications; they are conditional concepts, they are loosely bandied about, and they do not convey the essence.'[8] Unfortunately political thought during the Cold War years was preconditioned by such classifications and anyone who failed to fit neatly on the left-right continuum was doomed to misinterpretation by the stagnant ideologues on both sides of the divide.

Solzhenitsyn had already alienated many dissidents in Russia by his failure to genuflect before the altar of Western two-party democracy. Such a system was no panacea for the problems of totalitarianism, not least because it led to a choice little better than that between Tweedledum and Tweedledee. His pessimism was sometimes seen as authoritarian in nature, a misunderstanding exacerbated by some muddled thinking, or at least some muddled wording, in one of his essays in *From Under the Rubble*. Yet his views were far from anti-democratic as his enthusiasm for the political system in Switzerland indicated. He told Dr Fred Luchsinger, editor-in-chief of the *Neue Zürcher Zeitung*, a Zurich newspaper, that he admired Swiss democracy because it was organized in small local units, such as the village and the canton. Unlike the centralized democracies in other Western countries, the emphasis in Switzerland was on local self-determination and the active participation of the entire population. It reminded him, he informed Luchsinger, of the democratic system in medieval Novgorod. On another occasion he told his Swiss publisher, Otto Walter, that he was very impressed by the treatment Alexander Herzen had received when he sought political asylum in Geneva during the nineteenth century. The authorities in Geneva had asked the federal government in Bern whether they had any objections to Herzen's request for asylum, and the government had replied that it was a matter for Geneva to decide for itself. 'This,' Solzhenitsyn exclaimed, 'really is democracy from the base, when a city can decide questions of national policy for itself.'[9]

Solzhenitsyn repeated his praise of the Swiss political system in an interview on American television in June 1974:

> Swiss democracy has some amazing qualities. First, it is completely silent and works inaudibly. Secondly, there is its stability ... Thirdly, it's an upturned pyramid. That is, there's more power at the local level ... than in the cantons, and more power in the cantons than with the government ... Furthermore, democracy is everyone's responsibility. Each individual would rather moderate his demands than damage the whole structure. The Swiss have such a high sense of responsibility that there are no attempts by groups to seize something for themselves and

elbow out the rest ... Naturally one can only admire such a democracy.[10]

In Solzhenitsyn's eyes the Swiss system represented his own passionate belief in self-limitation incarnated on a national level. It was proof that the principles he lived by could be employed on a practical basis by societies as well as by individuals. Once again there are similarities between Solzhenitsyn's views and those of E. F. Schumacher, who had subtitled *Small is Beautiful* 'a study of economics as if people mattered'. In the Swiss democratic system Solzhenitsyn believed that he was seeing politics as if people mattered.

Solzhenitsyn's interview on American television was timed to coincide with publication of the long-awaited English translation of *The Gulag Archipelago*. As expected, its publication had a huge impact throughout the English-speaking world. 'To live now and not to know this work,' wrote L. W. Webb in the *Guardian*, 'is to be a kind of historical fool missing a crucial part of the consciousness of the age.'[11] His views were echoed around the globe as *The Gulag Archipelago* became an international bestseller. Two million copies of the American paperback edition were published, the book being described by George Kennan in the *New York Review of Books* as 'the most powerful single indictment of a political regime ever to be levelled in modern times'.[12]

Solzhenitsyn had achieved his aim, fulfilling the promise he had made while still a prisoner in the camps he described so graphically in *The Gulag Archipelago*. As a completely unknown prisoner, languishing in the oblivion of the Gulag, he had vowed to let the world know about the Soviet Union's sordid secret – an unspeakable secret that had hushed up the killing of tens of millions of people. Yet he could not have imagined the success which awaited him, the immensity of which was evoked by George Kennan: 'The Soviet leaders cannot, just by ignoring it themselves or attempting to smother it with falsehood, consign it to oblivion or cause it to remain without consequences. It is too large for the craw of the Soviet propaganda machine. It will stick there, with increasing discomfort, until it has done its work.'[13]

Of course the Soviet propaganda machine could always, in time-honoured fashion, simply dismiss such reviews in the American press as the anti-socialist rantings of bourgeois reactionary forces. More difficult was the devastating effect that the French edition was having on the views of the socialist intelligentsia in France. Following publication of *The Gulag Archipelago* the long-standing love affair between French intellectuals and the Soviet Union was brought to an uncomfortable end. Jean-Paul Sartre, Simone de Beauvoir, Louis Aragon and the other *illustrissimi* of the pro-Soviet old guard sank into gloom-laden old age, their lifelong delusions laid bare before their eyes. 'What shall we do?' asked Sartre in a plea to his lover. 'Where shall we go?' 'A whirlwind is carrying me to the grave,' mourned de Beauvoir, 'and I am trying not to think.'[14]

In contrast to the desolate atheism of Sartre and de Beauvoir, Solzhenitsyn was beginning to feel more hopeful about the problems facing the Orthodox Church in the Soviet Union. On 27 September his open letter to the Third Council of the Russian Church Abroad was published in the daily newspaper *Novoe Russkoe Slovo*. It was written at the request of Metropolitan Filaret who had asked him to present his views as to how the portion of the Russian Orthodox Church that existed in freedom could render assistance to the oppressed and captive portion in Russia. No doubt fuelled by nostalgia for the native soil upon which he was no longer free to walk, Solzhenitsyn's letter was full of heartfelt praise for the devoutness of his fellow-countrymen. He spoke of churches filled to the brim, stating that, in the midst of the current castration of faith in the West, there were probably nowhere else on earth such crowded churches as those in the USSR.

> Faith does not suffer when there is scarcely enough space to bow to the ground or to make the sign of the cross. Standing together shoulder to shoulder we support one another against persecution. And the number of faithful far exceeds the number who are willing and able to attend services. In the Ryazan region, with which I am most familiar, more than seventy per cent of all infants are baptized, despite all the prohibitions and persecution. In the cemeteries crosses are replacing the Soviet markers with their star and photograph.[15]

There were still many problems to be surmounted, such as state interference in church affairs, poorly organized or non-existent parishes, and the lack of Christian education for the nation's youth, but Russian young people were finding the way to church on their own and the Church was growing stronger in the fervour of its believers and converts, if not in its formal organization. With evident relish, Solzhenitsyn compared the resurrection of religious faith among the young with the militant atheism of Soviet youth in the honeymoon period following the Revolution. In the years immediately before and after the Revolution, the Church was shunned and subjected to ridicule by young people and the intelligentsia. Solzhenitsyn remembered how many fiery adherents were claimed by militant atheism in the 1920s. 'Those who went on rampages, blew out candles, and smashed icons with axes have now crumbled into dust, like their Union of the Militant Godless.' Fifty years on and the enemies of faith had adopted a different and more subtle, though no less pernicious, persona: 'Since the shiny bauble of unlimited material progress has led all of humanity into a depressing spiritual cul-de-sac, represented with only slight nuances of difference in the East as in the West, I can discover only one healthy course for everyone now living, for nations, societies, human organizations, and above all else for churches. We must confess our sins and errors (our own, not those of others), repent, and use self-restraint in our future development.'[16]

Even if he still remained contemptuous of the spiritual cul-de-sac into which the world had wandered, Solzhenitsyn's words had seldom resonated with such optimism. It seemed that life in the admirable Swiss democracy was, for the liberty-starved writer, as fresh with freedom as the alpine air.

In December 1974 Solzhenitsyn finally travelled to Stockholm to collect his Nobel Prize, four years after it had been awarded to him. In April 1975 he visited Paris, appearing on the popular television programme *Apostrophe*. The programme attracted five million viewers, twice the usual number, and most were captivated by his passionate sincerity and charm. According to *L'Express* Solzhenitsyn was 'a new prophet, the herald of a great religious movement' and *Paris Match* considered him 'a genius ... the equal of Dostoyevsky'.

On 30 June Solzhenitsyn delivered an address to two and a half thousand delegates of the AFL-CIO, America's main trade union organization, at the Hilton Hotel in Washington, DC. He expressed great admiration for America and the American people. The United States was 'a country of the future; a young country; a country of still untapped possibilities; a country of tremendous geographical distances; a country of tremendous breadth of spirit; a country of generosity; a country of magnanimity'.[17] Yet he also spoke about the situation in the Soviet Union where there was occurring a liberation of the human spirit. New generations were growing up which were 'steadfast in their struggle with evil; which are not willing to accept unprincipled compromises; which prefer to lose everything – salary, conditions of existence and life itself – but are not willing to sacrifice conscience; not willing to make deals with evil'.[18] As well as being an expression of praise for his fellow dissidents, Solzhenitsyn's words were a measured attack on the American policy of detente which he believed was a betrayal of his dissident friends in the Soviet Union and amounted to nothing less than a shameful compromise with evil.

Surprisingly considering his pro-American stance, Solzhenitsyn's visit to Washington was most conspicuous for the absence of any invitation to the White House. Henry Kissinger, the US Secretary of State, was known to be uneasy about Solzhenitsyn's outspoken opposition to detente and it was widely suspected that it was he who had blocked the invitation. Certainly the official excuses emanating from the White House were sufficiently lame to raise suspicions about the true motive for the official snub to Solzhenitsyn. President Ford was said not to want a meeting 'without substance'. It seems a little odd that the President of the United States could find nothing of substance to discuss with the author who was currently shaking the Soviet empire with the revelations in *The Gulag Archipelago*, not least because he had found time to pose with both a beauty queen and with Pele, the Brazilian soccer star, only a week or so earlier.

Simon Winchester, the *Guardian*'s Washington correspondent, praised President Ford for his reality and integrity in denying a hearing to the 'shaggy author', the 'hairy polemicist' who had become the 'darling of the redneck population' and who had talked to thousands of 'sagging beer bellies' at the Hilton Hotel. Gratuitous insults and stereotypes aside, Winchester's views were typical of those who now suspected Solzhenitsyn of political incorrectness. One State Department official managed to take the abuse against Solzhenitsyn one step further, foolishly rushing in where even Winchester had feared to tread. 'Let's face it,' he remarked, 'he's just about a Fascist.' This comment provoked the writer D. M. Thomas to justifiable words of contempt. How could anyone suggest that Solzhenitsyn, 'a man who had fought the Nazis and the Bolsheviks, demanded freedom of speech and religion, the rule of morality, grass-roots democracy, ecology before profit, an end to military conscription, and an end to the Soviet empire was ideologically akin to Himmler ...'?[19]

Many Americans were outraged at the White House's cold-shouldering of Solzhenitsyn and President Ford found himself politically embarrassed by the snub. Politicians were as annoyed as their electorates and on 15 July Solzhenitsyn addressed an audience of some eighty congressmen at a reception in his honour held in the Senate Caucus Room. In early October the Senate unanimously adopted a resolution to confer honorary citizenship on him but once again the State Department, in a further example of Kissinger's vindictiveness, intervened to prevent its implementation.

Having caused such controversy in the United States, Solzhenitsyn made his first visit to Britain in February 1976. He arrived as a celebrity and *The Times* reported on 23 February that his portrait had been presented to the Victoria and Albert Museum by Felix Fabian. An entourage of journalists accompanied him as he visited Oxford and Stratford-upon-Avon before his arrival in London. At the BBC Television Centre he criticized senior executives for the decline in the standard of its Russian service, calling for more information to be transmitted to a people bombarded with lies. He believed that the BBC should also broadcast to the minorities in the Soviet Union, for example in Estonian, Latvian and Ukrainian. Above all, the BBC Russian service should offer more religion to its listeners. Christianity, he explained, was the most vital form of dissent in Russia, and some communities were two or three hundred miles from a church. The BBC could and should bring the church into their homes.

The highlight of Solzhenitsyn's visit was an interview on *Panorama*, the BBC's flagship current affairs programme. Five million people watched the original broadcast, while a staggering fifteen million saw the repeat, an audience normally only achieved by popular comedy shows or soap operas. The nation watched and listened but Solzhenitsyn was already beginning to suspect that his words were falling on deaf ears: 'My warnings, the warnings of others – Sakharov's very grave warning directly from the Soviet Union – these go unheeded, most of them fall, as it were, on the ears of the deaf – people who do not want to hear them. Once I used to hope that experience of life could be handed on from nation to nation, and from one person to another ... But now I am beginning to have doubts. Perhaps everyone is fated to live through every experience himself in order to understand.'[20]

More controversially, Solzhenitsyn was beginning to criticize the decadence of the West as vociferously as he criticized the despotism of the East. He warned of the dangers inherent in the retreat of the older generation who had yielded their intellectual leadership. It was, he said, 'against the natural order of things for those who are youngest, with the least experience of life, to have the greatest influence in directing the life of society'.[21]

During the interview Solzhenitsyn took the opportunity to defend himself from the various labels that had been pinned on him by hostile critics on both sides of the Iron Curtain:

> Take the word 'nationalist' – it has become almost meaningless. It is used constantly. Everyone flings it around, but what is a 'nationalist'? If someone suggests that his country should have a large army, conquer the countries which surround it, should go on expanding its empire, that sort of person is a nationalist. But if, on the contrary, I suggest that my country should free all the peoples it has conquered, should disband the army, should stop all aggressive actions – who am I? A nationalist! If you love England, what are you? A nationalist! And when are you not a nationalist? When you *hate* England, then you are not a nationalist.[22]

A week after leaving England, Solzhenitsyn gave an interview on French television which provoked an official protest from the Soviet government. Yet this paled into insignificance beside the furore caused by the visit to Spain which followed. On 20 March he was interviewed on Spanish television and later the same day he gave a press conference. Spain was emerging from the authoritarian regime of General Franco, who had died the previous year after almost forty years as dictator, and it was natural that many of the questions from the press should concern the country's first tentative steps towards democracy. Solzhenitsyn offered tacit support for those seeking greater democratic freedom in Spain in the wake of Franco's demise but warned against proceeding too quickly. The Western democracies were weak and decadent and were not a good role model for Spain to emulate. He courted controversy by stating that 'the Christian world view' had triumphed in the Spanish Civil War and provoked outrage in liberal-socialist circles by suggesting that, compared with the Soviet Union, Spain was a free society. He had heard critics describe contemporary Spain as a dictatorship and totalitarian but after travelling around the country he could say that these critics clearly did not understand the meaning of the words they were using. No Spaniard was tied to his place of residence. Spaniards could travel abroad freely, and newspapers and magazines from all over the world were on sale in the kiosks. There was free and easy access to photocopying machines, strikes were permitted and there had recently been a limited amnesty for political prisoners. 'If we had such conditions in the Soviet Union today, we would be thunderstruck, we would say this was unprecedented freedom, the sort of freedom we haven't seen in sixty years.'[23] His words were well intentioned and, indeed, well reasoned and broadly accurate, but there was a predictable reaction from the world's press. Most outrageous of all the misrepresentations was the report in *Le Monde* which carried the headline, 'Solzhenitsyn Thinks that the Spaniards Live in "Absolute Freedom"'. Others followed the same line, attacking Solzhenitsyn for what they perceived as his exaltation of the Franco regime. Very few even mentioned that Solzhenitsyn had actually approved of the democratic reforms in Spain, merely urging that the country should be cautious in its approach.

As Solzhenitsyn watched the world headlines emerge, turning the half-truth into a lie, he was surely reminded of his treatment at the hands of the Soviet press. Indeed, a spokesman of the Left in Spain, reverting to a crude form of attack reminiscent of *Pravda*, alleged that he must 'be suffering from a mental illness'.[24]

It was grimly ironic, but the sensationalism of the press disguised the fact that most people had missed the point entirely. Solzhenitsyn's general tone throughout the conference had been not confrontational but genuinely conciliatory. He wanted to escape, he said, from the tyranny of left and right. Furthermore, the opposition between East and West was relative and was not of paramount importance. Humanity was in crisis but the crisis was essentially spiritual and not political. Both the communist East and the capitalist West suffered from the same disease: 'the ailment of materialism, the ailment of inadequate moral standards. It was precisely the absence of moral standards that led to the appearance of such a horrible dictatorship as the Soviet one, and of such a greedy consumer society as the West's.'[25]

The origins of the problem, he explained, were in the transformation from the Middle Ages to the Renaissance. This had been a materialist reaction to the exaggeration of the spiritual in medieval times. The process, once set in motion, was progressive, or rather regressive. Mankind had grown more and more materialistic, had more and more neglected its spirituality, the outcome being the universal triumph of materiality and the consequent decline in spiritual life. 'The picture today's world presents to the eye strikes me as appalling. I think that if mankind is not doomed to die, it must restore a proper appreciation of values. In other words, spiritual values must again predominate over material values. This does not mean that we should return to the Middle Ages. Every development is enriched by time. I am speaking of new horizons, or so it seems to me.'[26]

In these carefully considered sentences Solzhenitsyn had confessed his credo, his very *raison d'être*, but his words, his warnings, had once more fallen on the ears of the deaf, those who did not want to hear. Scandal, not spiritual values, sold newspapers and it was the scandal which made the following morning's headlines.

Perhaps Solzhenitsyn had already received a premonition of the way his words would be manipulated by the media. Towards the end of the press conference he had requested politely if he could make a little digression, pleading with reporters to use his answers in full or to omit certain topics altogether. 'I know from ... experience ... that newspapers usually take only what they need. They tear some phrase out of context, destroy all proportion, and distort my ideas ... Leave the scissors alone, do you understand what I mean?'[27] The assembled journalists said nothing but, sharpening their pencils like knives, they were already planning the perfect murder, the next day's character assassination.

Before long Solzhenitsyn despaired of ever getting a fair hearing from the Western media. Thereafter, he would rarely appear in public or grant interviews. Silence was the safest course of action because silence, unlike words, could not easily be distorted. If the world insisted on being deaf, he would become dumb, speaking only through his books.

In the meantime, his brief honeymoon with the West well and truly over, he yearned for his home in the East. 'I never intended to become a Western writer,' he told a reporter at the Spanish press conference, 'I came to the West against my will. I write only for my homeland ... I cannot worry about what someone somewhere makes of what I write and if he uses it in his own way.' Another reporter had asked him why he lived in Switzerland. 'I do not live in Switzerland,' he replied, 'I live in Russia. All my interests, all the things I care about, are in Russia.'[28]

Thrust out into the cold from the Russia he loved, he now found himself being cold-shouldered by the West that, increasingly, he loathed.

NOTES

1. Solzhenitsyn, *The Oak and the Calf*, p. 531.
2. Labedz, *Solzhenitsyn: A Documentary Record*, p. 362.
3. *New York Times*, 15 January 1974.
4. Solzhenitsyn, *The Oak and the Calf*, p. 538.
5. *New York Times*, 28 March 1974.
6. Alexander Solzhenitsyn, *Lenin in Zurich*, London: The Bodley Head, 1976, p. 223.
7. Solzhenitsyn, interview with the author.
8. Solzhenitsyn, *The Gulag Archipelago Volume One*, p. 475.
9. Scammell, *Solzhenitsyn: A Biography*, p. 883.
10. Ibid.
11. Quoted in Thomas, *Solzhenitsyn: A Century in His Life*, p. 446.
12. Ibid.

13. Ibid.
14. Ibid.
15. Niels C. Nielsen, *Solzhenitsyn's Religion*, p. 144.
16. Ibid., pp. 154-5.
17. Alexander Solzhenitsyn, *Detente: Prospects for Democracy and Dictatorship*, New Brunswick, New Jersey: Transaction Books, 1977, p. 37.
18. Ibid., p. 36.
19. Thomas, *Solzhenitsyn: A Century in His Life*, p. 433.
20. Solzhenitsyn, *Warning to the Western World*, p. 8.
21. Ibid., p. 9.
22. Ibid., p. 12.
23. Quoted in Scammell, *Solzhenitsyn: A Biography*, p. 946.
24. Ibid., p. 947.
25. Ibid.
26. Ibid.
27. Ibid., p. 948.
28. Ibid.

CHAPTER SIXTEEN

CHAMPION OF ORTHODOXY

In the aftermath of the storm surrounding his comments in Spain, Solzhenitsyn's public appearances, though less frequent as he became more defensive, met with increasing degrees of hostility. At the end of March 1976 his outspoken criticisms of British complacency and loss of will in the face of her international responsibilities prompted a dismissive response from the new Prime Minister, James Callaghan, who stated that he totally rejected Solzhenitsyn's views.[1]

A few weeks later Solzhenitsyn was interviewed by Georges Suffert, editor of *Le Point*. Throughout the interview, Suffert displayed a thinly disguised air of animosity and was unmoved by his quarry's efforts to describe his discovery of life and God in the labour camps. Instead he interjected with a quite unprovoked question about whether Solzhenitsyn wanted a world war, to which the Russian responded that only Suffert's 'cock-eyed' conception of history could have prompted such a query. 'Inner purpose is more important than politics' of any kind, he declared.[2]

On 27 April the screening of a BBC television interview with Solzhenitsyn on *The Book Programme*, during which he discussed the recently published English translation of *Lenin in Zurich*, met with a furious response from the Soviet Union. Sir Charles Curran, the BBC's director-general, had been warned on two occasions prior to the programme's transmission that broadcasting the interview would jeopardize Curran's proposed visit to Moscow. The Soviets carried out the threat and postponed the visit, informing Curran of their decision two days later. A telegram from Sergei Lapin, chairman of the state committee of the Soviet Council of Ministers for television and radio, stated that the BBC television programme of 27 April on Solzhenitsyn's slanderous book confirmed once again that the

BBC continued with Cold War attitudes and encouraged libellous attacks against the Soviet Union.[3]

Away from the prying eyes of the media, Solzhenitsyn was making plans to move his family from Zurich in the heart of Europe to Vermont in the backwaters of the United States. He was looking for an escape from the insanity of media manipulation to the tranquillity of a country retreat where he could concentrate once more on his writing. He had first struck upon the idea of living in Vermont during his travels through Canada, Alaska and the United States in 1975. A three-day visit to Vermont's Norwich University, at the invitation of its Russian department, had impressed him immensely, and he had been comforted by the echoes of his beloved Russia in the state's climate and countryside, its crisp, cold air and evergreen forests. He had asked a young architect called Alexis Vinogradov to look out for a suitable property in the area and authorized him to purchase and oversee the renovation of a property on the outskirts of Cavendish, a Vermont village. In the summer of 1976 Solzhenitsyn asked for, and was granted, a permanent residence visa for the family and in September the Solzhenitsyns left Switzerland for the United States.

For several months after his arrival the villagers saw no sign of the famous writer who had moved into their midst. A large fence was erected around the property and the reclusive Russian showed no intention of emerging into public life. It was not until the following February that Solzhenitsyn was finally seen in public when he and Alya attended the annual town meeting in the school gymnasium.

Yet the peace that the Solzhenitsyn family had managed to salvage from the intrusive eyes of the media belied the international turmoil that their very existence was still causing. On 3 April 1977, the Soviet government continued its ultimately futile war of attrition by stripping Alya of her Soviet citizenship for making statements prejudicial to the Soviet Union.[4] Meanwhile in London, Collet's International Bookshop confessed that the books of Solzhenitsyn and Andrei Sakharov were not being sold for fear of offending the Soviets. The shop admitted that it had received extended credit from the Soviet Union, running into six figures.[5]

Amid the hostility there were a few voices of sympathy speaking out in Solzhenitsyn's defence. In England the formidable Bernard

Levin came to his aid. In an article entitled 'Solzhenitsyn's Roar of Defiance on the Long Winter March into Night', published in *The Times* on 18 November 1977, Levin offered an alternative view to the dismissive way in which *Prussian Nights* had been discussed by some of the reviewers. He spoke of Solzhenitsyn's arrival in the West as being

> like some huge volcano, his expulsion representing the most complete confession of moral bankruptcy and turpitude yet made by his country's rulers...
>
> It soon became clear that the volcano was by no means extinct; Solzhenitsyn's television appearances in this country (and in the United States) had an effect so great and continuing that the only appropriate analogy is with the way in which some astronomers think the universe started; the echoes of Solzhenitsyn's Big Bang continue to vibrate in the mind, and the fallout is still fluttering to earth.

Having defended Solzhenitsyn so evocatively, Levin proceeded to evoke the power of his poem:

> Epic poems, and that is what *Prussian Nights* is, are not much in fashion nowadays: Chesterton's *Lepanto* was a long time ago. And I suspect that this very fact has coloured the reaction of some of those who have written about Solzhenitsyn's. For it has to be read in a single sitting, if the sweep and force of the work are to be properly felt ... the most powerful aspect of the poem is the way the poet matches the drive of his verse, its pulsing metre and varying pace, to the demands of his account of the Russian armies' drive. The reader is swept along with the advance, checking when it does, watching Solzhenitsyn's men pause to eat, loot or rape; this sense of being part of the poem is what makes me say that the reader should treat it as a single span across history, to take individual lines or even scenes being little more use in grasping the whole than to scoop a single pailful from a rushing river.

Levin concluded by describing *Prussian Nights* as a mighty achievement which confirmed Solzhenitsyn's place as a spiritual and artistic giant.

Yet if he was a giant in the spiritual or artistic sphere he was still a David in the face of the Goliaths of international power politics. In February 1978 Alya issued a statement about the latest attempts by the KGB to destroy a fund founded by her husband to help dissidents in the Soviet Union. The fund – known somewhat awkwardly as the 'Russian Social Fund to Help Those Who Are Persecuted and Their Families' – had been set up by Solzhenitsyn soon after his expulsion from the Soviet Union. He had donated royalties from *The Gulag Archipelago* to provide the initial finance and the fund had subsequently helped hundreds of families, mainly in the form of clothing or medicine or by the provision of travelling expenses for relatives to visit prison camps.

Alya was president of her husband's fund, while its main executor inside the Soviet Union had been Alexander Ginsburg, a prominent dissident, who had held the post for three years until his arrest in February the previous year. Soon after Ginsburg's arrest, security authorities had exiled the other main figures working for the fund to Siberia or persecuted them into emigration. Alya explained in her statement that Ginsburg's wife, Irina, had taken over from her husband as the main executor but was being hindered by Soviet prison authorities in her efforts to provide assistance to prisoners and their families. The authorities had refused to pass on warm clothes and a Bible, and had severely limited the contents of food parcels. Alya also claimed that KGB agents operating in Switzerland were attempting to obtain details of those people receiving assistance from the fund so that they could step up the government's efforts to block its work.[6]

As the KGB fumed at his efforts on behalf of imprisoned dissidents, Solzhenitsyn was preparing a speech which would incur the wrath of the world's other superpower. On 8 June he delivered the commencement address at Harvard University, during which he condemned the Western world as being morally bankrupt. 'It is time, in the West,' he said, 'to defend not so much human rights as human obligations.' The triumph of rights over obligations had resulted in a destructive and irresponsible freedom, leading to 'the abyss of human decadence'. He cited the 'misuse of liberty for moral violence against young people, such as motion pictures full of pornography, crime, and horror', which illustrated the inability of the West to defend itself against the corrosion of evil.[7]

Solzhenitsyn singled out the media for particular scorn, criticizing the press for its shameless intrusion into the privacy of well-known people so that its readers were having 'their divine souls stuffed with gossip, nonsense, vain talk'. Having been misrepresented on numerous occasions himself, he seemed to relish the opportunity to strike back against media distortion: 'Hastiness and superficiality – these are the psychic diseases of the twentieth century and more than anywhere else this is manifested in the press. In-depth analysis of a problem is anathema to the press; it is contrary to its nature. The press merely picks out sensational formulas.' The media, he maintained, had become 'the greatest power within the Western countries, exceeding that of the legislature, the executive, and the judiciary'. Yet its power was deeply undemocratic: 'According to what law has it been elected and to whom is it responsible?'[8]

Having vented his spleen on the media, he turned his critical attention to the West as a whole, stating that Russia could not look to the West as a model to emulate.

> No, I could not recommend your society as an ideal for the transformation of ours. Through deep suffering, people in our country have now achieved a spiritual development of such intensity that the Western system in its present state of spiritual exhaustion does not look attractive ... After the suffering of decades of violence and oppression, the human soul longs for things higher, warmer, and purer than those offered by today's mass living habits, introduced as by a calling card by the revolting invasion of commercial advertising, by TV stupor, and by intolerable music.[9]

These glittering trinkets of trash-technology were the ephemeral effects of a materialist philosophy born out of the anticlerical impatience of the Renaissance:

I refer to the prevailing Western view of the world which was born in the Renaissance and has found political expression since the age of Enlightenment. It became the basis for political and social doctrine and could be called rationalistic humanism or humanistic autonomy: the proclaimed and practiced autonomy of man from any higher force above him. It could also be called anthropocentricity, with man seen as the centre of all.[10]

This was a development of the view he had endeavoured to convey at the press conference in Spain. By turning its back on the scholastic philosophers and enthroning itself as the highest authority and judge in the universe, humanity had sown the seeds of its own malaise:

The humanistic way of thinking, which has proclaimed itself our guide, did not admit the existence of intrinsic evil in man, nor did it see any task higher than the attainment of happiness on earth. It started modern Western civilization on the dangerous trend of worshipping man and his material needs. Everything beyond physical well-being and the accumulation of material goods, all other human requirements and characteristics of a subtler and higher nature, were left outside the area of attention of state and social systems, as if human life did not have any higher meaning. Thus gaps were left open for evil, and its drafts blow freely today.[11]

The results of such humanism were evident for all to see. The world was in a harsh spiritual crisis and a political impasse, so that all the celebrated technological achievements of progress could not redeem the twentieth century's moral poverty.

Solzhenitsyn then expounded the philosophy of sacrifice and self-limitation he had learned in the labour camps. If, as claimed by the humanists, man's only purpose was to be happy, he would not have been born to die. 'Since his body is doomed to death, his task on earth evidently must be more spiritual: not a total engrossment in everyday life, not the search for the best ways to obtain material goods and then their carefree consumption.' On the contrary, the purpose of life must be linked to the fulfilment of a higher duty 'so that one's life journey may become above all an experience of moral growth: to leave life a better human being than one started it'.[12]

Perhaps the most memorable observation of any of the ten to fifteen thousand people who endured the drizzly rain to hear Solzhenitsyn speak was made by Richard Pipes, professor of history at Harvard University and former director of its Russian Research Center: 'we had heard a devastating attack on the contemporary West – for its loss of courage, its self-indulgence, its self-deception. It was as if the speaker, a refugee from hell, had excoriated us, denizens of purgatory, for not living in paradise.'[13]

Solzhenitsyn's speech sparked a storm of protest in the media. The *Washington Post* on 11 June accused him of grossly misunderstanding Western society while the *New York Times* two days later believed that 'Mr Solzhenitsyn's world view seems to us far more dangerous than the easy-going spirit which he finds so exasperating ... Life in a society run by zealots like Mr Solzhenitsyn is bound to be uncomfortable for those who do not share his vision or ascribe to his beliefs.' On 20 June Rosalynn Carter, the US President's wife, attacked Solzhenitsyn's Harvard speech during a speech of her own at the National Press Club in Washington, claiming that there was 'no unchecked materialism' in the United States.[14]

As of old, there were a few friendly voices straining to be heard above the general discordant din of Solzhenitsyn's growing army of foes. George F. Will, a syndicated writer with the *Washington Post*, compared Solzhenitsyn to an Old Testament prophet who allowed no rest and who stirred a reaction that revealed the complacency of society.[15] Will accused Solzhenitsyn's critics of intellectual parochialism, suggesting that 'the spacious skepticism of the *New York Times* extends to all values except its own'.[16] Compared with the narrow-minded parochialism of his critics, Solzhenitsyn's arguments were, Will observed, broadly congruent with the ideas of Cicero, Augustine, Aquinas, Pascal, Thomas More and Edmund Burke. Perhaps the *New York Times* would have dismissed these eminent thinkers as zealots like Mr Solzhenitsyn who had nothing of importance to say to the modern world.

The controversy surrounding the Harvard address dragged on for several weeks, crossing the Atlantic on 26 July when *The Times* decided to print the entire text of Solzhenitsyn's speech. Several letters were published in response, most of which seemed singularly to have missed the point. Only one, from a Mr R. J. Berney of Norfolk, appeared to appreciate 'its depth and clarity of vision of our, the Western world's, "easy, easy" extinction of the human spirit'. It was a speech of penetration which illuminated the real challenge, real life, real hope. Mr Berney contrasted Solzhenitsyn's address with a speech by the British Prime Minister James Callaghan, which had been printed in *The Times* on the same day. Unlike Solzhenitsyn's prescient warnings, Callaghan's speech 'woos us still further into the cosy hold of that funeral conveyance, the modern Western democratic state, in whose death throes we feel no pain, just nothing'.[17]

When the dust of discourse and dissent on both sides of the Atlantic had finally settled, it was clear that the overriding verdict on Solzhenitsyn's speech was negative, reinforcing the Russian exile's sense of alienation and strengthening his desire to retreat into his fortress-like home in Vermont. In this domestic sanctuary, surrounded by no one except his wife and three sons, he could work unhindered, heedless of the clamour from a hostile world. Furthermore, it was in the security and seclusion of his home that the increasingly reclusive writer came alive in a way seldom seen except by his family and closest friends. His son Ignat regrets that the public image of his father is one of sternness and severity, stating that the 'common public impression is entirely inaccurate'.

> My father has many facets to his character that are often overlooked or else are unknown to those who see him merely as stern or severe. For example, he has several talents over and above his gifts as a writer. He has tremendous acting ability and as a young man felt attracted to the theatre. He is also a brilliant teacher and he gave my brothers and I daily lessons in history, algebra, geometry and physics. He had all of us in stitches with his imitations, whether of public figures or one of the family. He could do all the different voices. It was stand-up comedy. He would also use his powers as a mimic, and his talents as an actor, to great effect when telling a story. He was a great story-teller. He would change his voice for each of the characters. It

was so funny. Yet he could also be terribly sombre on occasion, if troubled by affairs in Russia or by some difficult chapter in his writing. The point is that my father is very dynamic. He has a very dynamic personality. But that does not make him unusually stern or severe. In fact, everybody who ever met him expecting to be confronted by this severity came away with the opposite impression.[18]

Ignat's childhood memories of his father were an echo of Dimitri Panin's memories of Solzhenitsyn during their days as prisoners in the Marfino *sharashka* thirty years earlier: 'a man of exceptional vitality who is so constituted that he never seemed to get tired ... He often put up with our society simply out of courtesy, regretting the hours he was wasting on our idle pastimes. On the other hand, when he was in good form or allowed himself some time for a little amusement, we got enormous pleasure from his jokes, witticisms, and yarns.' On such occasions, Panin remembered, the flush on Solzhenitsyn's cheeks deepened and 'his nose whitened, as if carved from alabaster':

> It was not often that one saw this side of him – his sense of humour. He had the ability to catch the subtlest mannerisms, gestures, and intonations – things that usually escape the rest of us – and then to reproduce them with such artistry that his audience literally rocked with laughter. Unfortunately, he only indulged himself in this fashion very occasionally among his close friends – and only if it was not at the expense of his work.[19]

It is a great pity that this aspect of Solzhenitsyn's character, his *joie de vivre*, his sense of humour, his abilities as a comic and a mimic, were lost on the general public. Why was the public image so much at variance with the reality? Was it a product of media stereotyping or merely a failure on the part of Solzhenitsyn to display his lighter side? Ignat believed the former to be the case:

> I think it is because people, and particularly the press, think in stock responses. They already have a template for

the image of Solzhenitsyn as 'reclusive, severe, a modern-day Jeremiah' ...

The trouble is that the press in the UK and the US did not read Solzhenitsyn's books. Those who accuse him of the most outlandish views have not read his books. The only basis for the unjustifiable image is that his tone of voice and delivery is not what the West is used to. For instance, when my father made his controversial Harvard address, he was being genuine and passionate, but the depth of his passion was seen as impolite. Harsh. Perhaps this was made worse by the fact that he spoke in Russian and his words were heard through an interpreter. Possibly this depersonalized the passion making it sound harsher than it was. Either way, my father's approach is not comprehended in anglo-saxon circles. His approach is not anglo-saxon. He is not polite enough for anglo-saxons. I would add, however, that this attitude to my father is confined only to the anglo-saxon world. It does not apply elsewhere. In France, for instance, he is truly widely read and widely appreciated. People there have really read what he wrote. In France, a man named Bernard Pivot hosts a highly popular television show on books, which in itself would be unimaginable in the US. My father has been interviewed by Pivot on three separate occasions, once in the seventies, once in the eighties, and once in the nineties. On each occasion the ratings went through the roof. One simply cannot imagine such a thing happening in the US or UK. In France, intellectual or spiritual issues, philosophy for instance, are taken seriously. In the anglo-saxon world they are sometimes trivialized or marginalized.[20]

Ignat Solzhenitsyn's analysis of his father's anomalous position in the Anglo-Saxon world arises from his own unique and privileged vantage point, not only as Solzhenitsyn's son but as someone brought up straddling the Anglo-Saxon and the Russian cultural traditions. He and his brothers attended the local high school, receiving an American education, but spoke Russian at home and were given a Russian perspective through the home tutoring they received from their parents. In addition to the lessons and stories from their father, their mother gave them frequent lessons in Russian, especially Russian poetry. She was very enthusiastic about teaching her children the poetry of their homeland.[21]

'We were raised as Russians living in exile,' Ignat explains:

> We followed current events as they unfolded, first through father, who would update the family on any pertinent news he may have gleaned that day from the BBC or VOA [Voice of America] (I remember distinctly father informing us of Soviet tanks invading Afghanistan, for instance), and later of course on our own, through newspapers and television. Russia's past, present and future were always central in the family consciousness, and this was imbibed by us children naturally. Outside the home, when we began attending the local schools, we learned English, made friends, played sports, and did most of the things that kids in Vermont do. In retrospect, I certainly felt comfortable among our friends and neighbours, and the surrounding culture. The duality of Russia at home and America outside unfolded very naturally and with no effort to self-insulate or, vice versa, to integrate furiously.[22]

Ignat and his brothers also enjoyed a very loving relationship with both parents:

> I think I can confidently speak for my brothers also, when I say that we have been fortunate to have such parents as ours. Burdened as they were by the seemingly impossible tasks of writing and publishing twenty volumes of father's collected works with practically no help, and certainly without the stable of secretaries, editors, and publicists that most writers in America employ; and of fighting in the public arena for an understanding of the communist threat, etc., they were still able to devote more time and effort to our upbringing than less busy parents usually do. We were, and remain today, a very tightly knit family, and the stability and closeness of family life were quite wonderful. Of

course I am very close with my father, and this has never been measured by the amount of hours he actually spent with us ... he could pack more into two hours than most fathers could in twenty.[23]

On 13 February 1979, the fifth anniversary of his expulsion from Russia, Solzhenitsyn emerged from self-imposed reclusive life to be interviewed by the BBC Russian service. The interview was broadcast to his homeland and Solzhenitsyn's message to his fellow-countrymen contained a complex, though not contradictory, mixture of pessimism and optimism. There was pessimism in the belief that events were clearly moving toward a world war, although Western statesmen deceived themselves that the superpowers were advancing toward detente, while the optimism sprang from the hope that forces could still emerge in the West which would awaken and restore it to health. 'I particularly hope for the United States, where there are many untapped, unawakened forces quite unlike those which operate on the surface of newspaper, intellectual, and metropolitan life. For example, the people reacted to my Harvard speech in quite the opposite way to the way the newspapers did. There was a great flood of letters to me and the editors in which the readers mocked their newspapers' attitude.'[24] He saw a source of hope in the fact that many young people were becoming more sensitive to the truth and 'seem to be able to forge through the welter of rubbish, striving and seeking'. There was the possibility that these young people could form the vanguard of a genuine rise towards religion. 'And of course, we must consider the new Pope a banner of the time. It's ... words fail me ... it's a gift from God!'[25]

Throughout the interview Solzhenitsyn displayed a resolute optimism about the fate of his own country. 'Communism is a dead dog,' he proclaimed triumphantly. The most important gain from sixty years of Soviet rule was that Russians had been liberated from the socialist contagion. There was now a totally different moral atmosphere in Russia as though the people were not living under Soviet rule at all. 'People are behaving as though those vampires, this dragon that sits over us, simply didn't exist. The air is different now.' This led him to express a hope, a dream, which he was convinced was more than mere wishful thinking: 'Without doubt I shall soon return to my native land through my books, and I hope in person too.'[26]

Six weeks later Solzhenitsyn received welcome, if unexpected, support from the Prince of Wales. During an address to the Australian Academy of Science in Canberra on 26 March, Prince Charles agreed with Solzhenitsyn about the loss of courage in the West. The Prince referred to the devastating but constructive lecture at Harvard University and concurred with its conclusions, stating his own belief that it was 'now essential to consider the human aspects and to examine industrial society from the standpoint of what it does to the human qualities of man, to his soul and his spirit'.[27]

Questions of the soul and the spirit were paramount in Solzhenitsyn's mind as he commenced his sixth year in exile. He was now more concerned with spiritual renewal in Russia and the world than he was with political reconstruction. Indeed, he believed that the latter would be impossible, and efforts to achieve it consequently futile, if it were not preceded by the former. A conversion of heart must precede any conversion of society. With this in mind, he was to emerge during the 1980s as a champion of Orthodoxy, in both its specifically Russian and its broader Catholic manifestations.

Solzhenitsyn's Russian Orthodox faith was becoming an increasingly important part of his life. Everyone in the house in Vermont wore a cross, Lent was observed rigorously and Easter was more important than Christmas. The children's saints' days were celebrated as enthusiastically as their birthdays and there was an Orthodox chapel in the library annexe where services were said whenever a priest came to the house.

It was scarcely surprising that Solzhenitsyn's stance, his moral objections to modern materialism and his outspoken defence of spiritual values should attract the attention of other Christian writers. In 1980 the American writer and critic Edward E. Ericson published *Solzhenitsyn: The Moral Vision*, intended as an exposition of Solzhenitsyn's religious faith. Ericson was concerned that Solzhenitsyn for the most part had been misinterpreted and misunderstood:

> The main impediment, in my opinion, to understanding Solzhenitsyn has to do with the spirit of the times. Although Solzhenitsyn is thoroughly conversant with the currents of

thought which prevail in his own day, he chooses to stand largely opposed to them ... Even more important, though not unrelated, is the fact that in a day when secular humanism flourishes among the cultural and intellectual elite, he holds fast to traditional Christian beliefs.[28]

The foreword to Ericson's book was written by Malcolm Muggeridge, a man whose path through life had paralleled that of Solzhenitsyn in significant respects. He had, of course, not suffered the intense physical trials of Solzhenitsyn but his spiritual trials were akin to those of the Russian writer. He had passed from being a pro-Soviet socialist in the twenties and thirties, through a heart-searching period of disillusionment and rigorous self-assessment, to a final acceptance of orthodox Christianity. In his foreword Muggeridge displayed his admiration for Solzhenitsyn, highlighting 'the sheer greatness of the man in face of afflictions and dangers'. Muggeridge believed that Solzhenitsyn 'speaks out more bravely and understands more clearly what is going on in the world than any other commentator'. Yet even praise such as this was insufficient as Muggeridge echoed the reverence shown by others who saw the Russian as a modern-day prophet. 'I see him as being in the same category as, in the words of the psalmist, one of the holy prophets which have been since the world began; like the great Isaiah, he writes and speaks splendid words of encouragement and hope to people in darkness and despair.'

If Solzhenitsyn was the champion of orthodoxy, Muggeridge wanted to be his ally, defending the Russian from the attacks of the media. Solzhenitsyn's Christianity was something that the media had glossed over or ignored:

to fulfil the media's requirements, he should have felt liberated when, as an enforced exile, he found himself living amidst the squalid lawlessness and libertinism that in the western world passes for freedom. What amazing perceptiveness on his part to have realized straight away, as he did, that the true cause of the West's decline and fall was precisely the loss of a sense of the distinction between good and evil, and so of any moral order in the universe, without which no order at all, individual or collective, is attainable.

So, instead of pleasing the media by saluting the new-found Land of the Free, Solzhenitsyn sees western man as sleepwalking into the selfsame servitude that in the Soviet Union has been imposed by force ... On the campuses and the TV screen, in the newspapers and the magazines, often from the pulpits even, the message is being proclaimed – that Man is now in charge of his own destiny and capable of creating a kingdom of heaven on earth in accordance with his own specifications, without any need for a God to worship or a Saviour to redeem him or a Holy Spirit to exalt him. How truly extraordinary that the most powerful and prophetic voice exploding this fantasy, Solzhenitsyn's, should come from the very heartland of godlessness and materialism after more than sixty years of the most intensive and thoroughgoing indoctrination in an opposite direction ever to be attempted!

NOTES

1. *The Times*, 25 and 31 March 1976.
2. Dunlop, *Solzhenitsyn in Exile*, p. 262.
3. *The Times*, 1 May 1976.
4. *The Times*, 4 April 1977.
5. *The Times*, 26 July 1977.
6. *The Times*, 22 February 1978.
7. Ronald Berman (ed.), *Solzhenitsyn at Harvard*, Washington, DC: Ethics and Public Policy Center, 1980, pp. 8–9.
8. Ibid., p. 10.
9. Ibid., pp. 12–13.
10. Ibid., p. 16.
11. Ibid., pp. 16–17.
12. Ibid., p. 19.
13. Ibid., p. 115.
14. *The Times*, 21 June 1978.
15. Berman, *Solzhenitsyn at Harvard*, p. 33.
16. Ibid.
17. *The Times*, 1 August 1978.
18. Ignat Solzhenitsyn, interview with the author, 24 September 1998.

19. Panin, *Notebooks of Sologdin*, p. 265.
20. Ignat Solzhenitsyn, interview with the author.
21. Ibid.
22. Ignat Solzhenitsyn, letter to the author, August 1998.
23. Ibid.
24. Alexander Solzhenitsyn, *East and West*, New York: Harper & Row, 1980, pp. 174–5.
25. Ibid., pp. 175–6.
26. *Daily Telegraph*, 14 February 1979.
27. Ibid., 27 March 1979.
28. Ericson, *Solzhenitsyn: The Moral Vision*, pp. 2–3.

CHAPTER SEVENTEEN

RUSSIA REBORN

On 13 October 1979 Solzhenitsyn found himself once more the victim of government censorship. This time, however, it was not the Soviet government that sought to block his work but an ostensibly friendly regime. The Finnish authorities blacked out transmission of a Swedish television adaptation of *One Day in the Life of Ivan Denisovich* to the Swedish-speaking population of the Aland Islands. The transmission was banned in Finnish territory because the Supreme Court had ruled that it might harm Finland's relations with the Soviet Union.[1] Yet if the icy politics of the Cold War still continued to raise its frosty head, Solzhenitsyn could shrug it off with the knowledge that the iciness was the chill of the morgue. He already believed that the Soviet regime was dead on its feet and he sensed that his return to Russia was a distinct possibility.

> I am firmly convinced ... that I will return, that I will be in time for this business. You know, I feel so optimistic that it seems to me it is only a matter of a few years before I return to Russia ... I have no proof of it, but I have a premonition, a feeling. And I have very often had these accurate feelings, prophetic feelings, when I know in advance what is going to happen, how things will turn out, and that's the way it is. I think – I am sure – that I will return to Russia and still have a chance to live there.[2]

When these words were spoken few would have taken them very seriously. The Soviet Union stood secure, or so it seemed, an indestructible monolith squatting its vast immovable bulk over the whole of Eastern Europe and extending its influence to every corner of the globe. In fact the Brezhnev era was in many respects a period of relative stability. Consumer goods were heavily subsidized and shoppers could be comfortable in the knowledge that basic food-stuffs such as meat and bread cost the same as they had done under Stalin thirty years earlier. The stability masked deeper problems such as food shortages, a burgeoning black market and unprece-dented levels of corruption, but none of these appeared to represent a serious threat to the fabric of Soviet society. To suggest in 1980 that the whole Soviet edifice was about to collapse was as unthinkable as to suggest that the United States was on the verge of falling apart. It was assumed, tacitly at least, that both superpowers would be a fixture in world politics for decades to come. In this light, Solzhenit-syn's words must have seemed absurdly, blindly optimistic.

Brezhnev was succeeded in November 1982 by the hard-line for-mer head of the KGB, Yuri Andropov, reinforcing the impression that the Soviet monolith was as immovable as ever. In the same month a play in Moscow about Lenin, *Thus Shall We Win*, was brought to a halt by a lone man shouting 'down with Soviet fascism' and demanding Solzhenitsyn's return.[3] His solitary act of defiance may have displayed the indomitable nature of Solzhenitsyn's supporters but the gesture was at once both heroic and hollow, a Jacobite plea for the impossible.

In May 1983 Solzhenitsyn arrived in Britain for a high-profile visit during which he was more favourably received than he had been during his previous visit seven years earlier. The political complexion had changed considerably in the intervening years. Callaghan's Labour government had been toppled in 1979 by the Conservatives' triumph at the polls and Britain was enjoying the af-terglow of its victory in the Falklands war. On 11 May Solzhenitsyn was received by Margaret Thatcher at Downing Street in a private, hour-long courtesy call during which they discussed the cause of freedom.

On 9 May *The Times* had carried a photograph on its front page of Solzhenitsyn bearing an icon during an Orthodox service at the Russian Church in Exile in Kensington. The following day he gave the Templeton Address at London's Guildhall, the text of which was published by *The Times*. Entitled 'Godlessness, the First Step to the Gulag', this speech was perhaps more overtly religious than any of his previous appeals for a rediscovery of sanity amidst the madness of modern life. He began with a memory of his childhood which served as a moral template for the rest of his speech, as indeed for the rest of his life and that of the century in which he had lived. 'Over half a century ago, while I was still a child, I recall hearing a number of older people offer the following explanation for the great disasters that had befallen Russia: "Men have forgotten God; that's why all this has happened".'

Since then, he explained, he had spent nearly half a century researching the history of the Russian Revolution which had 'swallowed up some sixty million of our people', but if he was asked to formulate as concisely as possible the main cause of all that had happened he could not put it more accurately than to repeat the same words. 'And if I were called upon to identify briefly the principal trait of the *entire* twentieth century, here too, I would be unable to find anything more precise and pithy than to repeat once again: "Men have forgotten God".'

Quoting Dostoyevsky's observations about the seething hatred for the Church which had characterized the French Revolution – 'revolution must necessarily begin with atheism' – Solzhenitsyn asserted that 'hatred of God is the principal driving force' behind Marxism. As a result the USSR had witnessed an uninterrupted procession of martyrs among the Orthodox clergy. Although the West had not suffered the communist experience it, too, was 'experiencing a drying up of the religious consciousness ... The concepts of good and evil have been ridiculed for several centuries; banished from common use, they have been replaced by political or class considerations of short-lived value. It has become embarrassing to appeal to eternal concepts, embarrassing to state that evil makes its home in the individual human heart before it enters a political system.'

He concluded his address with an appeal to eternal verities:

> Our life consists not in the pursuit of material success but in the quest of worthy spiritual growth. Our entire earthly existence is but a transitional stage in the movement toward something higher ... Material laws alone do not explain our life or give it direction. The laws of physics and physiology will never reveal the indisputable manner in which the Creator constantly, day in and day out, participates in the life

248

of each of us, unfailingly granting us the energy of existence; when this assistance leaves us, we die. In the life of our entire planet, the divine spirit moves with no less force: this we must grasp in our dark and terrible hour.[4]

Solzhenitsyn's voice was as uncompromising as ever, his words as strident, but for once they seemed to be received by sympathetic ears. On 12 May the leader article in *The Times* had nothing but praise for the Russian writer's timely reminder of 'what happens to a society when men have forgotten God ... Fashionable opinion might be tempted to dismiss Solzhenitsyn as an embittered exile whose religious enthusiasm, born under Soviet oppression, is inappropriate for the liberal societies in the West. Fashionable opinion, as so often, would be wrong.'

Once again Solzhenitsyn was succeeding in fanning the flames of controversy as few others could. On 14 May *The Times* published an angry rebuttal of both Solzhenitsyn's Templeton Address and its own leader article in a joint letter from representatives of the British Humanist Society, the National Secular Society and the Rationalist Press Association. In the same issue several other letters were published which supported the tenets of Solzhenitsyn's argument. For the next fortnight debate simmered and boiled on *The Times*' letters page as Solzhenitsyn's supporters and detractors laid claim and counter-claim to the role of religion in modern society.

On 23 May, in the midst of this debate, *The Times* published an interview with Solzhenitsyn by Bernard Levin, in which he reiterated his conviction that 'the goal of Man's existence is not happiness but spiritual growth'. He admitted that in the modern world such a conviction 'is regarded as something strange, something almost insane'. Levin asked him whether there was anything intrinsically wrong with the right of the mass of the people to enjoy the material possessions that previously were enjoyed by only a few, to which Solzhenitsyn replied that one must distinguish between material sufficiency and consumer greed. The whole of history, he maintained, consisted of a series of temptations to which humanity had normally succumbed, showing itself to be unworthy of its higher purpose. 'Now we stand before the temptation of the material, more than a sufficiency of the material, of luxury, of everything, and again we show ourselves unworthy. Our historical process is really – consists of – man standing before the things which are temptations to him and of showing himself able to overcome them.'

Again Solzhenitsyn expressed his admiration for Pope John Paul II, 'his personality, the spirit which he has brought into the Roman Catholic Church and his constant and lively interest in all the various problems all around the world'.

Asked by Levin whether suffering was necessary for people to turn to things of the spirit, Solzhenitsyn confirmed that 'suffering is essential for our spiritual growth and perfection'. Furthermore, 'suffering is sent to the whole of humanity ... it is sent in sufficient measure so that if man knows how to do so he can use it for his growth'. Suffering must be freely *accepted* for it to have any positive power. 'Now, if a person doesn't draw what has to be drawn from suffering but instead is embittered against it he is really making a very negative choice at that moment.'

Asked whether he believed that communism would finally collapse in the Soviet Union, he refused to be drawn on a specific timescale but repeated his premonition that 'I am personally convinced that in my lifetime I will return to my country.'

Solzhenitsyn had granted this exclusive interview to Bernard Levin because Levin had been one of the few writers in Britain to speak up in his defence. For the same reason, several weeks later he granted an interview to Malcolm Muggeridge. For some time Muggeridge had been eager to interview Solzhenitsyn and the Russian finally agreed to his requests during the British visit. The interview was broadcast on BBC2 on 4 July 1983 and covered much of the familiar terrain explored in the earlier interview with Levin, including the brutalities of the Soviet regime, the resurgence of Christianity in the face of these brutalities, the betrayals of Western liberalism and the need for spiritual renewal in the non-communist countries. There was also the same prophetic premonition: 'In a strange way,' Solzhenitsyn told Muggeridge, 'I not only hope, I'm inwardly convinced that I shall go back.'[5] In fact, Muggeridge was one of the few people who took Solzhenitsyn's hopes of a return to Russia seriously. He had been predicting the imminent collapse of the Soviet Union since the mid-1970s. In the event, both men would live to see their prophecies fulfilled.

Commenting on the televised interview, Peter Ackroyd wrote that Solzhenitsyn's 'convictions animate him and in this short interview he seemed entirely self-assured, with a directness of glance and an economy of gesture which are the marks of someone who has "come through"'.[6] Ackroyd was also amused by the mutual respect that the two protagonists displayed throughout the proceedings: 'the spectacle of Solzhenitsyn and Muggeridge agreeing with, and complementing, each other had its comic moments ... "Hallelujah!", said Muggeridge to one remark by Solzhenitsyn; "what you have said has a profound significance," said Solzhenitsyn after one of Muggeridge's own contributions ...' For his part, Solzhenitsyn has nothing but positive memories of his meeting with Muggeridge, describing him as 'enchanting'.[7]

In October Solzhenitsyn was interviewed at home in Vermont by Bernard Pivot, who recorded their dialogue for his French television programme. The interview was broadcast on 10 December, on the eve of Solzhenitsyn's sixty-fifth birthday. It revealed that Solzhenitsyn 'chops wood in true Russian style for exercise' and that he had taken up tennis late in life. 'When I was a boy in Ryazan,' he explained, 'I dreamed of playing tennis, but I never had enough money for a racket. At the age of fifty-seven, I managed to allow myself my own court.' There was also the same familiar, seemingly mandatory, refrain that his dearest wish was 'to return to Russia alive, not just in my books'.[8]

On 9 December, the day before the interview with Pivot was broadcast, Solzhenitsyn's French publishers brought out a revised and expanded version of *August 1914*, which was described as the first volume of a cycle of books entitled *The Red Wheel*. Solzhenitsyn announced that he had completed two further volumes covering October 1916 and March 1917 but these still awaited publication. He was working on a fourth volume and several more were planned. 'Probably my life will come to an end before I complete it,' he told Pivot. In fact, he survived to see the full cycle through to completion, considering *The Red Wheel* the most important book of his life.[9]

Given Solzhenitsyn's own estimation of *The Red Wheel* as the culmination of his literary achievement, it was scarcely surprising that he became animated when discussing it, enthusing about it both as a work of literature and as a much-needed work of history:

In the West it is often said that I have proved with my book the inevitability of the February revolution. Actually that is not at all the case. This point of view was held by those who didn't actually read the book; one journalist would write something and another would read what he had written and repeat it. In reality, the February revolution might have happened or it might not have happened. That is the key question and that is the main event for Russia in the twentieth century, but after the February revolution these liberals and revolutionaries in eight months so quickly dismantled everything. Everything fell apart, all Russia fell apart. They didn't really know what to do, they didn't even want power any more. The Bolsheviks came along and found power just lying there on the ground and they picked it up. Therefore the October revolution is an event of secondary significance.

This book ended up being such a significant volume because it was important not to let go, not to ignore the importance of the development of events. I could of course have written it in a shorter fashion. It would have made for a good read as a description of lies that people tell but it would not have obtained historical proof. One could have said that he argued in this fashion but one could argue for the opposite case, but I laid out such a multitude of facts that it is impossible to give it a different interpretation since the facts themselves yield up one interpretation. And also of course given the volume, the size, of this work I utilized a number of different literary devices and switched between genres; prose, citations of documents, overview of the current press, a collection of short fragments of glimpses of the life in the different regions, cinematic scripts, Russian folk sayings embedded in the text in the sense that for instance a chapter would commence with a traditional saying. The meaning of it is as follows, that some old man would have been reading all of this and would then pass judgement on what he had just read with a traditional folk saying.[10]

Solzhenitsyn ascribed a great deal of perennial wisdom to folk sayings which in the context of their use in *The Red Wheel* 'lays bare,
presents clearly, the meaning of that which the previous chapter had
described'. In fact, folk wisdom can do more than merely summarize
what has been said: 'It is in some ways an unexpected judgement
of the people regarding that which we are doing.' To illustrate the
point, Solzhenitsyn discussed the proverbial lines 'Don't search
the village, search your heart', with which he had ended a chapter in
August 1914: 'In Russian there is also a rhyme which is lost in the
English translation. It means that when you try to explain strange
occurrences, things that are going on, don't look around and say,
"Oh, it's because people are this or that way", but recognize that
you also may be that way and that perhaps the key to what has transpired may also be found inside yourself.'[11]

It is clear from the irrepressible enthusiasm with which Solzhenitsyn discusses *The Red Wheel* that his work on this mammoth enterprise was the most important part of his life throughout the
1980s, taking precedence over everything else.

While Solzhenitsyn laboured away at *The Red Wheel* in the secluded isolation of Vermont, the Red Wheel of Soviet politics was
labouring onwards into the swamps of stagnation. Yuri Andropov
died in February 1984, barely a year after taking power, and was succeeded by the seventy-three-year-old Konstantin Chernenko. He
also died only a year later and in March 1985 Mikhail Gorbachev –
at fifty-three the youngest member of the Politburo – took over the
leadership. Within months of his accession the famous buzzwords of
the Gorbachev era, *glasnost* (openness) and *perestroika* (restructuring), could be heard on the lips of excited Russians. Perhaps at last
the end of communist oppression was in sight. Older Russians, remembering the false dawn under Khrushchev, remained cautious.

Ironically, the emergence of *glasnost* in the Soviet Union coincided with rumours that Solzhenitsyn was about to become an
American citizen. On 24 June 1985 the press waited expectantly for
his arrival at an American court where a special ceremony had been
arranged to confer citizenship on Solzhenitsyn and his family. In the
event, Alya arrived with their eldest son Yermolai (the two younger
sons had automatically become citizens under US law), both of
whom were granted citizenship, but it was Solzhenitsyn's failure to

appear which excited the interest of the media. Unconvinced by the official explanation given by the clerk of the court that he was ill, the press quoted a family friend who suggested that he may have wished to avoid the crowd of reporters.[12] Years later the mystery surrounding his non-appearance was explained by Alya. Throughout the years of exile, her husband 'never wanted to, and did not, become a US citizen, since he could not imagine himself to be a citizen of any country except Russia (not the USSR!)'. During the early eighties, at the height of the Afghan war and at a time of failing hopes for short-term change in the USSR, Solzhenitsyn did in fact experience a moment of some doubt, but ultimately he decided to 'remain stateless – right up until Russia's liberation from communism, an event for which he had always hoped'.[13] In short, he appears to have changed his mind at the very last minute, possibly prompted by recent changes in his homeland.

The cracks in the Soviet monolith were symbolized dramatically in April 1986 by the world's worst nuclear disaster at Chernobyl, the sort of ecological tragedy that Solzhenitsyn had forecast in his *Letter to Soviet Leaders* more than a decade earlier. The Soviet authorities desperately tried to smother all news of the catastrophe, concealing the matter for a full three days in cynical contradiction of the much-heralded *glasnost*. Muscovites suspected that something was amiss when trainloads of evacuated children began arriving at Kiev station, but it was only when meteorological observers in Sweden detected the radioactive cloud that the Soviet Union was forced to confess the worst.

In a similar cynical denial of his own principles of openness, Gorbachev brazenly denied the existence of political prisoners until Andrei Sakharov's unexpected release from exile in the 'closed' city of Gorky. Sakharov returned to Moscow to a hero's welcome and vowed to fight for the freedom of all.

In spite of such double standards, the Soviet stranglehold was being greatly loosened under Gorbachev's presidency. Corrupt officials who had abused their positions in the Brezhnev era were investigated publicly, as were allegations of black marketeering within the Party apparatus. The changing atmosphere within Soviet society inspired rumours that Solzhenitsyn's books would at last be published. In March 1987 a Danish newspaper reported that Soviet authorities were shortly to lift the ban on *Cancer Ward*.[14] A year later, in April 1988, *The Gulag Archipelago* finally breached the Iron Curtain with its publication in Yugoslavia.[15] On 3 August a Soviet weekly newspaper, *Moscow News*, hailed *One Day in the Life of Ivan Denisovich* as one of the great classics of Russian literature and an outstanding event in literary, moral and spiritual life. Ten days later, the Soviet State Publishing Committee announced that it was liberalizing its official attitude to Solzhenitsyn's works. Referring to *One Day in the Life of Ivan Denisovich*, the committee agreed that it was up to individual publishing houses to decide whether or not to reprint those works which had been previously published in the Soviet Union. Publication of those of Solzhenitsyn's books which had thus far only been published abroad, in other words the vast bulk of his work, was not to be authorized at present.[16] Significantly, *Novy Mir* announced on the same day that it planned to publish George Orwell's *Nineteen Eighty-Four*.

Encouraged by the liberalizing tendencies within the state apparatus, Soviet dissidents stepped up their campaign for Solzhenitsyn's return. In summer 1988 a short article appealing for his citizenship to be restored was published in the weekly journal *Book Review*.[17] At the end of August an unofficial committee lobbying for the erection of a monument to Stalin's victims in Moscow invited Solzhenitsyn to join its board. He politely declined the invitation. In October the first meeting of a Soviet human rights group called Memorial, set up to commemorate the victims of Stalinism, demanded public recognition for, and the restoration of Soviet citizenship to, Solzhenitsyn.

In a panic-stricken response to the growing reform movement, the Soviet old guard began to fight a furious rearguard action. At first it seemed that they might be successful. Boris Yeltsin, the highly popular reformist mayor of Moscow, was sacked, and in the summer of 1988 Gorbachev abandoned his delicate balancing act between old guard and avant garde and realigned himself with the hard-liners. It looked like the same old story: all the promises of reform were to be broken in a renewed totalitarian backlash. With the neo-Stalinists again in the ascendency, Gorbachev set about installing hard-liners in prominent positions of power. On 30 September Vadim Medvedev was appointed as the Politburo member responsible for ideology. Two months later he dramatically vetoed publication of Solzhenitsyn's books in the Soviet Union on the basis that they were 'undermining the foundations of the Soviet state'.[18]

On this occasion, however, the hard-liners had underestimated the forces aligned against them. Even as Gorbachev was siding with the old guard, liberals within the Communist Party formed the Democratic Union, the first organized opposition movement to emerge since 1921. Gorbachev banned its meetings and created a new Special Purpose Militia unit to deal with any disturbances. Meanwhile in the Baltic republics, nationalist Popular Fronts were attracting mass membership. In November 1988 the small nation of Estonia audaciously broke away from the Soviet Union. In February of the following year the Estonians raised the national flag above their parliament building in place of the hammer and sickle. At around the same time, two newspapers in the neighbouring Baltic states of Latvia and Lithuania published Solzhenitsyn's essay 'Live Not by a Lie', which had appeared in *samizdat* just before his exile.

In the face of such defiance Gorbachev's hard-line government caved in beneath the weight and momentum of the opposition. In March 1989, during elections for the Congress of People's Deputies, Soviet voters were for the first time in years allowed to choose from more than one candidate, some of whom were not even Party members. Despite the heavily rigged election process, prominent reformers such as Yeltsin and Sakharov were elected. When Sakharov, as combative as ever, called for an end to one-party rule, his microphone was switched off – a gesture which only highlighted the desperate nature of the communist hierarchy's efforts to cling to power, especially as Sakharov's speech was being broadcast live on Russian television.

In the same month as the elections, *Twentieth Century and Peace*, a magazine published by the officially sanctioned Soviet Peace Committee, defied the Kremlin's ban on Solzhenitsyn's works by following the example of the Baltic journals and publishing 'Live Not by a Lie'. A commentary accompanying the essay credited Solzhenitsyn with helping to prepare the way for the present reforms.[19] Meanwhile, in remote Kuban, another small journal also flouted the official ban by publishing a three-part guide to Solzhenitsyn's work.[20]

Following the success of the reformers in the March election, Solzhenitsyn found that he had many friends in influential places. In April several delegates in the Soviet parliament called for the restoration of his citizenship. The struggle, so long confined to the back-streets of the dissident fringe, was now being waged in the corridors of power.

On 2 June, while thousands of Chinese students were occupying Tiananmen Square in the abortive hope that totalitarianism could be overthrown in the other communist superpower, Sakharov was shouted down in parliament as he accused the Soviet army of atrocities in Afghanistan. On the same day another delegate, the writer Yuri Karyakin, caused a similar furore by proposing that the government should restore Solzhenitsyn's citizenship and that it should inscribe the names of the millions killed under Stalin on the walls of KGB headquarters.[21]

Solzhenitsyn must have sensed final victory at the beginning of July when the Soviet Writers' Union not only voted for his reinstatement as a member, but also urged the authorities to sanction publication of *The Gulag Archipelago*.

In spite of last-ditch efforts by hard-liners on the Central Committee to block its publication, the seemingly impossible happened in October when *Novy Mir* published the first long extract from *The Gulag Archipelago*. The journal published one-third of the work in three issues, adding a million to its readership in the process. Three million copies were sold. Interest in Solzhenitsyn was enormous and the state-run publishing house Sovietski Pisatel announced plans for a collected works.

In the same month that the first extracts of *The Gulag Archipelago* were published there were unprecedented counter-demonstrations in Red Square during the October Revolution celebrations. One of the banners read: 'Workers of the World – we're sorry'.

For the Stalinist old guard, the previous year had been one of unmitigated disaster. Not only had problems within the Soviet Union escalated out of control but the Soviet grip on its empire in Eastern Europe was being prised loose. During 1989 reformist movements had triumphed throughout the Eastern bloc, culminating in the fall of the Berlin Wall and the Velvet Revolution in Czechoslovakia.

In December 1989 the Soviet authorities indicated begrudgingly that Solzhenitsyn's citizenship would be returned to him if he applied for it. His rejection of the offer was conveyed by Alya to the *New York Times*: 'It's shameful, after all that they have done to him, that the Parliament doesn't have the simple courage to admit that they were wrong. They try to turn a moral and political question into a matter of bureaucracy and paperwork ... They kick him out and after that they want him to come and bow and ask permission to enter ... We've waited a long time. We will wait until they become wise.'[22]

Wisdom was not particularly evident in Gorbachev's decision on 19 January 1990 to send Soviet tanks into Baku, the Azerbaijani capital, to crush the independence movement there. More than a hundred people were killed that night, fomenting further hatred of the Soviet regime and intensifying the struggle for independence. In February scores of thousands converged on Red Square in the largest demonstration in Russia since the Revolution. The following month voters registered their disgust with the communist regime in the local elections. In the Soviet republics, nationalists swept the board paving the way for the declarations of independence which followed. In Russia the anti-communist Democratic Platform gained majorities in the powerful city councils of Leningrad and Moscow. During the May Day celebrations Gorbachev suffered the humiliation of being jeered by sections of the crowd in Red Square and by the end of the month his arch-rival Boris Yeltsin had secured his election as chairman of the Russian parliament. Two weeks later, on 12 June, Yeltsin played his master card, declaring Russian independence from the Soviet Union in imitation of the Baltic states.

After nearly three-quarters of a century of communist rule, Russia was reborn as a nation state. One by one, the outlying republics had declared their independence from the communist yoke and now Russia itself had opted out. It was the beginning of the end for the Soviet Union which had ceased to exist in anything but name, claiming to rule a vanished empire. In July 1990, the Soviet Communist Party held its last Congress. Yeltsin tore up his party card in full view of the cameras and two million others followed his example before the end of the year.

Meanwhile, thousands of miles away in Vermont, Solzhenitsyn observed the unfolding of events with a rising sense of joy. Surely it was now only a matter of time before he and his family could return home. Yet even amid the triumph there was no time for triumphalism. Such was his irrepressible personality that he was already writing a bold, polemical manifesto for the new Russia. He sensed that the end of the Soviet Union might be an exciting new beginning for his native land. Russia had been reborn but now she needed to be rebuilt.

NOTES

1. *Daily Telegraph*, 15 October 1979.
2. Scammell, *Solzhenitsyn: A Biography*, p. 993.
3. *The Times*, 20 November 1982.
4. *The Times*, 11 May 1983.
5. Ibid.
6. *The Times*, 5 July 1983.
7. Solzhenitsyn, interview with the author.
8. *The Times*, 12 December 1983.
9. Solzhenitsyn, interview with the author.
10. Ibid.
11. Ibid.
12. *The Times*, 26 June 1985.
13. Natalya Solzhenitsyn, written answer to the author's questions, October 1998.
14. *The Times*, 4 March 1987.
15. *The Times*, 12 April 1988.
16. *The Times*, 15 August 1988.
17. Thomas, *Solzhenitsyn: A Century in His Life*, p. 498.
18. *The Times*, 30 November 1988.
19. *The Times*, 21 March 1989.
20. Thomas, *Solzhenitsyn: A Century in His Life*, p. 498.
21. *The Times*, 3 June 1989.
22. *The Times*, 12 December 1989.

CHAPTER EIGHTEEN

REBUILDING ON
GREEN FOUNDATIONS

In January 1990 Solzhenitsyn took his war of words with Russia's modernists to the literal as well as the literary level. He announced through his Paris publisher Nikita Struve that he would be writing a specialized glossary of ancient Russian words and rare dialect as a means of defending the purity and beauty of the language from the encroachments of foreign neologisms and Soviet bureaucratic jargon.

The glossary, to be published in monthly instalments in the Soviet review *Russian Speech*, was welcomed by traditionalist writers who had voiced their abhorrence of both the inelegant, politically correct vocabulary of the Soviet era and the emerging *arriviste* vocabulary of the new capitalism. The westernizing flavour of Gorbachev's *perestroika* had added new words to the menu of the contemporary Russian language, including the capitalist buzzwords *biznesmen* and *menedzher*.

The whole debate was far more politically charged than its roots in dry philology may have suggested. Many traditionalist writers viewed the arrival of certain aspects of Western popular culture, such as *rok* and *narkotiki*, to be as great a danger to the Russian way of life as the emergence of the words themselves was a threat to the language. Western cultural and linguistic imperialism was following hard on the heels of the deadening effects of Soviet sloganizing. In the late 1960s the writer Konstantin Paustovsky had claimed in an article in *Literaturnaya Gazeta* that the language was degenerating into bureaucratic slang and as recently as July 1989 an article in *Literaturnaya Rossiya* had urged the Supreme Soviet to pass laws of linguistic defence. Solzhenitsyn was, therefore, stepping into a highly topical minefield when he chose to side with the traditionalists against the modernists.

'The Russian language is his element, his substance in life,' Nikita Struve explained. 'It is natural for an exiled writer.'

Solzhenitsyn's desire to nurture and preserve the purity of the language did not spring from motives of a retrogressive or reactionary nature but was derived from a passionate belief that the richness of the Russian language itself gave rise to opportunities for innovation. It was his intention to emphasize these opportunities and to stress that, as a living tongue, Russian could evolve vividly and vibrantly without recourse to alien appendages. 'Russian, with its suffixes and prefixes, is still a living language, where it is possible to create new words,' Struve said. 'Solzhenitsyn's works are testimony to its regenerating power.'[1]

Solzhenitsyn had been inspired to write the dictionary after he had seen Stephan, his youngest son, typing. 'It was a way to bring his Russian son closer to the language,' Struve explained. In fact Struve, in making this statement, unwittingly summarized the vocational trinity at the heart of Solzhenitsyn's inspiration during the years of exile. First and foremost he was a writer, and the literary aspects of his life invariably took precedence over everything else. Yet, as his son Ignat had testified, he was a naturally gifted teacher and a considerate father. It was not surprising, therefore, that as patriarch and tutor he should gain inspiration for his literary endeavours from the desire to educate his children. Fatherhood was itself a creative force.

Fatherhood was, however, an obligation as well as an inspiration and he and Alya made every effort to fulfil their parental duties in the difficult and unusual cultural circumstances in which they found themselves. Yermolai, Ignat and Stephan were encouraged to assimilate with the indigenous culture in which they were living without losing their Russian culture and heritage. It was a difficult balancing act which, to judge by results, was achieved with distinction.

Yermolai, the eldest of Solzhenitsyn's sons, was a particularly gifted schoolboy who was graded three years ahead of his age. Yet even this superlative achievement may not have done the child prodigy the justice he warranted; the Russian scholar Alexis Klimoff, visiting Vermont to discuss translations, found the three teenagers studying subjects at a level ten years ahead of their peers. Without doubt this was due largely to the quality of the home schooling they had received from their parents, along with the religious instruction from Father Tregubov, a priest from the Orthodox Church at Claremont. According to D. M. Thomas it was 'all part of the rich and rigorous demands placed upon them'.[2] As a twelve-year-old Yermolai had helped his mother by setting one of his father's works on their computer. Desiring to maximize his son's evident potential, Solzhenitsyn sent Yermolai to Eton for his final two years at school. 'I would say that my father sending me to school at Eton was a reflection of his respect for the quality of education available there,' Yermolai wrote, 'and I am grateful for his decision to do so.'[3]

> My two years at Eton did not I think leave me with any specifically English traits (to the extent that I do not feel I could usefully disaggregate them), although I certainly grew to love and appreciate the wealth and possibilities of the English language – something that I had not encountered in Vermont to nearly the same degree. That is perhaps the greatest gift I took away from that A-Level experience. When I was at Eton my fellow students would often say that the true measure of our opinion of the school was whether or not we would send our own children there. I would hesitate to answer such a question today, not the least for having little idea of what kind of place Eton would be a decade and more down the road. I think Eton could benefit through losing some of its 'stiffness'. As for the quality of the learning – it was tremendous. A great faculty and a real stimulus for probing deeper into the subjects of study are characteristic of the College.[4]

On a more general level, Yermolai's memories of England itself were necessarily coloured by those of the school – seeing as it was of the boarding variety – and were thus somewhat limited. Nevertheless his view, limited or otherwise, was extremely positive: 'I very much like England, and am always happy to visit there when I get the chance. Its contributions to world civilization are monumental, and British humour will (most of the time) find in me a great fan.'[5]

After his time at Eton, Yermolai returned to the United States where he read Chinese at Harvard.

Ignat was no less gifted than his older brother. He made his solo debut as a pianist with the Windham Community Orchestra, performing Beethoven's Piano Concerto No. 2, when he was still only eleven years old. Like Yermolai he continued his studies in England. Not unreasonably, D. M. Thomas concluded that Solzhenitsyn 'must have valued English education',[6] yet Ignat insisted that 'there was no master-plan to send us there' and that 'it was essentially a coincidence'.[7]

My moving to England was for one specific reason, which was to study with the extraordinary piano pedagogue Maria Curcio, who taught (and continues) privately in London. Concurrently, I enrolled to complete my A-Levels at the Purcell School, then located in Harrow, since I had not completed high school in the US before moving to London. I spent a total of three years in London. It was not easy at first. I think England is not the easiest country for a fourteen-year-old to move to on his own. But gradually I made some wonderful friends, and of course soaked up the great concert life and museums of London. I now look back fondly on those years as formative in my personal and musical life. I have come back often to visit, and will continue to do so.[8]

After completing his studies in England, Ignat returned to the United States and enrolled at the Curtis Institute of Music in Philadelphia, one of the finest music schools in the world, to pursue a double degree in piano and in conducting. While there, his performing activities continued to expand and eventually he signed with Columbia Artists, a major music management in New York.

Stephan, the youngest of the brothers, received his BA from Harvard and a Master's in City Planning from the Massachusetts Institute of Technology, so completing the successful educational careers of the Solzhenitsyns' prodigious offspring. The three boys had harvested the fruits of their parents' labours on their behalf, as well as labouring diligently on their own account. D. M. Thomas depicted the home life which the boys had enjoyed since infancy and which was the secret of their ultimate success, as an 'ordered harmony ... a productive hive, a rich simplicity'. Solzhenitsyn and 'his loving disciples', wrote Thomas, had 'farmed the grain of the spirit'.[9]

Thomas also singled out the importance to the boys of the 'stimulation of meeting interesting people who came as guests', perhaps the most notable of whom was Mstislav Rostropovich, Yermolai's godfather, who was a frequent visitor. The internationally renowned cellist was one of Solzhenitsyn's oldest friends and one of his greatest allies. In July 1974, only a few months after Solzhenitsyn's expulsion from the Soviet Union, Rostropovich had defected under duress, mainly due to his own persecution at the hands of the Soviet state for his public support for Solzhenitsyn. In January 1990 Rostropovich and his wife, the soprano Galina Vishnyevskaya, had been given back their Soviet citizenship. The following month he made his first return to Moscow since his defection to conduct the Washington National Symphony Orchestra. At a crowded press conference, he relayed a message from Solzhenitsyn: 'Tell our people I will come back, but only when every person has a chance to read my books.' Rostropovich stated optimistically that 'when we left, the Soviet Union was a huge island of lies, now it is cleansing itself', but he added that he and his wife would not be totally content until Solzhenitsyn was returned to his people. Stung into an official response, Nikolai Gubenko, the Soviet Minister of Culture, said that he would work to restore citizenship to anyone who left under duress.[10]

Solzhenitsyn's demand that everyone should have the chance to read his books at last seemed likely to be met. Plans were already under way in Russia to publish all his works over the next two years. Throughout the following months many of his works were published in his own country for the first time, becoming instant bestsellers. Seven million copies of his books were sold in the first year alone so that 1990 became known as 'The Year of Solzhenitsyn'.[11] The huge success added to the pressure on the authorities to restore his citizenship. In April 1990 the staff of *Literaturnaya Gazeta* sent an open letter to Gorbachev calling for Solzhenitsyn's rehabilitation. Ominously, the news was accompanied by reports that the conservatives and liberals in the Soviet Communist Party were on the verge of a major split.[12] Yet even while it looked as though the people of Russia were about to suffer another bout of the Soviet Union's insufferable politics, Solzhenitsyn sent a timely reminder that there were more important issues than the deadening dichotomy of left and right. At the end of April he announced that he would be donating his share of the royalties on the Soviet sales of *The Gulag Archipelago* to help with the restoration of a sixteenth-century monastery.[13]

With pressure mounting, it was only a matter of time before the inevitable happened. On 16 August Solzhenitsyn's citizenship was finally restored nearly seventeen years after it had been taken from him. Twenty-two other victims of Soviet oppression had their citizenship restored on the same day, including Viktor Korchnoi, the chess grandmaster, and Oskar Rabin, the artist whose open-air exhibition had been bulldozed on the orders of Brezhnev. A Soviet spokesman said it was 'a way of apologizing, belatedly, but apologizing'.[14] Within days Ivan Silayev, the Russian Prime Minister, sought to make political capital from the decision by inviting Solzhenitsyn to the Soviet Union as his personal guest. Solzhenitsyn refused.[15] He was not prepared to be used as a pawn in the highly volatile game of power politics unfolding in Russia. Instead, he was preparing a major move of his own.

On 18 September an important new essay entitled *Rebuilding Russia* was published simultaneously in two Soviet newspapers, *Komsomolskaya Pravda*, the communist youth daily, and *Literaturnaya Gazeta*. The fact that his essay was being published as a sixteen-page supplement in two journals which previously would only have mentioned him in scathing pejoratives was further evidence of his sudden and dramatic rehabilitation. Solzhenitsyn specified that his author's fee should be donated to the fund for the victims of Chernobyl, a gesture indicative of the environmental concerns at the heart of his vision.

The essay commenced with a catalogue of the disasters which had befallen Russia as a result of the 'laboured pursuit of a purblind and malignant Marxist-Leninist utopia'. This included the destruction of the peasant class together with its settlements, which in turn had 'deprived the raising of crops of its whole purpose and the soil of its ability to yield a harvest'. Large swathes of the countryside had been flooded 'with man-made seas and swamps' and the cities had been 'befouled by the effluents of our primitive industry'. Furthermore, 'we have poisoned our rivers, lakes, and fish, and today we are obliterating our last resources of clean water, air, and soil, speeding the process by the addition of nuclear death, further supplemented by the storage of Western radioactive wastes for money ... we have cut down our luxuriant forests and plundered our earth of its incomparable riches – the irreplaceable inheritance of our great-grandchildren'.[16]

The danger for the new Russia, Solzhenitsyn warned, was of a mindless leap from the wanton waste of Marxism to the uncontrolled greed of unbridled materialism. 'For centuries both manufacturers and owners took pride in the durability of their merchandise, but today (in the West) we see a numbing sequence of new, ever new and flashy models, while the notion of *repair* is disappearing: items that are just barely damaged must be discarded and replaced by new ones, an act inimical to the human sense of self-limitation, and a wasteful extravagance.'[17] This was inherent to a decadent system hell-bent on permanent and ultimately unsustainable economic growth at whatever cost to the future of the planet. The West had succumbed to a 'psychological plague' which was 'not progress, but an all-consuming economic fire',[18] a plague more than merely economic in nature. It had contaminated the very moral fabric of Western life and was threatening to do the same in Russia:

> The Iron Curtain of yesterday gave our country superb protection against all the positive features of the West: against the West's civil liberties, its respect for the individual, its freedom of personal activity, its high level of general welfare, its spontaneous charitable movements. But the Curtain did not reach all the way to the bottom, permitting the continuous seepage of liquid manure – the self-indulgent and squalid 'popular mass culture', the utterly vulgar fashions, and the by-products of immoderate publicity – all of which our deprived young people have greedily absorbed. Western youth runs wild from a feeling of surfeit, while ours mindlessly apes these antics despite its poverty. And today's television obligingly distributes these streams of filth throughout the land.[19]

Against the rising tide of licentiousness there was Solzhenitsyn's perennial call for self-limitation and the plaintive appeal of the poet for peace from the unendurable stream of information, much of it excessive and trivial, which was diminishing the soul. Modern man was being crushed by the omnipresence of technology. There was ever more clamour of a propagandist, commercial, and diversionary nature. 'How can we protect the *right* of our ears to silence, and the right of our eyes to inner vision?'[20]

Above all, however, and as the title suggested, *Rebuilding Russia* was more than the product of a plaintive voice crying in the wilderness, or a prophetic warning of what awaited a heedless generation. It was a positive vision of a new Russia, restructured according to sound and sensible principles and based upon sustainable and traditional values. It welcomed the resurgence of nationalism in the various constituent parts of the Soviet Union and looked forward to the final dissolution of the Soviet empire and the re-emergence of independent nations in its place. 'Every people, even the very smallest, represents a unique facet of God's design.' To reinforce the point, Solzhenitsyn quoted the religious philosopher Vladimir Solovyev, who had written, paraphrasing the Christian commandment: 'You must love all other people as you love your own.'[21]

Solzhenitsyn also believed that the spirit of decentralization should go beyond the rights of small nations to be free from the yoke of internationalism or imperialism. It should extend to the rights of small communities, and even families, to be free from the yoke of central state planning. 'The key to the viability of the country and the vitality of its culture lies in liberating the provinces from the pressure of the capitals,' he wrote. Provinces should 'acquire complete freedom in economic and cultural terms, together with strong ... local self-government'.[22] The need patiently and persistently to expand the rights of local communities would be an essential part of the gradual reshaping of the entire state organism. Only through a strong and revitalized local government could genuine democracy exist:

All the failings noted earlier would rarely apply to democracies of small areas – mid-sized towns, small settlements, groups of villages, or areas up to the size of a county. Only in areas of this size can voters have confidence in their choice of candidates since they will be familiar with them both in terms of their effectiveness in practical matters and in terms of their moral qualities. At this level phony reputations do not hold up, nor would a candidate be helped by empty rhetoric or party sponsorship.

These are precisely the dimensions within which the new Russian democracy can begin to grow, gain strength, and acquire self-awareness. It also represents a level that is most certain to take root because it will involve the vital concerns of each locality ...

Without properly constituted local self-government there can be no stable or prosperous life, and the very concept of civic freedom loses all meaning.[23]

The enduring influence of Solzhenitsyn's years in Zurich and his admiration for the Swiss political system is clearly discernible, although he was certainly aware of, and enamoured by, similar systems which had existed in Russia's medieval past. Whatever the principal motivation behind his advocacy of decentralization and subsidiarity in political life, he had nailed the lie that he was in any way undemocratic in his beliefs – not that this would stop the accusations being made, particularly by those who could not see beyond the futile oscillations of the Western two-party democracies.

Similar radical thinking energized Solzhenitsyn's calls for the restructuring of the Russian economy. What was needed was the re-establishment of independent citizens: 'But there can be no independent citizen without private property.' Seventy years of propaganda had instilled in Russians the notion that private property was to be feared but this was merely the victory of a false ideology over 'our human essence'. The truth was that ownership of modest amounts of property which did not oppress others must be seen as an integral component of personality, and as a factor contributing to its stability.[24] Solzhenitsyn professed to having no special expertise in economics and had no wish to venture definitive proposals, but the overall picture was clear enough:

healthy private initiative must be given wide latitude, and small private enterprises of every type must be encouraged and protected, since they are what will ensure the most rapid flowering of every locality. At the same time there should be firm legal limits to the unchecked concentration of capital; no monopolies should be permitted to form in any sector, and no enterprise should be in control of any other. The creation of monopolies brings with it the risk of deteriorating quality: a firm can permit itself to turn out goods that are not durable in order to sustain demand.[25]

There is a remarkable affinity between these proposals and those advocated by Schumacher in *Small is Beautiful* and by G. K. Chesterton and Hilaire Belloc in their calls for distributism. Schumacher, Chesterton and Belloc had all gained a large degree of their initial inspiration from the social teaching of the Catholic Church, particularly as espoused by Pope Leo XIII in *Rerum novarum*. By 1990 Solzhenitsyn was certainly conversant with the ideas of these kindred spirits and indeed with the Pope's crucial encyclical. He had come across the works of Schumacher and Chesterton soon after his arrival in the West but stressed that he had already arrived at similar conclusions himself entirely independently.[26] Since the central tenets of *Rebuilding Russia* were largely a development and a maturing of the ideas he had originally expressed years earlier in his *Letter to Soviet Leaders*, it is clear that the affinity was a question of great minds thinking alike rather than one mind borrowing from another. 'There was no direct influence because I was always submerged and immersed in things Russian. I touched upon world issues to the extent that these touched upon Russian questions and Russian concerns but that which I was drawing from and writing towards was Russian so it would be a coincidental affinity not a direct one.'[27]

In many respects *Rebuilding Russia* was one of Solzhenitsyn's most remarkable endeavours – and perhaps will prove to posterity one of his most important. Although it was written with Russia specifically in mind there is much of general interest. It deserves to stand beside Schumacher's *Small is Beautiful*, Chesterton's *The Outline of Sanity* and Belloc's *Essay on the Restoration of Property* as a permanent monument to the concepts of smallness, subsidiarity and economic sanity during a century characterized primarily by its headlong rush towards unsustainable growth and politico-economic giantism.

Solzhenitsyn concluded *Rebuilding Russia* on a note of genuine humility blended with words of sober realism. It was 'impossibly difficult to design a balanced plan for future action', he wrote, and there was 'every likelihood that it will contain more errors than virtues and that it will be unable to keep pace with the actual unfolding of events. But it would also be wrong not to make the effort.'[28] In making the effort he had fulfilled his duty, but perhaps he already sensed that, not for the first or the last time, his words would fall on deaf ears.

By 1990 most Russians were simply sick and tired of politics. All they wanted was an easy way out of the post-communist mess in which the Soviet Union had found itself. An easy life. To a disillusioned people intent on the path of least resistance, Solzhenitsyn's solution seemed too much like hard work. Much better to listen to the prophets of boom who were promising a land of limitless consumer goods. A people intent on self-gratification was not likely to feel attracted to Solzhenitsyn's plea for self-limitation. In fact, in *Rebuilding Russia* Solzhenitsyn had seen the danger and had foretold its consequences: 'If a nation's spiritual energies have been exhausted, it will not be saved from collapse by the most perfect government structures or by any industrial development: a tree with a rotten core cannot stand.'[29]

When *Rebuilding Russia* was published a spokesman for President Gorbachev promised that the Soviet leader would study the document.[30] Whether he did so is unknown. What is certain is that Solzhenitsyn's practical proposals for a revitalized Russia had not, to borrow a phrase of Chesterton, been tried and found wanting but had been wanted and not tried. Worse, they had been both unwanted and untried.

In fairness, it was very unlikely that Gorbachev had much time to study Solzhenitsyn's proposals, even had he any desire to do so, and even less likely that he would have been able to do anything about them. By the autumn of 1990 he was being outmanoeuvred on all fronts by his opponents. Yeltsin and his liberal allies in the Russian parliament had outflanked Gorbachev with the declaration of Russian independence, while the hard-liners within the Soviet hierarchy were gaining the ascendancy within the Communist Party and were putting the increasingly isolated Soviet leader under ever greater pressure.

In the midst of this feuding, Solzhenitsyn was being used as a convenient political pawn. In December the liberals in the Russian parliament awarded him the Russian state literature prize for *The Gulag Archipelago*, an honour which was tied up with the desire of the Yeltsin camp to score points against their Soviet communist opponents. In the meantime, the hand of the communists had been strengthened by a series of leadership reshuffles which had placed control of both the Interior Ministry and the media in the hands of old-guard reactionaries. On 20 December, in protest at these developments, the liberal Soviet Foreign Minister Edvard Shevardnadze resigned, warning ominously that 'dictatorship is coming'.

The effects of Gorbachev's hard-line reshuffle became apparent on 13 January 1991 when thirteen Lithuanians defending the national television centre were killed by Soviet troops. Yeltsin flew immediately to the Baltics and signed a joint declaration condemning the Soviet violence. A week later, a quarter of a million people protested on the streets of Moscow against the killings, the largest demonstration ever seen on the streets of the Russian capital. Only hours later, with a callous disregard for public opinion, Gorbachev's forces stormed the Interior Ministry in Riga, the capital of Latvia, killing a further five people. The Russian press, overwhelmingly on the side of Yeltsin and the liberals, backed the Baltic states against Gorbachev's repression. In response Gorbachev threatened to tighten control of the media and, as if to back his threats with action, he added more hard-liners to the Politburo and gave wider powers to the security forces.

A popular backlash against Gorbachev's efforts to turn back the communist clock was evident in June when the citizens of Leningrad voted in a referendum to rename the city St Petersburg. In the same month Boris Yeltsin emerged triumphant in the Russian presidential election, winning an overwhelming majority in spite of Soviet attempts to block his campaign.

The stage was set for the final conflict between the Soviet old guard and Yeltsin's liberals. It came on 19 August when the country awoke to the soothing sounds of Chopin on the radio and *Swan Lake* on the television. There was no cause for alarm, the listeners and viewers were informed, but a state of emergency had been declared 'in the public interest'. In an uncanny echo of Khrushchev's removal from office almost thirty years earlier, it was announced that Gorbachev had resigned for health reasons. The country was now ruled by the self-appointed 'State Committee for the State of Emergency in the USSR', a grandiose title for the group of hard-liners appointed to their posts by Gorbachev during the recent reshuffles. With little or no public support, the hard-liners soon realized that Russians would no longer kowtow to the tactics of terror. In defiance of a curfew order, a hundred thousand people took to the streets and defied the tanks. On the morning of 21 August, only two days after the state of emergency had been declared, it was announced that several tank units had defected to Yeltsin's side and by the afternoon the takeover had collapsed completely. Its leaders fled. One group flew to the Crimea where they were arrested on arrival and several others committed suicide. Meanwhile Gennady Yenayev, the group's nominal leader, took neither of these drastic courses of action, choosing instead merely to drink himself into an oblivious stupor. Thus began and ended what Russians call the putsch, what history would record as the final farcical collapse of the Soviet Union and, with it, the humiliating end of seventy-four years of communist rule.

One practical result of the dramatic events in Russia, from Solzhenitsyn's point of view, was the announcement in September that the treason charges against him had been officially revoked. This had been the last official obstacle barring his return to Russia. Its removal coincided with the completion, at long last, of the final book in *The Red Wheel* cycle. His work on this had been the other obstacle to his return: he had been determined to finish it before the inevitable disruption which the move from Vermont to Russia would entail.

In April 1992 Solzhenitsyn was visited in Vermont by Vladimir Lukin, the new Russian ambassador to the United States. It was the first official recognition on the part of Russia's new anti-communist leaders that Solzhenitsyn, to quote an article in *The Times* of 14 May, 'has become a legend in his homeland and revered by many as a saint'. Shortly afterwards he was visited by Stanislav Govorukhin, the film director who had achieved fame and notoriety in 1990 for his anti-Soviet film *You Can't Live Like This*. Govorukhin spent the Orthodox Easter with Solzhenitsyn and his family, filming a documentary to be shown on Russian television. It was the first time that Solzhenitsyn had granted an interview to anyone from the former Soviet Union since his expulsion in 1974. During the course of the interview he revealed that his wife would be travelling to Moscow in May to find a suitable home for the family's return to Russia.

On 12 June President Yeltsin announced his intention to telephone and possibly meet Solzhenitsyn during his forthcoming state visit to the United States. Four days later, within hours of his arrival in Washington, Yeltsin made an emotional thirty-minute call to Solzhenitsyn, during which he expressed repentance over the way former regimes had treated him and urged his return home, promising that 'Russia's doors are wide open'. Yeltsin promised to do everything he could to ensure that 'one of the great sons of our nation' could work for the Russian people from within Russia and not from a foreign land. The two men discussed the urgent and painful problems facing their country and Solzhenitsyn urged particularly that Russia's peasants should be given land of their own as soon as possible. For his part, Yeltsin assured Solzhenitsyn that he was trying to restore Russia's spiritual values and that Solzhenitsyn had 'blazed a trail of truth' which he was seeking to follow. Unlike the leaders of the previous regime, he would tell the Russian people 'the truth, the whole truth and nothing but the truth'.

Yeltsin's words were certainly warm, even if more cynical commentators suspected a colder motive for his courting of Solzhenitsyn's support. As a writer in *The Times* observed, 'Mr Solzhenitsyn still enjoys huge moral authority in Russia, and his support would be of considerable value to Mr Yeltsin.'[31] Yet if actions spoke louder than words it was clearly true that much had changed in Russia since Yeltsin's dramatic rise to power. In fact, on the very day that Yeltsin phoned Solzhenitsyn, Russia made a significant break with its Soviet past by granting political asylum to a research student from communist North Korea who had applied to stay in Russia to become a Christian priest.[32]

With the pace of change accelerating daily in Russia, it was no longer a question of if, but when, the Solzhenitsyns would return. Yet the months passed and little altered as far as their domestic arrangements were concerned. On 11 June 1993, almost a year to the day after his conversation with Yeltsin, Solzhenitsyn, still firmly rooted in Vermont, attended his son's graduation ceremony at Harvard. Ten days earlier Alya, on another visit to Russia, had assured reporters that 'we are coming back and very soon, it is a matter of months'.[33]

News of Solzhenitsyn's imminent return prompted an article in *The Times* by Bernard Levin, one of his most loyal allies throughout the years of exile. Entitled 'A Giant Goes Home', it was a eulogy to the Russian's courage and achievement overlaid with Levin's scarcely concealed delight at the providential turn of events: 'We have it on Shakespeare's authority, no less, that the whirligig of time brings in his revenges. But can there ever have been any revenge so sweet, or any revolution of the clocks so meaningful, as the news that Alexander Solzhenitsyn is shortly to return to his homeland, Russia, after almost exactly twenty years of forced exile?'[34]

The weeks and then the months slipped away and still there was no sign of the exile's long-awaited return. In September 1993, Ignat made his first journey back to Russia since he had left it as a bemused infant. On tour with the National Symphony Orchestra and Mstislav Rostropovich, he described it as 'an unforgettable experience, twelve days that are a separate chapter in my life'.[35] For the first time he could *see* Russian words all around him, on shop fronts and road signs, everywhere: '*seeing* Russian with my own two eyes ... hearing Russian spoken all around me – a din of hundreds of people walking along Tverskaia, and all speaking Russian'. With childlike excitement he explored various corners of Moscow, the home town of a dimly discerned childhood, and met people who had been until then only legendary shadows from his father's past: 'meeting friends of my parents, their comrades-in-arms, sitting and drinking tea with people who had risked their lives or livelihoods together with my father, and who were always present with us in spirit during the long years of exile'. The flow, the flood, of first impressions surged through his consciousness: The Kremlin, the blinding beauty of St Petersburg, 'and of course the concerts themselves with passionate Russian audiences'.[36] One can picture Solzhenitsyn's response as his son recounted his first excited impressions of Russia, and can only guess at the sense of longing it must have induced in his own exiled bones. Yet still he did not return.

Instead, on 14 September, even as Ignat was giving concerts to ecstatic Russian audiences in Moscow and St Petersburg, Solzhenitsyn was in the Liechtenstein village of Schaan receiving an honorary doctorate from the International Academy of Philosophy. His speech to the Academy was destined to be his valedictory address to the West, an appropriate finale to his years of exile.

Commencing with the divorce of politics from ethics which, he said, had begun with the Enlightenment and had been given added theoretical justification by John Locke, Solzhenitsyn presented a masterful analysis of the world's malaise. Whereas in *Rebuilding Russia* he had sought to solve society's problems on a socio-political level by laying green foundations, now he was seeking deeper solutions to the fundamental problems of life by laying philosophical foundations. Moral impulses among statesmen had always been weaker than political ones, Solzhenitsyn admitted, but he stressed that the consequences of their decisions for society as a whole necessitated that 'any moral demands we impose on individuals, such as understanding the difference between honesty, baseness and deception, between magnanimity, goodness, avarice and evil, must to a large degree be applied to the politics of countries, governments, parliaments and parties'.[37] Within a Christian context he quoted Vladimir Solovyov who had stated that 'political activity must a priori be *moral service*, whereas politics motivated by the mere pursuit of *interests* lacks any Christian content whatsoever'.[38]

Solzhenitsyn proceeded to discuss the nature and meaning of 'progress'. The whole of humanity had embraced the term but few seemed to give any thought to what it actually meant: 'progress yes, but *in what*? And *of what*? And might we not lose something in the course of this Progress?'[39] 'It was,' he reminded his audience, 'from this intense optimism of Progress that Marx, for one, concluded that history will lead us to justice without the help of God.'[40] In the twentieth century Progress had indeed marched on, and was 'even stunningly surpassing expectations', but it was doing so only in the field of technology. Was this sufficient in itself and had it been purchased at a price; perhaps at too high a price? Unlimited Progress was threatening the limited resources of the planet, 'successfully eating up the environment allotted to us'. It was also threatening the life of the human soul. In the face of technocentric Progress with its 'oceans of superficial information and cheap spectacles', the human soul was growing more shallow and the spiritual life reduced.

> Our culture, accordingly, grows poorer and dimmer, no matter how it tries to drown out its decline with the din of empty novelties. As creature comforts continue to improve for the average person, so spiritual development grows stagnant. Surfeit brings with it a nagging sadness of the heart, as we sense that the whirlpool of pleasures does not bring satisfaction, and that, before long, it may suffocate us.
>
> No, all hope cannot be pinned on science, technology, economic growth. The victory of technological civilization has also instilled in us a spiritual insecurity. Its gifts enrich, but enslave us as well ... an inner voice tells us that we have lost something pure, elevated and fragile. We have ceased to see *the purpose*.[41]

As Solzhenitsyn concluded his address he was bidding farewell to the West with a final plea for sanity. Yet as he prepared for a return to Russia he knew that the same problems of 'progress' awaited him in his homeland. The new Russians were accepting the new religion of consumerism with open, grasping arms, worshipping the latest gadgets as enthusiastically as their Western brothers. East and West were now marching together in a new unity, blinded not by the Light, but by the lights of a flashing, glittering technolatry. Unity without purpose.

NOTES

1. *The Times*, 6 January 1990.
2. Thomas, *Solzhenitsyn: A Century in His Life*, p. 473.
3. Yermolai Solzhenitsyn, letter to the author, 27 September 1998.
4. Ibid.

5. Ibid.
6. Thomas, *Solzhenitsyn: A Century in His Life*, p. 473.
7. Ignat Solzhenitsyn, letter to the author, September 1998.
8. Ibid.
9. Thomas, *Solzhenitsyn: A Century in His Life*, p. 474.
10. *The Times*, 13 February 1990.
11. *Daily Telegraph*, 28 February 1998; Thomas, *Solzhenitsyn: A Century in His Life*, p. 498.
12. *The Times*, 12 April 1990.
13. *The Times*, 1 May 1990.
14. *The Times*, 17 August 1990.
15. *The Times*, 25 August 1990.
16. Alexander Solzhenitsyn, *Rebuilding Russia*, London: Harvill/HarperCollins, 1991, pp. 9–10.
17. Ibid., pp. 34–5.
18. Ibid., p. 35.
19. Ibid., p. 40.
20. Ibid., p. 49.
21. Ibid., p. 23.
22. Ibid., p. 37.
23. Ibid., pp. 71–2.
24. Ibid., p. 33.
25. Ibid., p. 34.
26. Solzhenitsyn, interview with the author.
27. Ibid.
28. Solzhenitsyn, *Rebuilding Russia*, p. 90.
29. Ibid., pp. 44–5.
30. *The Times*, 19 September 1990.
31. *The Times*, 17 June 1992.
32. Ibid.
33. *The Times*, 1 June 1993.
34. *The Times*, 4 June 1993.
35. Ignat Solzhenitsyn, letter to the author.
36. Ibid.
37. Alexander Solzhenitsyn, *The Russian Question*, London: The Harvill Press, 1995, pp. 114–15.
38. Ibid., p. 115.
39. Ibid., p. 117.
40. Ibid.
41. Ibid., p. 119.

CHAPTER NINETEEN

A PROPHET AT HOME

Towards the end of 1993 Solzhenitsyn had an audience with Pope John Paul II in Rome. It was a meeting of considerable significance. The two men represented, each in his own way, the triumph of the human spirit over the evils of totalitarianism. Furthermore, both men had contributed to the downfall of communism to an extent that probably surpassed any of their contemporaries.

Solzhenitsyn had been a great admirer of John Paul II since the earliest days of his pontificate, describing the election of a Polish Pope as a gift from God. He had supported the Pope's policies throughout the world, not merely in John Paul's outspoken attacks on communism in eastern Europe but in his measures against Marxist-inspired liberation theology in South America. In a meretricious age, the Pope shone in Solzhenitsyn's eyes as a towering, and all too rare, paragon of virtue. The danger was that the Russian might feel a sense of disappointment when he finally met the Pole in the flesh. It was a danger that never materialized; Solzhenitsyn retained vivid memories of his audience, describing their meeting and discussions as 'very positive'. As a man, the Pope was 'very bright, full of light'.[1]

The audience lasted for an hour and a half and was characterized by what Solzhenitsyn described as very interesting conversations. In particular, the Pope appeared to be well acquainted with Solzhenitsyn's socio-political writings. He mentioned the importance of *Rerum novarum* to the Church's social teaching, perhaps sensing the affinity between the Church's teaching and Solzhenitsyn's views. As Solzhenitsyn remembered,

> Our only point of dissension was that I reminded him of the time in the 1920s when the Bolsheviks were crushing the Russian Orthodox Church. Some members of the

Vatican hierarchy at the time entered into dialogue with the Bolsheviks as to how the presence of the Catholic Church could be expanded in Russia. The Pope responded that this was unfortunate and was the result of those individuals' own initiative, but I do not believe it was only individual initiative. It is simply that the Catholic Church did not at the time understand to what degree the Bolsheviks were consistently against all religions. They thought perhaps that the demise of Russian Orthodoxy might represent an opening for Catholicism.[2]

'We were in complete affinity except for that one point,' Solzhenitsyn insisted, stating that the bulk of their conversation centred on the place of religion in the modern world and its role. The audience took place on the fifteenth anniversary of the Pope's ascension to the papacy and Solzhenitsyn felt saddened that he appeared to have physically weakened by this point.[3]

By comparison, the seventy-four-year-old Russian was in excellent health. It was not he who was visibly ailing but his country, which was emerging from communism in poor and deteriorating circumstances. As if he needed any reminder of the grim reality, news reached him in February 1994 that his Russian publisher had been gunned down in Moscow by the mafia. It was, therefore, with no illusions that he and Alya began preparations for their return to Russia which, at last, had passed beyond the realm of interminable rumour to that of imminent reality.

On 1 March he made only his third appearance at a public event in Cavendish, Vermont, in the eighteen years he had lived there. The purpose was to bid farewell to the neighbours who hardly knew him but to whom, nonetheless, he felt a debt of gratitude. 'Exile is always difficult,' he told the two hundred villagers who attended the meeting, 'and yet I could not imagine a better place to live and wait and wait and wait for my return home than Cavendish, Vermont ... You forgave me my unusual way of life, and even took it upon yourselves to protect my privacy. Our whole family has felt at home among you.'[4]

The farewells completed, Solzhenitsyn braced himself for a future that appeared to offer nothing but uncertainty. In the December 1993 elections there had been a dramatic swing to the ultra-nationalists under the leadership of Vladimir Zhirinovsky. In the so-called business world, crime and corruption were reaching new heights, as the murder of Solzhenitsyn's publisher had graphically demonstrated. Car-bombs, not conferences, had become the favoured means of settling business disputes. Even before his arrival on Russian soil, Solzhenitsyn had fearlessly made enemies in the worlds of both politics and commerce, attacking Zhirinovsky as a 'clown' and declaring war on the mafia. In an interview with the *New Yorker* Solzhenitsyn distanced himself in disgust from the crypto-fascism of the ultra-nationalists and stated that 'the mafia understand that if I was not going to make peace with the KGB I certainly would not with them'.[5] It was clear that there were many in the new Russia who were not looking forward to the writer's return.

In the same interview with the *New Yorker*, Solzhenitsyn admitted that he had overestimated the threat of a Soviet world takeover when he had first been exiled and that, in hindsight, his tone had seemed shrill. 'When I fought the dragon of communist power,' he explained, 'I fought it at the highest pitch of expression.'[6]

At the end of April Solzhenitsyn gave his last interview on Western television before his departure for Russia, appearing on the CBS programme *Sixty Minutes*. Perversely, considering his recent outspoken attack on the xenophobic nationalists in Russia, he was asked to respond to an American commentator who had branded him 'a freak, a monarchist, an anti-semite, a crank, a has-been, not a hero'. His reply was both measured and direct: 'The Western press works in the following way: they don't read my books. No one has ever given a single quotation from any of my books as a basis for these accusations. But every new journalist reads these opinions from other journalists. They have been just as spiteful to me in the American press as the Soviet press was before.'

Concerning his return home, he merely answered vaguely that 'my hope is maybe I'll be able to help somehow' but one suspected that, whatever the future held in Russia, he would be pleased to leave the distortions of the Western media behind him.[7] In the interim, however, they continued to dog his last days in the West. Anne McElvoy, writing in *The Times*, admitted that Solzhenitsyn had described Vladimir Zhirinovsky as 'an evil caricature of a

Russian patriot' but still insisted that Solzhenitsyn's *Rebuilding Russia* was 'dangerously nationalistic'.[8]

If Solzhenitsyn nurtured any hope that there might be more clarity of vision in the East than there had been in the West, from either politicians or the media, he would soon be disillusioned. On the morning of 27 May, as he set foot in Russia for the first time in more than twenty years, every shade of opinion in the political spectrum scrambled to appropriate him as one of their own. Alexander Rutskoi, a Russian imperialist and leader of the right-wing Accord for Russia, Boris Yeltsin, still the leader of the liberal reformers, and even Anatoli Lukyanov, a hard-line communist, all claimed Solzhenitsyn as a supporter of their own particular position.[9]

Meanwhile Solzhenitsyn was more interested in meeting ordinary Russians. After a ten-hour flight from Alaska, he took his first steps on Russian soil at Magadan which, appropriately enough, had once been the centre of the Soviet labour camp system. It was a poignant moment for the former prisoner. 'Today, in the heat of political change, those millions of victims are too lightly forgotten, both by those who were not touched by that annihilation and, even more so, by those responsible for it. I bow to the earth of Kolyma where many hundreds of thousands, if not millions, of our executed fellow-countrymen are buried. Under ancient Christian tradition, the land where innocent victims are buried becomes holy.'[10]

Arriving in the eastern city of Vladivostok flanked by his family, Solzhenitsyn received a hero's welcome. The authorities greeted him with flowers, hugs and the traditional welcome gift of bread and salt. Mobbed by journalists and applauded by a crowd of two thousand, Solzhenitsyn spoke of his hopes and fears for the future:

> Through all the years of my exile, I followed intensely the life of our nation. I never doubted that communism would inevitably collapse, but I was always fearful that our exit from it, our price for it, would be terribly painful. And now I feel redoubled pain for Russia's last two years, which have been so very trying for people's lives and spirits ... I know that I am returning to a Russia tortured, stunned, altered beyond recognition, convulsively searching for itself, for its own true identity.

He told the crowd that he planned to travel through the heart of Russia, beginning in the east and going through Siberia which he had only ever seen previously through the grate of a prison train window. He wanted to meet ordinary people along the way so that he could test and revise his own judgement, 'understand truly' their worries and fears, and 'search together for the surest path out of our seventy-five year quagmire'.[11]

Solzhenitsyn's triumphant return was witnessed by the world's media and was covered in depth by the BBC who had bought the rights to film the homecoming. The BBC filmed the whole journey from the Solzhenitsyn home in Vermont to the joyful arrival at Vladivostok, interviewing the writer at his desk in Vermont minutes before he took his final leave of it. There was time for a moment's melancholy. He told his interviewer that this, after all, was his home too and that in some respects his years in Vermont had been the happiest and most productive of his life. All departures were a kind of death, he said. He had finished his great work. There was no time to start anything else, anything of substance. That too was a death. He could not hope to live for long back in Russia. He was going home to die.

During his interview with the *New Yorker* three months earlier he had been asked whether he feared death. His face had lit up with pleasure. 'Absolutely not! It will just be a peaceful transition. As a Christian, I believe there is life after death, and so I understand that this is not the end of life. The soul has a continuation, the soul lives on. Death is only a stage, some would even say a liberation. In any case, I have no fear of death.'[12]

Although the BBC had purchased the exclusive rights to film the return, the best view of events as they unfolded was seen by the family itself. Recalling his father's return to Russia, Ignat described the weeks leading up to it as unforgettable:

> the daunting logistical preparations, including, prosaically, packing hundreds of boxes of books and papers; the mounting suspicion of the media that 'something is up', and smiling to myself thinking, 'Just you wait; none of you expect *this*'. And indeed, much of the world press were not only taken by complete surprise with the manner of my

father's return, but appeared personally offended that they were not consulted on whether or not returning through the Far East was a good idea! I sensed very clearly that a historic moment was approaching, not just in our family life but in a wider sense as well; but, as usual, such things were quietly understood among us, nobody ever said 'isn't this momentous?'; everybody knew and, with complete trust in one another, we moved as a team, each with his own place and responsibility. Thus, Stephan travelled with my parents from Cavendish to Boston to Salt Lake to Anchorage to Magadan to Vladivostok, while Yermolai flew there from Taipei, where he was working, to greet them off the plane and then to accompany father throughout the two-month-long journey across Siberia, while mother and Stephan flew ahead to Moscow to prepare a home, etc. Meanwhile, I stayed on in Cavendish with grandmother to ship out all those boxes, deal with the media on the Western side, and in general to 'hold down the fort' on that end.[13]

The story of the odyssey is taken up by Yermolai:

It was hardly anything I could have imagined even a few years before – travelling together with him across the vast stretches of Russia, for nearly two months. It was wonderful on a personal level to spend 'quality time' with him, and to see how much he stirred people. Some were stirred toward hope and faith, others – to anger, and to claims of his irrelevance. What I always found telling in the case of the latter (then, before, and since, in both Western and Russian media), was that their agitation – at times bordering on hysteria – in declaring his marginality undermined their own contentions. Why should they get so worked up about it if he was 'irrelevant'?[14]

As father and son traversed the country throughout June and July, Solzhenitsyn made forthright speeches claiming that Russia was in the grip of a ruling clique and required grassroots democracy. He urged spiritual revival and called for a crusade against the country's moral and cultural decline. He was a prophet coming home but, as so often with prophets at home, his own people were the last to be receptive to his words. Two thousand people greeted him on his arrival in Moscow on 21 July but the city had changed almost beyond recognition, both physically and metaphysically. D. M. Thomas evoked the transformation in starkly symbolic terms: 'Pushkin's statue faced a McDonald's. The West was moving in. Send us your trivia, your TV game shows, your dazzling trash, your pornography! Russia was begging.'[15]

The trivializing of culture was reflected in Russian tastes for literature. In 1994 the bestselling titles in Moscow bookshops included novelized versions of the Charles Bronson film *Death Wish*, an Italian television series *Octopus*, and a Mexican soap, *Simply Maria*. A British journalist looking for Solzhenitsyn's books found none in the fiction department of House of Books, Moscow's largest bookshop. He was told to try the secondhand department. Such stories reinforced claims that Solzhenitsyn was out of fashion and out of date in modern Russia, the ultimate heresies in a novelty-addicted culture.

Far from feeling horrified at the neglect of Russian literature in the face of this invasion of Western pulp fiction, many critics appeared to relish their nation's cultural decline and gloated over Solzhenitsyn's popular demise. 'Everyone knows his name, but no one reads his books,' wrote Grigori Amelin, a young Moscow critic, in May 1994. 'Our Voltaire from Vermont is a spiritual monument, a hat-rack in an entrance hall. Let him stay in mothballs forever ... put this eunuch of his own fame, this thoroughbred classic with a hernia-threatening Collected Works, a Hollywood beard and a conscience polished so unbelievably clean it glints in the sun, out to pasture ...'[16] In similar vein, the novelist Victor Yerofeyev felt qualified to dismiss Solzhenitsyn's work without any apparent understanding of it. 'The humanistic pathos of Solzhenitsyn, which informs all his writings, seems no less comic, no less obsolete, than Socialist Realism as a whole ... A Slavophile Government Inspector has come to call on us, dragging behind him all the traditional baggage of Slavophile ideology ...' Yerofeyev then added a dose of petty snobbery by deriding Solzhenitsyn as 'a provincial schoolteacher who has exceeded his authority and overreached himself'.[17]

An explanation for the hostility which Solzhenitsyn provoked in Russia was offered by Dr Michael Nicholson of University College, Oxford. Dr Nicholson, who with Professor Alexis Klimoff was the translator of Solzhenitsyn's *Invisible Allies,* had been studying Solzhenitsyn from *samizdat* documents since the 1960s, had written his thesis on 'Solzhenitsyn and the Russian Literary Tradition' and had taught the Russian's works with evident enthusiasm to generations of Oxford undergraduates. He believed Solzhenitsyn was only considered irrelevant in modern Russia because of the 'anarchic, amoral zeitgeist' which had replaced Marxist dogma. Relativism looked good after the years of communist prohibition and inhibitions and was easier to accept than Solzhenitsyn's alternative set of values.[18] It was this turnaround which was responsible for Solzhenitsyn's hostile reception in the new Russia:

> The fact that Solzhenitsyn had contributed more than most to the collapse of the Soviet Union did not ensure his assimilation into a new Russia, which he knew, even before his departure from Vermont, to be showing signs of embarrassment and boredom with the monumental features of its past – the heroic no less than the villainous. Literary Russia had become more sympathetic towards postmodernism than to *engagement,* to pluralism than to truthseeking, while the legendary voracity of the Soviet reading public seemed to have evaporated with the Soviet Union itself ...[19]

Nicholson suggested that Solzhenitsyn may have felt similarly to another returning émigré, Zinovy Zinik, whose sense was that Russia in the 1990s had become like a land of disorientated immigrants: 'The people here [have] emigrated to a new country. The old country slipped off from under their feet, and they are now in the new one. And it is as alien to them as it is to me.'[20]

Solzhenitsyn was thrown into this alien environment in the autumn of 1994 when he was given his own fifteen-minute television talk show on Channel One. *Meetings with Solzhenitsyn* was given a prime-time slot and attracted a respectable twelve per cent of Moscow viewers, though it could not compete with the twenty-seven per cent who tuned into *Wild Rose*, another Mexican soap, on one of the rival channels. By this time, Russian viewers were as addicted to soaps as were their counterparts in the West. D. M. Thomas reported that a terminally ill man had written to a newspaper offering his life savings to anyone who could tell him the ending of yet another Mexican soap, *The Rich Also Cry*.[21]

One of Solzhenitsyn's rival talk-show hosts, Artyom Troitsky, a rock critic with a post-midnight programme called *Café Oblomov*, spoke for many new Russians when he questioned the need for Solzhenitsyn's show: 'Why should anyone now care about *The Gulag Archipelago*? I'm afraid Solzhenitsyn is totally, totally passé.' In his own efforts not to become passé and to remain relevant Troitsky had metamorphosed from serious 'rock' dissident to editor of Russian *Playboy*. Another new Russian quick to pass judgement on Solzhenitsyn's emergence as a television celebrity was Victor Yerofeyev, who took the opportunity to indulge once more in petty snobbery: 'It's better to have him speak than write. He writes such ugly Russian. He is once again what he always was at heart – a provincial schoolteacher.'[22]

Perhaps it was inevitable that Solzhenitsyn would not survive for long in the world of television. On 23 April 1995, a report in the *Sunday Times* suggested he was facing a television ban for 'criticizing the regime' and five months later the programme was finally axed. Solzhenitsyn remains convinced that the decision was politically motivated. 'The programme was terminated because the powers-that-be were afraid of the issues being discussed.'[23] Whether his removal was due to these outspoken attacks on the government or whether it was merely that he did not fit into the modern scheduling requirements, is a matter of conjecture. The new upbeat programme which replaced Solzhenitsyn boasted as its first guest La Cicciolina, an Italian parliamentarian and porn queen. Russia was getting what it wanted – and it wasn't Solzhenitsyn.

The sense of despondency induced by Russia's cultural decline was expressed in Solzhenitsyn's speech at Saratov University on 13 September 1995. 'We are still holding together as a single unified country,' he told his audience, 'but our cultural space is in shreds.'[24] The despondency was also evident in his announcement in December that he would refrain from voting for either Yeltsin or his communist opponent in the presidential elections. 'I was approached by television asking for my opinion,' Solzhenitsyn explained. 'I asked them whether they would broadcast what I had to say. Yes, they said. I replied that both Yeltsin and the communists are not worthy of being elected, that they have not put forward programmes, that no programmes have been discussed. Neither of these sides has repented anything that they have done in the past and I propose to vote against both. (There was an option to vote against both.) They did not broadcast this!' His eyes glinting with amusement, Solzhenitsyn pointed out with evident relish that five per cent of the population did vote against both. 'These people figured it out for themselves,' he laughed.[25]

Increasingly disgruntled at the road Russia was taking, Solzhenitsyn retreated into the sort of reclusive life that had characterized his years in Vermont. The large house where he and Alya now resided in acres of isolated woodland in leafy countryside just outside Moscow was not dissimilar to their former home in the United States. Seeking seclusion he returned to his writing, ever the source of solace throughout his troubled life, and began to observe Russia's demise more passively, though still as passionately, from the sidelines. Yet his increased isolation did not stifle his ability to make carefully planned assaults on the Russian leadership when the opportunity arose. One such opportunity presented itself in November 1996 when he timed an attack on the government in the French newspaper *Le Monde* to coincide with a two-day visit to Paris by Viktor Chernomyrdin, the Russian Prime Minister.

Such was the force of his fulminations that the Reuters news agency described it as a 'blistering attack ... on Russia's new political leaders, saying they were no better than the communist rulers he spent much of his life opposing'.[26] In his article, entitled 'Russia Close to its Deathbed', Solzhenitsyn wrote that Russia was not a democracy and would never develop a genuine market economy. Russia's rulers 'get away with ... genuine crimes that have plunged the country into ruin and millions of people into poverty, or condemned thousands to death – yet they are never punished'. During the last decade 'the ruling circles have not displayed moral qualities that are any better than those during the communist era'. Indeed, in many cases the same communist cliques remained in power: 'Former members of the communist elite, along with Russia's new rich, who amassed instant fortunes through banditry, have formed an exclusive ... oligarchy of 150 to 200 people that run the country.'

Solzhenitsyn claimed that the Duma parliament was crushed by presidential power, that local assemblies were more like servants obedient to local governors, and that television channels were subservient to President Boris Yeltsin, who had been elected without any debate on his past rule or any articulated programme for the future. 'The government ... enjoys the same impunity as the former communist power and cannot be called a democracy.' Such a situation would have unleashed a social explosion in other countries, he wrote, but this would not happen in Russia because society, bled for seventy years under communist rule and weeded of political opponents, had no strength left. In July 1998 Solzhenitsyn was to reiterate his belief that communism had weakened and exhausted the Russian spirit: 'It is as if, just having survived the heaviest case of cholera, to immediately upon recuperation get the plague. It is very hard to withstand.'[27]

Meanwhile the government had no coherent economic strategy, and ill-conceived and ill-prepared privatization had proved disastrous, handing over national wealth for a fraction of its value to incompetent individuals. 'Such easy gains are unprecedented in the history of the West,' Solzhenitsyn wrote, adding that corruption had reached a level the West could not imagine. 'Market economy has not yet seen the light, and, as things are going, it never will.'[28]

Two years on, Solzhenitsyn's views had not moderated. In 1998 he wrote *Russia in the Abyss*, in which he elaborated on the scathing sentiments expressed in his article for *Le Monde*. Discussing these with the present author, Solzhenitsyn's disgust with the status quo in Russia was all too evident:

> We are exiting from communism in the most unfortunate and awkward way. It would have been difficult to design a path out of communism worse than the one that has been followed. Our government declared that it is conducting some kind of great reforms. In reality, no real reforms were begun and no one at any point has declared a coherent programme. The name of 'reform' simply covers what

is blatantly a process of the theft of the national heritage. In other words, many former communists, very flexible, very agile, and others who are basically almost confidence tricksters, petty thieves coming in from the sides, have together in unison begun to thieve everything there is from the national resources. It used to belong to the state ... but now under the guise of privatization all of this has been pocketed. For massive enterprises, for large factories, large firms, sometimes only one to two per cent of its value is paid when they are privatized. The top, the oligarchy, are really so preoccupied with this fever of thieving that they really did not stop to think of the future of Russia. They didn't even think of trying to maintain the government treasury, to think of the government finances, it is simply a frenzy of thieving. Suddenly they realize that as the government they have to rule the country but there's no money left. So now in a very humiliating way they have to bend the knee and ask the West for money – not just now but there has been an ongoing process. Now they are borrowing money to pay for wages from last year and the beginning of this year so that now at least one-third, perhaps one-half, of the nation has been cast into poverty, has been robbed. In addition, education has deteriorated and decayed. Higher education also. Science has decayed, medicine, manufacturing has stopped, factories have closed down, and now for almost twelve years no major new factory has been built. In this sense they are stabbing to death all the viable, in the sense of alive, direction of the people's life. And all these loans from abroad are merely stopgap measures designed to keep the oligarchy in power.[29]

'Imagine,' he continued, 'the people have been thrust into poverty, such that a woman teacher does not have suitable clothes to wear when she goes to teach a class.' Teachers no longer have access to published material because it is too expensive, scientists 'now receive less money than street sweepers ... doctors do not receive their salaries for half a year, nine months or more ... workers need to strike in order to get their pay cheques'. Furthermore, 'people have lost the opportunity to travel around the country to visit relatives or to go to some cultural event because the cost of travel is prohibitive'. This material devastation has had damaging ramifications in the cultural sphere so that 'the cultural space of the country has been torn ... There is almost a cultural atomization, a cultural rift certainly, in the country. What else could people in this position feel but that they have been abandoned, spiritually abandoned?' The link between material poverty and cultural impoverishment is inextricable: 'If people cannot receive the necessary education, or at least access to that cultural level which that person has set for himself, if that cultural level remains somewhere up above, unreachable to him, he has therefore lost both materially and spiritually.'

In *Russia in the Abyss*, Solzhenitsyn stated that Russia had entered a blind alley. The central government possesses no plan of finding the way out of this blind alley, he reiterated. They have been pursuing a course of simply trying to stay in power by any possible means.

> Across the country, Russians, whether political or otherwise, have some kind of ideas about how to save the country, about how to find the way out. There are a lot of clear thinkers everywhere. They may suggest some project, some plan for the future. I know this because a significant portion of these get mailed directly to me. These people hope that I will be able to say something and move it upwards, but in these circumstances I cannot do this ... It is said that we have freedom of speech here but the thing is that I can talk to you freely but Russia will not hear. If my voice is not heard then these people who are proposing various ways out of this blind alley will certainly not be heard.

When asked what he felt about the influx of Western multinationals into the economic life of Russia, Solzhenitsyn was unequivocal about his misgivings. Russia was losing its economic sovereignty and was 'becoming in many ways, I won't say fodder, but is becoming available to multinationals'. Whereas in the past 'we were able to rely on our own economic strength', today 'we have resigned ourselves from the resolution of simply standing on our own two feet'.

Coupled with this economic influx from the West was the accompanying influx of other Western influences. Was this a form of cultural imperialism? 'It could be termed cultural imperialism if the West's current cultural level was high,' Solzhenitsyn replied. 'Certainly our young people readily accept that which flows from the West' but this is 'exclusively materialist in character and is devoid of spiritual content so I would call this not a Western imperialism but the imperialism of materialism'.

Solzhenitsyn believed that the process of globalization was inevitable but that it could proceed in different ways. 'One would be a full standardization of life on earth. The other would be a careful preservation of national differences and cultures, and not only of national peculiarities and characteristics but those of civilization.' It should always be remembered that in addition to many different nations, there also exist 'several large civilizations, large cultures'. At present, it seems that the world is moving towards the former alternative, that of global standardization. This is unfortunate.

> This international standardization eats away at and destroys national self-identification. In the struggle for our own personal identity we have no other way but to also in the process struggle for our communal contact with our own homeland. This sense of homeland is tied to the continuum of many traditions, spiritual ones, cultural ones, and certainly religious ones. Internationalization tears people away from all traditions. It is almost as if it rids the person of individuality. Perhaps not their own personal individuality but something which could be described as its spiritual nucleus, a spiritual kernel perhaps. There is an illusion of world unity which carries with it the threat to local cultures. It is an illusory unity.

Nevertheless the globalizing of the modern world has inextricably linked the paths of Russia and the West. Over the previous twelve years Solzhenitsyn had stopped viewing Russia as something very distinct from the West.

Today, when we say the West we are already referring both to the West and to Russia. We could use the word 'modernity' if we exclude Africa, and the Islamic world, and partially China. With the exception of those areas, we should not use the word 'the West' but the word 'modernity'. The modern world. And yes, then I would say there are ills that are characteristic, that have plagued the West for a long time and now Russia has quickly adopted them also. In other words, the characteristics of modernity, the psychological illness of the twentieth century is this hurriedness, hurrying, scurrying, this fitfulness – fitfulness and superficiality. Technological successes have been tremendous but without a spiritual component mankind will not only be unable to further develop but cannot even preserve itself. There is a belief in an eternal, an infinite progress which has practically become a religion. This is a mistake of the eighteenth century, of the Enlightenment era. We are repeating it and pushing it forward in the same way.

There is, Solzhenitsyn believes, a stark and unavoidable choice facing humanity as it enters the third millennium. 'There could be a model of what has been called sustainable development, Schumacher's view of stable development, or there could be a model of unbridled, unlimited growth.' The former path was one of sanity, the latter potentially disastrous. At present the world is locked into the latter course, putting the future of both humanity and the planet at risk.

It was clear that in 1998, his eightieth year, Solzhenitsyn was still as unwilling to compromise with a system he despised as he had been thirty years earlier. Dr Michael Nicholson accredits this to 'a massive degree of integrity ... You can call it inability to change or cantankerousness, but he has managed to annoy a whole range of people over the years ... He's been accused of being an anti-semite, he's been called a crypto-Jew, he has managed to provoke on a very large scale ... It's not bad you know, ever since 1962, and he was certainly still causing a stir thirty years after *Ivan Denisovich* ...'[30]

Few could argue that Solzhenitsyn has managed to provoke hostility on a huge scale over the years. Yet his son Yermolai senses a sea

change in the public's perception of his father. Perhaps, at last, the
tide is beginning to turn in his favour.

> I must say that the attitude toward him in Russia has
> changed quite significantly. Quietly but surely many in the
> (print) media have begun to write of how much truth there
> is in what he says, of how it would be wise for all to think
> of many of the issues he holds dear. It is as if he is always a
> step ahead of his time. A Russia drunk with the novelties
> of the 'new life' hardly had time to pause and think of
> where it was going, and treated insightful words of caution
> as those of unjustified gloom. That was 1994. Four years
> on, more and more people seek to pause and think.[31]

Since Yermolai now lives and works in Moscow he is certainly well
placed to monitor any changes in the media's stance towards his father, yet one must suspect an element of bias in his words, a degree
of wishful thinking. He is on safer ground when he states his belief
that his father's reception among those who read him 'has always
been and remains overwhelmingly positive'. This, in itself, is
grounds for optimism: 'At the risk of stating the obvious,' Yermolai
continues, his father's books are the means by which 'he will (and
does) influence Russian society the most'. Consequently, 'the va-
garies of the media's stance are in many ways of much less lasting
significance than might appear at first glance'.[32]

A similarly positive appraisal of Solzhenitsyn's reception and role
in today's Russia was given by Ignat:

> He has come back, as he promised to do; and he is doing
> exactly what he said he would do: he is actively involved in
> public life, he has travelled extensively around the country,
> and met thousands of people from all walks of life; he
> maintains correspondence with dozens of people and re-
> ceives hundreds upon hundreds of letters; he has contin-
> ued steadfastly to speak out about current events, usually
> to the chagrin of current leadership; and, of course, he has
> continued to write, returning to his beloved forms of short
> story and prose-poem, which he was forced to abandon

for thirty years by the immense project of the *Red Wheel*. His political opponents predicted with metaphysical certitude that he would return and lead some kind of Russian nationalist movement (although he indicated repeatedly that he would not get involved in politics nor hold any official opinion). He has kept his word, and so their strategy had to be updated: now the standard line is that 'Solzhenitsyn is irrelevant, he has returned too late, his significance is diminished, and no one reads his books' – all notions that are either patently untrue or whose fallacy will shortly become self-evident. Particularly in the light of Russia's present crisis, it is obvious that very little has been learned or absorbed by Russia's political and cultural elite ... It is clear to me that my father and his ideas will contribute enormously to Russia's rebirth, now and for generations to come – precisely because he has always viewed political and social issues in the dual context of history and the moral dimension.[33]

Again, one could be tempted to dismiss such comments as indicative of excessive filial loyalty rather than being illustrative of the objective nature of Solzhenitsyn's role in modern Russia. A less biased, though admittedly sympathetic, view was given by Michael Nicholson. Discussing Solzhenitsyn's place in the literary life of modern Russia, Nicholson believed that 'the coherence of the fictional world Solzhenitsyn creates, the heroic dimensions of his life, his moral reputation – all present an irresistibly broad target to those jostling for elbow room in the literary life of post-Communist Russia'. Nicholson pointed to the rise of 'avant-gardism', which Solzhenitsyn had dismissed as the product of 'shallow-minded people' who had no feel 'for the language, the soil, the history of one's mother country', as the principal cause of this literary hostility, adding that 'the septuagenarian Solzhenitsyn seems unlikely to benefit in his lifetime from a reverse swing of the pendulum'. Nevertheless Solzhenitsyn's 'readiness over the years to endure and even provoke unpopularity has lent his position an integrity which even adversaries have grudgingly acknowledged'. Ever since his literary debut in 1962 he had functioned in both the East and the West as 'a touchstone, litmus or creative irritant' and there was 'virtue in his unfashionable rejection of relativism and his enduring capacity to provoke'.[34]

One adversary who had 'grudgingly acknowledged' the integrity of Solzhenitsyn's position in modern Russia was the writer Alexander Genis who paid the following magnanimous tribute to Solzhenitsyn's role as a thankless prophet to a heedless generation:

> In its own way, it is, I feel, a courageous and dignified role – to be one of the last remaining prophets of Apollo in the abandoned temple of absolute truth.[35]

NOTES

1. Solzhenitsyn, interview with the author.
2. Ibid.
3. Ibid.
4. *The Times*, 2 March 1994.
5. *New Yorker*, 14 February 1994.
6. Ibid.
7. *The Times*, 26 April 1994.
8. *The Times*, 20 May 1994.
9. *The Times*, 30 May 1994.
10. *The Times*, 28 May 1994.
11. Ibid.
12. *New Yorker*, 14 February 1994.
13. Ignat Solzhenitsyn, letter to the author.
14. Yermolai Solzhenitsyn, letter to the author.
15. Thomas, *Solzhenitsyn: A Century in His Life*, p. 503.
16. *Nezavisimaya Gazeta*, May 1994; quoted in Thomas, *Solzhenitsyn: A Century in His Life*, pp. 514, 523.
17. *Guardian*, 28 May 1994.
18. Dr Michael Nicholson, interview with the author, University College, Oxford, 2 November 1998.
19. Dr Michael Nicholson, 'Solzhenitsyn, Exile and the *Genius Loci*', unpublished manuscript.
20. Ibid.
21. Thomas, *Solzhenitsyn: A Century in His Life*, p. 528.
22. Ibid.
23. Solzhenitsyn, interview with the author.
24. Quoted in Nicholson, 'Solzhenitsyn, Exile and the *Genius Loci*'.
25. Solzhenitsyn, interview with the author.
26. Reuters press release, 26 November 1996.

27. Solzhenitsyn, interview with the author.
28. Reuters press release, 26 November 1996.
29. Solzhenitsyn, interview with the author.
30. Dr Michael Nicholson, interview with the author.
31. Yermolai Solzhenitsyn, letter to the author.
32. Ibid.
33. Ignat Solzhenitsyn, letter to the author.
34. Dr Michael Nicholson, 'Solzhenitsyn as "Socialist Realist"', in Hilary Chung (ed.), *In the Party Spirit: Socialist Realism and Literary Practice in the Soviet Union, East Germany and China*, Amsterdam/Atlanta, Georgia: Rodopi, 1996, p. 68.
35. Ibid.

CHAPTER TWENTY

SOLZHENITSYN AT EIGHTY: PESSIMISTIC OPTIMIST

On 26 October 1998 Solzhenitsyn gave a short speech in Moscow at the unveiling of a statue to Anton Chekhov. 'For millions of Russian readers,' Solzhenitsyn began, 'Chekhov is not just a Russian classic but is close to one's soul, almost a family member.' He proceeded to evoke the spirit of Chekhov's short stories: of an old peasant enumerating the damage done to nature in his own lifetime who concludes that 'the time has come for God's world to perish'; of an old man driving his wife to hospital, speaking to her mentally even though she has silently passed away; of the remarkable way that Chekhov 'could transmit the mind-set, the *weltanschauung*, of the exile-prisoner without ever being a prisoner himself'. Chekhov wrote about Orthodoxy with great understanding and warmth in stories such as 'Holy Night' and 'Passion Week'. According to the 'quality of his soul or spirit', Solzhenitsyn asserted, 'each reader can feel his own way and pick a little chain close to his heart' from Chekhov's short stories. 'I will not speak here of his plays,' Solzhenitsyn stated at the conclusion of his address, 'but let us be happy that Chekhov who for so long pined away in his unjust medical Yalta captivity and who so desired to be with his beloved art theatre, has now finally reached its walls forever.'[1]

The content of Solzhenitsyn's speech was largely ignored by the Western media, the Reuters report concentrating instead on the small print run of Solzhenitsyn's latest book, the fact that his television show had been cancelled three years earlier, and the observation that some in the crowd talked among themselves as he spoke. It appeared that conveying the impression of Solzhenitsyn's irrelevance was more important, and paradoxically more relevant, than his views on Russia's greatest playwright. Ignat Solzhenitsyn dismissed the Reuters report as the 'usual nonsense', describing it as 'so inconsequential that I didn't bother to mention it to my father'.[2]

In fact, Solzhenitsyn's address at the unveiling ceremony was considered sufficiently relevant in Russia itself for Yuri Luzhkov, the mayor of Moscow, to place himself at the Russian writer's shoulder as he made the speech. Many political observers saw Luzhkov's attendance as a strategic ploy in the wake of President Yeltsin's ill-health. He was considered one of the prime candidates to succeed Yeltsin and was clearly using the unveiling ceremony as a photo-opportunity. His opportunism paid off as newspapers published photographs of Solzhenitsyn delivering his address with Luzhkov positioned behind him.

For his part, Solzhenitsyn declined reporters' questions about Russia's current plight, an indication of his own disillusionment with the political establishment and his desire to concentrate on higher themes and aspirations. As he approached his eightieth birthday he was more inwardly convinced than ever that politics was not enough. In his own work he maintained that the spiritual or philosophical dimension was more important than the political.

> First would be the literary side, then the spiritual and philosophical. The political side is required principally because of the necessity of the current Russian position. It is defined by the current moment in time and the environment...
>
> I must say that among educated people politics occupies far too great a proportion of time. All the periodicals, all the newspapers are saturated with politics, although many of the objects they are discussing are very transient and short term. Of course, everywhere in the world people do occupy themselves with higher themes, and not just writers, but they always have a narrow audience, sometimes even appear to be some strange group on the edge of things, peripheral. In truth, questions of higher spirit cannot even be compared to the sort of blinking frivolity of politics. The ultimate problems of life and death show up the colossal nature of this difference even more. Modern humankind is characterized precisely by the loss of the

ability to answer the principal problems of life and death. People are prepared to stuff their heads with anything, and to talk of any subject, but only to block off the contemplation of this subject. This is the reason for the increasing pettiness of our society, the concentration on the small and irrelevant.[3]

In fact, he maintained, it is the over-emphasis on politics to the detriment of humanity's grasp of spiritual or philosophical truth, which is at the heart of the modern dilemma. 'Man has set for himself the goal of conquering the world but in the process loses his soul.' He then reiterated the theme at the centre of his address to the International Academy of Philosophy five years earlier:

That which is called humanism, but which would be more correctly called irreligious anthropocentrism, cannot yield answers to the most essential questions of life. Certainly it is hard to answer these questions for all, but for this irreligious anthropocentrism, this humanism, it is most difficult of all to answer such questions. We have arrived at an intellectual chaos, not all understand this, not all grasp this crisis of the world view of the past three or four centuries.

One example of this lack of grasp, Solzhenitsyn suggested, was the way that he is often accused of being a prophet of 'doom and gloom'.

This is a consequence of the fact that people don't read, they just glance through. For instance, let me give you another example: *The Gulag Archipelago*. There are horrific stories in there but throughout that book, through it all, there comes through a spirit of catharsis. In *Russia in the Abyss*, I have not painted the dark reality in rose-tinted shades but I do include a clear way, a search for something brighter, some way out – most importantly in the spiritual sense because I cannot suggest political ways out, that is the task of politicians, so it is simply that those who accuse me of this do not know how to read. It is an example of that hurriedness, that rushing quickly about. The current world is characterized by this hurriedness of glance, by this too hurried a glance, which is linked to this attempt to live everything as fast as possible.

Although Solzhenitsyn insists that politics must be subjugated to the higher goals of life, it is nevertheless true that he remains critical of both communism and consumerism. His criticisms, however, have spiritual, as opposed to political, roots:

> In different places over the years I have had to prove that socialism, which to many Western thinkers was seen as a sort of kingdom of justice, was in fact full of coercion, of bureaucratic greed and corruption and avarice, and consistent within itself that socialism cannot be implemented without the aid of coercion. Communist propaganda would sometimes include statements such as 'we include all the commandments of the Gospel in our ideology'. The difference is that the Gospel asks all this to be achieved through love, through self-limitation, but socialism only uses coercion.

Yet if Bolshevism was a bully, capitalism was a cad. Whereas the former crushed the human spirit, the latter corrupted it with comforts and, as such, was equally insidious. To illustrate the point, Solzhenitsyn stated that he would like to begin not with himself but with Pope John Paul II. 'He simply said that the third totalitarianism is coming, the absolute power of money, "the inhuman love of the accumulation of capital for capital's sake" ... I would summarize as follows: Untouched by the breath of God, unrestricted by human conscience, both capitalism and socialism are repulsive.'

In essence, he said, both systems have common materialistic roots and are therefore, of necessity, at loggerheads with Christianity. They are in opposition to the Christian position because they exist on totally different planes, on different levels. Neither system can 'tolerate Christian commandments, they do not concern themselves with the spiritual sphere, they reject the spiritual sphere ... it is simply a life lived in a different dimension, the dimensions are separate.'

Consequently, those Christians who succumb to the lure of materialism may understand Christianity 'but they don't accept it with their soul'.

The hedonism inherent in a materialist view of life is an important component in the rise of consumerism and liberal morality. Another component is legalism, the juridical.

> Current modernity boasts of the fact that everything is in accordance with 'the law'. In modern society if one is correct from the legal point of view then no one will demand of him or her a higher level of moral action. A famous statement of modernity is 'that which is not prohibited by law is permitted', which is a rejection of applying a moral valuation to action. In truth, the legal measure, the juridical way of measuring is lower than the ethical. It is the atmosphere of spiritual or soul-connected mediocrity. In the foundations of current Western morality we have both hedonism and legalism.

In biblical terms this juridical approach would be called pharisaical and it has become the foundation upon which selfishness, the lowest common denominator of humanity, has been established in law as the highest common factor of modern morality. The moral essence of humanity has been forgotten 'so that now for the past few decades the most fashionable slogan is human rights'.

> But human obligations, human duties people forget. You cannot have rights without obligations. They must be in balance, if indeed obligations are not to be greater. Just as it is impossible to say to myself that I will breathe with my left lung but I will not breathe with my right – they both need to work together – in such a way, duty and obligation and right must go together. Our situation has become so twisted that we now even have the expression that there is an ideology of human rights. And what is that? That is anarchism, known for a long time, and so we are moving towards this anarchism.

The fact that modernity makes a virtue out of selfishness is one of the keys to its enduring success. Solzhenitsyn claims that Protestantism made a major contribution to this:

> Of course, one cannot declare that only my faith is correct and all the other faiths are not. Of course, God is endlessly multi-dimensional so every religion that exists on earth represents some face, some side of God. One must not have any negative attitude to any religion but nonetheless the depth of understanding God and the depth of applying God's commandments is different in different religions. In this sense we have to admit that Protestantism has brought everything down only to faith. Calvinism says that nothing depends on man, that faith is already predetermined, and also in its sharp protest against Catholicism, Protestantism rushed to discard together with ritual all the mysterious, the mythical and mystical aspects of the faith. In that sense it has impoverished religion.

Agreeing with G. K. Chesterton's view that each heresy takes a part of the truth and caricatures it until only a distortion of the truth remains, Solzhenitsyn maintained that this falling away from the truth in recent centuries could have apocalyptic consequences. 'If mankind does not subordinate itself to moral demands, to moral conditions, then egos will destroy the world.' Taking the example of the ecological crisis, he believed that, like so many of society's other problems, it has an irreligious origin.

> Having left religion, man has forgotten that he is part of a unified creation. He has stopped thinking of himself as part of nature and so we move to a destruction of the environment to such an extent that perhaps we will destroy the environment before we destroy society. As we can see by the number of international conferences where the United States and other leading countries are refusing to take measures to stem the destruction of the environment. This is a direct path towards the destruction of the world.

Confronted with such a doomsday scenario, was the only hope a return to religion? 'Not a return to religion,' Solzhenitsyn replied, 'but an elevation towards religion. The thing is that religion itself cannot but be dynamic which is why "return" is an incorrect term.' There could be no return to the past. 'On the contrary, in order to combat modern materialistic mores, as religion must, to fight nihilism and egotism, religion must also develop, must be flexible in its forms, and it must have a correlation with the cultural forms of the epoch. Religion always remains higher than everyday life. In order to make the elevation towards religion easier for people, religion must be able to alter its forms in relation to the consciousness of modern man.'

Solzhenitsyn's call for a dynamic dialogue between religion and modern culture seemed at variance with the implicit sympathy for the Old Believers which is evident in *The Gulag Archipelago* and several of his other works. 'I spoke exclusively through the historical aspect, the historical plane, the historical lens,' Solzhenitsyn explained. The Old Believers were

> treated amazingly unjustly, because of some very insignificant, trifling differences in ritual which were promoted with poor judgement and without much sound basis. Because of these small differences they were persecuted in very many cruel ways, they were suppressed, they were exiled. From the perspective of historical justice I sympathize with them and I am on their side, but this in no way ties in with what I have just said about the fact that religion in order to keep together with mankind must adapt its forms towards modern culture. In other words, do I agree with the Old Believers that religion should freeze and not move at all. Not at all!

Related to this from a Western point of view was the debate within the Catholic Church in the 1960s at the time of the Second Vatican Council. One side welcomed the Council because it modernized the Church, while the other, the traditionalists, saw it as a surrender to the modern values with which Christianity was essentially at war. Solzhenitsyn referred to the similar difficulties facing the Russian Orthodox Church:

A question peculiar to the Russian Orthodox Church, is should we continue to use Old Church Slavonic or should we start to introduce more of the contemporary Russian language into the service? I understand the fears of both those in the Orthodox and in the Catholic Church, the wariness, the hesitation and the fear that this is lowering the Church to the modern condition, the modern surroundings. I understand this fear but alas I fear that if religion does not allow itself to change, it will be impossible to return the world to religion because the world is incapable on its own of rising as high as the old demands of religion. Religion needs to come and meet it somewhat.

This perennial tension between tradition and reform in religious affairs was at the heart of Chesterton's image of the Church as a heavenly chariot careering through the centuries, reeling but erect. It was, however, a little surprising to find Solzhenitsyn, so often perceived as the arch-traditionalist, apparently coming down on the side of the reformers. Perhaps it was time to apply a liturgical litmus test. Was there a point at which relevance to the modern world would sever religion's links with its traditional tenets? Take, for example, the issue of women priests which has caused such division in the Anglican Church?

'Certainly there are many firm boundaries which cannot and should not be changed,' Solzhenitsyn replied. 'When I speak of some sort of correlation between the cultural norms of the present it is really only a small part of the whole thing.' There was a pause, punctuated by a mirthful, almost youthful gleam in the ageing blue eyes. 'Certainly I do not believe that women priests is the way to go!' he continued, chuckling infectiously.

This infectious chuckling was another aspect of Solzhenitsyn's demeanour which came as something of a surprise. Somehow it seemed at variance with the pugnacity of his public image. The mirth, the relaxed humour were as much a part of his general character as the seriousness with which he approached many of the subjects under discussion. One example of Solzhenitsyn's effervescence emerged when he was shown a list of Western writers with whom he shared an affinity. Solzhenitsyn was, I suggested, part of the same network of minds as these writers who had also adopted traditional Christianity as a response to modernity. He cast his eyes over the list, reading the names of Chesterton, Belloc, Eliot, C. S. Lewis, Tolkien, Sassoon, Sitwell, Waugh and Newman: 'I do know that such writers exist,' he quipped with the same recurrent chuckle, 'and I also know that they are equally unpopular in the West!'

Did he believe that the outlook of such writers, taken together with the socio-economic vision of E. F. Schumacher, was the key to society rediscovering its sanity? 'I do believe that it would be the key but I don't believe this will happen because people succumb to fashion, and they suffer from inertia, and it is hard for them to come round to a different point of view.' Did this pessimism, for want of a better word, apply to society's prospects of rediscovering, or rising to, religion? There was a potent pause, during which his soul's azure windows visibly saddened. 'I would have to say that the road is very difficult and the hope is very small but it is not excluded. History has in different questions laid out some tremendous turnabouts and curves.' In that case did he see the likelihood that religious belief would continue much as it was at present, the preserve of a misunderstood minority? 'Yes I do, but that doesn't mean that believers should let their hands drop or that they should give up.'

In Russia at least, there were grounds for a limited degree of optimism. Since the fall of communism there had been an increase in the number of Christianity's adherents. 'Many under an atheistic press, a vice grip, had forgotten, so we do have something of a return to Christianity. Yet simultaneously there is a decay of values which accompanies the rise of the consumer society. It is a simultaneous process.' The present upheavals in Russia made it difficult to determine what the future held in store. 'For the entire future of Russia, I would say that the situation is in a balance and it is unclear which way this balance will go. As this is true for the whole of Russia, and all the issues to do with Russia, it is also unclear to what degree the development of Christianity will be intertwined in Russia and will influence the way the whole country goes. We cannot predict that now.'

Amidst the confusion, many in Russia had even begun to rue the downfall of communism. 'In any case,' Solzhenitsyn laughed, 'many people here condemn me and censure me by saying "well, you demolished it but what do we have now?"' Although few would venture to suggest that Solzhenitsyn was a communist, he has often been smeared by association with the extreme nationalists who have risen from the ashes of communism's collapse. It is interesting, therefore, that he rejects unequivocally any racial basis for nationhood. 'Much in man is determined not so much by his physical side or by blood but by the spirit,' he insisted. 'For instance, I often speak of Russians and I am asked "Who are the Russians? Russia covers large territories with different peoples mixed together. You cannot trace the blood." I answer, He who is Russian is so by spirit, is so by heart, by the direction of his loyalties and interests. So there is a spiritual unifying of people and not a blood-based one.'

It is one of Solzhenitsyn's most passionately held beliefs that this spiritual basis is central to any understanding of life itself, as much for individual people as for whole peoples. One of the *leitmotifs* of his novel *Cancer Ward*, he explained, was 'the correlation, the relationship, between the physical and spiritual facets of love. It is tied with the direct development of the book's plot since before Oleg there stands the possibility of the loss of the physical side and the question that lies before him is what might be left to hope for, to live for ... Love without the spiritual side is not love.' Linked with this spiritual dimension was the characterization of the female characters in the book who are developed with strength and sympathy but in an implicitly anti-feminist, although not anti-feminine, direction. 'I do feel that feminism is anti-natural,' Solzhenitsyn asserted. 'It does destroy the feminine and in so doing it also destroys humankind. It disassembles the female side of humankind and the male side also suffers. This is one of the manifestations of the fact that people have lost the high image of man as a creation of God. Instead we have this unbridled, almost frenzied, moving about of liberalism which fails to understand human nature itself, not just the feminine, but human existence, being blinded by this wild, liberal dancing.'

Spiritual preoccupations aside, Solzhenitsyn's greatest love remains his work. Even at eighty his eyes glistened and the words rolled ebulliently from his lips as he discussed his writing. He was happy to talk about his past work but, as he said, 'the favourite work is always the one on which you are currently working'. It was with added enthusiasm, therefore, that he spoke about the eight double-part short stories he had written since his return to Russia. 'It is a special kind of genre,' he explained.

> These two parts need to be linked by something. Sometimes they are linked by the same characters but in very different time periods perhaps. Sometimes characters, completely disparate, would seem at first glance to have nothing in common with each other whatsoever and the trick there is to try to guess what is the common theme linking each part. In some ways this creates an additional space, an additional dimension, so this link that you have to guess at is not present in either the first part or in the second part, but in putting the two together one is able to deduce something else.

In continuing to define new genres, even in his latter years, Solzhenitsyn was highlighting the apparent paradox embodied by the marriage of creative innovation and cultural tradition. This is a facet of his work which Michael Nicholson finds particularly exciting. 'Solzhenitsyn has been more concerned than most writers with the practical problems attached to his writings,' Nicholson states. It is a 'fascinating struggle not between genius and mediocrity, but with the problem of preventing the weight of the material from steamrolling you flat'. The difficulties have been overcome by innovation. 'He uses sub-titles that define new genres. *The Gulag Archipelago* was "an experiment in literary investigation". *The First Circle* has no linear development beyond about three days, it works on parallel echoes and circular images.' Even *One Day in the Life of Ivan Denisovich*, one of the most understated of Solzhenitsyn's works, is 'a novel which is bursting at the seams with the impulse to say far more than it can, so you get a terrific tension here. The text seeps these emblematic, symbolic moments.'[4]

One sublimely beautiful passage in *Cancer Ward* includes what purports to be a definition of the meaning of life itself: 'The meaning of existence was to preserve untarnished, undisturbed and undistorted the image of eternity which each person is born with – as far as possible.' Did Solzhenitsyn believe that his own life and work had succeeded in preserving this image of eternity? 'I certainly try that in every work there are such moments when I try to preserve the image of eternity – in each one of my works. Of course not throughout the entire scope of the work, and that, I would add, applies to life as well as work. And I would also add that the older a person becomes the more they are concerned with such issues, such questions.'

This led to a discussion of the rarely discerned similarities between Solzhenitsyn's starkly 'realist' novels and J. R. R. Tolkien's supposedly 'escapist' fantasies. Tolkien had defined those moments when a work succeeds in preserving or perceiving the image of eternity as the 'sudden joyous "turn"', the 'sudden glimpse of the underlying reality or truth ... a brief vision ... a far-off gleam or echo of *evangelium* in the real world'.[5] 'Yes, yes,' Solzhenitsyn exclaimed, concurring wholeheartedly. 'In many of the episodes and certainly in the wider flow of events in my work I tried to both see, locate and to evoke towards life such a turn.'

Tolkien and Solzhenitsyn also shared a preoccupation in their work with the ennoblement of souls through the trials and tribulations of adversity. 'It is not only the pure souls that are able to rise but those which have resilience and strength,' Solzhenitsyn explained:

> Long periods of well-being and comfort are in general dangerous to all. After such prolonged periods, weak souls become incapable of weathering any kind of trial. They are afraid of it. But strong souls in such periods are still able to mobilize and to show themselves, and to grow through this trial. Difficult trials and sufferings can facilitate the growth of the soul. In the West there is a widespread feeling that this is masochism, that if we highly value suffering this is masochism. On the contrary, it is a significant bravery when we respect suffering and understand what burdens it places on our soul.

It is, however, very important to differentiate between the form of ennoblement epitomized by the Crucifixion and Resurrection, and the triumph of the will espoused in the Nietzschean maxim 'every blow which doesn't destroy me makes me stronger'. 'When we speak of crucifixion and resurrection the image foremost in our minds is that of Christ, and the image of those who followed the path of martyrdom or suffering in the context of Christianity. It is the pure struggle of spirituality against suffering or trial. In Nietzsche we see the physical counter-stance against suffering. It is almost like a training, almost like a sparring. These are phenomena of different natures, one is spiritual the other is physical.'

Encouraged by Solzhenitsyn's ready acceptance of the affinity between his own creative vision and that of Tolkien, I ventured to read him two quotes from Tolkien which appeared to encapsulate the spirit of his own work:

> the essence of a *fallen* world is that the best cannot be attained by free enjoyment, or by what is called 'self-realization' (usually a nice name for self-indulgence, wholly inimical to the realization of other selves); but by denial, by suffering.

('Absolutely ... absolutely,' Solzhenitsyn whispered.)

> Out of the darkness of my life, so much frustrated, I put before you the one great thing to love on earth: the Blessed Sacrament ... There you will find romance, glory, honour, fidelity, and the true way of all your loves on earth, and more than that: Death: by the divine paradox, that which ends life, and demands the surrender of all, and yet by the taste (or foretaste) of which alone can what you seek in your earthly relationships (love, faithfulness, joy) be maintained, or take on that complexion of reality, of eternal endurance, which every man's heart desires.[6]

'Is that Tolkien?' Solzhenitsyn asked, eyes widened in surprise. 'Yes, again correct.'

As those piercing eyes met mine across the table another image from Tolkien entered my head. This time the quote remained unspoken but the image of Treebeard, the wizened voice of wisdom in *The Lord of the Rings*, with his 'deep eyes ... slow and solemn, but very penetrating', filled my mind. For an instant Solzhenitsyn's eyes and those of Treebeard were one: 'One felt as if there was an enormous well behind them, filled up with ages of memory and long, slow, steady thinking; but their surface was sparkling with the present: like sun shimmering on the outer leaves of a vast tree, or on the ripples of a very deep lake.' Like Pippin I felt that those eyes were considering me with the same slow care they had given to their own inside affairs for endless years.

'I recently started writing once more small prose poems,' Solzhenitsyn continued, breaking the spell. 'One of these is called ageing, growing old. It's only a few lines. The conclusion, the point that emerges from those few lines is that growing old is not a path downwards but in fact movement up.'

This, of course, is opposite to the vision of the materialists who see the ageing process only as evidence of physical decay, heralding nothing but the unmentionable approach of death. This in turn had led to the modern idolization of youth with further detrimental effects on society. 'The old possess a collective experience. There's no substitute for experience. Youth may only have premonitions, guesses, but it does not yet possess the foundations upon which to build that up. Therein lies the advantage of an advanced age.'

Inevitably the subject of advanced age brought the conversation back to thoughts of retrospection. In his autobiography *The Oak and the Calf*, Solzhenitsyn had hinted at the role of providence in his life. To what extent did he believe that his life's labours had served a purpose greater than the sum of their parts?

> There are two questions here. The first question is how do I view providence and I have already said today that I am deeply convinced that God participates in every life, and the other issue is that people understand this in varying degrees. Some clearly recognize this, others do not. In addition, life does not necessarily have to be externally significant. It can be the most humble of lives but it can always feel this contact with God. So the fact that I have this feeling is no exception. It is simply another example of this. That is the first question. The second question about whether what I have done is more than the sum of its parts. That which I have done is divided into the books I have written, each book has its own weight and its own meaning, and the concept of a 'sum' does not readily fit in

with this artistic creativity. The second would be my sort of societal actions. My societal actions have sum and they have had an influence on the process both in my homeland and in the West ... Currently I consciously step back from this because I do not see in my own homeland the ability to be able to influence the course of events, in the conditions of which I was telling you concerning the cultural atomization of the country. The other method is to write books addressing the problems directly, but books aren't going to penetrate anywhere. For instance, this book *Russia in the Abyss* is sold in Moscow and St Petersburg and who knows when it will penetrate into the provinces. It is impossible to determine. And my age demands that I finish the work that I have previously begun which is what I am now doing.

As Solzhenitsyn enters the twilight years of his life it seems that an air of resignation has swept away any last remaining plans, desires or ambitions. There is little he still wishes to achieve. 'I only want to finish those works which I have already begun and not more than that. Of course, I would try to influence the course of events here in Russia but I don't see the ways of doing so. I have already had two mild heart attacks.'

The melancholy atmosphere evaporated with the very suggestion that Solzhenitsyn's prodigious productivity could be coming to an end. The mention of retirement triggered one of those infectious chuckles, accompanied as ever with the reassuringly boyish glint of the eye. 'I'm afraid that I will not be able to finish everything and after death I think I will still have enough unpublished material for several volumes ... so now is not the time to retire!'

If the cheerful octogenarian did not have time to retire, it was almost time that I did so. I had been the recipient of the Solzhenitsyn family's hospitality for many long hours and the audience was drawing to a close. There was time, perhaps, for one last question. How, I asked, would Solzhenitsyn like to be remembered to posterity? 'That's a complex question,' he responded, pausing a moment before commencing.

I would hope that which has been lied about me, slandered about me, in the course of decades, would, like mud, dry up and fall off. It is amazing how much gibberish has been talked about me, more so in the West than in the USSR. In the USSR it was all one-directional propaganda, and everyone knew that it was just communist propaganda. But in the West anyone can lie, some person can say something in a little article and thirty people start reproducing it. It is the fashion to imitate.

The complaint about media distortion was not new. Solzhenitsyn had been making the same plaintive pleas for objectivity and fairness for many years. I had read similar words by him on several occasions and on the dry page they sounded stern, possibly even bitter. Now, however, as he spoke them across the table to me, there was the softened countenance, punctuated periodically with smiles which transformed regularly into laughter. The complaint against the media was real enough, and certainly heartfelt, but his contempt was tempered by contentment. He was happy and could shrug off the lies with apparent ease.

But you are still smiling?

'Of course. I am indifferent to all this because I was always occupied with my work and I wasn't listening to what they were saying, or reading what they were writing. But when you ask, "after my death", it is then that I will not be able to justify myself and that is why I hope that it would, like mud, fall off of its own accord.'

As our interview reached its conclusion, I was addressed by Alya in faltering English. She told me with evident pleasure that her husband was again writing prose poetry, something he had been unable to do during the years in exile. The poems were, she intimated, evidence that he was once more at peace with life. Some were directly inspired by events in their own garden, such as a storm which he had taken as allegorical inspiration for aspects of human behaviour. Solzhenitsyn had finally come home, artistically as well as physically. Michael Nicholson, on reading these prose poems, was particularly struck by the resonant use of the imagery attached to bells and bell-towers in two of them.

The most typical in its 'spiritual optimism' is *'Kolokol'nia'*, in which a lone bell-tower is seen protruding high above the waves of the Volga, while what survives of the half-flooded town of Kaliazan has the air of a ghost-town populated by deceived abandoned souls. Though Kaliazan suggests a gloomy *pars pro toto*, the bell-tower stands nevertheless: 'As our hope. As our prayer: no, the Lord will not permit *all* of Russia to be drowned beneath the waves.' The link with the homes, churches and bell-towers of Solzhenitsyn's earlier fiction does not need further elaboration.[7]

Nicholson compares the spiritual optimism of these poems with what he perceives to be Solzhenitsyn's underlying pessimism about the future:

> Now back in Russia, he finds that the muddied waters of freedom have silted up the space once occupied by communism, or, to use another of his images, an evil prince still casts his spell over Lake Segden, and the people still scuttle about in his shadow denied access to the healing lucidity of its waters. As for Solzhenitsyn, he finds himself sounding a tocsin that has pealed through centuries of Russian history and grappling in his declining years with the fear that perhaps he rings in vain.[8]

It is crucial to any understanding of Solzhenitsyn's life and work to understand that this combination of pessimism and optimism is a paradox and not a contradiction.

At the conclusion of my time with him, I asked Solzhenitsyn whether there was anything else of particular importance which he would like me to cover in the proposed biography. 'That's an unexpected question,' he responded. 'I'll have to think that one over.' Eventually he expressed the desire that the charge of pessimism be confronted. 'I must tell you that, on the contrary, I am by nature an ineradicable optimist. I've always been an optimist. When I was dying of cancer I was always an optimist. When I was exiled abroad nobody believed that I would return but I was convinced that I would return. So no, it's not full of dark and gloom. There's always a ray of light. But of course,' he added with a broad grin, 'there may not be enough optimism to last a full eighty years!'

Solzhenitsyn is paradox personified: the pessimistic optimist. His pessimism springs from the creeping knowledge that human history may be little more than a long defeat in a land of exile. Yet such a defeat, however long, is rooted in time: temporal and therefore temporary. Solzhenitsyn knows that his exile in time, like his exile in the West, must eventually come to an end. Perhaps only then will the fullness of his destiny be revealed. Solzhenitsyn is, for the time being, a temporary pessimist, but he is also, and remains, an eternal optimist.

NOTES

1. Translated for the author by Ignat Solzhenitsyn from his father's notes.
2. Ignat Solzhenitsyn, conversation with the author, November 1998.
3. Solzhenitsyn, interview with the author.
4. Ibid. Unless otherwise specified, all other quotes by Solzhenitsyn in this chapter are from his interview with the author.
5. Dr Michael Nicholson, interview with the author.
6. J. R. R. Tolkien (ed. Christopher Tolkien), *The Monsters and the Critics and Other Essays*, London: George Allen & Unwin, 1984, pp. 153–4.
7. Humphrey Carpenter (ed.), *The Letters of J. R. R. Tolkien*, London: George Allen & Unwin, 1981, pp. 53–4.
8. Dr Michael Nicholson, *Solzhenitsyn, Exile and the* Genius Loci, unpublished manuscript.
9. Ibid.

NEW PROSE POEMS
BY ALEXANDER SOLZHENITSYN
Translated by Michael A. Nicholson, with Alexis Klimoff

Translator's Note

Among the many genres at which Solzhenitsyn has tried his hand are these *Krokhotnye rasskazy* (Microstories) or *Krokhotki*, the more colloquial form that he has favoured in later years. They are essentially prose poems, typically reflections on journeys, landscapes, natural phenomena. In them Solzhenitsyn's polemical involvement with issues facing contemporary Russia tends to be framed by a contemplative, even elegiac intonation. The first cycle of prose poems, seventeen in number, was written at various times between 1958 and 1960, while the nine new ones were begun almost four decades later, after Solzhenitsyn had returned to Russia from his twenty-year exile. This latest cycle was first published in 1997, in Nos. 1, 3 and 10 of *Novy Mir* – the same Moscow literary journal in which he had made his debut thirty-five years before. In the original Russian these short pieces well illustrate the dynamic, elliptical syntax and non-standard lexis of Solzhenitsyn's mature style. The present translation is based on the slightly modified text in Alexander Solzhenitsyn, *Na izlomakh: malaya proza* (Yaroslavl': Verkhnyaya Volga, 1998). The following lines from Solzhenitsyn's letter to the editor of *Novy Mir* were reproduced as an epigraph to the new cycle:

> *It was only when I got back to Russia that I found I could write them again; living abroad – I simply couldn't do it.*

THE LARCH

What an extraordinary tree this is!

All we see when we look at her are needles and more needles. Obviously another conifer then? But not so fast! As autumn sets in, the deciduous trees around her start to shed their leaves, almost as if death were upon them. And then – is she commiserating? I won't desert you! the rest of my kind can winter safely here without me – she too begins to shed. And how suddenly her needles shower down – in festive, glinting sparks of sunlight.

Do we conclude that there is a softness at her very heart? Wrong again! The texture of her wood is among the toughest in the world – not every axe can get the better of it, it is too dense to drag and float downstream, and, far from rotting when abandoned in the water, it draws ever closer to the eternal strength of stone.

But when the gentle warmth of spring creeps back, a gift that each year takes us by surprise ... it seems another year of life has been bestowed upon us, then why not spread our foliage anew, why not rejoin our kin, arrayed in needles soft as silk?

One could point to people who share those same qualities.

LIGHTNING

Only in books had I read of lightning splitting a tree in two; it was not something I had ever seen.

But I have now! It came from a thunderstorm passing overhead in broad daylight – a blinding flash of lightning that bathed our windows in coruscating gold, followed, a split second later – by an almighty clap of thunder – it couldn't have been more than two or three hundred yards from the house.

The storm passed. And sure enough – there it was, in a patch of trees close by. Why, among all those towering pines, should the lightning have singled out a lime tree – and not even the tallest one? From just below its crown the bolt had coursed downwards – down the length of the trunk, slicing through its core, its vitality and self-assurance. But for all the lightning's power, it had not reached the very bottom – had it glanced off to one side? or simply exhausted itself? ... All one could see was the gouged-up earth near the scorched roots and the coarse wood-chips, hurled fifty yards in every direction.

One section of trunk, reaching midway down the tree itself, had split off and toppled over to one side, coming to rest against the branches of its blameless neighbours. The other half lingered on for another day, though with such a gaping hole torn clean through it that who can say what force sustained it? Finally, it too heeled over to be welcomed into the forked arms of another of its tall sisters.

And so it is with some of us: when conscience does hurl its chastening bolt, it strikes through our inmost being and down the length of our days. And after such a blow there is no telling who of us will emerge tempered from the storm.

THE BELL AT UGLICH

What Russian has not heard of the bizarre punishment meted out to this bell? How its tongue was plucked out, how they broke off one of the lugs by which it hung so that it should never again grace a belltower and how, for good measure, they whipped it, then exiled it twelve hundred jolting miles by cart to Tobol'sk, drawn not by horses – no, this accursed load was hauled every inch of the way by condemned townsfolk of Uglich – over and above the two hundred already put to death for tearing apart 'the Tsar's retainers' (sent to murder Dmitry, the young heir to the throne), and in addition to those whose tongues were sliced off lest they tell their own tale of what really happened that day at Uglich.

Returning to Russia by way of Siberia, I chanced upon the traces left behind by this former exile in the Tobolsk Kremlin: I stood in the tiny chapel where it had served out its three-hundred-year solitary confinement before being pardoned and allowed to go home. And now here I am in Uglich itself, in the Church of Dmitry-on-the-Blood. And the bell, only half a man's height for all its seven hundredweight, hangs here in a place of honour. Long suffering has dulled its bronze to grey. Its clapper hangs idle. And I am invited to ring it.

I strike just once. And a marvellous deep boom resounds through the church! How richly evocative these intermingling bass tones, appealing from the distant past to our foolishly bustling, turbid souls! A single blow – yet for half a minute it reverberates, then lingers a full minute more before dying away in slow and solemn majesty, preserving to the last its rich palate of sounds. How well our forebears knew the secrets of metal!

Within minutes of learning that Prince Dmitry had been butchered, the sexton of the cathedral church had raced into the bell-loft – he had the foresight to bolt the door behind him – and however hard the scoundrels battered at the door, he rang and rang, sounding the tocsin on this very bell. In the horror and lamentation of the townspeople of Uglich the bell proclaimed its fear for the very survival of Russia.

Those rolling peals, signalling a great Calamity, heralded Russia's first Time of Troubles. And now it has fallen to me to ring this bell, so steeped in suffering, amidst the clinging, lingering decay of a third Time of Troubles. There is no escaping the comparison: the prophetic alarm of the people is but a pinprick to the throne and to the thick-skinned nobles clustered round it. This is as true today as it was four hundred years ago.

Historical Note

Historians are divided in their interpretation of this event, but popular tradition holds firmly to the view that Dmitry, the young son of Tsar Ivan IV of Russia, was murdered in Uglich in 1591. Boris Godunov, who succeeded to the throne in 1598 upon the death of Fedor I, Ivan's other surviving son, was immediately suspected of complicity. The end of Boris's reign inaugurated a period of unrest and civil war, known as the 'Time of Troubles' (1605–1613), which ended with the accession of Mikhail Romanov. Solzhenitsyn sees the Revolution and civil war which brought the Romanov dynasty to a close as a second Time of Troubles, and the period since the end of the 1980s as a third.

THE BELLTOWER

Whoever seeks to grasp, to compass at a glance our Russian land before it is finally submerged – should take the time to look upon the belltower of Kalyazin.

It once stood hard by the cathedral in the thick of a flourishing trading town near the covered market of the Gostinyi dvor, and streets of two-storey merchant houses ran down on to the square at its feet. And no prophet could then have foretold that after eight centuries of life this ancient town, survivor of successive onslaughts by marauding Tatars and Poles, would be deliberately submerged at the ignorant behest of petty tyrants, leaving two-thirds of the town beneath the Volga – the Bolsheviks begrudged the money for a second dam, which would have saved it. (Two-thirds submerged? Why, the entire town of Mologa is lying down at the bottom of the river too.) Kalyazin, swallowed up like the fabled town of Kitezh, lies in ten fathoms of water, and if you stand today at the river's edge no effort of the imagination can raise this reluctant Atlantis from the abyss.

But what survives of the drowned town is its tall, graceful belltower. The cathedral was blasted apart or dismantled to provide the building bricks for our radiant future, yet for some reason they didn't get round to flattening the belltower, didn't lay a finger on it – you'd think it was a protected building! And here it stands, jutting out of the water, its white brickwork built to last, its six tiers tapering as they rise (one and a half of them submerged) – in the last few years they have been tipping rubble against her sides to form a protective platform round the base – here it stands with no sign of a tilt or twist, thrusting heavenward the open-work pattern of its five visible tiers, surmounted by an onion-dome and spire. And on the spire – what miracle is this? – the cross survives intact! Bulky Volga steamers forge by – yet when viewed from afar they reach barely halfway up the first of the belltower's exposed tiers – and their wake sends the waves slapping against its white walls, while from the decks Soviet passengers gape at the tower, just as they have these fifty years.

You roam the surviving little streets – dismal, mutilated and still showing here and there the buckled hovels of those first, hastily resettled flood victims. Along the false new embankment the women of Kalyazin, devoted as ever to the renowned gentleness and purity of the Volga water, are trying to rinse out their linen. The ravaged town lingers on, a broken stump, more dead than alive, with but a handful of its once splendid buildings left intact. Yet even amidst this desolation, cheated and abandoned as they are, people have no choice but to go on living. And where are they to live but – here?

And still, for them, as for all who have once beheld this marvel – the belltower stands! Like the hope we cherish. Like the prayer we raise on high. No, the Lord will not permit *all* of Russia to be plunged beneath the waves...

GROWING OLD

Much has been written about the horrors of death, but scarcely less about death – at least, death by natural causes – as an organic link in the chain of life.

I remember a Greek poet I knew in the labour camps: he was still in his thirties but not long for this world. Yet his gentle, wistful smile betrayed no fear of death. This amazed me. But, he told me, 'Before the onset of death we go through an inner process of preparation; we grow and mature to meet it – and then it no longer holds any terror for us.'

Barely a year was to pass before – at thirty-four years of age – I experienced the same thing at first hand. Month by month, week by week, as I drew ever nearer to death and adapted to it – my readiness and resignation outstripped that of my own body.

How much easier it is then, how much more receptive we are to death, when advancing years guide us softly to our end. Ageing thus is in no sense a punishment from on high, but brings its own blessings and a warmth of colours all its own.

There is warmth in watching little children at play, seeing them gain in strength and character. There is even warmth to be drawn from the waning of your own strength compared with the past – just to think how sturdy I once used to be! You can no longer get through a whole day's work at a stretch, but how good it is to slip into the brief oblivion of sleep, and what a gift to wake once more to the clarity of your second or third morning of the day. And your spirit can find delight in limiting your intake of food, in abandoning the pursuit of novel flavours. You are still of this life, yet you are rising above the material plane. The shrill cry of the tomtits in a snow-clad wood in early spring holds twice the charm, for soon you will hear it no more – so listen to your heart's content! And what an inalienable treasure your memories prove! This is something the young are denied, but you carry them all with you, unfailingly, and a living portion of them calls upon you each day – during the infinitely slow transition from night to day, and again from day to night.

Growing old serenely is not a downhill path, but an ascent. But, Lord, spare us from an old age racked by poverty and cold.

The fate to which we have consigned so very, very many...

SHAME

How agonizing it is to feel ashamed for your own Motherland!

Whose callous hands are these, whose scheming hands that rule Her life so rashly and corruptly? What faces these – haughty, cunning or void of character – that represent Her to the world? What rancid swill is She now served in place of wholesome spiritual fare? To what depths of ruin and penury are Her people reduced, powerless to clamber from the pit?

The sense of humiliation is unremitting. It has none of the transience of those everyday personal emotions, which change readily to match the fleeting play of circumstance. No, it oppresses you constantly, dogs your every step – it is with you when you wake, with you as you drag out each hour of the day and with you as you sink back into night. And even death, which sets us free from personal afflictions, can offer no escape from this Shame – it will simply continue to hang over the heads of the living, and you, after all, are a particle of their being.

You peruse the depths of Russia's past in search of encouraging precedents. And yet you know equally well the implacable truth – that nations of the earth have sometimes perished utterly. This would not be the first time.

But no, there are other depths to draw upon – those two dozen regions of the Russian heartland that I visited on my travels – it is they that whisper words of hope to me. There I saw aspirations still untarnished, a questing spirit as yet uncrushed, and living, generous-hearted countrymen of mine. Can it be that they will never break out of this pale of doom? No – they *shall* break free! It is yet within their power.

But day after day the Shame hangs over us, like a pinkish-yellow cloud of poison-gas, corroding our lungs. And even when at last it is dispersed, the blot upon our history will never be erased.

THE EVIL WEED

To think of the labour expended by the tiller of the soil in preserving the seed grain until its time, sowing it to best advantage and lovingly tending the good plants until they bear fruit! Yet weeds spring up with a savage exuberance, knowing neither care nor nurture, but thriving in scornful defiance of them. That is what the proverb has in mind when it says: 'The evil weed is slow to wither.'

But why should the good plants always be the weaker ones?

Looking back over the clinging morass of human history – from the dimmest recesses of the past to the vivid freshness of the present moment – we bow our heads despondently: yes, this seems to be a universal law. And for all our well-meaning contrivances and all our earthly schemes, we shall never, ever escape its dictates.

Not till the end of humankind.

And to each of the living is granted nothing more than his labour – and his soul.

MORNING

What happens to our soul in the course of the night? Amidst the numb inertia of sleep it seems to detach itself from this body, to soar free through vast, pure expanses, stripping away the petty, murky accretions of the past day, and even of whole years. It returns, in pristine snowy whiteness, to open up for us the boundless, calm lucidity of our morning state of mind.

What better moments than these for thought and reflection! Your perceptions seem unimaginably heightened, as if you were on the brink of grasping something which you have never before ... something which...

You pause, motionless. Something seems poised to burst into growth within you, something hitherto unknown and unsuspected. Scarcely daring to breathe, you summon forth this radiant shoot – the white tip of a tiny lily, soon to pierce the smooth unbroken surface of the eternal waters.

These are moments of grace! Moments which raise you high above yourself. There is something incomparably precious that you are capable of discovering, resolving, conceiving – if only you do not ruffle, or let others disturb the glassy calm of this lake that lies within you...

But all too soon something comes along to unsettle and disrupt that heightened sensibility whether it be another person's word or deed, or some petty thought of your own. And at once the spell is broken. That wondrous glassy stillness and the lake itself have vanished in a trice.

And all through the day, try as you might, you will not retrieve it.

Nor will every new morning bring it back to you.

THE CURTAIN

Heart disease can serve as an image of life itself – darkness shrouds its future course, we never know just when our end will come: is that it lurking at our door, or might it still be a long way off?

When a tumour swells ominously within you, at least you can face the implacable truth and work out how long there is to go. But heart disease plays cunning tricks: at times you seem quite healthy – so you're not doomed after all! why, it's as if you'd never been ill!

Blissful ignorance. What a merciful gift!

But in its acute phase heart disease is like being on death row. Each evening you sit and wait – is that the sound of footsteps? Are they coming for *me*? But then, each morning – what relief! and what a blessing! God has granted me a whole new day. One can live and do so very much in the space of but a single day.

INDEX

Ackroyd, Peter, 251
Akhmadulina, Bella, 171
Akhmatova, Anna, 187
Amelin, Grigori, 284
Andropov, Yuri, 201–2, 247, 253
Animal Farm (Orwell), 106
Aquinas, St Thomas, 236
Aragon, Louis, 189, 221
Armes, Keith, 148
art, S's concept of, 192–4
Attlee, Clement, 105–6
Auden, W. H., 190
Augustine, St, 236
Ayer, A. J., 190
Azhayev, Vasiley, 104

Bach, Johann Sebastian, 208
Barabash, Yuri, 158–9
Barbarossa (Clark), 48
Belgorodtseva, Elena, 15
Belloc, Hilaire, 269, 305
Bellow, Saul, 215
Beria, Lavrenty, 132
Berney, R. J., 237
Böll, Heinrich, 189
Brezhnev, Leonid, 162–3, 202,
    246–7, 254, 265
Bronevitsky, Nikolai, 50–52, 57
Bronson, Charles, 284
Burke, Edmund, 236
Butor, Michel, 189
Byron, Lord, 22

Callaghan, James, 230, 237, 247
Capote, Truman, 189
Carter, Jimmy, 206
Carter, Rosalynn, 236
Carver, David, 188–9
Chakovskaya, Liusha, 197, 211
Chalmayev, Victor, 184–6
Charles, Prince, 242
Cheever, John, 189
Chekhov, Anton, 22, 41, 297
Chernenko, Konstantin, 253
Chernomyrdin, Viktor, 287
Chesterton, G. K., 92, 232, 269–70,
    302, 304–5
Chukovsky, Kornei, 168
Cicero, 236
Clark, Alan, 48
communism, *passim*
Curcio, Maria, 263
Curran, Charles, 230

Dahl, Vladimir, 16
Daniel, Yuli, 170, 216
Dante, 208
Das Kapital (Marx), 45
Death of Ivan Ilyich, The,
    (Tolstoy), 170
de Beauvoir, Simone, 221
Dementyev, Alexander, 185–6
Dickens, Charles, 16
Divnich, Father Evgeny, 94
Doctor Zhivago (Pasternak), 144,
    148

Dostoyevsky, Fyodor, 16, 118,
  161, 222, 248
Dürrenmatt, Friedrich, 189

ecology, 204–8, 265–70, 302
Ehrenburg, Ilya, 180
Eliot, T. S., 305
Emmanuel, Pierre, 188–9
Epicurus, 93
Ericson, Edward E., 242–3
Ermilov, Vladimir, 155
Esenin, Sergei, 45
Essay on the Restoration of
  Property, An, (Belloc), 269
Evtushenko, Evgeni, 154
Ezepov, Captain, I. I., 75
Ezherets, Lydia, 22, 75

Fabian, Felix, 224
Far From Moscow (Azhayev), 104
Fastenko, Anotoly, 76
Fedin, Konstantin, 188–9
Fedorovsky, Vladimir, 20–21, 27
Filaret, Metropolitan, 221
Flood, Charles Bracelen, 189
Ford, Gerald, 223–4
Franco, General Francisco, 99,
  226
Fuentes, Carlos, 189

Galanskov, Yuri, 191
Gammerov, Boris, 80–81, 91, 124
Genis, Alexander, 295
Ginsburg, Alexander, 216, 233
Ginsburg, Irina, 233
Glanville, Brian, 90
Gogol, Nikolai, 16, 94, 149
Gorbachev, Mikhail, 253–6, 258,
  260, 264, 270–72
Gorlov, Alexander, 201–2
Govorukhin, Stanislav, 272
Granin, Danil, 159
Granovsky, Bishop Antonin, 8
Grass, Gunter, 189–90

Greene, Graham, 190
Griboyedov, Alexander, 23–4
Grunau, Anastasia, 22
Gubenko, Nikolai, 264

Haugh, Richard, 193
'Heirs of Stalin, The',
  (Evtushenko), 154
Herzen, Alexander, 219
Himmler, Heinrich, 224
Hingley, Richard, 182
Hitler, Adolf, 48, 56, 78, 80,
  97–9
Huxley, Julian, 190

John Paul II, Pope, 241, 250,
  278–9, 300
Johnson, Rev. Hewlett, 105

Kaganovich, Lazar, 132
Kalinin, Mikhail, 8, 28
Kamenev, Lev, 28
Karyakin, Yuri, 257
Kedrina, Zoya, 170
Kennan, George, 220
Kennedy, John F., 151
Ketlinskaya, Vera, 175
Khodkevich, Tanya, 10
Khrushchev, Nikita, 132–3, 148,
  150–51, 154, 157–8, 161–2, 253,
  271
Kirov, Sergei, 28, 132
Kissinger, Henry, 223–4
Klimoff, Alexis, 261, 285
Kopelev, Lev, 63, 100–102, 104,
  107, 131, 136–7, 139, 144, 171,
  186, 211 216
Korchnoi, Viktor, 265
Kornfeld, Boris, 114–15
Kosygin, Alexei, 202
Kramarenko, Georgi, 77
Krysko, W. W., 13–14

Lapin, Sergei, 230

139–41, 160–61, 163–4, 169–71, 173, 180, 182, 307; *For the Good of the Cause*, 158–9; *From Under the Rubble*, 207–11, 219; *Gulag Archipelago, The*, 163–4, 173–4, 180, 202–3, 214, 216, 218, 220–21, 233, 255, 257, 265, 271, 286, 299, 303, 307; *Incident at Krechetovka Station, An*, 157; *Invisible Allies*, 217, 285; *Lenin in Zurich*, 217–18, 230; *Lenten Letter*, 148, 197–200, 211; *Letter to Soviet Leaders*, 204–7, 211, 254, 269; *Light Within You, The*, see *Candle in the Wind*; *Love Girl and the Innocent, The*, 131, 171, 184; *Matryona's House*, 145, 149, 157–9; *Oak and the Calf, The*, 102, 217, 310; *October 1916*, 211; *One Day in the Life of Ivan Denisovich*, 112, 141–3, 148–51, 154–7, 159–61, 246, 255, 292, 307; *Prisoners*, 122–3; *Prussian Nights*, 25, 62–3, 122, 217, 232–3; *Rebuilding Russia*, 265–70, 281; *Red Wheel, The*, 24, 251–3, 272, 294; *Russia in the Abyss*, 288, 290, 299, 311; *Victory Celebrations*, see *Feast of Conquerors, A*
Solzhenitsyn, Ignat (son), 180, 237–41, 261, 263, 274–5, 282–3, 293, 297–8
Solzhenitsyn, Isaaki (father), 3, 195
Solzhenitsyn, Natalya (second wife), 179–82, 203, 212, 216–17, 231, 233, 240, 253–4, 258, 261, 273–4, 279, 283, 287, 312
Solzhenitsyn, Stephan (son), 261, 263, 283
Solzhenitsyn, Taissia (mother), 3–6, 19–21, 44, 47, 54–6

Solzhenitsyn, Yermolai (son), 253, 261–4, 283, 292–3
Somov, Vsevolod, 111, 137–8
Spark, Muriel, 190
Stalin, Josef, 6, 23, 28–30, 55, 61–2, 67, 69, 74–7, 80–82, 97–9, 105–6, 115, 119, 125–6, 129, 132–4, 143, 148, 154–5, 161, 182, 187, 201, 216–17, 247, 255, 257
Stolyarova, Natalya, 180
Stravinsky, Igor, 189
Struve, Nikita, 260–61
Suffert, Georges, 118, 230
Susi, Arnold, 77
Svetlova, Natalya, *see* Solzhenitsyn, Natalya
Symons, Julian, 182

Thatcher, Margaret, 247
Thomas, D. M., 224, 262–4, 284, 286
Tikhon, Patriarch, 7, 8
Tolkien, J. R. R., 305, 308
Toller, Ernst, 30
Tolstoy, Leo, 16, 25, 41, 45, 161, 170
Toynbee, Philip, 190
Troitsky, Artyom, 286
Trotsky, Leon, 1, 28
Tseretelli, Tamara, 38
Turgenev, Ivan, 16, 41, 54
Tvardovsky, Alexander, 148–51, 154, 157, 160–62, 164, 170, 175, 196–7
Tyurin, Andre, 180

Updike, John, 189

Veniamin, Metropolitan, 8, 9
Vinogradov, Alexis, 231
Vishnyevskaya, Galina, 264
Vitkevich, Nikolai, 21, 34–6, 39–42, 44, 55, 68–9, 75, 133, 143–4, 146

Vonnegut, Kurt, 189
Voronyanskaya, Elizaveta, 202

Wall, Bernard, 190
Walter, Otto, 219
War and Peace (Tolstoy), 16, 25, 45, 194
Waugh, Evelyn, 305
Webb, Beatrice, 105, 130
Webb, L. W., 220
Webb, Sidney, 105, 130
Wells, H. G., 29–30, 130
Wilbur, Richard, 189
Will, George F., 236
Wilson, Michell, 189

Winchester, Simon, 223–4
Woe from Wit (Griboyedov), 23

Yeltsin, Boris, 255–6, 258, 270–74, 281, 286–8, 298
Yenayev, Gennady, 272
Yerofeyev, Victor, 284, 286

Zakharova, Matryona, 144
Zaozersky, A. N., 8
Zernov, Nikolai, 5
Zhirinovsky, Vladimir, 280
Zimyanin, Mikhail, 178–9
Zinik, Zinovy, 285
Zinoviev, Grigori, 14, 28